T0331863

Cases on Enterprise Information Systems and Implementation Stages:

Learning from the Gulf Region

Fayez Albadri
ADMO–OPCO, UAE

A volume in the Advances in Business Information Systems and Analytics (ABISA) Book Series

Information Science
REFERENCE
An Imprint of IGI Global

Managing Director:	Lindsay Johnston
Editorial Director:	Joel Gamon
Book Production Manager:	Jennifer Romanchak
Publishing Systems Analyst:	Adrienne Freeland
Development Editor:	Hannah Abelbeck
Assistant Acquisitions Editor:	Kayla Wolfe
Typesetter:	Travis Gundrum
Cover Design:	Nick Newcomer

Published in the United States of America by
Information Science Reference (an imprint of IGI Global)
701 E. Chocolate Avenue
Hershey PA 17033
Tel: 717-533-8845
Fax: 717-533-8661
E-mail: cust@igi-global.com
Web site: http://www.igi-global.com

Library of Congress Cataloging-in-Publication Data

Cases on enterprise information systems and implementation stages: learning from the Gulf / Fayez Ahmad Albadri, editor.
    p. cm.
  Includes bibliographical references and index.
   ISBN 978-1-4666-2220-3 (hbk.) -- ISBN 978-1-4666-2221-0 (ebook) -- ISBN 978-1-4666-2222-7 (print & perpetual access) 1. Information technology--Persian Gulf Region. 2. Management information systems--Persian Gulf Region. I. Albadri, Fayez Ahmad, 1958-
  HC415.3.Z9I553 2013
  658.4'038--dc23
                              2012020241

This book is published in the IGI Global book series Advances in Business Information Systems and Analytics (ABISA) Book Series (ISSN: 2327-3275; eISSN: 2327-3283)

British Cataloguing in Publication Data
A Cataloguing in Publication record for this book is available from the British Library.

Advances in Business Information Systems and Analytics (ABISA) Book Series

ISSN: 2327-3275
EISSN: 2327-3283

Mission

The successful development and management of information systems and business analytics is crucial to the success of an organization. New technological developments and methods for data analysis have allowed organizations to not only improve their processes and allow for greater productivity, but have also provided businesses with a venue through which to cut costs, plan for the future, and maintain competitive advantage in the information age.

The **Advances in Business Information Systems and Analytics (ABISA) Book Series** aims to present diverse and timely research in the development, deployment, and management of business information systems and business analytics for continued organizational development and improved business value.

Coverage

- Big Data
- Business Decision Making
- Business Information Security
- Business Process Management
- Business Systems Engineering
- Data Analytics
- Data Management
- Decision Support Systems
- Management Information Systems
- Performance Metrics

IGI Global is currently accepting manuscripts for publication within this series. To submit a proposal for a volume in this series, please contact our Acquisition Editors at Acquisitions@igi-global.com or visit: http://www.igi-global.com/publish/.

Titles in this Series

For a list of additional titles in this series, please visit: www.igi-global.com

Managing Enterprise Information Technology Acquisitions Assessing Organizational Preparedness
Harekrishna Misra (Institute of Rural Management Anand, India) and Hakikur Rahman (University of Minho, Portugal)
Business Science Reference • copyright 2013 • 345pp • H/C (ISBN: 9781466642010) • US $185.00 (our price)

Information Systems and Technology for Organizations in a Networked Society
Tomayess Issa (Curtin University, Australia) Pedro Isaías (Universidade Aberta, Portugal) and Piet Kommers (University of Twente, The Netherlands)
Business Science Reference • copyright 2013 • 432pp • H/C (ISBN: 9781466640627) • US $185.00 (our price)

Cases on Enterprise Information Systems and Implementation Stages Learning from the Gulf Region
Fayez Albadri (ADMO-OPCO, UAE)
Information Science Reference • copyright 2013 • 370pp • H/C (ISBN: 9781466622203) • US $185.00 (our price)

Business Intelligence and Agile Methodologies for Knowledge-Based Organizations Cross-Disciplinary Applications
Asim Abdel Rahman El Sheikh (The Arab Academy for Banking and Financial Sciences, Jordan) and Mouhib Alnoukari (Arab International University, Syria)
Business Science Reference • copyright 2012 • 370pp • H/C (ISBN: 9781613500507) • US $185.00 (our price)

Business Intelligence Applications and the Web Models, Systems and Technologies
Marta E. Zorrilla (University of Cantabria, Spain) Jose-Norberto Mazón (University of Alicante, Spain) Óscar Ferrández (University of Alicante, Spain) Irene Garrigós (University of Alicante, Spain) Florian Daniel (University of Trento, Italy) and Juan Trujillo (University of Alicante, Spain)
Business Science Reference • copyright 2012 • 374pp • H/C (ISBN: 9781613500385) • US $185.00 (our price)

DISSEMINATOR OF KNOWLEDGE

www.igi-global.com

701 E. Chocolate Ave., Hershey, PA 17033
Order online at www.igi-global.com or call 717-533-8845 x100
To place a standing order for titles released in this series,
contact: cust@igi-global.com
Mon-Fri 8:00 am - 5:00 pm (est) or fax 24 hours a day 717-533-8661

Table of Contents

Detailed Table of Contents

Chapter 1

Firas Albataineh, Oracle Systems, UAE

A project is a complex, no routine, one-time effort limited by time, budget, resources, and performance specifications designed to meet a customer's needs (Gray & Larson, 2010). Consequently, although projects may seem similar, largely they are different, and each project represents a unique experience reflecting the variations in the projects' scopes, objectives, specifications, time, budget, resources, constraints, and risks. In line with this, the author's experience as a consultant in different ERP projects indicates that each project has its own unique issues, concerns, and problems, although some of them are common across different projects. This chapter attempts to examine the nature and causes of issues, problems, and concerns that were observed in one of the author's Gulf ERP implementations and suggests the introduction of new and enhanced features in ERP system implementation methodologies as a means to cope with potentially damaging issues, problems, and concerns, and prevent them from evolving into malicious risks that could lead to project failures.

Chapter 2

Amer Dabbagh, CATS, Jordan
Eissa Khoori, ADMA-OPCO, UAE

This major Oil and Gas producing company in the Gulf went through an implementation experience of EIS system in 2005. The EIS Implementation involved the replacement of the existing Maintenance, Supply, and Commercial system with a new EIS and an upgrade of the HR and Financial systems to the latest releases. The exercise was prompted by management's desire to replace the outdated ERP system in order to address shortcomings in functionality, to control the high cost of upgrades and modifications, and to enable implementation of the newly formulated Maintenance Policy. The project was deemed a success, even though it took longer than planned and the results were less than anticipated.

Chapter 3

Rima Shishakly, Ajman University of Science and Technology, UAE

Implementing Enterprise Resource Planning (ERP) is one of the major IT innovations in this decade. ERP solutions seek to integrate and modernize business processes and their associated information and work flows. Nonetheless, ERP usage in educational management is still new. Educational institutions for various appropriate factors have begun to implement this technology. The school ERP enterprise solution system offers complete school management software, which covers all the functions related to the smooth functioning of school activities. This chapter provides a complete analysis of ERP solutions in the educational sectors and focuses on ERP usage and utilization in the United Arab Emirates (UAE) public (government) schools.

Chapter 4

Nooruddin Ahmed, ADNOC, UAE

Any ERP/EAM implementation is a complex journey. No matter how prepared, more often than not you end up like a traveler on a tour of countries where most people look, dress, and speak differently from you. The feeling is of a lost tourist with a map and language guide ambling through unfamiliar terrain, barely coping to do some of the normal things one took for granted. The analogy goes further; it takes time to familiarize oneself with routes, signs, language, and people to barely get along, and you find your trip ending and you move on to the next country on your tour. Similarly, just as you think you are finding your way with your ERP/EAM, someone announces it is time to upgrade, and you start to move again. After nearly 15 years of conventional projects, the case of a particularly interesting implementation came along in the UAE for a major Oil and Gas Services Company. A novel approach was mandated by necessity. The project was managed remotely and executed primarily by internal resources, making it a lean and green implementation.

Chapter 5

Nabil Ghalib, Business International Group, UAE

Application software development has always been viewed as a massive challenge by companies that view IT services as a support function rather than a core function. The term "core" here implies that IT plays an enabler role to facilitate technology and services that support users to meet set business objectives in an efficient way. Furthermore, IT development is perceived by many managers as a burden; hence, they prefer the fast track implementation of specialized packages to deliver the majority of service levels over the long wait for systems to be built in-house, even though the latter option is more advantageous in the long run, as it offers a much better fit to all user requirements. With this dilemma in mind, this case is an example of how an in-house development solution was implemented. The case touches on positive and negative aspects of the decision to build the application and covers a range of issues encountered during every phase of the development life cycle.

Chapter 6

ERP systems life cycle may extend in some business organizations up to fifteen years or more. Nevertheless, the time comes in the life of an ERP system when there is a need to evaluate and compare the value of continuing to use the existing ERP system version against the option to upgrade to a higher version of the same system or having it replaced all together by a different system. In many cases, this translates into a critical management-sponsored mission designating a dedicated team or task force to investigate the feasibility of the alternative options, and to report on the preferred option with a recommendation of the way forward and implementation approach. This case reflects the investigations of Gulf Telecom Company (GTC) in exploring the viability and feasibility of its ERP options to support and provide the grounds for a management decision to mark the next phase of the ERP in the organization. The case describes the approach that was adopted by Gulf Telecom and highlights the challenges to accomplish the mission successfully and any lessons learned from this experience.

Chapter 7

Considering the high rate of failures in ERP implementation projects, there is an urgent need to identify the causes of such failures and the preventing actions associated with these causes. ERP practitioners and academics are unanimous that competencies and abilities of the ERP project manager have a direct impact on the project and its well-being. In fact, it is widely accepted that specific project manager's attributes such as oversight, leadership, communication, problem solving, and conflict-resolution are critical to the success of ERP projects. This case highlights some of the important issues and challenges that the author has encountered as a project manager of ERP system implementation in an Oil and Gas company in Kuwait. The focus of the case is on lessons learned and tips that can be handy and useful for people who may resume this important role in implementation projects.

Chapter 8

The high academic posture of Gulf Private School (GPS) and its outstanding students' performance in the gulf region is a translation of its vision to be the leading school in the region. Technology applications were always viewed by GPS as tools to leverage change and drive continuous improvement, and thus, the utilization of Information Technology applications was weaved into GPS strategy to maintain its high ranking among private schools in terms of the delivery of quality education and the provision of distinguished services to students and parents. This positive attitude to new technologies explains why GPS is always on the lookout for the latest advancements in educational technology aids and tools to support its functions and processes. This case reflects on the ups and downs associated with GPS decision to implement an ERP system with a promise for major business gains that can help GPS to reinstate its position in the leaders' quadrant.

Chapter 9

The "End-Users" factor is singled out as the one of the most important ERP Critical Success Factors (CSF). It is evident from reported ERP failure cases that commonly used approaches to ERP end-users' "training and competency building" are inadequate and ineffective. The case reports on an alternative structured approach that was developed and adopted in GCC Project. The new approach redefines the traditional role of "ERP Training" from isolated project activities that aim to introduce end-users to "how-to" use applications to an integral component of a comprehensive "knowledge and change management" strategy that advocates a holistic life-cycle approach to managing ERP. The proposed approach, which was successfully adopted in GCC ERP project, was built around "end-user characterization" as the main input into "competency building." It is also flexible enough to plug into standard ERP methodologies and could be projected throughout the ERP life cycle. The end-users characterization and Competency Building Approach (ECB) is expected to contribute to increased business gains and return on investment as a result of boosting levels of ERP usage and utilization.

Chapter 10

Computerized Maintenance Management Systems (CMMS) are designed to manage asset maintenance in a professional manner, by means of integrating all related transactions (financial, material, purchasing) and maintenance activities (work requests, work orders) and converting them into high level information to drive users towards best practices and optimize cost and improve asset reliability. However, CMMS will only remain a tool with limited use unless proper attention is given to dynamic data feeding by end-users to build up a reliable asset maintenance history that can be used as a basis for managing assets over the life cycle. This investigation reflects on the challenges encountered in the cases of three UAE CMMS Projects, comparing the effectiveness and suitability of the dynamic data-feeding strategies and approaches adopted in the three cases and the level of business improvement through proper usage and utilization.

Chapter 11

Wafi Al-Karaghouli, Brunel University, UK
Ahmed Al Azri, Ministry of Higher Educationt, Oman
Zahran Al Salti, Sultan Qaboos University, Oman

Transformational e-government projects and large-scale Enterprise Information System (EIS) implementation projects have one thing in common: they both overrun their time and budget due to unclear vision and unrealistic expectations. The aim of this chapter is to report on a success story of implementing e-government in the Higher Education Admission Centre (HEAC) that is beneficial in providing an insight to both categories of projects. The case is unlike many other case studies that look at project failures; it is concerned with exploring and discussing the key critical factors that facilitate the success of the projects of both categories (Brady & Maylor, 2010). The research is a qualitative approach, and the investigation uses a single case study, with data collected by means of semi-structured interviews and organisational documents from the Ministry of Higher Education in Oman. The research findings suggest that there are three paradigms with a set of factors that impact the success of projects, namely organisational paradigm, technology paradigm, and end-user paradigm.

Chapter 12

Asim Hussain, KOC, Kuwait

The chapter focuses on the challenges encountered and strategy used during Integrated Enterprise Asset Management (IEAMS) project from its inception to Go-Live. It has integrated all of the related processes from the project initiation to Asset Write-off (project initiation/ approval, asset creation/ operation/ maintenance/ write-offs, contract initiation/ execution/ payments) with the involvement of all concerned stakeholders. IEAMS has replaced over 100 legacy, standalone, and custom applications with Maximo®. The consolidation of these applications and associated data represented a challenge in data integrity, cleansing, transformation, migration, and upload to Maximo® as a unified data repository. A comprehensive training program was carried out before Go Live of the system to train all prospective users of the system. The extensive change management program included comprehensive campaigns, game shows to promote awareness about IEAMS in the company. A number of key personnel in their respective organizational units were designated as Change Agents to promote IEAMS and to ensure smooth transition upon Go Live.

Chapter 13

Mohamed Elhefnawi, UDEAL, UAE

The experience of many organizations that have automated their business capabilities using enterprise information systems indicates that the realization of the sought business gains and promised returns on investment are conditional to having in place an effective strategy to support and maintain such systems technically and functionally during the post-implementation phase. It is argued that the proper implementation of Information Technology Infrastructure Library (ITIL) represents an ideal forum for providing effective support tools that include service/help desk and incident reporting functions for end-users to report problems and issues or request enhancements, change management and configuration management functions to manage and document changes to the applications and functionalities, as well as IT infrastructure inventory and tracking applications. ITIL framework is widely used as a best-practice framework for IT services management. It outlines a set of integrated processes and procedures that will structure and re-engineer IT services activities, shifting IT function to be enterprise-wide business-focused while making the best use of the deployed technology. The case described in this chapter reflects the approach adopted by the IT function of an Arabian Gulf Company (AGC) used for ITIL implementation, highlighting the main challenges that have been encountered in this project.

Chapter 14

Nabil Ghalib, Business International Group, UAE

Application software projects have always been viewed as a massive challenge by companies, particularly when it comes to replacing legacy in-house developed systems with package solutions. Challenges start by the resentment to change typically demonstrated by a good percentage of the user community, followed by the many pitfalls encountered due to the changes that are included / excluded while the project progresses with user hesitance to accept the new system. The project had many challenges that are not typical of a properly managed one and to make matters worse, it had challenges that were related to poor priority settings that were attached to some non-professional aspects. Cultural issues came as a bonus in this project. The challenges and the counter measures taken to ensure the timely delivery of the project with minimum damage possible will be addressed as the chapter progresses, reflecting on how the objective shifted towards the end of its life to a win/win scenario.

The project aimed at developing a system to manage the development of young university graduates and equip them with the experience and skills necessary for integrating them in the company workforce. The case study focuses on three sections. The first section addresses the development of the Proof Of Concept (POC) that aimed at creating a prototype that was then enhanced in terms of its functional capabilities and data management tasks to meet the set objectives. The second section addresses how the POC was transformed to a fully functional multi-user system that was later utilized by all the divisions within the company. The third section touches on how the experience obtained was later used to help in building a unified system for the oil and gas sector in the country. The case also discusses the challenges, measures, and counter measures taken to address them, and the lessons learned to ensure the project was delivered to stakeholders.

The challenge of transforming data and information in enterprise information systems into knowledge that can be rolled up and presented to management as key performance indicators is business-critical. The implementation of a business intelligence layer on top of the transaction processing systems and management information systems is viewed as an opportunity to move up a level to promote knowledge-based decision-making and strategic planning. This chapter attempts to examine the issues and challenges associated with the initiative by Abu Dhabi Finance to implement business intelligence solutions that extract information from the enterprise information systems, present them as KPIs for senior management, and produce knowledge that can be used to support decision-making and strategic planning.

Foreword

In an age when Information and Communication Technology (ICT) has been rapidly perceived as a vehicle for business excellence, Enterprise Information Systems in particular have been evolving since the 90s as business-critical technology-based solutions that are widely accepted by Arabian Gulf organisations, as is the case with global businesses of all types and sizes accepting such systems as the backbone of their resource planning, operations, and management. Today, it is unimaginable that any business can survive without using one or more information systems to support its business functions and automate its business processes.

Despite the promised business gains, many companies underestimate the risk associated with implementing and utilizing such systems, and all kinds of problems are encountered in conjunction with system selection, implementation, dissemination, and utilization. In fact, an alarming number of EIS projects were deemed either complete failures or partial failures financially, technically, functionally, or due to end-users' resistance or rejection of the system.

This book includes the valuable contributions of EIS practitioners with reflections on their hands-on experiences in EIS projects in Gulf organisations, highlighting issues, problems, challenges, and lessons learned along with hidden costs related to such projects.

The scope includes case studies related to all stages of the EIS life-cycle, from the view point of both clients and vendors, including project managers, consultants, analysts, trainers, quality assurance coordinators, and subject matter experts. It covers a rich assortment of topics including system selection models, system implementation methodologies, post-implementation strategies, system usage and utilization, end-users' issues, project governance and oversight, project risks and threats, and critical success factors.

This volume is an excellent reference for practitioners, academics, and university students preparing to take up EIS-related posts in the industry. It will help them to identify the problems encountered during the conception of information systems. Furthermore, it provides measures to alleviate these problems and simultaneously identify new directions for future consideration.

Sami Abi Esber
Mideast Data Systems, UAE

Sami Abi Esber *is a prominent figure and a pioneer in the information technology arena of UAE and the region. Mr. Sami Abi Esber has managed, since 1987, when he started as an engineer, to move through different positions and resuming different roles to become the President of Mideast Data Systems (MDS) UAE in 1996. Mr. Abi Esber has successfully Developed MDS UAE from a single IT company to one the leading IT Groups in UAE and the region. Sami is well known for his affiliation and active participation in important local and regional information technology forums and conferences, such as: Member of Young Arab Leaders Organization (www.yaleaders.org); Member, through MDS, in World Economic Forum; Member of Board of Trustees and Executive Committee of University of Balamand, Lebanon; Vice President of the Lebanese Business Council in Abu Dhabi; Presenter and Speaker in Major International events (Planete Lebanon, TechLeb in MIT, etc.). Sami was also chosen by Channel Middle East Arabic Magazine (an ITP publication) as the number one Executive of UAE Information Technology Companies (System Integrators/Service Providers category) in 2008.*

Preface

It is nearly two decades since my first Enterprise Information System (EIS) implementation assignment at City of Melville, Western Australia, when I was nominated by my boss, Mr. Werner Corbe, Head of the Asset Management Unit, to lead the implementation of the Integrated Asset Management System (IAMS), an enterprise modular system with engineering and financial applications to support the management of infrastructure assets pertaining to road pavement, footpaths and crossovers, buildings, street furniture, drainage system, sewage system and landscape. I guess when Mr. Corbe selected me specifically to carry out this business-critical task, he was convinced that the nature of this type of system requires special knowledge and competencies in both business and technology, and since I was then a practicing asset management engineer and I was at the same time completing my Masters degree in Intelligent Information Processing Systems at the University of Western Australia, my chances to be designated this task were better than colleagues who were specialized in either business or technology but not both.

What I was not fully conscious of then is that the successful accomplishment of this mission, which was concluded with the satisfaction and endorsement of the City Mayor and the members of the City Council, was in a very mysterious way shaping my career path and paving the way for a highly challenging yet enjoyable journey of academic and professional specialization track in Enterprise Information Systems (EIS) and Enterprise Resource Planning (ERP) systems in particular.

Academically, over the past two decades, I have completed a doctorate level action research, which has included in its investigation scope twenty-seven major EIS projects in both Australia and the Gulf region. This research has not only deepened my understanding of the EIS and ERP issues, but has also culminated in the development of the Integrated Project Risk Management Model (IPRM) offering an alternative implementation approach with the potential to substantially reduce the likelihood of EIS and ERP failures. The results of this research reflected different aspects of EIS / ERP implementations in numerous Gulf organizations, and the findings were the subject of tens of research papers that were presented at prominent conferences

My related publications include three books and more than twenty peer-reviewed articles and research papers, which were the subject of seminars, workshops, and public presentation.

Also as university faculty, I have taught EIS and related subjects in undergraduate and post-graduate level courses at Abu Dhabi University and other institutions in Australia and the Gulf region.

Professionally, I have firsthand experience with ERP issues from the view points of both the vendor (as a consultant or manager) and the client (as subject matter expert or team leader). My ERP roles were not only diversified in the nature of the designation and responsibility, but also in terms of direct involvement in all stages through the ERP life-cycle (pre-implementation, implementation, and post-implementation).

This unique and successful experience in the early nineties has evidently signaled the beginning of an interesting career track that was enriching, exciting, and self-gratifying in many aspects, although not lacking in stress, pressures, frustration, and pain, which were frequently encountered in different projects.

Since the mid 90s, many business organizations have accepted EIS / ERP applications as their preferred platforms for integrating disparate enterprise functions and automating business processes. Organizations were longing for substantial business gains as an outcome of implementing such costly systems. However, nearly a decade after the introduction of these systems, organizations are weighing the diverse functional issues they have encountered, including technical problems, security threats, persisting end-user resistance, and excessive hidden costs. The big number of reported ERP implementation failures has also contributed to cynical views about the usefulness and worth of such systems, especially after taking into account the business risks associated with excessive hidden costs, complex business models, business process re-engineering, change management, and negative impacts on end-user perceptions.

The experiences of EIS projects successes and failures are worth consolidating for both professionals and academics to use as teaching cases and lessons learned. How successful have enterprise solutions been in Gulf countries? What were the persisting issues? Have the promised benefits and investment returns been realized by the Gulf organizations? What is the outlook of enterprise systems in the Gulf? What are the lessons learned? Arabian Gulf countries (Saudi Arabia, Qatar, UAE, Kuwait, Oman, and Bahrain) have led the region in the adoption and utilization of enterprise information systems. Gulf region organizations' expenditures on enterprise systems since the 90s have exceeded those of many developed countries, and have outpaced those of other countries in the Middle East region. Observers attribute this phenomenon primarily to the unprecedented increase in oil prices, but also acknowledge the role of expatriate employees in technology investment decision-making at senior or middle management levels or even as specialists, advisors, and consultants.

There are many EIS stories to tell and experiences to share that are of interest to both specialists and academics. The cases in this book investigate important EIS implementations in different Gulf organizations, reflecting the first hand experiences of consultants, managers, and experts working on real projects.

This unique book on enterprise systems is an indispensable source of EIS cases from organizations in the Gulf region. These cases are distinguished by high technology investment over the past 15 years in a culture that highly regards human values. EIS practitioners and academics in the region and globally will find the book cases to be both informative and enjoyable to read. The book focuses on EIS specialists' experiences implementing enterprise systems, delivers a comprehensive multi-perspective account of EIS issues, and explores the concerns, problems, risks, and critical success factors of EIS for a variety of organizations.

Conscious of the difficulty in finding relevant EIS material and documented cases to benefit from, and use by both practitioners and academics, the book attempt to fill in this gap by meeting different audiences' requirements and demands.

The book is a useful resource to support demand of teaching (academics and students), to use as a text supporting cases and material for IS/IT and MIS undergraduate and post-graduate courses, and could also be used by academic researchers as a reference and source of cases for further research.

The book could also be a useful reference for analysts, consultants, managers, and staff (vendors and clients) who may be involved in any of the following phases in the life of such systems: system selection, system adoption, system implementation, and system post-implementation.

The cases covered in the book highlight and investigate important aspects of enterprise information system issues in Gulf organizations in any of the systems' life-cycle stages, providing detailed accounts of the settings and highlighting the problem situations, challenges, opportunities, and decisions.

The textbook is organized in 16 chapters, covering through the reflections of practitioners and experts a multitude of EIS aspects and issues encountered in different implementations in Gulf organizations. Each chapter presents one or more cases for examination with a focus on a selected issue or question using analytical tools to highlight strengths and opportunities or identify weakness, vulnerabilities, and threats as an input for drawing on the lessons learnt from the experience.

Chapter 1 attempts to examine the nature and causes of issues, problems, and concerns that were observed by an ERP consultant in one of Kuwait's Oil and Gas ERP implementations, and suggests the introduction of new and enhanced features in ERP system implementation methodologies as a means to cope with potentially damaging issues, problems, and concerns, and prevent them from evolving into malicious risks that could lead to project failures.

Chapter 2 reports on the successful implementation of EIS system in UAE Oil producing company. The author, who was in the project, reflects on the experience, which involved the replacement of the existing maintenance, supply, and commercial system with a new enterprise information system and the upgrade of the human resources and financial systems to the latest releases. The chapter discuses the challenges that were encountered and how change was managed, and extracts important lessons learnt from the experience.

Chapter 3 moves away from business organizations to the education sector, to emphasize the importance and potential of Enterprise Resource Planning in educational organizations. It discusses the main objectives and benefits from utilizing such applications to support the integration, automation, and optimization of educational processes and functions. The chapter is specifically concerned with school ERP solution systems that offer complete school management software and cover all the functions that contribute to the smooth functioning of school activities. As it examines ERP solutions in the educational sectors, the study focuses on the case of ERP usage and utilization in the United Arab Emirates (UAE) public (government schools).

Chapter 4 is concerned with green implementation of EIS systems. It describes any EIS implementation as a complex journey and suggests that ERP end-users compare to confused travelers in an alien land. It takes them time to be familiarized with routes, signs, languages, and people, and similarly, just as they think they are finding their way with the system, someone announces it is time to upgrade and to start to move again. The case reflects an interesting implementation of a major UAE Oil and Gas Services Company. It highlights a novel approach that was mandated by necessity as the project was managed remotely and executed primarily by internal resources, making it a lean and green implementation.

Chapter 5 is concerned with an important subject that echoes the debate and the comparison of the pros and cons of in-house development enterprise information applications to the deployment of configurable EIS packages. The case provides an insight into an in-house development of a paperless medical system for a Gulf Off-Shore Operating Company. The case study is an example of how a solution was decided and implemented. It touches on the positive and negative aspects of the decision to build the application in-house rather than implement a software package and covers a range of issues that were encountered during every phase of the development life cycle. The author's familiarity with ERP packages and his role as a designer and developer adds value to the argument and to the analysis of the structured approach that was adopted.

Chapter 6 touches on an important decision, that needs to be taken during the post-rollout stage of the ERP systems life cycle, whether to replace or upgrade. In many cases, this translates into a critical management-sponsored mission designating a dedicated team or task force to investigate the feasibility of the alternative options and to report on the preferred option with a recommendation of the way forward and implementation approach. This case reflects on the investigations of Gulf Telecom Company in exploring the viability and feasibility of its ERP options to support and provide the grounds for a management decision to mark the next phase of the ERP in the organization. The case describes the approach that was adopted by Gulf Telecom and highlights the challenges to accomplish the mission successfully and any lessons learned from this experience.

Chapter 7 suggests that the high rate of reported failures in ERP implementation projects warrants the urgent need to identify the causes of such failures and the preventing actions associated with these causes. This case highlights some of the important issues, problems, and challenges that the author has encountered as a project manager of ERP system implementation in an Oil and Gas company in Kuwait. The focus of the case is on lessons learned and tips that can be handy and useful for people who may resume this important role in implementation projects.

Chapter 8 explores another interesting case from the education sector in the region, in its efforts to achieve excellence with the help of a technology-based solution. This positive attitude to new technologies explains GPS's continuous lookout for the latest advancements in educational technology aids and tools to support its functions and processes. However, the approach adopted for the selection and deployment of the new enterprise system had proven to be inadequate and the venture did not go smoothly. The case reflects on the ups and downs associated with GPS decision to implement an ERP system with the promise of major business gains that can help GPS to reinstate its position in the leaders' quadrant.

Chapter 9 highlights the criticality of the End-Users' factor to the success or failure of the ERP venture. This case highlights the ineffectiveness of the current approaches to ERP end-users' "training and competency building," that are commonly applied in ERP implementations and describes an alternative structured approach that redefines the traditional role of "ERP Training" from isolated implementation project activities concerned with introducing end-users to "how to" use ERP applications to an integral part of a comprehensive "knowledge and change management" strategy that advocates a holistic life-cycle approach to managing ERP Critical Success Factors. The proposed approach, which is built around "end-user characterization" as the main input into "competency building" is flexible enough to plug into standard ERP methodologies and may be projected throughout the ERP life-cycle.

Chapter 10 reflects on the challenges encountered in the cases of three UAE Computerized Maintenance Management System (CMMS) Projects, comparing the effectiveness and suitability of the dynamic data-feeding strategies and approaches adopted in the three cases and the level of business improvement through proper usage and utilization. Lessons learned are drawn from the experience to suggest improved methods for favorable outcomes.

Chapter 11 proposes that transformational e-government projects and large-scale Enterprise Information System (EIS) implementation projects have one thing in common: they both overrun their time and budget due to unclear vision and unrealistic expectations. The aim of this chapter is to report on a success story of implementing e-government in the Higher Education Admission Centre (HEAC) that is beneficial in providing an insight to both categories of projects. The case is unlike many other case studies that look at project failures. It is concerned with exploring and discussing the key critical factors that facilitate the success of the projects of both categories.

Chapter 12 focuses on the challenges encountered and strategy used during the Integrated Enterprise Asset Management (IEAMS) project from its inception to Go-Live. It has integrated all of the related processes with the involvement of all concerned stakeholders. IEAMS has replaced over 100 legacy, standalone, and custom applications with IBM MAXIMO system. The consolidation of these applications and associated data represented a challenge in data integrity, cleansing, transformation, migration, and upload to IBM MAXIMO as a unified data repository. With special attention to the human factor, a comprehensive end-users training program and extensive change management program was carried out to promote awareness about IEAMS in the company before the Go-Live.

Chapter 13 claims that the realization of the sought business gains and promised returns on investment of Enterprise Information Systems are conditional to having an effective strategy to support and maintain such systems technically and functionally during the post-implementation phase. It is argued that the proper implementation of Information Technology Infrastructure Library (ITIL) represents an ideal forum for providing effective support tools that include service/help desk and incident reporting functions for end-users to report problems and issues or request enhancements, change management and configuration management functions to manage and document changes to the applications and functionalities, IT infrastructure inventory, and tracking applications. The case reflects on the approach adopted by the IT Division (ITD) of Arabian Gulf Company (AGC) in its ITIL implementation and the main challenges that have been encountered in that project.

Chapter 14 reports on the challenges associated with the replacement of a human resources legacy in-house developed system with package solutions in Gulf Organization. These challenges range from the resentment to change by many end-users to system pitfalls that contribute to end-users hesitance to accept the new system and consequently leading to low usage and utilization. The case also highlights cultural issues and poor priority settings that were attached to some non-professional aspects. The case study is an example of how a project could take a dangerous turn from what was agreed on and also reflects on the results from additional detours that were made during its life cycle until sign off.

Chapter 15 reports on the case of a project to build a system to manage the development of young university graduates, and to equip them with the experience and skills necessary for integrating them in the company workforce. The case study focuses on: 1) the development of the Proof of Concept (POC) that aimed at creating a prototype, 2) how the POC was transformed to a fully functional multi-user system, and 3) how the experience obtained was later used to help in building a unified system for the Oil and Gas sector in the country. The case also discusses the challenges, measures, and countermeasures taken to address them, and the lessons learned to ensure the project was delivered to stakeholders.

Chapter 16 discusses the challenge of transforming data and information in enterprise information systems into knowledge that can be rolled up and presented to management as key performance indicators. The implementation of a business intelligence layer on top of the transaction processing systems and management information systems is viewed as an opportunity to move up a level to promote knowledge-based decision-making and strategic planning. This chapter attempts to examine the issues and challenges associated with the initiative by Abu Dhabi Finance to implement business intelligence solutions that extract information from the enterprise information systems, present them as KPIs for senior management, and produce knowledge that can be used to support decision-making and strategic planning.

To this end, the main objective of this case book is to bring together different and insightful experiences from EIS practitioners from the Gulf region to reflect on their personal experiences with EIS implementations issues, challenges, and lessons learnt. I expect this book to be an essential reference and a resource on Enterprise Information Systems in the Arabian Gulf region.

Fayez Albadri
ADMA-OPCO, UAE

Acknowledgment

To ensure that this book is unique in its offering to practitioners, academics, and graduating university students preparing to enter the industry, much time and effort has been expended on the quality, relevance, and knowledge-value of the selected cases. This has proven to be a major undertaking and the project could not have reached the shores of safety without the dedication and support of many people.

I would like to extend my gratitude to all people who have contributed directly or indirectly through support and encouragement to bring this amazing work to light. In particular, I thank the respected members of the editorial advisory board for their valuable support throughout this venture. However, my genuine appreciation goes to the chapters' authors for sharing their hands-on experiences, and for shrewdly presenting these experiences as distinguished scholarly work.

My special thanks are extended to my colleagues in ADMA-OPCO and the ERP Custodian team, colleagues I worked with on different projects during my two-decade EIS/ERP journey in both Australia and the Arabian Gulf region, and to my MIS, EIS, and EDT students at Abu Dhabi University, who I lectured (2007-2012), for their support and encouragement. I also extend special thanks to my dear colleague and friend Dr. Salam Abdallah, who was a co-editor in the early development stages of the textbook.

I dedicate this work to my beloved parents, brothers and their families, and to my direct family members: Baha, Ahmad, Ayah, Omar, Dima, and little Maya.

Chapter 1
ERP Implementation in Kuwait O&G:
Issues, Problems, and Concerns

Firas Albataineh
Oracle Systems, UAE

EXECUTIVE SUMMARY

A project is a complex, no routine, one-time effort limited by time, budget, resources, and performance specifications designed to meet a customer's needs (Gray & Larson, 2010). Consequently, although projects may seem similar, largely they are different, and each project represents a unique experience reflecting the variations in the projects' scopes, objectives, specifications, time, budget, resources, constraints, and risks. In line with this, the author's experience as a consultant in different ERP projects indicates that each project has its own unique issues, concerns, and problems, although some of them are common across different projects. This chapter attempts to examine the nature and causes of issues, problems, and concerns that were observed in one of the author's Gulf ERP implementations and suggests the introduction of new and enhanced features in ERP system implementation methodologies as a means to cope with potentially damaging issues, problems, and concerns, and prevent them from evolving into malicious risks that could lead to project failures.

DOI: 10.4018/978-1-4666-2220-3.ch001

ORGANIZATION BACKGROUND

The case subject to be discussed in this chapter belongs to Oil and Gas Company (OGC) located in the northern part of the Arabian Gulf and will be referred to throughout the chapter as OGC. The discussion is concerned with OGC implementation and integration of two international systems to support the majority of OGC business requirements and business areas namely, IBM MAXIMO, as best of breed system, and Oracle E-Business Suite, as the ERP system.

Oracle applications were used in OGC mainly to support the Human Resources, Payroll, and Financial requirements by utilizing Oracle Human Resource (HR), Payroll, and Financial modules within EBS.

However, IBM MAXIMO applications were used to support OGC requirements in the areas of Asset Management, Supply Chain, and Contracts by utilizing IBM MAXIMO Maintenance, Inventory, Purchasing, and Contracts modules.

The two systems (Oracle EBS and IBM MAXIMO) were integrated by a prominent international implementation vendor by means of a customized API application interface with an agreed definition of interface points and rules and modes of data exchange.

Oracle is the gold standard for database technology and applications in enterprises. Oracle is a public company and it is the world's leading supplier of information management software and the world's second largest independent software company. Oracle is a multinational corporation that specializes in developing and marketing hardware systems and enterprise software products. Oracle Revenue as of 2010 was US $26.82 billion (Wikipedia).

The corporation has arguably become best known for its flagship product, the Oracle Database. The company also builds tools for database development and systems of middle-tier software, Enterprise Resource Planning (ERP) software, Customer Relationship Management (CRM) software, and Supply Chain Management (SCM) software.

International Business Machines (IBM) is a multinational technology and consulting firm. IBM manufactures and sells computer hardware and software, and it offers infrastructure, hosting, and consulting services. IBM is a public company with revenue as of 2010 of US$ 99.870 billion. International Business Machines Corporation (Wikipedia). MRO Software, the provider of MAXIMO, was acquired by IBM in August 2006.

SETTING THE STAGE

A close look at how operations were handled by OGC prior to the ERP project indicates clearly that business areas and functions were isolated of each other resembling disconnected islands whereby each OGC department (island) had its applications, programs, activities, and own way of doing things without much consideration of how they would those impact or related to other parts of the organization. While some departments were running legacy systems, others were either using simple standalone software and MS applications or running virtually fully manually.

OGC had more than 30 legacy systems running at the same time on different databases including, Oracle, MS Access, and SQL Server, and were also running on different platforms. These legacy systems were used by nearly 2000 employees from different business areas, such as Maintenance, Inspection, Inventory, Purchasing, Contracts, Finance, Human Resources, and Payroll.

It was evident that not all the legacy systems were talking to each other (integrated) and fell short of covering all the business areas requirements and needs.

Recognizing the inadequacy of the existing softwares and their lack of integration, OGC was on the lookout for the best solution to integrate or replace these various legacy systems, improve the business processes and automate all the manual work. Eventually the final decision was in favor of replacing all the legacy systems with a proven ERP solution. The selection process was concluded with a recommendation to implement and integrate Oracle E-Business Suite and IBM MAXIMO to constitute the total ERP solution.

The duration of the implementation project was two years and was partnered and resourced by three companies: OGC (The project owner), IVEN (The ERP implementing vendor for both Oracle and Maximo), and CONSCO (The consulting company that was hired by OGC for auditing purposes and to make sure that IVEN was implementing and delivering the project correctly and according to the signed contract with OGC).

The project team was made up of 67 people representing the three companies as follows:

OGC: The project owners' resources and participants in the ERP implementation project included (9) Steering committee members, (1) Project sponsor, (1) Project manager (PM), and (33) Team members representing the following business and technical areas:

- Finance, human resource, and payroll business team leader 1 and members 6.
- Maintenance business team leader 1 and members 9.
- Supply chain and contracts business team leader 1 and members 11.
- Technical members 4.

IVEN: The ERP implementing vendor's resources included (1) Project manager and (18) Team members assigned to the following teams:

- Maintenance team leader/business consultant 1 and senior maintenance business consultant 1.
- Inventory team leader/business consultant 1 and senior inventory business consultant 1.
- Purchasing team leader/business consultant 1 & senior purchasing business consultant 1.
- Contracts team leader/business consultant 1 and senior contract business consultant 1.
- Financial team leader/business consultant 1 and senior financial business consultant 1.
- Human resource and payroll team leader/business consultant 1 and senior human resource and payroll business consultant 1.
- Technical consultant team leader 1 and technical senior consultants 5.

CONSCO: The consulting company resources included (1) Project manager and (6) Team members distributed as follows:

- Maintenance consultant 1.
- Inventory consultant 1.
- Purchasing consultant 1.
- Contract consultant 1.
- Financial consultant 1.
- Human resource and payroll consultant 1.

The author's role was the IVEN maintenance team leader business consultant and acting as a project manager whenever needed.

CASE DESCRIPTION

The following points have been defined as high level project objectives to ensure project focus and common understanding among all involved parties of the main deliverables and output from the project:

- One consolidated business processes document across all departments in OGC.
- Automation of all the manual work.

- One integrated ERP system across all departments in OGC.
- The introduction of a unified database.
- Improve data visibility throughout the company.
- Adopt excellence Key Performance Indicators (KPIs) and apply analysis mechanism for implementation.
- Automate the communication between all OGC departments.
- Increase the employees' efficiency and skills.

After OGC had selected the systems and selected the implementation vendor company (IVEN) to implement the selected systems, a contract agreement was signed off between OGC and IVEN.

Following the contract agreement sign-off, a kick-off meeting was held between the three companies to signal the launching of the ERP project. The one-day formal meeting was attended by all project team members from OGC, IVEN, and CONSCO. The main objectives for this meeting were to introduce the team members, agree on the logistical matters (i.e. working areas, safety procedures, security requirements, etc.) and to agree on a short-term action plan until the formal detailed project plan was produced and agreed on.

At a later time, after the launching of the project, the implementation vendor IVEN produced a detailed project plan that was duly reviewed and approved by OGC. The project plan had included the below main activities, and each main activity had detailed tasks assigned to it.

This case elaborates on each of the included activities and tasks in the detailed project plan highlighting the issues, problems, and concerns associated with the main ERP implementation project. The adopted implementation methodology was used as a guide to define the projects activities, tasks, deliverables, and milestones as part of the project plan. The following are the main activities that constitute the ERP implementation plan.

Project Office Activity

The first main activity on the project plan was the project office set up. The implementation methodology highly recommended to create a comfortable work environment and to have all project team members gathered and work in the same environment. Accordingly, OGC has prepared a project office for the project team members with workstations, computers, communication tools and logistics items including:

- Desks, filing cabinets, and stationeries.
- Communication: Phones, Internet, and intranet connectivity.
- Computers, servers, laptops, scanners, and printers.

- Meeting rooms with a projector and flip chart in each room.
- Training rooms equipped with desktop computers, projector, and flip chart.

Team Mobilization Activity

The second main activity on the project plan was the team mobilization and project teams' formation. The three companies involved; OGC, IVEN, and CONSCO have mobilized their personnel that they have been assigned as project team members and resources. The team members were divided into technical members and business or functional members.

The business (functional) team members were assigned the responsibility to handle business activities such as defining reports and carry out business processes workshops. The technical team members' responsibilities were to deal with technical project activities such as developing reports and system customizations and configurations. The main responsibilities of the project's business and technical consultants were defined as follows:

- **Business (functional) consultant:** Responsible to provide application training, business processes reengineering, business workshops, data gathering guidance, reports definitions, application testing, application support, etc.
- **Technical consultant:** Responsible to provide technical training, system installation, data loading, configuration, customizations, tailoring the software, setup security profiles, building reports, technical workshops, systems integrations, etc.

Some of IVEN consultants were relocated from their home country and others were allocated locally. When the project was kicked off, not all the team members from OGC and IVEN were present. Many of the team members joined the project after it was started.

Building the System and Databases Environments Activity

The third main activity was installing IBM Maximo and EBS systems and creating the databases. Many different environments were created to serve different purposes, with each environment has its own set of applications, database and workflow rules.

The following five environments were developed by the IVEN technical consultants:

- **Test Environment:** The main purpose for this environment was to carry out the system testing by OGC.

- **Training Environment:** The main purpose for this environment was to deliver both OGC core team training and end user training.
- **Development Environment:** The main purpose for this environment was to carry out all the system configurations, customizations, and building reports.
- **Production Environment:** This was the environment that OGC went live with.
- **Data Migration Environment:** The main purpose for this environment was to test the migrated data. The data was migrated from different databases, Excel sheets and from Word documents by the IVEN technical consultants.

OGC Core Team Training Activity

The fourth activity on the project plan was OGC's project core team training. The training courses were delivered by the IVEN's technical and business consultants depends on the nature of the training course.

Although, OGC project team members were considered business experts in their respective business areas and had the deep business knowledge, the core team training objectives were to transform them into subject-matter experts in almost unreasonably short two to three weeks period, because they were going to be responsible for managing the ERP implementation project from the OGC side.

The IVEN consultants trained the OGC team on the system functionalities to prepare them for participating in the business process workshop. The core team training had a hand-on practice to familiarize the trainees with the system main features and functionalities.

Business Process Workshop Activity

The main purpose of this activity is to define OGC 'To Be' business processes, not to convert the 'As Is' business processes to 'To Be' business processes. After OGC core project team members were trained on the system functionalities, the business process workshop was launched. The business process workshop involved three distinct steps:

- The first step was an intensive workshop session that was held between the OGC team and the IVEN business consultants. Both teams walked through the 'To Be' business process in details. During this workshop, the data loading strategies had been discussed and agreed (for e.g. inventory codes, labour and craft codes, location hierarchies, levels of detail for instrumentation, etc.). In addition, comprehensive gap notes were taken by both team members. Wherever gaps were identified, solutions were discussed and agreed.

These solutions changed some of the business processes and added some configurations to the system.

- The second step involved formal documentation of the workshop outcomes. Three documents were produced; the first document was the Gap Notes Document, which listed all the identified gaps listed during the workshop, the second document was the Business Processes Document, which outlined the OGC proposed new business processes, and the third document was the System Configurations Document, which identified the system configurations and customizations requirements.
- The third step was the presentation of the Business Processes Document and the System Configurations Document to OGC team and management for approval. After the approval was obtained, the Business Processes Document was formed the basis for OGC operations and the System Configurations Document was formed the basis for the system changes.

Reports Workshop Activity

The purpose of the reports workshop was to define OGC new report requirements and to classify them into different report types, namely; Static reports, KPI reports and Drilldown reports.

Usually The ERP system is shipped with many standard reports; however, it is inevitable that the client request his own specialized reporting requirements and so did OGC. The agreed number of new reports was10 for each module, which were to be developed by IVEN, of course 10 reports were evidently insufficient.

The reports workshop involved three distinct steps:

- The first step was an intensive workshop session, which was held between the OGC team and IVEN business consultants. Both teams walked through the new reports requirements in details. During this workshop, each report requirements such as data to be displayed, format of the data, and how the data will be displayed were discussed.
- The second step involved formal documentation of the reports identified in step one. This document identified the list of reports required and the reports specifications (Reports Requirements Document) and outlined the reports mock up.
- The third step of this workshop was the presentation of the Reports Requirements Document to OGC team and management for approval. After the approval has been obtained, the Reports Requirements Document was forwarded to the IVEN technical team or to the reports writer consultant to start developing the reports.

System Configurations Activity

'Configuration' and 'Customization' are two terms that are widely confused in the context of ERP system implementation and which need clarification for their importance.

They are defined as follows:

- **Configuration:** It is applying changes to the standard ERP applications by using readily available configuration tools, without touching the system source code or changing the way the system behave. Such configurations will be part of future system upgrade.
- **Customization:** It is applying changes to the standard ERP applications by means of changing the system source code and / or the way the system behave. In future system upgrades, these customizations will not be part of the upgrade process and need to be redone and tested it again.

It was inevitable to identify areas were elements of configurations were required, including the following:

- Re-labeling of screens fields to suit OGC terminologies.
- Creating new fields to hold additional data not provided by standard package.
- Hiding of non-required fields from screens.
- Changing the field lengths.
- Adding additional values to the standard value lists.
- Creating new tabs, screens, and applications.

After the Business Processes Document and the System Configurations Document were signed and approved by OGC during the business process workshop activity. The IVEN technical consultants started configuring the system based on these documents. In this project, there were a lot of configurations as well as some customizations.

As a rule of thumb, it would be strongly recommended to adopt minimum customization strategy to guide the ERP implementation by exploring other options and workarounds unless the customizations are very vital for the business.

Data Mapping and Migration Activity

The data mapping and migration exercise had three main steps; data gathering, data mapping and data migration.

- **Data Gathering Step:** This step was completed by OGC core team. The data was collected from the following areas: Legacy systems, Excel sheets, Word documents and hard copy documents. This step included the following sub steps carried out by the OGC core team:
  ○ OGC reviewed all the history data and then decided which data needed to be migrated to the new system and which data was not needed to be migrated.
  ○ For the data that needed to be migrated, OGC core team did a lot of cleansing and cleaning before it was handed over to IVEN.
  ○ After the data was cleansed and cleaned, it was gathered and prepared by OGC core team in an agreed format to be handed over officially to IVEN for data migration.
- **Data Mapping Step:** This step was completed by the IVEN technical consultant, who mapped the data submitted by OGC to the new system fields and tables. The data was mapped and pointed to the new system fields and tables and the technical consultant had to make sure that the new system field's characteristics were correct to accept the migrated data. This step were reviewed and approved by OGC core team.
- **Data Migration Step:** The IVEN technical consultant physically migrated (moved) the data to the new system. The IVEN technical consultant had to make sure that following points were successfully completed before handing the migrated data to OGC core team for testing:
  ○ All the history data records have been migrated.
  ○ The total number of records migrated were correct.
  ○ The data was migrated to the correct fields.
  ○ The data was populated on the screen correctly.
  ○ The data integrity.
  ○ The data relationship.

The data migration step was done on the data migration database and finally before the go live was done on the production database.

Systems Integration Activity

OGC had two options either opt the "packaged tour" with an integrated system from one vendor, or plan its own itinerary; the so-called "best of breed" approach and this subject is a complete separate discussion. For the optimal solution in each area, the best of breed option usually provides richer functionality, satisfying more users. However, savings, convenience, and efficient data sharing can make the integrated approach very appealing.

The "packaged tour" or integrated systems provide multiple applications with a common database and consistent user interface so that all modules have a familiar look and feel. The downside is that some applications may have anemic functionality, causing users in these areas to become disgruntled.

Best of breed systems, designed specifically to excel in just one or a few applications, can also pose challenges, such as increased training and support, complex interfaces with other systems, duplicate data entry, and redundant data storage.

The following are key factors that can be considered in weighing the pros and cons of the two options and selecting the most suitable option:

- Cost.
- Support.
- Data sharing.
- Leverage.
- Functionality.

In comparing and choosing an integrated system approach or best of breed approach, much may depend on the client's organization's size, culture, and management style. If sub-entities within the organization are large or complex, they may require the advanced functionality that only a best of breed system can provide.

In a highly centralized decision making organization, easier access to shared data would likely take a higher priority. In such case, specialized systems that do not provide mission critical functionality would be sacrificed for the "greater good" of shared data and other integrated system efficiencies.

Trends show that many organizations are beginning to prefer and adopt an integrated systems strategy and are filling in the gaps with best of breed systems. Many integrated vendors now offer a "one-stop shopping" experience by either acquiring or partnering with best of breed vendors. In such cases, data sharing problems may still occur, but the vendor is committed to making the integration appear seamless.

In this project, the best of breed approach was selected by the vendor. The two systems, MAXIMO and Oracle EBS were selected to be implemented and integrated as a total ERP solution supporting OGC's main business functions.

Because OGC decided to go with the best of breed approach, he had two options: either to purchase out of the box integration directly from one of the owners of the systems, and in this case would be either Oracle or Maximo, or ask the implementation vendor to build the integration between both systems. However, OGC had selected the second option whereby IVEN is given the responsibility to build the integration.

An integration workshop was held between OGC team and IVEN business and technical teams to capture OGC integration requirements and decide on the integration points and strategy. The information captured during the workshop, were used as a base for writing the Integration Document.

The Integration Document was written by the IVEN technical consultant and it was reviewed and approved by OGC core team.

Systems Testing Activity

System testing is a very important activity in any ERP implementation. It is the procedure that usually timed prior to the software goes live, in order to identify certain situations that may occur after the implementation has been completed.

OGC had tested the business processes, the system configurations and customizations, the reports, the data migrated, and the integration on the test environment to ensure the readiness of the system to go live.

The test scripts were written by the IVEN business and technical consultants to ensure that the results that OGC would get were in line with their expectation and to their satisfaction.

The tests were conducted in two steps and at two different levels: unit system tests, where each module was tested separately, and complete system tests, where all the system modules were tested together.

End Users Training and Training Materials Activity

The main objective for the end user training was to minimize the productivity losses associated with the software transition period. This meant that OGC had to get its end users up to the skill level required to do their jobs at least as quickly and accurately as they were doing before with the old software or manually, especially that OGC was believed that the new systems would help the end users to do their jobs more quickly, accurately, and more securely than before.

The IVEN technical and business consultants wrote all the customized training materials that would be used during the end users training. These materials were reviewed and approved by OGC core team.

OGC and IVEN teams spent a lot of time to plan for the end user training. They agreed as a strategy that all the users must attend an overview course before attending the specialized courses. They also explored and agreed on important training related issues such as:

- Training courses schedules.
- Which users will attend which specialized training courses.
- Training venues and the tools needed during training.
- The adoption of a backup plan for users that could miss the training courses.

The training method that was agreed on was the hands-on style instructor-led training, whereby an instructor shows users how the software works and how to perform common tasks, with users performing the tasks themselves in a classroom on their own computers. The training facilities were prepared to accompany 15 to 20 trainees.

System Rollout

The implementation project was completed with the system 'Rollout' or 'Go-live' phase signaling the beginning of the post-implementation phase, which was agreed as important as the implementation phase itself.

Therefore, and in order to move smoothly from the implementation phase to the post-implementation phase, OGC had set up a fully support help desk to assist end users in any problems they face as they start using the new system and also OGC has prepared super users to coach and support end-users with any questions or problems.

The following points were observed during the system rollout or go-live:

- The rollout during the first days had experienced many technical issues, such as the system was stopped and restarted few times due to the high number of users accessing the system concurrently. The technical consultants had to work day and night to fix the issue.
- As a result of the frequent restarting of the system, the interface had failed to start and needed attention by the technical consultant.
- Most of the users were not able to run reports because they did not know how to do it and we found out that most of them did not get trained on how to generate reports specially the complicated reports where the user had to enter some parameters.
- Most of the users were confused with workflow processes because again during the training there was no proper exercises on how to work with workflow processes.

PROJECT ISSUES, PROBLEMS, AND SUGGESTED IMPROVEMENTS

This section is mainly to scrutinize and discuss the actual project execution, highlighting any deviations from the plans and any providing suggestions for improvement in future implementations. The discussion follows the project activities as were described in the previous section.

Project Office Activity

The project owner, OGC prepared the project office but it was incomplete and important items were missing at the time of the project kick-off including; telephone lines, Internet and intranet connections and the servers. Although the telephone lines are not that very important, but the team members used their own cellular phones instead for nearly 2 weeks inconveniently carrying the associated costs. Similarly, the lack of Internet and intranet connections had caused the team members extra effort and time and some activities were delayed.

The two months delay of the delivery of the implementation servers caused a huge delay in some activities in the project; and other activities were delivered with very low quality like team training. For instance, the team training was delivered in a very low quality because the system was installed on temporary low specifications servers. Another example, all the technical work had to be done on the temporary low specifications servers leading to extra effort and time from project members to shift all the technical work to the new servers.

Based on the above, it is strongly recommended that the project should not start unless the project office is equipped at least with the main and critical items.

Team Mobilization Activity

After the project started and the team members were assigned, the following serious issues and problems were encountered, which caused the project a lot of delay and budget over run.

The IVEN team members knew the software very well, but they did not have the industry business experience. This caused a lot of problems, because the IVEN consultants could not understand the client requirements because they could not speak the industry language, so it was difficult to offer OGC the best solution. In fact, during the business process workshop the IVEN consultant could not offer enough examples to OGC team because again they did not have enough industry knowledge.

An experienced consultant should have both the software experience as well as the industry experience. OGC should have interviewed all the IVEN team members to make sure that they had both the software and the industry experience.

Some of the IVEN consultants were on and off the project, because they were involved in more than one project. This was not a good practice, because during the project some issues were raised that needed an immediate action from these consultants and they were away, again this delayed the project. Other consultants were on and off the project, because they could not relocate from their home country, because they needed a work permit; I believe they should not be on the project from the first place unless a work permit is issued to them.

The project team members should be full time members that are dedicated for the project, especially for big and long projects and locally residing consultants should be preferred over consultants stationed abroad.

Some IVEN consultants have been taking off the project and reassigned to other projects permanently during the implementation. This had delayed the project because this practice of reassigning consultants to other projects and bringing on another consultants to take over will delay the project one-way or another. To eliminate the delay, there should have been at least a full one month of hand over period, where both consultants work on the project at the same time.

OGC and IVEN should not have agreed to reassign any of the team members unless it was urgent and critical.

Building the System and Database Environment Activity

This activity added a lot of extra days to the project, because the servers were delayed, so the IVEN technical consultants had to create these environments and databases on temporary servers to be able to deliver the team training on time as well as some other project activities.

The quality of the team training was low and not up to the standards because the temporary server's response were slow and not effective. Additionally, OGC technical team was not involved in this activity.

It is important to ensure the availability of the servers and to have a contingency and backup plan in case of delivery delay. It is vital to involve the client technical team for knowledge transfer and to be able to provide future support.

OGC Team Training Activity

Some major issues were raised during this phase. All OGC core team members attended the detailed specific course that was related to their work, without attending the prerequisite course, plus the course training days were not enough and the practice exercises were not adequate.

It is recommended that the owner team members should have been educated not just on how to use the software but also on best practice techniques, so that they are clear about any implications of future actions. Additionally, all members of the core team should have attended as a minimum the following courses during the core team training: 1) overview training course and 2) specialized training course.

The overview-training course would provide the core team with adequate knowledge and hands-on experience, including manipulation of fields and navigation of screens, forms, and sessions. The specialized training course would provide functional representatives within the core team in-depth knowledge and hands-on experience in specific and relevant system modules that relate to their business function or department.

Business Process Workshop Activity

During this phase of the project, some major issues and concerns have been observed with respect to OGC team, such as they had the tendency to replicate the existing systems processes and behavior to the new system and convert the As-Is business processes to To-Be business processes and automate everything without proper validation.

In addition, IVEN consultants had problems of their own as they have lacked in industry practices and experience adversely affecting their credibility in front of the OGC users and also reflecting on the poor quality of their produced "To-Be" documents.

Many of the OGC team members did not fully comprehend the features of the newly installed system, which subsequently led to low performance and they resisted and objected to the changes in the business process.

The business process workshop purpose was to define the "To-Be" business processes. The biggest problem that was raised during the workshop was that the OGC users were looking at the "As-Is" business process and try to build on it, which was not the purpose of the workshop. The main purpose was to build the new business processes, in other words what the new business processes the users want.

OGC tried to automate existing redundant or non-value-added processes to the new system. The integrated environment of the new ERP system will require the organization to do business in a different way. Therefore, existing business processes had to be reengineered from the bottom up to join together with the ERP structure and requirements.

The vendor consultants supposed to help OGC users to build the "To-Be" business processes by providing them with the latest and best industry standard processes, unfortunately the IVEN consultants knew the software very well but not the industry business, so the OGC users were talking industry language and the IVEN consultants did not comprehend this at the right level, because the IVEN consultants were talking the software language.

The point is that the IVEN consultant should have had enough industry experience on top of their software experience. Another example was that the IVEN consultants could not give enough industry examples, again because they did not have the industry knowledge.

After the workshop, the IVEN consultants wrote the "To-Be" business processes document and again because of the above problems they IVEN consultant could not write an excellent "To-Be" business process document because the IVEN consultant did not understand OGC requirements probably and this led to a lot of delays in approving the Business Processes Document.

The running of a conference room pilot to simulate the running of the solution could have been useful for OGC to understand the proposed IVEN team members' solutions.

When the "To-Be" document went backward and forward between the OGC users and the IVEN consultants for comments and approval, there was no mechanism to capture all these changes and document them professionally; in other words, there was no document version control, so team members had too many different versions of the document and nobody was sure which one had the latest and the greatest information.

The fact that each vendor consultant had his/her own templates had resulted in OGC ending up with too many different document styles and formats.

Obviously, there should have been one standard format for each document type that was agreed at the begging of the project or even better use agreed project templates part of the project early deliverables.

The IVEN consultants were not communicating adequately or meeting regularly in relation to the cross issues that are shared or that may have effect on each other's areas. Therefore, consultants' analysis and solutions were done in silos without considering other modules that could be affected, to the extent that at a later stage there were huge conflicts and issues, which were raised from the solutions, offered by the IVEN consultants because they worked greatly alone.

The IVEN consultants should have met once a week to discuss solutions offered to OGC that may impact each other's areas. IVEN team members should have been consulting with OGC team members about all the solutions and do some demos about these solutions. These should have been included and agreed by the parties as part of the project manager's communication plan at early days of the project. Also this could have been done under the pretext of reviewing the project risk status of the project in regular meetings of OGC and IVEN team members

Another evident irregularity and malpractice in this phase was that both project members were improperly storing the project documents in their computers, laptops, flash drives, or external hard desks.

All project documents should be stored in a clearly structures project folder on a server. Privileges should be granted for the project team to allow proper storage and access. Formal controls and monitoring should be applied to ensure consistency and integrity of the documents published / updated.

Report Workshop Activity

The biggest problem encountered in this phase was that the OGC users were not sure what reports or KPIs they needed, so what they did was that they brought all the old reports and built on them and that was totally wrong approach.

The second biggest problem was the total numbers of reports. It was agreed in the contract to develop 10 new reports for each module. All the 10 reports that were defined during the reports workshop for each module were not the real needed reports, and OGC discovered this at a later stage of the project.

IVEN knew that 10 reports for each module were not enough and that OGC would ask for more reports at a later stage and that when IVEN asked for a variation order.

Ideally, OGC users should have been prepared with well defined new reports based on the new system before they attended the report workshop.

It is strongly recommended that a proper appraisal of the needed reports should be conducted at much earlier stages to come up with a more realistic number of reports and avoid variation orders.

Another observation that is worthwhile reflecting on is that during the developing phase of the new reports only IVEN technical consultants and IVEN report writers were involved, without any involvement by OGC report writers, missing the opportunity presented for the OGC designated report writers to learn and observe the knowledge of writing reports.

It is highly advised to always involve the client report writers who would be envisaged to take up the role of report writing at later project stages and during the post-implementation, so whenever there are new reports needed by the customer, they do not have to go back to the implementation vendor to develop the reports and get charged for it.

Best practices suggest that reports development be a function that is either supported by the IT within the company, or produced by the users using report generators or query builders. This again should have been formally discussed at the early days of the project.

The IVEN consultants did not have a unified template for the Reports Requirements Document, and each consultant had his own template, when this could have been resolved by having agreed template at early stage of the project.

Vendor consultant with fair knowledge about the industry could be very useful, as they should have educating roles about what is realistic and valid reporting requirements and what is merely a wish that does not serve a genuine purpose or represent a substantial improvement to business.

When the Reports Requirements Document was sent backward and forward between the OGC core team and the IVEN consultants for comments and approval, there was no mechanism to capture all these changes and document them professionally; in another words, there was no document version control, so team members had too many different versions of the document and nobody were sure which one had the latest and the greatest information.

It is suggested that the implementation vendor always delivers a quick overview session about the reporting tool capabilities to the customer before the report workshop starts.

System Configuration Activity

The following are some of the important project issues and problems that were raised in association with the 'System Configuration' activity, and which can be the used basis for lessons learnt and suggestions for improvement in future implementations:

The updating of the System Configurations Document (Functional Requirements Document) with the latest changes was a main concern due to the fact that the document was handled by both the technical and business consultants simultaneously, where the business consultant was updating the document regularly for new requirements or modifying exiting requirements, and the technical consultant was updating the functional requirements document with the technical details.

The System Configurations Document (Functional Requirements Document) must be always up to date. So there should have been a proper agreed mechanism in place to control the document versions and modifications.

The focus for the technical consultant was to get the technical job done and the updating of the documents with the latest system changes, configurations, and customizations was his lowest priority. The lack of document control has resulted in a number of different versions of the same document and using wrong documents.

It is critical to address this issue and introduce document versioning control due to the anticipated value of the technical configuration and customization document when OGC decides to upgrade to a higher version of the system in future, when there would be a need for reference of all the configurations and customizations done to the system.

The technical consultant developed all the configurations and customizations in the development database and then applied it to the test database to be tested by the business consultant, once approved by the business consultant then it was applied to the production database. The biggest issue here was that there was no mechanism to follow up on what have been applied to the different project databases and what was not applied.

It is suggested to have a proper mechanism to capture the synchronization between the databases.

During the project, the resignation of some of the technical consultants had resulted in a mess due to lack of documentation and the team had great difficulty trying to track the configurations and customizations which the resigned consultant was involved in and which were supposed to be according to a documented methodology.

A formal dictionary should be created for all changes made by consultants to labels on the forms, data field names, and newly introduced fields.

Restarting the environments was another issue; the project environments should not be started during the office hours because people need these environments for the work, so the process of restarting the databases environments should be agreed on between the team members.

Proper procedure was supposed to be agreed between OGC and IVEN to ensure that any such restarting of project environments would not affect or interrupt the work of the project team and consultants.

One of the critical issues that was observed during the project was the tendency of some IVEN technical consultants interfering in the IVEN business consultant's work, by directly communicating with OGC team and suggesting technical solutions that were in conflict with those endorsed by IVEN business consultant.

This should be avoided as the technical consultant job should be very clear and it is only to take care of the technical work of the project that the business consultant asked them to do, they should not talk or discuss any solutions with the client until they discuss it first with the business consultant.

Data Mapping and Migration Activity

One of the major concerns was that IVEN technical consultant lack of experience with new system database tables, structure, and relationships. He was an excellent data migration consultant but unfortunately was not very experienced with the new system tables' relationships and structures.

It is strongly suggested that the data migration consultant is to be trained specifically on the system tables' relationships and always to consult the business consultant on the data migration.

Additionally, the testing of the migrated data has consistently yielded errors, which were hard to track for cause due to lack of documentation.

There should be a proper documented methodology to check the migrated data and the accuracy of data.

Systems Integration Activity

In this project, OGC requested IVEN to design and build the integration between the two systems, effectively without the approval by the system owners Oracle and IBM. This integration was at the database level not at the application level, which is something was not recommended at all. The following integration-related issues were raised:

- The integration was built by a technical person who was not experienced in both systems.
- OGC suffered from the integration support after the go-live because the technical person who wrote the integration left when the project went live, so OGC had to employee him again.
- OGC suffered and will keep suffering from the fact that in case of any upgrade to any system then the interface has to be rewritten from scratch and test it.
- The most important question was what to do if the integration failed during the go live or any other day. There was not a proper mechanism for the worst-case scenarios.
- The integration document was not very detailed.

In view of the above issues, it is suggested that there should have been two different integration documents, one for the business users to understand it from business view and another document for the technical users to underhand it from technical view. It would have been also beneficial if OGC had one of its technical users involved throughout the integration phase to for knowledge transfer to be able to support and modify the interface at later stage when the implementation has been completed and the vendor has left.

Systems Testing Activity

Systems testing are very important part of the development and delivery of the solution to the client.

During the testing phase, the following points were raised:

- The test scripts were written by the IVEN consultant and were not end to end test scripts, in another words did not cover all the different type of scenarios, due to lack of industry knowledge by the IVEN consultant. OGC resources should have provided the business scenarios which then be converted into test scripts.
- The systems integration test should have been performed on all possible scenarios that may come out of the business process (different variations of the same process).

It is suggested that Subject Matter Expert (SME) be used to provide such business scenarios and help in building the test scripts that are comprehensive and reflective of the real business. Also, a structured approach for testing should be agreed and adopted.

During the testing, a stress software test must be done. The system should be tested when all the users are logged in at the same time.

It is strongly recommended to use a conference room pilot before handing the system to the client for testing the following aspects of the system:

- To see that the software can support all the things we need to do.
- To identify operational responsibilities.
- To identify new procedures needed, and to test draft procedures and policies.
- To identify training needs.
- To identify implementation method and issues to be resolved.
- To test problem management procedures.
- To confirm data definitions.
- To confirm data conversion rules.
- To confirm the system testing already carried out, for batch processes and job streams and interfaces, will work in a repetitive production environment.

Users Training and Training Materials Activity

During this phase, the following problems were noticed:

- The customized training materials were not up-to-date and were not reflecting the latest system configurations and customizations.
- The training system data (exercise and examples) setup was not properly done. Users were trying to do exercises according to the training materials, and the data was not found.
- The training materials did not have one unified template.
- The courses duration were short.
- Users' skills levels were not pre-assessed, so experienced users were in the same training class with non-experienced users.

It is suggested to conduct a pilot training program of a small, selected group of users that best represent the overall user base prior to conducting training classes to end-users. This will help to identify problems and issues and have them addressed before the actual training takes place.

Post Implementation Phase

The client, OGC has suffered from the following issues during the post implementation phase:

- The agreed three months support between OGC and IVEN had proven to be inadequate, as the system needs stabilization technically and functionally and a punch list of issues for resolving.

It is suggested always to have at least a one-year post support from the implementation vendor depending on the complexity of the implementation, the number of users and the company size.

It is suggested that such plans and procedures be there to continue running business for a short while if the system is down. This is not an IT contingency plan alone. It could be any risk to the operation, and it does not mean spare computers; it means, for example, being able to ship without a computer system.

CURRENT CHALLENGES FACING THE ORGANIZATION

Nearly three years after the system had been rolled out in OGC, the two most important challenges that OGC were facing as they are considering the upgrade of the system to a higher version are related to:

- Rewriting the customized integration interface, which was built by IVEN during the implementation.
- The fact that the system was over-customized is proven to be problematic in the context of the upgrade warranting the need to review and validate the need for such customizations in view of alternative functionalities introduced with the new version of the system.

LESSON LEARNED

In view of the fact the ERP implementation project in OGC had suffered from delays and budget over run and that the actual time used has exceeded the planned time by nearly 23%, it could be useful to look into the causes of such delay and view the experience as a lesson learned.

It is only normal that the project plan is developed by the implementation vendor and reviewed and approved by the client. It is also normal that the vendor would always try to minimize the number of days in the project plan to save money over quality, therefore the onus was on the client to pay attention to the number of days assigned for each activity and ensure that sufficient and realistic durations are incorporated in the project schedule considering various project uncertainties and constraints as well resources availability.

During this project, the project plan was not updated on regular bases, making it difficult to assess the project progress, so the project plan should have been updated weekly and published on the company intranet along with the contingency plans, communication plans, and quality plan documents.

REFERENCES

Chen, I. (2001). Planning for ERP systems: Analysis and future trend. *Business Process Management Journal, 7*(5), 374. doi:10.1108/14637150110406768

Clemmons, S., & Simon, S. (2001). Control and coordination in global ERP configuration. *Business Process Management Journal, 7*(3), 205. doi:10.1108/14637150110392665

Davison, R. (2002). Cultural complications of ERP. *Communications of the ACM, 45*(7), 109. doi:10.1145/514236.514267

Gray, C. F., & Larson, E. W. (2008). *Project management: The managerial process* (4th ed.). Burr Ridge, IL: Irwin/McGraw-Hill.

Gupta, A. (2000). Enterprise resource planning: The emerging organizational value systems. *Industrial Management & Data Systems, 100*(3), 114. doi:10.1108/02635570010286131

Hong, K., & Kim, Y. (2002). The critical success factors for ERP implementation: An organizational fit perspective. *Information & Management, 40*(1), 25. doi:10.1016/S0378-7206(01)00134-3

IBM. (2012). *Wikipedia.* Retrieved from http://en.wikipedia.org/wiki/Ibm

Kerbache, L. (2002). Enterprise resource planning (ERP): The dynamics of operations management. *Interfaces, 32*(1), 104.

Kettinger, W., Guha, H., & Teng, J. (1995). The process engineering lifecycle methodology: A case study. In Grover, V., & Kettinger, W. (Eds.), *Business Process Change: Reengineering Concepts, Methods and Technologies*. Hershey, PA: Idea Publishing.

Kremers, M., & van Dissel, H. (2000). ERP system migrations. *Communications of the ACM, 43*(4), 52–56. doi:10.1145/332051.332072

Oracle Corporation. (2012). *Wikipedia.* Retrieved from http://en.wikipedia.org/wiki/Oracle_Corporation

Stratman, J., & Roth, A. (2002). Enterprise resource planning (ERP) competence constructs: Two-stage multi-item scale development and validation. *Decision Sciences, 33*(4), 601. doi:10.1111/j.1540-5915.2002.tb01658.x

Tarafdar, M., & Roy, R. (2003). Analyzing the adoption of enterprise resource planning systems in Indian organizations: a process framework. *Journal of Global Information Technology Management, 6*(1), 31.

KEY TERMS AND DEFINITIONS

CONSCO: The Consulting Company.
CRM: Customer Relationship Management.
CRP: Conference Room Pilot.
EBS: E-Business Suite.
ERP: Enterprise Resource Planning.
HR: Human Resource.
IBM: International Business Machines.
IVEN: Implementation Vendor.
KPI: Key Performance Indicator.
OGC: Oil and Gas Company (the client).
PM: Project Manager.
SCM: Supply Chain Management.
SME: Subject Matter Expert.

Chapter 2
EIS Implementation in a Major UAE Oil Producing Company

Amer Dabbagh
CATS, Jordan

Eissa Khoori
ADMA-OPCO, UAE

EXECUTIVE SUMMARY

This major Oil and Gas producing company in the Gulf went through an implementation experience of EIS system in 2005. The EIS Implementation involved the replacement of the existing Maintenance, Supply, and Commercial system with a new EIS and an upgrade of the HR and Financial systems to the latest releases. The exercise was prompted by management's desire to replace the outdated ERP system in order to address shortcomings in functionality, to control the high cost of upgrades and modifications, and to enable implementation of the newly formulated Maintenance Policy. The project was deemed a success, even though it took longer than planned and the results were less than anticipated.

ORGANIZATION BACKGROUND

EIS evolve and develop to cater for the requirements of companies large and small. The Gulf Oil and Gas Company involved in this implementation is a major producer of oil, and of gas to a lesser degree, from marine fields in the Gulf.

DOI: 10.4018/978-1-4666-2220-3.ch002

The company headquarters are situated on the mainland with wells scattered over large marine areas and serviced by steel structure platforms and land based storage and processing facilities as well. Plants and facilities of the company are of considerable age, which makes maintenance efforts a major factor in the safe and economical production equation.

The company is an operating company on behalf of the Shareholders in the concession. The Company is headed by a Chief Executive Officer under the direction of a Board of Directors and assisted by a number of advisory committees.

Under the CEO, there are a number of vice presidents assisted by a number of managers. Apart from service and support divisions, e.g. Maintenance, Human Resources, Finance, Information Technology, General Services, Management Services, and Public Relations, there are separate divisions for each of the production sites. The production sites enjoy a certain degree of autonomy within standard company strategies and policies. Sites are custodian of the plants and facilities with maintenance responsibility entrusted with the Maintenance Division.

The company is a major Oil producer in the region contributing a major share of revenues to the country. Production and exploration policies are formulated by the shareholders to best serve their interests with the priority for the interest of the host country, populace, and environment. To achieve these goals the company strives to utilize world-class processes, policies, and ideas.

SETTING THE STAGE

Operations of the company are centered on the production of oil and gas after exploring and location of deposits in the concession areas. Drilling is the most costly activity in the oil production process, which makes planning an essential activity. Plans for the drilling operations for new and work-over wells are usually developed for a period of five years. The shareholders must review and approve budgets. Production policies are reviewed regularly to keep astride international markets regarding demand volumes and prices.

Extracted oil and gas undergo a number of treatment processes before delivery for export. These processes require sophisticated plants that are operated to a very high standard of safety, health, and environment protection.

To ensure the uninterrupted service of these plants a number of ERP systems were employed in the company. Because of the scale of the plants and facilities it is required that these systems support all business processes and cater for large volumes of data and transactions. These systems cover the areas of maintenance, procurement, and material management, HSE, finance, and HR.

A new performance study was carried out and recommendations for a Performance Driven Organization were published. It was felt by management that the existing ERP systems were incapable of supporting the new ideas, procedures, and policies.

At this stage, the business processes were not up-to-date and require some effort to enhance and improve. Business processes for Finance and HR were in pretty good shape. The Supply and Commercial business processes where well formulated but required some effort to document in full detail. The Maintenance business processes required major revamping because of the introduction of a new Maintenance Policy that was formulated recently by an international consultancy firm. Part of the findings of the study was that the current ERP system could not support the new policy. Another recommendation of the study was to rebuild the equipment and Location hierarchy to be in line with the new policy. Data in the existing ERP system was limited and major effort was required to fill the missing parts to support the new policy and to produce the required management information. In the current system, management could not get clear and correct information on the cost of plant maintenance.

The decision was taken to choose a new EIS system to replace the existing one and to utilize the expertise of an International Implementation Vendor (IIV) to carry out the implementation process under the control of an implementation project formed for this purpose.

CASE DESCRIPTION

Project Startup

Upon Shareholder approval, the company established a project team. In the terms of reference for the project, the stated aim was "the implementation of the latest version of the selected ERP package as a replacement of the existing system and to upgrade the Finance and HR systems to the latest versions, employing the most up-to-date Company's business processes and accessing cleaned, accurate, and consistent Company data."

The Scope of work for the project team was stated as "Core team training, Gap Analysis, ERP package configuration, Data migration, Finance system upgrade implementation, HR system upgrade implementation, Users' Acceptance Testing, End User training, Go-Live Tasks, and Post Go-Live Support."

The terms of reference also established a Steering Committee made up of Top Management, a Project Champion, and a Project Sponsor. The project manager was selected from IT Division and assisted by six team leaders as detailed in the organization below.

The Implementation teams were made up of part-time representatives of the user divisions and a number of permanent staff with a number of consultants from the International Implementation Vendor.

Project Charter

One of the first responsibilities of the project was the production of a Project Charter document for presentation to the Steering committee for approval. The project objective and the project terms of reference as quoted above were stated in the project charter document.

Project Organization

The organization of the project was specified in full detail in the project charter. A diagram of the organization is shown in Figure 1. Detailed duties and responsibilities of each member of the project were elaborated as part of the project organization. The Project Office Team is responsible for the Administration, Quality Assurance, Planning, and Documentation of all project activities. The Finance Team is responsible for the implementation of the Finance System upgrade. The HR Team is entrusted with the implementation of the Human Resources System upgrade. The Maintenance Team is responsible for the implementation of the Maintenance modules and associated data.

Figure 1. Diagram of the organization

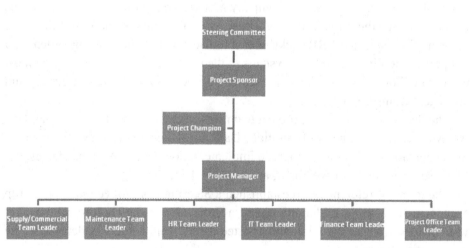

The Supply/Commercial Team is responsible for the implementation of the Commercial and Supply modules and associated data. The IT Team is charged with handling the infrastructure, operating system, database and related issues.

Project Strategy

The main points stated as the project strategy in the project charter are:

- Forming a project team representing all disciplines and locations in the Company.
- Reviewing and updating the business processes of the Company.
- Cleaning the Company's data prior to data migration.
- Minimizing package customizations to absolute minimum.
- Providing improved management information and reports.
- Involving User Management in all implementation stages.

Implementation Methodology

It was agreed to use a closed loop four-step implementation methodology consisting of four phases:

- Preparations to set up the project, document the business processes and to set up data cleaning.
- Pre-implementation phase involving planning the infrastructure, software installation and tuning and implementation core team training.
- Application configuration phase covering the Gap Analysis, Application Configuration/Customization, Data Conversion and System/User Acceptance Testing.
- System Implementation phase including the user training and implementation go-live.

Communication Plan

A schedule of regular meetings among teams within the project and with the project sponsor and the steering committee was set up. Frequency and attendees of these meetings were detailed in addition to the reports to be produced.

Project Plan

An overall project plan and a detailed plan where developed and included in the project charter. The overall plan was for presentation to the steering committee for approval. The detailed plan was included for follow-up and control of the project progress. The Project Office Team was charged with the follow-up and reporting of progress and delays in the project. Progress reports were to be developed and presented to the various stakeholders as detailed in the communication plan.

Service Level Agreements

These agreements between the Project Manager and the Project Team Leaders were developed and included in the project charter. These agreements were set up to ensure clarity and commitment of the team leaders to their roles and responsibilities for the project. Also included in these agreements were the team's organization and the high-level project plan.

Project Quality and Risk Assessment Plan

A quality and risk assessment plan was included in the charter to identify each implementation phase's risks and mitigation methods. For each stage of the project, deliverables are identified and the required quality assurance criteria outlined.

Change Control Management

A section on the Change Control Management was included in the charter to emphasize the importance of the subject. Changes inevitably occur during the course of development and implementation in a project. These changes can affect the scope, cost, delivery, and nature of the software deliverables as well as the functioning project team. In order to maintain a balance between requirements and cost/schedule, project teams need an effective process that allows for controlled change during the project life cycle.

Uncontrolled changes during the course of development and implementation can be extremely disruptive. Clear and effective procedures for evaluating and tracking change requests, analyzing potential impacts of change and implementing the change are essential for controlling cost and schedule overruns and to avoid the failure to meet user expectations.

Business Processes and Data Cleaning

The project plan was for the review and finalization of the business processes as the first major task. A parallel task was the data-cleaning task. These were the preliminary tasks to lay the ground for the next step of the project, i.e. gap analysis. The data cleaning was entrusted to user divisions in most cases. On the other hand, the data preparation for maintenance data, in line with the new Maintenance Policy and the new package, was contracted out to a consulting company. The data preparation took much longer than planned and the results delivered by the contracted company proved to be lacking and required further enhancements. Meetings arranged by the project team and the users and the Implementation Vendor dragged on and contributed to further delays.

The business processes were not recently updated; actually, they were the version prepared for the previous package implementation almost seven years earlier. Numerous workshops were arranged by the project teams to finalize the business processes and to align them to the new Maintenance Policy, the PDO concepts and the VAP for project control. There were around 120 processes in total that required review, agreement, updating, and management approval. This exercise required large effort from the team and commitment from the users, which was lacking. The vendors were involved in this to complete the task and move on to the gap analysis stage. This contributed to project budget overruns and to glossing over issues of contention.

Gap Analysis

The Gap Analysis stage was started when the approved business processes were delivered to the vendor. The process was performed through specialize workshops for each of the business area. To enable the team members to partake in the Gap Analysis exercise specialized training sessions were conducted by the vendor. All project members were trained and given access profiles in their areas of expertise. The vendor provided only two consultants to cover the two major business areas, namely maintenance and supply/commercial. This limitation stretched the abilities of these consultants to the limit and required them to work overtime to try to meet targets. Eventually extra help was provided by the vendor but the harm was done.

At this stage, the each of the teams had to cover each of the approved business processes and identify the gaps in the package. As an additional demand on the teams, they were required to identify areas of improvement that the package offered. These extras were to be documented for presentation and approval by management.

During this stage of the project, a number of issues became apparent. Office space availability for the project team proved to be insufficient. The teams were split over separate locations, which led to difficulty in interaction and coverage of common areas. Another issue that proved to be problematic to the project was the testing infrastructure. The vendor deployed the package onto a number of dedicated servers. During initial stages and the core team training the service was quite satisfactory. After the Gap Analysis Stage, it became apparent that the available system capabilities were lacking and an upgrade to the servers and the introduction of extra dedicated servers was required. This slowed progress for some time until the issue was addressed. A positive outcome of that was to give the project a better idea of the required infrastructure for the production service. This was very important because at go-live time both the old system and the new were to run in parallel for a number of weeks and until confidence in the new system by users was established.

The exercise continued with each identified gap in the package documented in full detail. The vendor consultants then decided whether these gaps could be overcome by relatively simple tweaks or they required customization to the package. Since customizations were to be avoided or kept to the absolute minimum management decision on these was required. In certain cases, work-around scenarios were found to address these gaps.

At this stage, it was decided to allow the users through the team representatives to change the feel and look of the package screens. This was deemed appropriate by management to reduce the effort of learning of the new package by the users. Also allowed were changes to field names on the screens to align with common names the users were familiar with.

A part of the exercise was the gap analysis of the workflow and documentation of these for each individual identified process. Because there was no preset workflow in the out-of-the-box system it was agreed to postpone this activity and to include it with user acceptance testing. This proved to be inappropriate because it delayed progress at the testing stage and had to be developed without proper to-be documentation for the workflow.

The deliverables from this stage were the to-be or functional specifications. These specifications were the basis for the system configuration and customizations. Missing specifications at this stage meant that the development of these processes in the following stage was not possible. The functional specifications were reviewed by the implementation teams and signed off by them, by the project management and by the user division management.

Development/Configuration/Customizations

At the conclusion of the Gap Analysis, the information was available with vendors to proceed with the development, configuration, and customization of the system. This stage is the major stage in the implementation process. It involves a number of activities by the vendor and by the implementation team. The first step in this stage of the implementation project was the preparation of the technical specifications, which are technical translations of the functional specifications that represent the user requirements as produced in the gap analysis stage. Preparation of the technical specifications was the responsibility of the vendor. These specifications had to be reviewed by the implementation teams and signed off. Because of the very technical nature of these specifications it was decided by the project management and the project sponsor to accept them as produced by the vendor with assurances that they reflect exactly the approved functional specifications produced in the gap analysis phase.

The chosen EIS package is a highly configurable system with a huge number of parameters. The parameters' settings had to be chosen carefully to suit each business process. Suitability and correctness of chosen values could be ascertained only after completing the configuration and carrying out the system testing. This meant that that the settings were revisited and reset a number of times to get the best results.

Another important activity was the changes to the standard out-of-the-box system. These changes covered screen layouts, arrangement of fields on screen, addition, and hiding of fields on screen, changes to field names on screen, changing menus and navigation. These activities were the responsibility of the vendor with feedback and advice from the implementation teams. Because of the users wish for screens and field names very much like the previous system, extra effort was required through meetings, demonstrations and workshops to discuss the desired changes and to agree on which were practical and acceptable to implement and which were rejected. All decisions were documented and had to be reflected in the technical specifications. The vendor had to complete the technical specifications and get them approved by the project before proceeding with the development. In addition to screens of the system, reports to be produced had to be agreed. The package had a number of standard reports that covered most of the modules. The company business requires a number of non-standard reports for the Shareholders and for Government entities that had to be developed from scratch. The vendor programmers worked on the required reports, changes to existing reports and on the changes to screens and menus. This effort was carried out in parallel with the Data migration and User Acceptance testing phases. Results of the testing feedback were used to further fine tune the configurations.

A major milestone took place in the middle of this stage and that was a change of project management. This was decided by the project sponsor and agreed by the steering committee. Throughout the Gap Analysis and the Development stages, there were deep differences among the Maintenance team members and with the users. Differences over the implementation of the new Maintenance Policy and over data preparations caused friction, bad feelings, and delays. Management decided that a revamp of the Maintenance team management and representatives will be more conducive to project success. Another shift in management thinking was that the project had to be led by the user units and not by outsiders. Hence the project manager was replaced with a senior Maintenance Division staff. This resulted in significant delay in the project. Decisions concerning maintenance contention issues had to be taken by the new project manager and Maintenance team. Eventually the project was on track again after drastic decisions on data migration were taken. Because of the changes to Equipment and Location hierarchy and the difficulty in cross-referencing it was agreed to drop migration of most of the maintenance transactions in the old system.

Data Migration

The data migration stage was a very important and tricky one. A data gap analysis exercise was arranged and carried out. The exercise involved mapping records and data items for the new and the existing systems. The exercise was an elaborate one and required thorough knowledge of the date structures and data elements of both systems. This definitely created a situation because the required knowledge was not available to a single source. Knowledge of the old system was largely with the implementation core team representatives. Required details for the new system were available with the vendor representatives. Development of the data gap analysis required very close cooperation between the two sides. It also involved decisions on the scope of the data to be included in the migration exercise and the new data to be created directly in the new system.

The vendor representative had at their disposal tools and scripts to carry out the data migration from the old system database directly to the new system. New data to be created had to be prepared in certain formats and scripts to upload it had to be prepared by the vendor.

Another aspect of the new system was the access profiles for system users. There were limitations on the access privileges' profile mapping to individual users. Representative access profile groups that apply to groups of similar users had to be created. A large number of access groups had to be created because of the system restriction of mapping each user to only one single access group. Each access group contained access to a number of screens and to actions available from these screens. The access levels to be granted had to be specified as a read only or update access. Active users had to be identified. This proved to be a tricky exercise. The user identification numbers and relevant personal details ere downloaded from the HR system. One of the problems was that not all employees registered in the HR system were active users. Another problem was that contracted employees, as opposed to direct hire employees, were not registered in the HR system, and had to be added using other sources. Such a source was the old system, which was used to extract the contractor information. Here a new issue surfaced which was that there was no identification of contractors who had already left the company. Extra efforts were required to clean the user data and get it to an acceptable state.

The chosen package had a very robust system administration module. A substantial number of value lists were required for the effective implementation of the system administration facilities. Some of this data was readily available while some had to be created and made ready for the implementation.

User Acceptance Testing

This stage of the project was started in parallel to the development and data migration exercises. The first activity in this stage was preparation of the test scenarios. The test scenarios had to cover all business processes that were specified and translated to functional specifications. These scenarios were prepared by the implementation core team members with the cooperation of the vendor consultants. The scenarios had to be documented and had to contain the data that is to be used in the tests and the expected results. Any exceptions to the expected results had to be documented and the outcome conveyed to the vendor for corrective actions.

The test scenarios are supposed to cover all possible variations and all possible error conditions and not only correct and standard cases. The large number of bugs, although most were of minor nature, indicated that the scenarios did not cover all possible variations.

The process was a reiterative activity that had to be repeated until clear test results were obtained. When a clean and error free test was completed, it was signed-off by the test panel and by the responsible team leader. At the end of the tests, the results were presented to the user divisions for sign-off as well.

User Training

The user training was an essential part of the implementation. The user training was delivered by vendor trainers. Training courses that covered the major disciplines in the company were prepared. The delivery of the courses was timed to start two months before the go-live date. This proved to be a bad timing because it coincided with employees summer vacations. The training material was not reviewed by the implementation team who were heavily involved in the user acceptance testing and data migration at the time. Another negative factor in the user training delivery was that the training material was not always updated to reflect the results of system configuration and customization. The data used in the training sessions was fictitious data that did not help the users in relating to real life experiences. The vendor trainers who were brought in to conduct the training courses were not conversant with the company's business. These elements led to user confusion and lack of confidence at go-live.

All training was conducted through classroom sessions with very little or no practical practice by the users. There was no training environment available to the users to practice after attending the training courses. The early-trained users confessed later to have not retained much of the benefits of the courses they had attended.

Timing problems were encountered with training course delivery to the offshore cycle workers. The result was that many missed the scheduled courses. Some additional sessions were arranged to overcome the shortage. Overall, the effectiveness of the delivered training was of very limited value as became apparent after go-live.

Go-Live

The go-live was timed to coincide with a first working day of the month. It was planned that the old system would be shut down four days earlier to allow sufficient time for data migration from the old to the new system. During this time, only essential transactions were carried out and documented on paper for entry to the new system after go-live. The old system was made available for data enquiries only. The blackout period was not excessive and partly spanned a weekend so that the volume of backlog was reasonable.

On a go-live day, the service was not available for few hours which caused a negative image of the package.

Post Go-Live Support

Users were issued with the sign-in instructions, user-ID, and password through the e-mail system earlier. A special call-centre type office was setup to receive and handle user calls and complaints. The support office was manned mainly by members of the implementation team.

The office was inundated with user calls. On the first day, a large number of the calls were related to sign-in and passwords. The system navigation was the next major obstacle for the users. It became apparent that a large number of the users needed coaching to start using the system.

Apart from a number of bugs that the users reported, a major issue surfaced in the early days. This was the workflow implementation. The users expected it to follow the old system pattern which was user controlled. Another concern to the users was that the user could not see the workflow path to the end stage before all assignees completed their tasks. Because of missing bits and pieces in the user information, objects were getting stuck in the workflow and had to be handled by the system administrator and vendor consultants. This clearly indicated that the acceptance testing did not cover the workflow well.

The reported bugs and issues were recorded in a special support environment. Access to the support office members was not set properly and the whole thing had to be shifted to the regular help-desk environment. The regular helpdesk staff were trained but lacked sufficient expertise to handle the calls so that the special support team had to carry on for a long period before handing over.

Custodianship

As time passed, it became apparent that there were still major issues in the system that required addressing. The Implementation vendor was responsible for fixing bugs for a period of three months after go-live. Management decided to form a team to take custody of the issues that transpired after the implementation. The team was charged with the follow-up on resolving the major issues, for validating the requests for system enhancement and for training and coaching of users.

CURRENT CHALLENGES FACING THE ORGANIZATION

User Competence and Training

Users' competence on the use of the system was very low and resulted in a very large number of calls to the fire fighting help desk. Since the feel and look of the new system was quite different from the previous system and the users did not have sufficient on-hand experience with the new system, they faced problems in signing in to the system, entering the information, navigating in and between system screens and using the system in general.

Many users were not trained because they were away when user training was delivered. Therefore, they were not familiar with the sign in procedure, did not know their user-IDs or passwords, and required coaching to use the system.

Financial Transaction

Vendors' invoices and payments were not processed for an unacceptable long time, which resulted in complaints and deterioration of the company image. Invoices were delayed because of change of the procedure for invoice payment in the new system. The volume of the invoices and dependency on other modules' data to complete the payment process was not well thought out and delays were inevitable.

Workflow

Transactions were not entered to the system or were stuck because process implementation through the workflow was not correct or not according to user wishes. In the previous system approvals were manually set by the originator and the full approval map was visible to all parties involved. In the new system, the workflow was supposed to reflect the business process approval policy. The full workflow map was not visible, only the completed approvals showed in the system and the following steps were to be carried out in line with approved business process. This made it apparent that some users were not fully aware of the correct process.

Users wanted to control the workflow and did not accept the automatic process. This is tied up with the previous point. Ignorance of the full approval process meant user resistance to adoption of the new system with the automatic implementation of the workflow.

Planning

The original implementation period was grossly exceeded. This resulted in budget overruns and upsets to other major project milestones. One of the main reasons for the delay was the change of project management in mid implementation. This change resulted in changes of outlook and priorities, especially that the new management was user oriented. The change had positive effects in resolving contentions and user differences. It also helped in putting an end to the dispute on data migration issues.

One of the major oversights and causes of post implementation issues were the interfaces. There were user representatives for all functional areas of the project except for the interfaces. These were gray areas that were not assigned direct responsibility but were sort of shared. Because of this many issues were not fully tested during the user acceptance phase and resulted in problems that had to be fixed post go live.

Some of the user requirements were dropped or overlooked because the chosen system did not cover these requirements and the vendor felt that development of solutions to these requirements would cause awkward delays to the implementation.

SOLUTIONS AND RECOMMENDATIONS

Most of the issues and problems encountered by the implementation project could have been eliminated by the adoption of simple steps before and during the exercise. The following is a list of the measures that can eliminate the issues discussed above.

Preparedness

The issue of very low user competence can be considered a result of insufficient preparations and ineffective communication with end users. The business processes must be prepared and be well documented before initiating the implementation project. Without up-to-date business processes, the Gap Analysis and the workflow resulted in faulty implementation that does not satisfy the user expectations.

User requirements should be developed by the company staff and possibly assisted by a specialized consultant company. The Implementation Vendor should not be involved in the requirement specification to avoid bias towards the chosen system's available functionality.

The issues encountered with the workflow can be related to a number of reasons. One of the main failures of the implementation teams was the failure to produce workflow maps to enable the users better assessment of the developed workflows and better judgment on errors and inadequacies in the implementation.

All users should be given full training in their areas of responsibility. The training scenarios should reflect actual production system screens and data. Out of the box training scenarios are ineffective and confusing to the users at go live time. The trainers brought in by the vendor were not familiar with the company's business and did not have access to documentation of these processes. In the training sessions, the trainers could not pass on the knowledge of the company's business to the trainees. They were not able to relate the training scenarios to the business processes, which resulted in less than desired results.

The timing of training is very important and should consider user work cycles and annual leave cycles. In addition, to be considered is the timing of delivery before go live date to enable retention by the users. In this respect availability of a training environment accessible by the users and a CBT training or e-learning programs are very helpful in preparing the users for the new system.

The unacceptable delay in the processing of financial transactions at go-live is also a result of insufficient preparation of the Finance Division staff. Since, with the implementation of the new system, a change in the invoice payment process was introduced, the users should have been well trained in the new procedure and the expected volume of transactions anticipated and solutions found to meet this challenge. Involving a larger number of Finance staff at go-live could have alleviated the situation. Proper analysis could have identified the issue beforehand and the process streamlined to reduce adverse effects.

Project Management

The failure in the project plans and the failure to meet the deadlines could be related directly to changes in the project management and team leadership in midstride. Project management and manning should be well planned ahead of the start of the project to avoid delays and last minute decisions on vital implementation issues.

Another important issue was the inadequacy of development/testing infrastructure and the office space allocation. A well-managed project would plan the acquisition and allocation of these resources at a very early stage before mobilization to curtail subsequent inconvenience and delay.

System interfaces must be assigned clear responsibility for specification and more importantly for user acceptance testing to avoid post go live failures and delays.

The data should be prepared in advance of the implementation to enable good acceptance testing of the system and later good go live scenario and avoiding user complaints over lacking data.

Support staff should have been better trained in system support with experience gained through positive participation in the implementation project as members involved in all stages of the project in addition to Vendor training on system anatomy, workflow, and system features. A decision on the post go live support responsibility should be taken early and staff, facilities, and procedures to implement it in place at go live time. Responsibility for system improvements and enhancements and future upgrades should be clearly defined.

LESSONS LEARNED

Project Management

A change in the project management involving the project manager and team leaders during major stages of the project is very counterproductive. The project management staff should be well chosen before launching the project and is advisable to be picked from the user community.

Training

Training timing should be well planned regarding the timing and the content to enable maximum benefit to the users. The course material should be tailored to the company business processes. The trainers should be familiarized with the company business processes to guarantee best delivery to the users.

Workflow

The workflow, which was a new feature introduced with the system, should have been developed and tested rigorously during the UAT stage and should have been included in the training courses to prevent go-live issues.

Business Processes

The business processes should be updated and documented before the launch of the project by competent company staff and if required assisted by consultants.

REFERENCES

Abdinnour-Helm, S., Lengnick-Hall, M., & Lengnick-Hall, C. (2003). Pre-implementation attitudes and organizational readiness for implementing an enterprise resource planning system. *European Journal of Operational Research, 146*(2), 258. doi:10.1016/S0377-2217(02)00548-9

Al-Mashari, M. (2003). Enterprise resource planning (ERP) systems: A research agenda. *Industrial Management & Data Systems, 103*(1/2), 22. doi:10.1108/02635570310456869

Al-Mudimigh, A., Zairi, M., & Al-Mashari, M. (2001). ERP software implementation: An integrative framework. *European Journal of Information Systems, 10*(4), 216. doi:10.1057/palgrave.ejis.3000406

Beretta, S. (2002). Unleashing the integration potential of ERP systems. *Business Process Management Journal, 8*(3), 254. doi:10.1108/14637150210428961

Esteves, J., & Pastor, J. (2003). Enterprise resource planning systems research: An annotated bibliography. *Communications of the Association for Information Systems*. Retrieved from http://profesores.ie.edu/jmesteves/cais2001.pdf

Mandal, P., & Gunasekaran, A. (2003). Issues in implementing ERP: A case study. *European Journal of Operational Research, 146*(2), 274. doi:10.1016/S0377-2217(02)00549-0

Payne, W. (2002). The time for ERP? *Work (Reading, Mass.), 51*(2/3), 91.

Rao, S. (2000). Enterprise resource planning: Business needs and technologies. *Industrial Management & Data Systems, 100*(2), 81. doi:10.1108/02635570010286078

KEY TERMS AND DEFINITIONS

CBT: Computer Based Training.

E-Learning: Electronic learning programs usually utilizing the Web.

Go-Live: The actual startup of the new system in the production service.

PDO: Performance Driven Organization.

SLA: Service Level Agreement.

UAT: User Acceptance Testing.

VAP: Value Assurance Process. VAP is a five step methodology for the control of major projects.

Chapter 3
ERP Promises in the United Arab Emirates Educational Sector:
A Descriptive Analysis of ERP Usage and Utilization

Rima Shishakly
Ajman University of Science and Technology, UAE

EXECUTIVE SUMMARY

Implementing Enterprise Resource Planning (ERP) is one of the major IT innovations in this decade. ERP solutions seek to integrate and modernize business processes and their associated information and workflows. Nonetheless, ERP usage in educational management is still new. Educational institutions for various appropriate factors have begun to implement this technology. The school ERP enterprise solution system offers complete school management software, which covers all the functions related to the smooth functioning of school activities. This chapter provides a complete analysis of ERP solutions in the educational sectors and focuses on ERP usage and utilization in the United Arab Emirates (UAE) public (government) schools.

INTRODUCTION

Firms around the world have been implementing Enterprise Resource Planning (ERP) systems since the 1990s. ERP systems can be regarded as one of the most innovative developments in Information Technology (IT) of the 1990s (Al-Meshari, 2003). ERP systems have been adopted by many organizations in the past decade

DOI: 10.4018/978-1-4666-2220-3.ch003

(Bradford & Florin, 2003). Wong and Tien (2004) agreed that in the past decade ERP have become one of the most important developments in the corporate use of information technology.

ERP is defining as an integrated information system that serves all departments within an enterprise. Somers and Nelson (2003) define ERP systems as a software tool used to manage enterprise data. Watson and Schneider (1999) describe ERP system as a term for an integrated enterprise computing system. Xia et al. (2010) and Upadhyay and Dan (2008) define an ERP system as an information system consisting of software support modules where information is flowing between them and they share a central database. ERP "is a standard software package that provides integrated transaction processing and access to information that spans multiple organizational units and multiple business functions" (Wu & Wang, 2006, p. 884). ERP systems automate organization activity with an integrated software application their purpose is to facilitate the flow of information between all business functions inside the boundaries of the organization and manage the connections to outside stakeholders.

Many organizations have sought to improve their competitiveness by investing in advanced information technology, such as Enterprise Resource Planning (ERP) systems. The implementation of an ERP system creates associated changes in business processes (Grabski & Leech, 2002). ERP integrate internal and external management information across an entire organization, embracing finance/accounting, HR, and service the stakeholders' relationship management. Adopting ERP solutions are used to improve stakeholders' service, transform enterprise processes, modernize computer systems, improve administration, maintain competitiveness, increase operating efficiency, and adhere to regulatory compliance (King, Kvavik, & Voloudakis, 2002). ERP systems are seen to be effective in tying the business functional units with the various organization information systems and their associated databases, which in the end can support the strategic aims of modern organizations (Soliman & Youssef, 1998). It enables companies to achieve their objective of increased communication and responsiveness to all stakeholders (Dillon, 1999). Pasaoglu (2011) agrees that ERP not only a technical system but also a social system requiring group work. Ragowsky and Romm Livermore (2002) mention that ERP requires a combination of technical and human expertise to select develop and implement successfully.

ERP APPLICATIONS IN EDUCATIONAL SECTOR

Educational ERP Solution is not only to automate every operation in a school, college, or university, but it is a solution for educational intuitions who automate all the internal and external processes and also help in improving communication among parents, students, teachers, management staff, and alumni. Watson and Schneider (1999) approve that the aim of ERP implementation in universities and educational sector is to provide colleges, schools, and departments, with an enhanced ability for research and teaching at reasonable or low cost. Allen and Kern (2001) agree that it has been implemented in many educational institutions of all levels from Nursery Schools to Colleges around the world.

Abougabah and Sanzogni (2010) distinguish between ERP usage in the educational institutions and organizations. According to them, the differences between universities and organizations seem to be that universities use ERP for academic purpose, but organizations use ERP system for business purposes. Educational institutions (schools, colleges, and universities) are becoming increasingly complicated and their operation is not limit to delivering education only but also managing a complex process and huge amount of data. Furthermore, in universities and schools, it is a more complicated process because faculty members, students, parents, and administrative staff request different data and information for various purposes and want to interact through ERP. Mehlinger (2006) mentions that Universities differ from other organizations because they have different environments and circumstances, and they use ERP technologies for academic purposes. Rico (2004) define ERP for universities as "an information technology solution that integrates and automates recruitment, admission, financial aid, student recorders, and most academic and administrative services" (p. 2). Abugabah, and Sanzogni (2001) suggest that higher education institutions are continuing in the IS era by adopting and implementing ERP system. The need to evaluate their benefits and impacts on organizations and individuals are increasingly essential. ERP is an integrated solution for complete computerization for educational institutions. Chung and Snyder (2000) say that ERP combines both organizational business processes and total organizational IT into one integrated system. ERP combines both organizational business processes and total organizational IT into one integrated system, data entered in one department does not require entering it again in another department and can be used for understanding and enhancing further according to requirements.

Most of the ERP's are highly configurable based on the requirements of schools and higher educational institutions in administration, management, accounting department, admission management, fees management, library management (Xia, et al., 2010; Jing & Qui, 2007). ERP provides an integrated solution for complete computerization for educational institutions. Different schools types and higher education have been strongly influenced by global trends, especially as a result of the demand by governments for schools and universities worldwide to invest more in innovation and to improve their performance and efficiency. Noudoostbeni et al. (2009) agree that ERP provides an opportunity for the organization to improved process flow, better data analysis and better enterprise performance and higher efficiency.

Implementing an ERP system is an organization is a complex process. Most organizations find that ERP implementation is long, complex, and expensive (Wu & Wang, 2006). It will likely be the most difficult and complex project that school, college or university will undertake, ERPsystems are highly complex information systems (Umble, et al., 2003). Olson (2004) agrees the "ERP implementations require a long time to put in place, have high levels of complexity, and involve new technology" (p. 112).

SCHOOL ERP SOLUTION

Student Information Systems (SIS) by definition is a software application for educational institutions to manage student data and to provide capabilities uses as entering student tests and other assessment scores, building student schedules, tracking student attendance, and managing many other student data. Lloyd (2010) defines "Student Information System (SIS) as a computer software that allows the school staff to input and share information about all the aspects of running their school" (p. 2). Fulmer (1995) describes Information system as an integration of the processes of automation with the process of information. Management Information Systems (MIS) is provides that which is needed to manage organizations efficiently and effectively (Lauden & Lauden, 2005). O'Brien (1999) approves that Management Information Systems (MIS) involves three primary resources: people, technology, and information for decision making. MIS are different from other information systems in that they are used to analyze operational activities in the organization. The school ERP Solution is to automate every operation in a school and also help in improving communication among parents, students, teachers, and management, ERP integrated software modules and common central database. The database collects data from different departments in the schools and makes the data available for applications to support all the schools' functioning. The benefits of school ERP solutions in educational sector are offering improved services for faculty, staff, and students, administrative, academic, and student data (Kvavik, et al., 2002). School ERP is different from an SIS in many ways. The biggest difference is in their functions. An SIS is typically limited to managing basic student information, whereas school ERPs are all encompassing solutions that manage all campus administrative functions (for example, admissions, registration, student records, financial aid, fiscal management, HR/payroll, development, alumni relations, facility management, academic affairs, document management, course management, and more).

Schools in general deals with large amounts of data on daily basis due the large number of students in an institute and almost double the number of parents tracking them. It is a difficult and error-prone process. The complexity comes from the flow of these amounts of data and information flow between the different school departments. School ERP solution data can be maintained confidential with better technical applications. It helps to understand the school business function, encourage good coordination between various departments and provides greater communication among the departments, avoiding uncertainty, which helps greater efficiency and productivity.

School ERP helps to decrease manual methods of applications, which are often repetitive and time consuming tasks. ERP covers all the functions related to the smooth functioning of schools. By the use of School ERPs' access can be controlled based on the different hierarchy levels existing in administrative functions in the school. Complex school business functions made simple and effective by School ERP features. School ERP helps to define school business functionally and provides complete solutions to school administrative functions. Swartz and Orgill (2001) mention that ERP automate school functioning enhances workflow, increases efficiency, and reduces reliance on paper, tightens controls. It also automates e-mail alerts, provides user-friendly Web-based interfaces, and streamlines processes. Enterprise resource planning is a system that integrates all data and processes of an organization into a unified system.

ERP system uses multiple components of computer software and hardware to achieve the integration. A key ingredient of the systems is the use of a unified database to store data for the various system modules. School ERP helps to decrease manual methods of applications, which are often repetitive and time consuming tasks. ERP covers all the functions related to the smooth functioning of schools.

School ERP can be configurable according to the changing demands of the schools business. It keeps each and every department posted thus avoiding manual communication methods and this will improve access to accurate and timely information (Kvavik, et al., 2002). It also simplified generating reports. School software is integrated with the best ERP features, which not only best suit school functions, but also make entire school functions more simple and effective. It is ideal school software which is customizable based on school requirements. Furthermore, data can be imported in the required software to further enhance the data for various needs. Instant reports help management to take rapid decisions and this will improve the efficiency and effectiveness of the school organization Arunthari (2005) agrees that ERP systems on user performance is a significant way to assess the utility of these applications and how they contribute to performance efficiency and effectiveness. Kvavik et al. (2002) approve that ERP in the educational institution achieve more efficiency and accessibility for all members and improve end users performance by providing better managerial tools.

ERP USAGE IN UAE SCHOOLS

The UAE is a federation of seven Emirates (Abu Dhabi, Dubai, Sharjah, Ajman, Ras Al Khaimah, Umm Al Quwain, and Fujairah). The government schools are managed by five educational councils and six educational zones, they are intermediate in administrative tasks between the public schools (government schools) and private schools in each Emirates and the Ministry of Education (MoE) in the UAE. The Abu Dhabi Education Council (ADEC) supervises and monitors 303 schools within the three educational zones. (Abu Dhabi, Al Ain, and Al Gharbieh).

In 2009, ADEC decided to computerize the educational sector in Abu Dhabi and implement the Electronic Student Information System (eSIS) as a platform system, Geographic Information System (GIS) and Enterprise Resource Planning (ERP), which assists school administrations, financial functions, and daily school record-keeping in Abu Dhabi public schools as well as a network connecting all schools to provide a central school monitoring service.

This move is part of ADEC's ongoing efforts to modernize and create a more effective processes and procedures for resource management across the education system in the Emirates. Furthermore, it follows the completion of ADEC's ERP system implementation for ADEC headquarters, teachers, and administrative staff. The ERP system will effectively consolidate different systems such as HR, procurement and finance within the organization. The new system is a tool that effectively saves time, and encourages a more seamless exchange of information by centralizing key processes on a common platform. ADEC places high importance on maintaining the best IT practices and plan to creating a technological infrastructure that will ease workflow, improve access to accurate data, and support decision-makers and education strategy development. The ERP will work through a centralized system of administrative and financial solutions based on a unified data center, which serves all of ADEC's systems.

This infrastructure is implemented to support and assist school administration, financial functions, and daily school record keeping. The investment in the best technological infrastructure in public government schools in order to maximize the potential of the education system is through enhancing methods of learning, teaching, and administration. Electronic systems should be applied across all schools in order to achieve ADEC's strategic goals and objectives.

eSIS platform was developed to provide a simple and easy-to-use data management system to modernize the storage and access to information pertaining to student records. Teachers access eSIS on a daily basis, using it to record grades, attendance, and other relevant student information. The platform can also assist with administrative tasks, such as school transfers, and new student registration.

Registration approvals and data transfer can all be managed online, improving efficiency and eliminating the need to send hard copy files between schools and the educational zone authorities.

IMPLEMENTATION STAGES

The first phase of eSIS implementation in schools has been a massive success with 5,000 users uploading information on 133,000 students in 303 schools; this amounts to a 95% usage rate across Abu Dhabi schools. The second phase of the eSIS implemented during the 2010-2011 school years, this involved development of a portal for parents to support direct communication with schools and teachers.

Geographic Information System (GIS) is defined as category of DSS that use data visualization technology to analyze and display data in form of digitized maps (Lauden & Lauden, 2009) which enables users to locate all schools in the emirate, and the nearest medical facilities, with a simple search tool; Users are also able to generate dynamic and comparative reports on everything from school profiles, to teacher and student statistics through this online resource. Decision-makers and school staff can compare students' test scores in their own school against average performance levels.

Enterprise Resource Planning (ERP) system has successfully automated, streamlined, and improved centralized back office operations. This includes general ledger transactions such as, payment and receipt of funds, cash management, and purchasing. In addition, the ERP system will effectively support online human resource management, and payroll functions. The organization-wide considered ERP as a strategic tool helping ADEC to automate and integrate its key business operations in the areas of human resources, procurement, and finance. Ashbangh and Rowen (2002) agree that the components of HR modules within an ERP system include HR management, benefits administration, payroll, time and labor management and employees' management self-service. However, due to the large quantity of information that is handled in schools, the job is becoming more difficult every day. ERP solution for supporting HR is represented like a useful tool to help and orient the users to focus their work in the direct relationship with the stakeholders.

ADEC has also implemented Oracle SSHR, a leading self-service human resource tool, and automated payroll to over 14,000 teachers and staff members. This service allows ADEC employees to automate practically every HR tasks and provides a single data model supplying a fast, immediate and accurate view of HR activities including payroll, benefits, access and update personal information, apply for leave, check leave balances from anywhere in the world at any time.

The ERP system is a strategic tool that will satisfy, control, and integrate the human resources and the financial procurements functions seamlessly and effectively. ERP provides the option to update the employment records on the basis of information, and updating collectively on a single screen for more than one staff member, as well as facilitate transparent and accurate communication between ADEC's staff and relevant departments. ERP project implementation in ADEC implementation done in two phases:

- The first phase of the ERP was implemented in 2009 on financial and procurement systems. ERP's second phase focuses on payroll and self-service systems, salaries of Abu Dhabi teachers and Administrative staff were transferred from the Ministry of Education's payroll to ADEC's payroll, and the later has sent to banks. The ERP phases were completed in a record time of four and a half months and had covered an enormous number of staff, 14658 employees.
- The second phase included the relocation of data and information of all ADEC Staff, including the three educational zones related to Abu Dhabi emirate (Abu Dhabi, Al Ain, and Al Gharbieh). In ERP solution, HR self-service ADEC staff can follow up on HR-related issues from any location, including leave application, requesting work-related certificates and letters, and many other services. There are currently 15,002 users registered to the system who have engaged in more than 57,000 transactions using the employee self-service tool. ERP is able to provide the management of the Human Resources area with an integrated solution to the different processes of these sections, ERP embracing management, and control report. The internal communication is a indispensable part of the daily tasks of the department (ADEC, 2010).

ERP offers ADEC staff the facilities, which no longer requires leaving offices or schools to follow up on any HR service. Applying for leaves, work-related certificates, letters, information update, and many other services can be made through the Internet anywhere and anytime. ERP system will allow teachers working in remote areas conduct online operations such as data updates, i.e. change of social status and adding new born baby, etc., with less time and without the need to be physically present in the headquarters.

The ERP Project emphasize knowledge transfer to all ADEC employees, and will support and enable the transformation through the deployment of best practices and integrated business processes followed by major institutions worldwide.

The biggest challenge ADEC faced during the implementation of the project was the on-time integration of more than 15,800 employees and teaching staff into the HR self-service and payroll system and establishes best practice for HR across the organization's various sites. And the major challenges is Automate processes, bringing ERP methods of modern business into an educational setting

FUTURE CHALLENGE

It can be stated that ADEC has awareness and a high level of recognition of the future challenges associated with this step toward using ERP to support not only HR but to provide complete services for their users and parents. Even though it is early and difficult to measure the benefits of implementing ERP as a strategic solution to improve the efficiency and effectiveness of the school organization, the system is a new concept to the users. After organizing several training courses, then users became qualified to support and train new users in the system. It is recommended that ideal management be used for the project in order to meet the future challenges that are facing ADEC such as: building an entirely new educational framework in a short period of time, providing 15,800 employees with all tools they require to use the systems; securely manage the names and identities of all staff members; establish best practices for Human Resources (HR), finance, and recruitment across the organization's various education sites and automate processes, bringing Enterprise Resource Planning (ERP) methods of modern business into an educational setting.

REFERENCES

Abugabah, A., & Sanzogni, L. (2010). Enterprise resource planning (ERP) system in higher education: A literature review and implications. *International Journal of Human and Social Sciences*, 5(6), 49–53.

ADEC. (2010a). *Enterprise student information system (eSIS) systems documents.* Retrieved from http://www.adec.ac.ae/English/Pages/NewsDisplay.aspx

ADEC. (2010b). *Completes the ERP system in a record time.* Retrieved February 10, 2012 from http://www.ameinfo.com/222431.html

ADEC. (2010c). *Implements enterprise resource management in Abu Dhabi institutions.* Retrieved February 11, 2012 from http://www.ameinfo.com/224841.html

Al Meshari, M. (2003). *Enterprise resource planning (ERP) systems:* A research agenda. *Emerald Industrial Management & Data Systems*, 103(1), 22–27. doi:10.1108/02635570310456869

Allen, D., & Kern, T. (2001). Enterprise resource planning implementation: Stories of power, politics, and resistance. In *Proceedings of the IFIP TC8/WG8.2 Working Conference on Realigning Research and Practice in Information Systems Development: The Social and Organizational Perspective.* Boise, ID: IFIP.

Arunthari, S. (2005). *Information technology adoption by companies in Thailand: A study of enterprise resources planning system usage.* (PhD Thesis). University of Wollongong. Wollongong, Australia.

Ashbaugh, S., & Rowen, M. (2002). Technology for human resources management: Seven questions and answers. *Public Personnel Management, 31,* 7–20.

Ben Zion, T. M., & Yaffa, G. (1995). Information technology in educational management: Maximizing the potential of information technology for management. In C. L. Fulmer (Ed.), *Strategies for Interfacing the Technical Core of Education.* London, UK: Chapman & Hall

Bradford, M., & Florin, J. (2003). Examining the role of innovation diffusion factors on the implementation success of enterprise resource planning systems. *International Journal of Accounting Information Systems, 4*(3), 205–225. doi:10.1016/ S1467-0895(03)00026-5

Calisir, F. (2004). The relation of interface usability characteristics, perceived usefulness and perceived ease of use to end -user satisfaction with enterprise resource planning systems. *Computers in Human Behavior, 20,* 505–515. doi:10.1016/j. chb.2003.10.004

Chung, S., & Snyder, C. (2000). ERP adoption: A technological evolution approach. *International Journal of Agile Management Systems, 2*(1). doi:10.1108/14654650010312570

Grabski, S. V., & Leech, S. A. (2002). Complementary controls and ERP implementation success. *Information & Management, 40*(1), 25–40.

Jing, R., & Qui, X. (2007). A study on critical success factors in ERP systems implementation. In *Proceedings of the IEEE International Conference on Service Systems and Service Management.* IEEE Press.

King, P., Kvavik, R. B., & Voloudakis, J. (2002). *Enterprise resource planning systems in higher education (ERB0222).* Boulder, CO: EDUCAUSE Center for Applied Research (ECAR).

Kvavik, R., Katz, R., Beecher, K., Caruso, J., & King, P. (2002). The promise and performance of enterprise systems for higher education. *EDUCAUSE, 4,* 5–123.

Kvavik, R. B., Katz, R. N., Beecher, K., Caruso, J., King, P., Voludakis, J., & Williams, L. A. (2002). *The promise and performance of enterprise systems for higher education (ERS0204)*. Boulder, CO: EDUCAUSE Center for Applied Research (ECAR).

Lauden, K., & Lauden, J. P. (2009). *Management information systems: Managing the digital firm* (11th ed.). Upper Saddle River, NJ: Prentice Hall.

Lloyd, S. (2010). *Why use school information software: Keys to making sense of K-12 software*. Victoria, Canada: Trafford.

Mehlinger, L. (2006). *Indicators of successful enterprise technology implementations in higher education business*. (PhD Thesis). Morgan State University. Baltimore, MD.

Noudoostbeni, A., Yasin, N. M., & Jenatabadi, H. S. (2009). To investigate the success and failure factors of ERP implementation within Malaysian small and medium enterprises. In *Proceedings of the Information Management and Engineering*, (pp. 157-160). IEEE Press.

O'Brien, J. (1999). Management information systems. In *Managing Information Technology: The Internet Worked Enterprises*. Boston, MA: McGraw Hill.

Olson, D. L. (2004). *Managerial issues of enterprise resource planning systems*. Boston, MA: McGraw Hill.

Pasaoglu, D. (2011). Analysis of ERP usage with technology acceptance model. *Global Business and Management Research, 3*(2), 157–181.

Ragowsky, A., & Romm Livermore, C. T. (2002). ERP system selection and implementation: Across cultural approach. In Proceedings of the Eighth American Conference on Information Systems, (pp. 1333-1339). Retrieved from http://www.davidfrico.com/rico04f.pdf

Soliman, F., & Youssef, M. (1998). The role of SAP software in business process reengineering. *International Journal of Operations & Production Management, 18*(9/10), 886–895. doi:10.1108/01443579810225504

Somers, T., & Nelson, K. (2003). The impact of strategy and integration mechanism on enterprise system value: Empirical evidence from manufacturing firms. *European Journal of Operational Research, 146*, 315–338. doi:10.1016/S0377-2217(02)00552-0

Swartz, D., & Orgill, K. (2001). *ERP project: Learned using this framework for ERP could save your university millions of dollars*. Retrieved from http://net.educause.edu/ir/library/pdf/eqm0121.pdf

Umble, E. J., Haft, R., & Umble, M. (2003). Enterprise resource planning: Implementation procedures and critical success factors. *European Journal of Operational Research, 146*(2), 241–257. doi:10.1016/S0377-2217(02)00547-7

Upadhyay, P., & Dan, P. (2008). An explorative study to identify the critical success factors for ERP implementation in Indian small and medium scale enterprises. In *Proceedings of the IEEE International Conference on Information Technology.* IEEE Press.

Watson, E., & Schneider, H. (1999). Using ERP in education. *Communications of the Association for Information Systems, 1*(9), 12–24.

Wikipedia. (2011). *Education in Saudi Arabia.* Retrieved 6 April, 2011, from http://en.wikipedia.org/wiki/Education_in_Saudi_Arabia

Wong, B., & Tein, D. (2004). *Critical success factors for ERP projects.* Retrieved from cms.3rdgen.info/3rdgen_sites/107/resource/ORWongandTein.pdf

Wu, J.-H., & Wang, Y.-M. (2006). Measuring ERP success: The ultimate users' view. *Journal of Operations & Production Management, 26*(8), 882–903. doi:10.1108/01443570610678657

Xia, L., Yu, W., Lim, R., & Hock, L. (2010). A methodology for successful implementation of ERP in smaller companies. In *Proceedings of the Service Operations and Logistics and Informatics (SOLI),* (pp. 380 – 385). SOLI.

KEY TERMS AND DEFINITIONS

ADEC: Abu Dhabi Educational Council.
ERP: Enterprise Resource Planning.
eSIS: Enterprise Student Information Systems.
GIS: Geographic Information System.
MIS: Management Information Systems.
MoE: Ministry of Education.
SIS: School Information Systems.

Chapter 4

Enterprise Asset Management System:
A Green Gulf Implementation Case

Nooruddin Ahmed
ADNOC, UAE

EXECUTIVE SUMMARY

Any ERP/EAM implementation is a complex journey. No matter how prepared, more often than not you end up like a traveler on a tour of countries where most people look, dress, and speak differently from you. The feeling is of a lost tourist with a map and language guide ambling through unfamiliar terrain, barely coping to do some of the normal things one took for granted. The analogy goes further; it takes time to familiarize oneself with routes, signs, language, and people to barely get along, and you find your trip ending and you move on to the next country on your tour. Similarly, just as you think you are finding your way with your ERP/EAM, someone announces it is time to upgrade, and you start to move again. After nearly 15 years of conventional projects, the case of a particularly interesting implementation came along in the UAE for a major Oil and Gas Services Company. A novel approach was mandated by necessity. The project was managed remotely and executed primarily by internal resources, making it a lean and green implementation.

DOI: 10.4018/978-1-4666-2220-3.ch004

ORGANIZATION BACKGROUND

The Organization is a major Oil Support Services Company in the GCC region, part of a much larger group. A large part of the Organization's business came directly from servicing the Group; however, there were plans in place to provide services across the region. The Organization employed either directly or indirectly several thousand staff and serviced many diverse Oil and Gas requirements. Although the revenue was in several millions of dollars, the net margins had significant room for improvement.

As with any Support Services Organization, to provide tangible value to customers and stakeholders, the business has to be run effectively and efficiently. Information Systems and Technology is a critical component in driving performance and delivery. It was clear that this critical component was functioning well below par, resulting in a direct impact on the overall Organization's performance.

SETTING THE STAGE

The assignment started as one of the many ad-hoc meetings called for by the Manager. I was pretty much used to getting calls from his office which invariably ended up with a "special assignment." He had almost cultivated an art of building up the suspense to make it appealing and exciting.

The closed door meeting room would invariably have few handpicked members who were trusted with assignments, usually considered not practical or possible, His excitement used to come from taking up such assignments, creating an exciting aura around them and challenging his team to deliver. I was privileged to be part of many such "Missions" which were quite successful. Being mentally prepared for this, I took my diary and headed to the meeting room expecting the same process.

This time though, it was different. It was just him and me; we got into a waiting car and were on our way to the Company's General Manager's Office. There was no one else involved. I was briefed on the way that the concerned organization was having major issues with their maintenance, inventory and procurement. They already had an existing financial system implemented and were looking to implement the same system for the rest of the functions. A lot of evaluations were done and a proposal was submitted to the board for approval. However, the approval had not come as the cost as well as duration was way beyond the expectations and budget. We were now on the way to meet with the GM to look at alternatives.

On entering the GM's office, we were welcomed by a team of people besides him. The problem was spelt out to us in more detail and a direct request to us if we could help in anyway. It was simple; they needed a solution to manage the above functions at a very low cost and in fewer than 6 months. The internal team was all for the existing system, so anything else would be an immense challenge.

My expertise was with another leading EAM and I was more or less sure that if they were willing to adopt a pretty much out of the box solution with minor changes we could give them something to work with within or below the budget. However, there were major constraints of time, availability of resources and more importantly my own availability. I had a personal commitment to travel for a family engagement and was not sure how it would work it out. All these thoughts were running to my head as I was sitting in the meeting room, simply because this was what I expected my Manager to ask me eventually.

As expected, my Manager did not commit anything. He just told the GM that he was confident we could address his concerns, however he would need to consult and review if the time frame was practical (he seemed completely unaware that he had already approved my vacation). We politely left the meeting with a commitment to revert the next day with a plan.

On the way back, I told him about the constraints and reminded him on my vacation. He seemed unperturbed. He looked me in the eye and said, "We need to get this done." In other words, find a way to do it. Several scenarios ran through my mind as we continued in silence. There was no way I could postpone my leave so I had to think of another model. By the time we reached our destination a basic plan (thinking out of the box, literally) started forming in my mind. I told my Manager that I need to hand pick a couple of people to work with me and I would have something for him (however crazy it might sound), the next day.

CASE DESCRIPTION

The first thought on my mind was agility. In order to achieve this it was important to assemble the right people with the right mindset. One core principle that I learned over the years and still firmly believe in is to put people first. The process comes later. If we had the right mix of people, things could work, otherwise it could go horribly wrong.

The right people, in my mind were those who could combine logic, practicality, process and control, in that order. A quick review and 3-4 people flashed. I picked them and put the most practical one in charge of the implementation. On my own role, after some internal debate, I decided to play the role of a Coach or more a Joker, someone who would be a go to person for any of the guys and the same time, someone who could get behind the wheel in case one of the drivers tire.

In addition to our team, we included two from the Organization's team. My belief was if this had to work, we had to be one team. Their guys were not new to EAM systems; they just needed to know the new tool. The implementer from our side was one of the best guys we had, down to earth and hard working, so, my role was just to build the right processes around him to control the project.

Looking back it is still hard to believe. Over 2 marathon sessions of 8-9 hours well into the evenings, we had a blue print of what this Project would look like. It was to be a core team of 5 people, two of whom had no experience on the tool supported from the outside by me, who was to be out of the country for half of the Project. Just to make it more interesting, the time line was 4 months out of which 2 months were in summer when most of the people are usually planning their vacation. The mission was exciting and to us it was just to do something that challenged our limits.

My manager was convinced and it took just one meeting to convince the GM that we meant business, provided he backed us with all the necessary support. He most willingly signed the charter and we walked out confident that we would be able to make it.

As they say, the devil is in the details. Despite the initial confidence, as things started to unfold it was becoming clearer that we had bitten off perhaps a bit more than we could chew. The next week saw intense sessions where we started to scope and draw out the functional specifications and requirements more clearly. Although we had agreed on a plain Vanilla implementation, we were shocked with the state of the data that was presented. It was clear that unless we had the data prepared, there was no way on earth we could meet the deadline. A key take away at this point that needs mention is the value of doing a Readiness Assessment before any commitments are made. In most cases, no one really knows precisely what is being accepted and you go with a degree of acceptable risk. However, doing even quick check across several dimensions (as presented later through a questionnaire), goes a long way in ensuring that commitments have a higher probability of delivery.

From the perspective of a Project, it really does not matter what the Charter says about Roles and Responsibilities. Once you are in, it is all hands to the wheel. The Data needed not just hands but heads and hearts too. In fact, during one point our Implementer gave up. It took a lot of cajoling and persuasion to get him back. The importance of personal relations during such extreme implementations cannot be overstated.

The implementation model was as lean and green as possible. Workshops were held only when absolutely necessary. Most information was obtained through pre-defined templates and communication of status was only for exceptions. This minimized the need to spend valuable time on writing status reports and maximized time on getting the job done.

- It was agreed that the Organization would use the new tool without any customization or Interfaces. Simple Data exchange would be setup for core financial reporting needs.
- Our team would manage the implementation and the Organization would be responsible for providing the data as per the prescribed format.
- We would provide training to the Organization's Users on the Tool processes AS IS.
- The Organization's IT team could participate with us team during the implementation to witness firsthand how things were done, however, there would be no separate time allocated for this. The IT team could gradually pick up working on the system after the initial GO-LIVE.
- The Organization could use our expertise and services until they needed it. They could decide whenever they felt necessary to take over the Tool completely at their site
- The priority as stated by the GM was to have their Users up and running with the new Tool as soon as possible, so all efforts we driven with that objective in mind.

The only processes that were documented were the exceptions. Anything that followed out of the box was just converted to a Help Document/File. These files became the processes, saving precious time documenting AS IS and TO BE's. Basically we documented "How Can I use the System for....?"

Several of the Data Records were entered manually. This combined to serve as hands-on training sessions minimizing the need to hold independent training sessions. It was also decided to reduce complexity of data migration scripting by entering data wherever the logic was complicated or the source data was not clean. This reduced time to some extent; however, the Data migration did prove to be the longest part of the implementation.

The GM's instructions and perhaps promised incentives to his team motivated them to work with sincerity. This was an extremely crucial factor for the acceptance. The personal agendas and bias for the existing system was somewhat neutralized by this. Perhaps the biggest factor was that they did not perceive us as external vendors, so the trust was implicit.

CURRENT CHALLENGES FACING THE ORGANIZATION

Despite the successful implementation (yes we did roll out the new Tool in 100 days with a core team of 3 people from our side and 2 from their side), the challenge of actually benefiting from the process persisted. As we often see, it is not the implementation that is important, it is the expected result from the implementation that is. Summarized below are some of the key findings:

Expectation Management

This is perhaps the real key to everything. Somewhere, much earlier to our arrival on the scene, the General Manager had the expectation implanted in his mind that all his problems would go away with an automated solution. To him however, there were still problems that persisted. These problems were such that could hardly be resolved by automation (for example if someone creates a Duplicate Supplier by adding a few more characters on the name, it is unlikely that a system can prevent it). Resetting expectations to what can be realistically expected and achieved is vital. In hindsight, this is something we could have done much better.

User Engagement

The approach lent itself well with several Key Users. They did not feel intimidated by us and felt part of the process. In typical lengthy implementations, a lot of suspicion pervades the atmosphere. There are so many documentation sign-offs that are needed which makes everyone fearful of mistakes and failure. This overkill of caution in many cases proves counter-productive. In our agile approach, the Users typically had to accept functions they saw and tested not sign off documents that for most parts they could not understand. This definitely facilitated the process a great deal.

Internal Expertise and Knowledge Transfer

If there is one thing that can make or break an implementation, it is the availability of motivated internal resources. A large part of my role involved getting them engaged at an early stage and making them honestly take ownership of the Project. At every step measures were taken to facilitate and enforce knowledge transfer. This is one of the key skills that must be a prerequisite for any Engagement Manager. The Project benefitted substantially since the internal resources provided by the Organization were of a high caliber, something that I had insisted upon. Once motivated, this helped us mitigate substantially the risks post-implementation. Although the hand over was by and large smooth, there were areas where we could have done better especially when it came to getting acceptance and sign-off's documented.

Process vs. Functional View

The impact of having Functional Units control and dictate Business Processes is a reality in this environment. In many cases, processes have to be built around individuals. Invariably, this works against streamlining the processes and impacts overall effectiveness and efficiency of the business. Having the support of the top management helped to a large extent and individual pockets of resistance were generally overcome. However, there is definite room for improvement.

SOLUTIONS AND RECOMMENDATIONS

On reviewing the outcome of the approach and implementation adopted for the Organization, it became abundantly clear that we were on to something here. Given the current realities where over 50% of all major IT Projects fail to meet expected outcomes, resulting in wasted investments as well as environmental damage, perhaps the approach adopted need not just be a one-off event.

As energy becomes more scarce and power consumption of ICT growing at over 10% annually there is definitely a need to consider alternative approaches more frequently.

The conventional wisdom of reusing components and implementing huge systems was challenged. Many of these components that are part of these systems are "obese" as they try to standardize and cater to multiple scenarios. The end product has so many unused "features" and even more features that are perhaps used not more than once or twice in its entire life. Additionally, there are the innumerable customizations, which also rely on the same obese components to be extended.

It just seemed natural at this point to understand the bigger picture. If we could do something different that resulted in a fraction of the cost, resources and time in terms of the footprint consumed, perhaps understanding the overall Green/Sustainable economy and the impact such approaches can have were worth pursuing further.

This journey of discovering the bigger picture is interesting in itself. To recommend solutions the importance of the bigger picture cannot be overstated. The following section throws some light on this.

Green or Sustainable IT is the technology industry's way of asking itself what role it should play in the global movement toward building a more sustainable civilization. The answer is typically to reduce the energy footprint of IT thereby reducing GHG emissions and using IT as a strategic enabler to help business processes reduce emissions, reduce costs, and improve efficiency.

ICT equipment has amongst the lowest lifecycle usage, with most equipment become e-waste in 3- 5 years. Further, besides the actual hardware involved, tangible differences in Organizational sustainability can be achieved through the Processes, in fact using IT to green the overall business is where almost 98% of the benefits of Green IT are visible. The conventional Green IT focused on Hardware saving, while important is not the critical part.

Besides "passing on a sustainable world to our children" there are also reasons that this is becoming a major concern for businesses such as the growing cost of energy, concerns over the future supply of energy the real threat of government regulation over energy consumption and growing political support for managing and regulating GHG emissions.

The realization dawned on me that perhaps our achievement was much more significant that we imagined. Our approach had drastically reduced the environmental footprint of the implementation.

It is of paramount importance, therefore to make all concerned aware of this issue by conducting specific Executive level briefings targeting decision makers in the organization, developing a Policy for Sustainable ICT, formulating and implementing strategic actions to drive eco-friendly ICT and rewarding compliance with the policy.

For our project, it was difficult since the system was rolled out already. However, for future projects it could definitely be worth considering.

It is therefore recommended to reevaluate the way ERP/EAM implementations are done and to consider the following phases as a mandatory part of forthcoming ERP/EAM implementations or upgrades:

- **Phase 1 Assessment:** A baseline of energy usage and emission is created and an overall plan to achieve greener practices is prepared as part of the AS IS Process analysis.
- **Phase 2 Planning:** Detailed roadmaps for specific green IT initiatives like procurement, data center optimization, and recycling are developed as part of the TO BE Process analysis.
- **Phase 3 Implementation:** Specific initiatives are focused on and implemented with an emphasis on quick wins such as power management, virtualization and the like embedded as part of the overall ERP/EAM project.
- **Phase 4 Evaluation:** Measurement of the emissions and energy usage are done after the implementation. This can be ongoing and periodic as well, not just one time.

Another recommendation is to consider the overall Business-IT Alignment. One of the largest contributors to success was the Alignment maintained in the Project. A more comprehensive impact assessment of IT Investment decisions is definitely needed. The GM by challenging his team not to accept the conventional EAM implementation approach was commendable. However, his challenge was primarily based on the dimension of cost.

Considerable improvement can be envisaged by considering some of the other dimensions as well prior to embarking on an ERP/EAM project. This following questionnaire could prove useful to answer and score prior to embarking on a Project:

1. **Strategy:**
   a. Has the Business Objective(s) linked to the Venture been identified? (1 – Not Sure, 2 – Not Identified, 3 – Partly Identified, 4 – Mostly Identified, 5 – Fully Identified).
   b. Have the measures that determine Business Success been defined? (1 – Not Sure, 2 – Not Defined, 3 – Partly Defined, 4 – Mostly Defined, 5 – Fully Defined).
   c. How strategic is the Business Objective to the Business Mission? (1 – Not Sure, 2 – Not Strategic, 3 – Partially Strategic, 4 – Completely Strategic, 5 – Vital).
   d. Has the Business Strategy been communicated to all the relevant stake-holders? (1 – Not Sure, 2 – Not Communicated, 3 – Partly Communicated, 4 – Mostly Communicated, 5 – Fully Communicated).
   e. Has the Venture been prioritized in the IT Strategic Plan? (1 – Not Sure, 2 – Not Prioritized, 3 – Low Priority, 4 – Medium Priority, 5 – High Priority).

2. **People:**
   a. What is the level of executive sponsorship? (1 – Not Sure, 2 – Low, 3 – Medium, 4 – High, 5 – Top Most).
   b. How many people are involved in the decision making process? (1 – Not Sure, 2 – More than 5).
   c. What level of team support does the ERP Manager command? (1 – Not Sure, 2 – Low, 3 – Medium, 4 – High, 5 – Very High).
   d. What is the maturity level of the Business Users? (1 – Not Sure, 2 – Low, 3 – Medium, 4 – High, 5 – Very High).
   e. What is the maturity level of the IT resources? (1 – Not Sure, 2 – Low, 3 – Medium, 4 – High, 5 – Very High).

3. **Cost:**
   a. What Delegation of Authority is needed to approve funding? (1 – Not Sure, 2 – Board, 3 – Directorate, 4 – Division, 5 – Department).
   b. What is the length of time for the funding process? (1 – Not Sure, 2 – Very Long, 3 – Average, 4 – Short, 5 – Very Short).
   c. How justified is the cost to the benefits? (1 – Not Sure, 2 – Low, 3 – Medium, 4 – High, 5 – Very High).

d. What level of details are the costs broken down to? (1 – Not Sure, 2 – High Level, 3 – Medium, 4 – Low, 5 – Lowest).

e. What percentage of the costs are evidenced, i.e. have documentary proof vs. speculative? (1 – Not Sure, 2 – Little Proof, 3 – Some Proof, 4 – Sufficient Proof, 5 – Completely Proven).

4. **Tools:**

a. What is the comfort level of the people with the tools being used? (1 – Not Sure, 2 – Low, 3 – Medium, 4 – High, 5 – Very High).

b. How much of internal support exists to trouble-shoot tool related problems? (1 – Not Sure, 2 – Low, 3 – Medium, 4 – High, 5 – Very High).

c. How important are tools for the task? (1 – Not Sure, 2 – Essential, 3 – Important, 4 – Low Importance, 5 – Not Important).

d. How much of the work done is affected by changes to the tool? (1 – Not Sure, 2 – All the Work, 3 – Most of the Work, 4 – Some Work, 5 – No Work).

e. How much of external support is available for the tool (Internet, vendor, etc.)? (1 – Not Sure, 2 – Some Support, 3 – Adequate Support, 4 – Proactive Support, 5 – Excellent Support).

5. **Work Culture:**

a. How much of importance is given organizationally to successful work? (1 – Not Sure, 2 – Low, 3 – Medium, 4 – High, 5 – Excellent).

b. What are the consequences of non-performance? (1 – Not Sure, 2 – Little Consequence, 3 – Some Consequence, 4 – Adequate Consequence, 5 – Immediate Preventive Action).

c. What are the rewards for superior performance? (1 – Not Sure, 2 – Some Recognition, 3 – Inadequate Timely Recognition, 4 – Adequate Timely Recognition, 5 – Immediate Exemplary Recognition).

d. How proactive are the organization units impacted by the venture? (1 – Not Sure, 2 – Low, 3 – Medium, 4 – High, 5 – Very High).

e. What is the approach towards failure? (1 – Not Sure, 2 – Blame, 3 – Cover Up, 4 – Move On, 5 – Treat it as a Stepping Stone to Success).

6. **Business Process:**

a. How much of the Business Processes Documented? (1 – Not Sure, 2 – LITTLE, 3 – Some Gaps, 4 – Adequate, 5 – Fully).

b. How much of the Process Documents are up-to-date? (1 – Not Sure, 2 – Little, 3 – Some, 4 – Most, 5 – Fully).

c. What is the level of control that exists for the Processes? (1 – Not Sure, 2 – Little, 3 – Some Control, 4 – Adequate Control, 5 – Excellent Control).

d. To what degree are the processes streamlined across departments? (1 – Not Sure, 2 – Low, 3 – Medium, 4 – High, 5 – Very High).

e. To what degree does the Process being affected by the automation contribute to the Business Objectives? (1 – Not Sure, 2 – Low, 3 – Medium,
4 – High, 5 – Very High).

7. **Data:**
   a. How much of the data is clean? (1 – Not Sure, 2 – Little, 3 – Some Gaps,
   4 – Adequate, 5 – Fully).
   b. To what extent does validation control exist for data capture? (1 – Not
   Sure, 2 – Little, 3 – Some, 4 – Adequate, 5 – Fully).
   c. To what extent is data custodianship defined and executed? (1 – Not Sure,
   2 – Hardly, 3 – Partially, 4 – Adequately, 5 – Fully).
   d. To what extent is a centralized data dictionary available for use? (1 – Not
   Sure, 2 – Hardly, 3 – Partially, 4 – Adequately, 5 – Fully).
   e. To what extent is data reused across systems? (1 – Not Sure, 2 – Hardly,
   3 – Partially, 4 – Adequately, 5 – Fully).

8. **Value:**
   a. To what extent have the metrics that capture value been defined? (1 – Not
   Sure, 2 – Hardly, 3 – Partially, 4 – Adequately, 5 – Fully).
   b. To what extent are metrics communicated and approved by the business?
   (1 – Not Sure, 2 – Hardly, 3 – Partially, 4 – Adequately, 5 – Fully).
   c. To what extent is a structured methodology for the process of IT value
   measurement being used? (1 – Not Sure, 2 – Hardly, 3 – Partially, 4 –
   Adequately, 5 – Fully).
   d. To what extent has the venture investment been evaluated against potentially more useful Ventures? (1 – Not Sure, 2 – Hardly, 3 – Partially,
   4 – Adequately, 5 – Fully).
   e. To what extent does executive management use venture value influence investment decisions? (1 – Not Sure, 2 – Hardly, 3 – Partially, 4
   – Adequately, 5 – Fully).

9. **X-Factors:**
   a. To what extent has a formal risk assessment done? (1 – Not Sure, 2 –
   Hardly, 3 – Partially, 4 – Adequately, 5 – Fully).
   b. How much of the venture is constrained by time? (1 – Not Sure, 2 – Fully
   Constrained, 3 – Partially Constrained, 4 – Hardly Constrained, 5 – Not
   Constrained).
   c. To what extent was the venture planned? (1 – Not Sure, 2 – Hardly, 3 –
   Partially, 4 – Adequately, 5 – Fully).
   d. To what extent is a competent resource pool buffer maintained? (1 – Not
   Sure, 2 – Hardly, 3 – Partially, 4 – Adequately, 5 – Fully).
   e. To what extent is the ERP managers appointed solely on merit? (1 – Not
   Sure, 2 – Hardly, 3 – Partially, 4 – Adequately, 5 – Fully).

10. **Compliance:**
   a. To what extent does the venture comply with the security policy? (1 – Not Sure, 2 – Hardly, 3 – Partially, 4 – Adequately, 5 – Fully).
   b. To what extent does the venture comply with the HSE/ sustainability policy? (1 – Not Sure, 2 – Hardly, 3 – Partially, 4 – Adequately, 5 – Fully).
   c. To what extent does the venture comply with the ethical policy? (1 – Not Sure, 2 – Hardly, 3 – Partially, 4 – Adequately, 5 – Fully).

The weight of each dimension and factor in the questionnaire can be defined based on the specifics of the Organization where the implementation is intended. To some extent, the answers to the questions will help determine the degree of alignment. It is safe to say that alignment is the key to successful delivery. I am certain based on the experience in this project and several others that the factor that makes or breaks alignment is People. An interesting list of the most important factors impacting success of Projects from Standish Group CHAOS report is presented below:

- User Involvement.
- Executive Management Support.
- Realistic Expectations.
- Competent Staff.
- Ownership.
- Hard work and Focus.

All of these have something to do with people. These factors basically reaffirm my core belief that it is not just methodology or certifications that lead to successful Projects, but People with an open mind that really make the difference.

To summarize, the case was a real opportunity to do things differently. This opportunity necessitated the use of several unconventional tools and techniques to deliver a successful implementation. The driving force behind most of the changes to convention came from finding the "Purpose" behind the "Process." It was remarkable to us that several Processes followed religiously for conventional implementations were not contextualized for Organizational Purpose. The simple contextualization helped us to eliminate a large number of processes.

This in turn, led us down a path that was far more effective. Yes, the 100 days were hard; however, it was far better than 400 days with results that may not have been too much different. The last we checked on the Organization they were using the tool for over 5 years. They did mention though that they were now thinking of an Upgrade/Replacement. I may be involved in another journey, but this time the road appears to be greener or is it? Only time will tell.

REFERENCES

Al-Mashari, M., Al-Mudimigh, A., & Zairi, M. (2003). Enterprise resource planning: A taxonomy of critical factors. *European Journal of Operational Research*, *146*(2), 352. doi:10.1016/S0377-2217(02)00554-4

Beal, B. (2003, October 15). *The priority that persists*. Retrieved February 14, 2012, from http://searchcio.techtarget.com/originalContent/0,289142,sid19_gci932246,00. html

Ip, W., & Chau, K., & Chan. (2002). Implementing ERP through continuous improvement. *International Journal of Manufacturing*, *4*(6), 465.

Nah, F., Lau, L.-S., & Kuang, J. (2001). Critical factors for successful implementation of enterprise systems. *Business Process Management Journal*, *7*(3), 285. doi:10.1108/14637150110392782

Sobotta, T., Sobotta, N., & Gotze. (2010, May 31). *Greening IT*. Retrieved February 14, 2012 from http://greening.it/wp-content/uploads/downloads/2010/06/greening-it_isbn-9788791936029.pdf

Standish Group. (1995). *Website*. Retrieved February 14, 2012, from http://www. projectsmart.co.uk/docs/chaos-report.pdf

Umble, E., Haft, R., & Umble, M. (2003). Enterprise resource planning: Implementation procedures and critical success factors. *European Journal of Operational Research*, *146*(2), 241. doi:10.1016/S0377-2217(02)00547-7

KEY TERMS AND DEFINITIONS

Alignment Dimensions: The various areas that need to be considered prior to investing or commencing an IT project.

Alignment: A state in which all IT investments in an organization are aligned with business objectives of the organization.

EAM: Enterprise Asset Management – IT systems that help organizations manage their enterprise assets.

Factor: An entity that is believed to have an influence on the outcome of a venture. The influence could either be positive or negative.

GHG: A greenhouse gas is a gas in an atmosphere that absorbs and emits radiation within a range. This process is the fundamental cause of the greenhouse effect.

The primary greenhouse gases in the Earth's atmosphere are water vapor, carbon dioxide, methane, nitrous oxide, and ozone.

Green: An approach that facilitates that is environmentally-friendly and sustainable.

Greenhouse Effect: The greenhouse effect is a process by which thermal radiation from a planetary surface is absorbed by atmospheric, and is re-radiated in all directions. Since part of this re-radiation is back towards the surface, energy is transferred to the surface and the lower atmosphere. As a result, the average surface temperature is higher than it would be if direct heating by solar radiation were the only warming mechanism.

IT Investment: An investment quantified in $ value made in information technology or systems. This could be implementation of systems, acquisition of systems, or technology upgrades.

IT Strategy: The strategy developed by the information systems and technology unit in the organization that touches on the vision, mission, goals, and plans of the IT department.

Chapter 5

The Design and Implementation of Paperless Medical System (PMS) for Offshore Operating Company:
A Structured Approach

Nabil Ghalib
Business International Group, UAE

EXECUTIVE SUMMARY

Application software development has always been viewed as a massive challenge by companies that view IT services as a support function rather than a core function. The term "core" here implies that IT plays an enabler role to facilitate technology and services that support users to meet set business objectives in an efficient way. Furthermore, IT development is perceived by many managers as a burden; hence, they prefer the fast track implementation of specialized packages to deliver the majority of service levels over the long wait for systems to be built in-house, even though the latter option is more advantageous in the long run, as it offers a much better fit to all user requirements. With this dilemma in mind, this case is an example of how an in-house development solution was implemented. The case touches on positive and negative aspects of the decision to build the application and covers a range of issues encountered during every phase of the development life cycle.

DOI: 10.4018/978-1-4666-2220-3.ch005

CASE STUDY OBJECTIVES

This case study highlights issues and challenges pertaining to the different phases of the "System Development Life Cycle—SDLC," with emphasis on the cultural constraints and limitations encountered at each phase.

The case study aims at providing the audience with examples on how cultural and regional factors could affect the SDLC regardless of the technology and methodology used.

For organization, the case study is divided into the following sections: 1) setting the stage, 2) background of the business requirements, 3) the project starting days, 4) the analysis phase, 5) the design and development phase, 6) the go-live phase, 7) achievements, and 8) lessons learnt.

SETTING THE STAGE

The company is multi-site organization with operational sites distributed over a wide geographical area. It employs thousands of employees and contractors, with working conditions being risky in most of the company's locations. Medical Services is a unit of the company that serves employees and contractors in all locations on 24 by 7 basis.

The assignment of Medical resources to the project was mostly based on availability since the welfare of patients was an objective that could not be compromised under all conditions.

BACKGROUND OF THE BUSINESS REQUIREMENTS

The Medical Services unit of the company required a system that would enable its Medical Officers to offer the expected service levels to all employees and contractors with emphasis on aspects such as personal health, particularly for employees suffering from "chronic diseases" and "allergies" as well as hazards caused by the nature of the job or job location.

Due to the fact that the system was to be developed in-house, a number of project pre-requisites were not completely adhered to. One such critical pre-requisite was the "Project Charter," where the project team accepted to start the project from the point when the project plan was prepared.

The system was expected to deliver the following:

1. A simple user interface with minimum use of the keyboard by all users.
2. A seamless user workflow, which triggered users to do their role automatically.
3. A colored graphical representation of patient queues and service queues (service here being laboratory, x-ray, pharmacy, etc.).
4. An easy to use reporting facilities based on user privileges.
5. A monitoring and control tool for privileged staff members providing them with a bird's eye view of the status at the different sites.

Different Views

Stakeholders had different views pertaining to the requirement, the involvement of others, the overall objectives, and the points that could be scored from such a case. There were other parameters relating to risks involved and stakeholders were striving to isolate themselves from risks such as failure to deliver. The section below addresses the different views applying the Strengths, Weaknesses, Opportunities, and Threats (SWOT) analysis technique and. understandably, one could argue that this case is based on an internal implementation; hence, SWOT would be rather restricted with limitations applicable to the organization. This is true but SWOT was used to establish some common grounds for the different view of the stakeholders. This common ground enabled the project manager oversee some of the hurdles that would be encountered with different flavors (depending on the stakeholder's view).

IT Management Point of View

That project was a golden opportunity for IT management to assign a few graduates to the project. This would give these graduates the opportunity to enhance their skills in a number of areas such as Systems Analysis, Design Techniques, Data and Process Modeling, as well as applying the design tools. It also meant that the IT team assigned was capable of utilizing more resources to conduct more tasks in parallel hence optimizing delay, and of course that was seen here as a strength. On the other hand, the risk of having resources assigned as part time members of the team would encourage slackness particularly during the light workload period. This threat was genuine as employees have the tendency to minimize workload whenever possible. From the management point view, the threat of failure was the biggest challenge.

IT Project Senior Members of Staff View Point

The project was a golden opportunity for the senior IT team to demonstrate skills that were rarely used in an environment that depended heavily on packaged software solutions, and that meant the ability to inject ideas and concepts that were acquired by different senior members of staff. It also gave the senior members of staff the chance to transfer knowledge to the newer staff members in a real situation project with tasks being assigned to each one of them.

Some of the graduates assigned to the project took this challenge seriously and capitalized on the opportunity to learn. The gradual build up of skills applied during the project proved useful as they were given more complex tasks over time.

There was one weakness that was identified from the first day, and it related to the tool used. The design tool assumes one repository; hence, changes / enhancements to the design had to be filtered via one and only one member of staff who had the privileges to apply such changes to the repository. This was seen as a weakness and a threat and was a major factor throughout the project lifecycle.

No Project Charter was a huge risk and proved to be a threat to the project in a number of incidents, particularly where it involved management approvals from the user end at different project milestones.

IT Project Junior Members of Staff View Point

The project was a golden opportunity for the junior IT team members to demonstrate their competence, willingness to learn and ability to contribute to the success of such an important project. It was also a chance for them to challenge senior members of staff in areas that relate to the latest technology trends, which related to skills they acquired from their academic preparation. The graduates assigned to the project who demonstrated keenness to participate capitalized on the opportunity by maximizing the time they assigned to the project. Their gradual build up of skills applied during their project assignment proved useful to their career build up.

However, there was one weakness that was identified from their point of view, which was their inability to use the design and development tool. There was one threat they could see and that related to the impact of project failure on their career path (each one has a development program that had to be completed within a specific period of time) and regular assessments were made to ensure the progress of each). This threat was seen by most of the graduates as trivial since they were aware of the competence level of the senior team members.

THE PROJECT STARTING DAYS

The system request came from the main "Medical Services Unit" serving the company at its prime offshore site and aimed at raising the health status and awareness for the employees and contractors serving the company.

There were a number of earlier attempts to provide IT solutions including "package" software, but all these attempts ended up unsuccessfully. Three main reasons for earlier failures, the first was attributed to the not comprehending the specific nature of the user requirements on the vendor (supplier) side, were certain requirement areas were addressed, while other areas where left as manual or were never addressed. The second reason for failure was the inability to change the package/system since changes were considered as "variations" to the source code of the package and had to wait for a long time before being invoked in later releases. A third reason was the cost factor where changes that had to be addressed quickly were very expensive to develop and implement. They also proved very expensive to maintain with later releases of the packages software.

The above situation triggered a request for evaluating an in-house developed system, so that the exact requirements are captured and developed and enhancements were easier to address and include in the system. Easy future enhancements at a reasonable cost were used as the strongest justification for why the system is best developed in-house.

Due to the pressing need to reduce the losses and with the aim of starting the project as soon as possible, management sponsorship was quickly obtained and a team of qualified professional was assembled with a competent project manager assigned the task of delivering the system in a relatively short period (in fact the team was given less than six months to design and develop the fully functional system).

To ensure that the deadlines were met, a number of users from different offshore locations were requested to participate in the "Analysis" sessions so that a comprehensive 'Scope Of Work—SOW" was developed along with an extensive list of functional requirements.

Finally, a reporting mechanism was agreed so that the project sponsors are updated frequently and project control was steered on time to ensure the project's success.

There were (6) Key Project Success Factors that were identified at this stage:

1. The completeness and correctness of the user requirements and the indicator for this was the sign off by the Senior Medical Officer(s) concerned on the document that was labeled "Functional Specifications."
2. The agreement of all ITD senior staff on the "Logical Data Model." The milestone for its completeness and correctness was a signed Entity Relations Diagram (ERD).
3. The agreement of all ITD senior staff on the "Process Model," which was extracted from the "Functional Specifications" document.
4. The acceptance of the key Medical Staff team of the presentations and walkthroughs that were made to ensure he correct understanding of the requirements particularly the areas where Lists of Values were used such as Diseases,

Symptoms, Allergies, Medicines, and Drugs, Vaccinations, etc. This was important as it meant an early introduction to the Medical Officers of how the data will be retrieved once the system is live.

5. Upon delivering the first cut of the system, the key success factor was the acceptance of the system and the measure of resentment encountered. The objective was set to offer additional assistance to the users that were less capable to ensure that all users were willing and prepared to use the system. This factor was fairly difficult to address as users in this part of the world tend to raise false alarms upon facing the least significant challenge, and such alarms tend to reach their supervisors rather quick and rather loud. One story that I still remember from 1987 was in a different country in the area, where a general manger of one company called the development manager of the company I worked for and was threatening that he will throw the computer and the software that were installed for them a couple of days earlier and was not paid for yet. The development manager asked me to pay them a visit and advise action. To my shock (in fact I was terrified) to see that the complaint was baseless and the reason for the complaint was that the computer was not plugged in (no electricity). That in fact is typical for users that are incompetent and are less willing to adopt technology changes, as they perceive it as a threat to their job security.

6. The last factor was the satisfaction of the users after the system was in use for a few months. This factor was important for the users as it offered them a comfort zone that followed the go-live but offered them time to use the system before signing the final acceptance. For management, this factor was an indicator of how well the IT team delivers this project.

Reflecting Back on the Starting Days

Due to the many restrictions and constraints applied, and using SWOT to reflect back on the early days of the project, one could see that Risks and Threats outweighed the positive sides.

The risks included, but were not limited to, the time constraint (project had to be delivered within time frame set by the need). The rotational nature of Medical Officer work also meant that time assigned to meet them had limited windows (certain dates), and the nature of work in the field added the extra risk that their time could be given to higher priority assignments (saving lives and responding to emergencies).

Furthermore, there were areas of debate between the user community (Medical Officers from different locations that lead to delays in obtaining a unified and agreed reply to an issue).

There were even more threats that could not have been foreseen, and one of the examples is the inability to visit the site due to conditions beyond anyone's control such as the weather, flight reschedules, and emergency situations.

The biggest threat of all was obtaining user's time to train them. With the large population of staff and contractors being served, the limited number of resources and the nature of work in offshore locations, the project senior staff members could see that this would be a huge threat to the success of the project. One suggested resolution to ensure training all Medical Services staff members was to train them on their way going back to work from their cyclic leave. This meant a rescheduled shift for all, but was one practical solution that proved correct.

There were not many strength points identified then, but after reflecting back, the mere acceptance of the Medical Services staff members to go the extra mile and attend all the required sessions (analysis, walkthroughs, presentations, and training) are seen as part of the project success strength factors.

The majority of the users saw an opportunity arising from learning and applying new skills arriving with the new system.

A "Project Charter" must have been created and as a minimum should have had a provisional endorsement from the user management as well as IT management.

Project Sponsorship was also an area of uncertainty. Although it was the user pressing need that initiated this project. Different stages of the project saw dramatic shift of winds, particularly when it came to conflict areas. Under the organization chart applicable at the time of the project, Medical Services reported to two Business Units, where offshore sites reported to one unit and the Medical Services in the main office reported to a different unit. The senior IT staff had to make a number of decisions to minimize delay on one side and to offer solutions that were not rejected by different stakeholder in the project. As seen now, these two project areas were not handled best for reasons beyond the project team.

THE ANALYSIS PHASE

The team of IT analysts assigned to the project were split into (2) sub-teams. The first team aimed at collecting the requirements from the offshore sites while the second one worked closely with the different hospitals and clinics in town that were contracted by the company to deliver medical services to its employees and contractors.

Two products were generated at the end of the analysis phase, the first was labeled as "Functional Specifications" and was passed to the concerned user community for review and endorsement (comments, changes, and enhancements were recorded as Gaps and were compiled in a document that was labeled "System Gaps"), while the second was a "System Design" document, which addressed the

Data and Process Models, the Workflow, and the Business Rules extracted from the "Functional Specifications" document, which is a reflection of what the user wants and was developed in a simple to follow structure and easy to understand language. In that document, users could read what functions were going to be developed and delivered, he/she could see the flow of events and the triggers that would initiate / terminate each stage of the flow, and would reflect on inputs expected by the system, validations perfumed at every field (when applicable) and outputs the user would anticipate the system to deliver.

Each section of the document had an area that addressed interfaces to other systems used by the company and the flow of data / events in that interface.

A section on user profiles and functionality privileges was also included to allow for a clear "Who can do what?" understanding by the management, since confidentiality of the data is a prime factor in the medical services area.

The analysis phase was given sufficient time to ensure that the system design covered all the functional aspects and that the "System Gaps" were identified and a comprehensive list of all these gaps was available to the IT team for addressing at the right time.

At the end of this phase, the IT team had a verbal endorsement of the "Functional Specifications" document by the Senior Medical Officers, and the "System Gaps" document was quite long.

Some of the gaps on that list included:

- Different interpretations of the priorities. Some medical officers wanted the system to cover the whole spectrum of function (occupational and non-occupational) health issues is one example here, while others wanted concentration on the basic medical aspects such as consultations, laboratory tests and dispensing medication.
- Different interpretations of disease classifications by different medical officers.
- Different ways of handling the packaging and dispensing of medicines and drugs.
- Different ways of issuing and transferring medicines between different locations.
- Different ways of priorities given to patients waiting to see the Medical Officers.
- The need to issue medicine for long periods particularly for cycle leaves.

A note worth addressing at this point relates to what the first key Success Factor stated in terms of user sign off and the fact that the project team had to move on with the project based on a verbal endorsement. It is worth noting that such cases are not rare in this area of the world, particularly if the development is carried out by a team of company employees. Users tend to prefer a comfort zone of "yes I agreed but I want to add or change." That comfort zone is typical twilight zone for IT projects.

In the case at hand, the "Medical Services" users were genuine in terms of their requirements and were keen to work jointly with the IT team to continuously improve the system, but verbal agreements and/or acceptances are a typical big risk in projects no matter how big or small a project is.

Reflecting on the Analysis Phase

Using SWOT to reflect back on the analysis phase of the project, one could see that Risks and Threats once again outweighed the positive sides. The risks included, but were not limited to, having to accept verbal endorsements which of course were a risk to the project lifecycle and a threat to the ultimate objective. (written acceptance had to be obtained as per the project plans).delivered within time frame set by the need). The rotational nature of Medical Officer work also meant that time assigned to meet them had limited windows (certain dates), and the nature of work in the field added the extra risk that their time could be given to higher priority assignments (saving lives and responding to emergencies).

Furthermore, there were areas of debate between the user community (Medical Officers from different locations that lead to delays in obtaining a unified and agreed reply to an issue).

There were even more threats that could not have been foreseen, and one of the examples is the inability to visit the site due to conditions beyond anyone's control such as the weather, flight reschedules and emergency situations. However, the biggest threat of all was obtaining user's time to obtain, review and verifies the detailed requirements.

THE DESIGN AND DEVELOPMENT PHASE

To meet the agreed deadline and due to the time taken to complete the analysis phase, "Prototyping" was the approach agreed to design and develop the application. This approach enabled the IT team to utilize "design" tools that generated first cut prototypes, which were demonstrated to the key users for endorsement and comments. The IT team worked hard to ensure that the prototypes were later transferred to fully functional modules that were made available to the users for data entry of medical records so that the database was ready by the time the system was delivered in full. During this phase, the IT team was split to even more groups to cover the logistical challenges in training users at different offshore sites, continue the design and development phase and correct / modify as per the comments passed from the users in training and testing.

Due to the perception created from the ease of changes, it was noticed that medical officers were often asking for changes that were conflicting in nature and would not add value to the overall goal of the system. The prime reason for this was of course that the system was in-house designed and developed, and terms such "to offer cutting edge functional and technical capabilities" were often used as the justification by the medical officers to ensure the inclusion of the requested changes.

A second challenge appeared while collecting and populating test and production data, where some of the data structuring required changes to the database design to ensure that the data sets provided by the medical officers were properly saved.

A third challenge popped up when access rights were being addressed, since medical officers took different stands at different sites and times when access rights and privileges were discussed for Nursing, Pharmacists and Laboratory Technicians.

A fourth one was related to the tools used, since some of the errors encountered had to be reported to the tools suppliers and that meant waiting for a reply from the supplier that took a couple of days on some occasions. The tools used imposed additional challenges at the application, database servers, and reporting servers.

THE GO-LIVE PHASE

By the time the system was ready for rollover, medical officers were able to instantly monitor and follow up the status of every patient at every point in the hospital using the automated paperless process flow.

Supporting modules to the system included a fully operational Laboratory, X-Ray Unit, Nursing area and In-Patient follow up module as well as a full functionality Pharmacy. Immediate access to store and retrieve soft copies of all related X-Rays, Test results, and Prescriptions issued per patient were standard system features.

The system warned medical officers of Allergies, Chronic Diseases, and potential risks per patient at a glance; hence, it enabled them to deal with such patients with utmost care as well as plan necessary campaigns for different potential risk groups, and thus improve the quality of life of all concerned.

With over 5000 employees and contractors records populated for the company and its offshore sites, the system delivered better services in terms of accurate, consistent, confidential and secured information, expedited retrieval of medical history records, immediate warnings for patients with allergies and chronic diseases hence improved the service quality and reduced the time spent on investigations and diagnosis.

With records instantly accessible by medical officers and service providers, seeking medical advice and second opinion was easily achieved since the network of medical officers and service providers was limitless.

With better health services delivered to all concerned in the company, the company and the group reputation in the "Health and Safety" areas was improved.

This improved image will be addressed in the "Achievements" section below.

ACHIEVEMENTS

A long list of innovative ideas and applications were bundled in the solution.
Technology wise, the following achievements were accomplished:

1. A fully automated paperless workflow.
2. A full set of supporting records stored in the database, including Consultation history, Health status and indicators, Lab tests and X-Ray results, Vaccination and Immunization history, Sick Leaves history, and Prescriptions.
3. The latest Technology was used to design and build the fully Web-based system enabling secured linking to different kinds of confidential documents and offering a protected and safe environment.

Operationally, the following applied:

1. Medical Officers have better command and control of the process.
2. Warning signals related to patient Allergies and Chronic diseases minimized chances of erroneous medication, i.e. health implications, particularly with emergency situations pertaining to personnel with allergy to specific medicine(s).
3. Drug/Medication inventory are better controlled by the fully automated receiving and issuance processes.

At the human behavior front, the following applies:

1. Employees and contractors are better assured with medical records accessible practically anywhere, which is essential for emergencies.
2. Health monitoring resulted in better services hence better health for all concerned.
3. Lost time due to sick leaves as optimized and better controlled.

At the Cultural level, the following was achieved: Graduate employees in the IT Department were equipped with a good level of knowledge that was accompanied by "hands on" practical work in the different stages of the System Development Life Cycle (SDLC).

The system had a wide range of IT support personnel, which meant that users were given an extra "Cushion" when it came to assistance with specifics. This is rather typical in this part of the world were different cultures tend to have different ways of adaptation to new ways / methods of doing things including new systems.

REFERENCES

Al-Mashari, M., Al-Mudimigh, A., & Zairi, M. (2003). Enterprise resource planning: A taxonomy of critical factors. *European Journal of Operational Research, 146*(2), 352. doi:10.1016/S0377-2217(02)00554-4

Beal, B. (2003, October 15). *The priority that persists.* Retrieved February 14, 2012, from http://searchcio.techtarget.com/originalContent/0,289142,sid19_gci932246,00.html

Ip, W., Chau, K., & Chan, S. (2002). Implementing ERP through continuous improvement. *International Journal of Manufacturing, 4*(6), 465.

Nah, F., Lee-Shang Lau, J., & Kuang, J. (2001). Critical factors for successful implementation of enterprise systems. *Business Process Management Journal, 7*(3), 285. doi:10.1108/14637150110392782

Sobotta, T., Sobotta, N., & Gotze. (2010, May 31). *Greening IT.* Retrieved February 14, 2012 from http://greening.it/wp-content/uploads/downloads/2010/06/greening-it_isbn-9788791936029.pdf

Standish Group. (1995). *Website.* Retrieved February 14, 2012, from http://www.projectsmart.co.uk/docs/chaos-report.pdf

Umble, E., Haft, R., & Umble, M. (2003). Enterprise resource planning: Implementation procedures and critical success factors. *European Journal of Operational Research, 146*(2), 241. doi:10.1016/S0377-2217(02)00547-7

KEY TERMS AND DEFINITIONS

7-S Model: A tool typically used for analyzing organizations but was applied here at the project level. It views the company from the 7 parameters that all start with the letter "S." The parameters are: Strategy, Structure, Systems, Style (culture), Staff, Skills, and Shared Values.

Business Process Re-Engineering (BPR): A widely used term to reflect changes to the business processes. There are two schools of thought here. One suggests that re-engineering means major changes with major impacts. The other school accepts re-engineering as the term reflecting even minor changes to the processes. Other related terms include Business Process Improvements and Business Process Enhancements.

Data Normalization: The method used to group data attributes in a logical manner so that data duplications are eliminated and fields defined later within physical tables are all related to the purpose of that table. An example would be a table labeled as "Person." The attributes defined as fields of the table will all be describing the person. Data such as the Person family and first names, date of birth and gender would be included, but there will be no reference to his job for example.

Project Charter: The document that describes the project, its teams with the responsibilities assigned to each team member and agreed terms an conditions (including quality parameters).

Scope of Work (SOW): It is the document that specifies in sufficient details what the requirements are and that in turn is typically transformed into the more details "Requirements Specifications" document.

Strengths: Weaknesses, Opportunities, and Threats (SWOT): SWOT is typically depicted as a 4 quadrants in a "+" shaped matrix. Each quadrant addresses one of the four parameters.

Chapter 6
ERP Upgrade vs. ERP Replacement:
The Case of Gulf Telecom

Fayez Albadri
ADMA-OPCO, UAE

EXECUTIVE SUMMARY

ERP systems life cycle may extend in some business organizations up to fifteen years or more. Nevertheless, the time comes in the life of an ERP system when there is a need to evaluate and compare the value of continuing to use the existing ERP system version against the option to upgrade to a higher version of the same system or having it replaced all together by a different system. In many cases, this translates into a critical management-sponsored mission designating a dedicated team or task force to investigate the feasibility of the alternative options, and to report on the preferred option with a recommendation of the way forward and implementation approach. This case reflects the investigations of Gulf Telecom Company (GTC) in exploring the viability and feasibility of its ERP options to support and provide the grounds for a management decision to mark the next phase of the ERP in the organization. The case describes the approach that was adopted by Gulf Telecom and highlights the challenges to accomplish the mission successfully and any lessons learned from this experience.

DOI: 10.4018/978-1-4666-2220-3.ch006

ORGANIZATION BACKGROUND

The history of the Gulf Telecom goes back to the early 90s when it was a single telecommunication player is the country. However, the emergence of new technologies and the global industry transformations that followed have prompted a major deregulation of the telecommunication industry in the early days of 2000, presenting Gulf Telecom with major challenges to survive global competition.

Consequently, Gulf Telecom has gone through a major restructuring and expansion of its lines of products and services and a new vision for excellence and customer service and intimacy. This transformation was guided by a new vision and strategy that also views Information and Communication Systems (ICT) and applications as business enabler and strategic assets. Consequently, investment in state-of-art ICT infrastructure and enterprise information systems applications had a high ranking in the Gulf Telecom list of priorities.

A review of ICT in Gulf telecom by an external management consulting in 2001 has led to a strategy to guide investment in ICT that is included in a five-year forward plan. Among the high priority items in the plan was the selection and implementation of s suitable ERP system to support its main function business functions including Human Resources, Finance, and Procurement.

The Information Technology function was entrusted by management to lead the ERP selection team, which included representative members from all concerned business areas. The selection team has consolidated the main business requirements and used them as the basis for defining the project Scope Of Work (SOW) and Request For Proposal (RFP) to invite ERP vendors' submissions.

SETTING THE STAGE

Introduction

By opting to replace its disparate software applications by a single ERP system, Gulf Telecom decision was driven by the need for an integrated business solution that connects the organizations core functions and to automate the business processes. However, in order to reap the benefits of a system with such features is only possible through proper and effective system selection in the pre-implementation stage, proper and effective system configuration in the implementation stage and certainly proper and effective usage and utilization of the ERP applications in the post-implementation stage which could extend over many years. However, there is clear evidence from many ERP projects that proper usage and effective utilization is correlated with managing system, data and end-users issues (see Figure 1).

In view of the above and to ensure that Gulf Telecom is continually up-to-date with new emerging technologies that can potentially improve its business and support the realization of its goals and objectives, Senior Management of Gulf Telecom has indicated their interest to review the current status of the ERP system after five years of use, and to explore the feasibility of upgrading the current system or replacing it by a different system.

The prime aim of this chapter is to report on the experience and the findings of Gulf Telecom investigations to review, compare, and validate options pertinent to ERP systems for the upcoming phase, five years post go-live. This mission constitutes several investigations to be carried out by a dedicated Task Force that is exclusively internally resourced. The ERP Task Force was created by virtue of Management Order, which spelled out the main objective and deliverables of the task force, the members of the task force and the time by which the task force needs to complete its mission and report findings to GTC General Manager.

Background: ERP in Gulf Telecom

Following the deregulation of the telecommunication industry, Gulf Telecom embarked on a major restructuring initiative and technology adoption venture as measures to survive global and local competition and to cope with challenges to improve customer satisfaction. Senior management view of technology as a strategic option and a business enabler to ensure its survival in a competitive environment has translated into a major review of the existing ICT infrastructure and computer software applications. This review has led to the creation of a five-year plan (2001-2005), defining and prioritizing different technology projects and initiatives to implement during that period. The acquisition and implementation of an ERP system to support the core business functions of Gulf Telecom was of high priority and was planned for 2001/2002.

The current status of ERP in Gulf Telecom can be understood better by reviewing the history of the ERP system in the organization which went through three stages:

- ERP Pre-Implementation (Selection) Stage.
- ERP Implementation (Configuration) Stage.
- ERP Post-Implementation (Usage and Utilization) Stage.

Figure 1. ERP life cycle

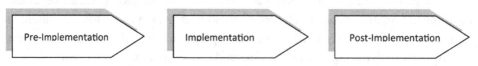

Each of the stages (above) is briefly described to form together a reasonable context and background to the ERP Upgrade-Replacement study on hand.

ERP Pre-Implementation (Selection) Stage

In March 2001, the IT department announced the creation of ERP selection team with a mandate to select a suitable ERP system that is Y2K compliant and that matches business and functional requirements consolidated by representatives from the main business areas namely; Human Resources, Finance, and Procurement. The requirements were consolidated and prioritized to reflect business importance. The requirements were used to produce a Request For Proposal (RFP) that was used to invite different ERP vendors' submissions. Initially, well-known ERP local agents were invited to present their systems to the selection team and some have triggered visits to reference sites.

This was followed by the commercial procedures that included both technical and commercial evaluation. The technical evaluation was focused on the level of matching of the ERP system functionalities to the business requirements and has resulted in a short list of the three highest fit systems. The technical evaluation was concerned with the total cost of the ERP system including licenses, implementation, training and yearly maintenance. The commercial evaluation was concluded with 'award' of the contract to a local ERP partner and an agreement was signed between the two parties to mark the end of the ERP selection and the beginning of the ERP implementation.

ERP Implementation (Configuration) Stage

The ERP implementation project was kicked-off in October 2001 and was resourced by both Gulf Telecom and the Implementation vendor; From the Gulf Telecom, the project had a steering committee and a sponsor, a project manager and representatives of different business and technical functions. From the vendor's side, the project had a project manager, business discipline leaders, functional and technical consultants, and trainers. The project planning and scheduling was guided by an agreed implementation methodology that defines the project phases, objectives, deliverables as well as control and monitoring tools.

The project started with core team training, followed by gap workshops, solution design and specifications. The development was about configuring and tailoring the system to deliver the required functionalities avoiding customizations. This was followed by extensive testing and training prior to rolling out the system in a big bang mode. The project encountered different issues and problems and a creep in the scope due to additional requirements of high priority that were requested by Gulf

Telecom which translated into additional cost (variation) and two month extension of the planned project time from twelve to fourteen months.

ERP Post-Implementation (Utilization) Stage

The Go-Live of the ERP system in December 2002 has signaled a new and critical stage in the life of the ERP system in Gulf Telecom. The responsibility to manage the ERP issues in the stage was delegated to a small team to resolve arising problems and to support end-users. Over five years, the Post-Implementation team encountered many ERP issues ranging from system performance issues, to data scarcity and end-users resistance to use the system.

In addition, important changes had to be made to fix problems or introduce enhancements. Five years down the track, the system configuration, reports and workflow automated processes are more in line with Gulf Telecom business, although there are important applications that are still unutilized or under-utilized. Investigations indicated that the low utilization rates in certain areas were mainly due to system limitation or lack of data. With the release of new versions of the same ERP system and the introduction of new applications and functionalities in other ERP systems, there was increasing calls by different parties within the organization to consider upgrading or replacing the existing system. This has prompted senior management to create a task force to explore the feasibility of such options and report findings and recommendations to management.

CASE DESCRIPTION

The ERP Go-live in December 2002 has signaled the conclusion of the ERP implementation project and the beginning of the post-implementation phase, which was considered critical for realizing the promised benefits and business gains in the core functions (Finance, Human Resources, Procurement, and Customer Service) as well as other secondary functions. During the five years, several challenges were encountered that had a direct impact on the end-users acceptance of the ERP and also had also contributed to low levels of ERP applications usage and utilization.

The persisting problems were diversified in nature and were mainly linked to:

- System Limitations.
- Data Quantity and Quality Status.
- Analytical Reporting Limitations.
- Workflow Limitations.
- End-User Resistance to Change.

Although the ERP post-implementation team has managed to stabilize the system, resolve many of the persisting issues and train end users, some important system applications were still either unutilized or under-utilized. The latest version of the ERP has evidently improved in functionality and in some of the areas which represented a pain in the current version. Similarly, new versions of competing ERP systems have also improved a great deal in different areas.

Management Directives

Considering the natural life cycle of any ERP system and due to the rapid advent in technologies it was deemed normal after five years of system use since the rollout to consider either of the following two options:

- **The Upgrade Option:** To upgrade the current system version and build on a system that has been relatively stabilized, functionalities used and utilized and end-users acceptance increased.
- **The Replacement Option:** To replace the existing system by another ERP system to benefit from its enhanced functionalities and features.

In order to carry out the above investigations, senior management decision has clearly spelled out the main objectives, scope, and deliverables of the Task Force.

Task Force Objectives

To explore viable options pertinent to the upcoming stage in the life of the ERP system in Gulf Telecom by considering feasible options to upgrade or replace the current ERP system. Also, to agree with stakeholders and end-users on an effective business strategy to guide the transition associated with upgrade or replacement, by identifying cross-functional processes and addressing related issues, problems and concerns, and to work towards agreement between all parties on effective means to mitigate risks and manage change associated with the upgrade or replacement.

Investigation Approach

In order to review the two options (upgrade and replacement), an investigation framework and structured approach were developed and adopted to ensure rigor of work and reliability of results. The investigation comprised two parts:

- **Part One: Feasibility Investigation**: To identify and weigh the pros and cons associated with the two options as an indicator of feasibility from functional, technical, and financial perspectives.
- **Part Two: Gain-Readiness Assessment:** To gauge the levels of Business Gain and Organization Readiness associated with the two options.

PART ONE: FEASIBILITY INVESTIGATION

Feasibility Investigation Objectives

The prime objective of the feasibility investigation was to explore viable options pertinent to the upcoming stage in the life of the ERP system in Gulf Telecom by considering feasible options to upgrade or replace the current ERP system.

Functional Feasibility Investigation SOW

The scope of the functional feasibility includes the following tasks and activities:

- To consolidate business requirements in relevant business areas (Finance, HR, Procurement, etc.).
- To assign priorities (1-5) to each requirement reflecting business importance.
- To assess and rate (Current ERP version) functionalities / Usability against each requirement.
- To assess and rate (Upgrade ERP higher version) functionalities / Usability against each requirement.
- To assess and rate (New ERP system) functionalities / Usability against each requirement.
- To calculate functional (usability) gain associated with the upgrade option.
- To calculate functional (usability) gain associated with the replacement option.

Technical Feasibility Investigation SOW

- To assess and compare the technical gain associated with the upgrade option, considering security, resilience, scalability, compatibility, etc.
- To assess and compare the technical gain associated with the upgrade option, considering security, resilience, scalability, compatibility, etc.

Financial Feasibility Investigation SOW:

- To assess and compare the financial aspects and costs (licenses, consulting, management, training, and maintenance) associated with the upgrade option.
- To assess and compare the financial aspects and costs (licenses, consulting, management, training, and maintenance) associated with the replacement option.

Feasibility Investigation Deliverables

- **Functional Feasibility:** Comparing the upgrade and replacement options.
- **Technical Feasibility:** Comparing the upgrade and replacement options.
- **Financial Feasibility:** Comparing the upgrade and replacement options.
- Recommendation of (preferred) most feasible option.

Feasibility Investigation Measures

The investigation involved examining the functional, technical, and financial feasibility pertinent to each of the following cases:

- **Existing ERP system:** Current version.
- **Existing ERP system:** Higher version (Upgrade Option).
- New ERP system (Replace Option).

The functional feasibility investigation employs a measure of 'Usability' to indicate functionality gain associated with the level 'Usability' of each of the upgrade and Replace options and compare it with that of the existing system. The Usability measurements and functionality gain is applied at functionality level and rolled up to system modular levels.

The term 'Usability' that is used in the feasibility is an indicator of system potential, capability, and preparedness of different ERP module, application, functionality, or feature to be used in GTC. For the purpose of the investigation, 'Usability' was preferred to be used as an indicator of anticipated use (after the system is implemented) in contrast to the terms 'Usage' and 'Utilization' which are measures of a past action (the use and utilization of an existing system).

Compared to the above definition of the terms 'Usability,' the term 'Usage' is defined as a measure of the level of use (quantity) of a certain ERP module, application, functionality or feature and the term 'Utilization' is defined as the effective usage (quality) of a certain ERP module, application, functionality or feature.

Feasibility Investigation Findings

The outcome of the feasibility favored option 2 (Replace) as the most feasible option functionally with overall gain (16%) compared to (10%) in the case of the (Upgrade Option). It was also evident that the preferred option was also technically feasible considering the current infrastructure and technical architecture. Also, the option it was financially viable (see Table 1).

However, the most important outcome of this investigation is that Human Resources and Finance functions were identified as the main beneficiaries from the option 2 'Replace' with substantial boosting of functionality in Financial Management, Asset Management, Accounts Payable and Receivables, General Ledger, Payroll, Personnel, and Manpower Development. The finance functions associated with the 'Replace' function has a functionality gain of (25%) compared to only (11%) in the case of option 01 (Upgrade).

It is clear from Table 1 that the Usability ratings of the General functionalities of the current system is (86%) comparing to Option 1 (92%) and Option 2 (97%). This indicates a good functionality gain, boosting the usability of by (11%) in the case of the 'Replace' option and 06% in the case of the 'Upgrade' option. This represents a positive improvement that is expected to contribute to end-users acceptance and perception of ease of use of the system.

Table 1. Functionality comparison: usability and business gain

Functionality Perspective	Usability %			Functionality Gain %	
	Current System	Option 1: Upgrade	Option 2 Replace	Option1 Upgrade	Option 2 Replace
General: Integration, Security, Reports, Documents, Administration, Help, Navigation, Control, Searching, Workflow	86%	92%	97%	06%	11%
Finance: General Ledger, Financial Management, Payables, Receivables, Assets, Reports, KPIs	66%	77%	91%	11%	25%
Human Resources: Personnel, Learning Management, Payroll, Recruitment, Interfaces, Time Keeping, Reports, KPIs	68%	78%	86%	10%	18%
Procurement: Contracts, Purchasing, Pre-Qualifications, RFQ, Tendering, Cataloging, Reports, KPIs.	78%	90%	88%	12%	10%
Overall	75%	84%	91%	10%	16%

Table 2. A summary of the technical feasibility comparing the two options

Issues	Technical Perspective: Option 1 (Upgrade) vs. Option 2 (Replace)
Configuration	Database, network, hardware, and software currently existing in GTC are sufficient to handle new ERP system. However, existing Servers processing configuration need to be upgraded by 23%. This conclusion is based on the Hardware sizing recommendation provided by the ERP implementation Vendor and based on the 1 ERP Modules within the scope of the implementation
Workflow	Owing to the anticipated change in structure, work flow processes need redeveloping. ITD continuously raised that the replication of the Work Flow processes across environments is not following ITD standards; where final approved Workflow in the Acceptance area is to be transferred through a procedure to the production environment.
Interfaces	With the new tightly integrated ERP system, there would be no need to interface to scheduling and planning tools. However, the financial module may still need to consider interface to risk management software and the HR system to a time sheet module. Users that utilize Business Objects have to regenerate the Business Objects Structure and Queries.
Administration	The new ERP configuration is more flexible than the current ERP, a reasonable percentage 8% of customization and reports could be configurable. New ERP Administration is bundled within the Application. Administration module is more flexible.
Security	New ERP has improved in security where passwords are encrypted, it provides an optional audit tracking.
Reports	The Reports in the current ERP and Customization need to be redeveloped, due to major difference in structure between the current system and the new ERP. The current reporting tool is replaced by a new reporting analytical tool.
Overall	General technical improvement in administration, security, workflow, reporting, screen configurations, interfaces, KPIs

Table 2 provides a summary of the technical feasibility comparing the two options. It shows clearly that both options are valid; however, the 'replace' option might need an upgrading of the servers and boosting of the network capacity. On there would be no need for some of the current interfaces due to the fact that the new ERP has its scheduling, planning and other applications

Table 3 outlines the cost comparisons of the two options part of the financial feasibility investigation. The summarized findings in the Table 1, Table 2, and Table 3 were presented to senior management with a message that the Option 2 'Replace' represents an opportunity for GTC to boost the integration across different business functions, streamline the processes, and improve the overall functionalities in different areas. This could translate into improved performance especially as new technologies have been used to introduce functionalities that are superior to the equivalent in the 'upgrade' version of the existing system.

However, it was highlighted that although option 2 is the preferred option, there is a genuine need for stakeholders to agree on new inter-related processes and practices and issues related to data and resources have to be supported by management to reap the fruit of this investment. Furthermore, the change to a new system with different approach to business in important finance, human resources and

Table 3. Provides a summary of the financial feasibility comparing the two options

External Cost	Budgetary Figures ($)	
Items	Option 1: Upgrade	Option 2: Replace
Time / Duration	9 months	11 months
Software Licenses: Based on 2500 users	NA	YYYY
Database Licenses: Based on 2500 users	XXXX	NA
Implementation (including project management and end-user training)	XXXX	YYYY
Total	XXXX	YYYY
Savings / through load sharing using internal resources:	(-)XXX	(-)YYY
Revised Total	XXXX	YYYY

procurement processes represent a major cultural change that dictates having in place a comprehensive change management program addressed to a community of end-users who have been accustomed and tuned over the past 5 years to do business in synch with the existing system.

In a larger context, the answer to the question of 'why to replace' has summarized the main reasons and drivers as follows:

1. **Functionality and Business Improvement:**
   As highlighted above, the functionality comparison based on the levels of usability indicates that the replace option represents an opportunity for business improvement for the following reasons:
   a. General enhancements in the interface and general features related to searching and querying, reporting, navigation, control, security, administration, documents, etc.
   b. New applications in finance and human resources
   c. Best Practices-Based: Provides the opportunity to adopt best practices to help improve the productivity and efficiency of their critical assets.
2. **Reliable System Support:**
   a. Having in mind the support issues experienced with the current system vendor, from system support reliability the score is in favor of the new system vendor. This has been one of the main concerns that have been voiced by end-users who suffered from delays to attend to fixing reported problems and addressing system bugs.

3. **Strategic Value:**
   a. The fact that the new ERP system under consideration to replace the current system uses new technologies such as Mobility, RFID, APIs, and Add-Ons grants GTC the advantage and the benefits associated with future technology trends that support best-practices and global standardized based solutions. GTC can used this transformation conveniently to benchmark against other international telecom company as means to identify weaknesses and act on them for business improvement.

Why Option Two is Recommended

1. **Functionally:**
   a. Functional gains in important business areas (Finance 25%, HR 18%, Overall 16%).
   b. New applications in; Finance, HR, Planning and Scheduling.
   c. General enhancements in interface and general features related to searching and querying, reporting, navigation, control, security, administration, documents, etc.
   d. Limited enhancements in Procurement 10%.
2. **Technically:**
   a. Benefits from new technologies used.
   b. Improved and new technical functions, applications and tools for administration and support of technical environment, including security profile, administration tools, configuration tools, screen editing, security, new analytical reporting tool, improved analytical reporting and KPIs, improved workflow tools.
   c. New anticipated value of tight integration and new technologies such as mobility and RFID.
   d. Compatibility with the environment in GTC.
3. **Financially:**
   a. Testing the worth considering functionality gain and relative costs of option 2; functionality gain (16%) and a relative cost increase (12%), is a strong evidence of worth and value.
   b. Technical gains compared to limited technical cost favors the option 2.
   c. Various anticipated tangible and intangible benefits and positive potential to realize ROI.
4. **Support:**
   a. The local support of the new ERP is proven and more reliable than the existing ERP vendor.

The presentation of the above to management has provided an insight about the potential business gains that would culminate from the replacing the system as compared to upgrading it to a higher version. Nevertheless, senior management has raised concern about the scale of change associated with the 'replace' option, and raised a question about the level of readiness of GTC to undergo to undergo this change, prompting the General Manger to order the creation of a new Task Force, with a clear objective to work together with the stakeholders to: 1) confirm the findings of the feasibility investigation, 2) to gauge the level of readiness in the different business areas, and 3) to examine the impact of change associated with replacing the current system on different business functions.

PART TWO: GAIN AND CHANGE-READINESS ASSESSMENT (GCRA)

GCRA Task Force: Key Objectives

The Gain-Change Readiness Assessment builds on the findings of the Feasibility Investigations in Part one. In line with senior management directions, the main objective of the assessment was to verify the identified business gains and to examine the level of readiness of the concerned functions to cope with the change associated with the usage and utilization of new ERP applications, functionalities, and tools.

The outcome of this exercise would be used as input to agree with stakeholders and end-users on an effective business strategy to guide the transition associated with the system upgrade or replacement, by identifying cross-functional processes and addressing related issues, problems, and concerns, and to agree with all parties on effective means to mitigate risks and manage change associated with the ERP upgrade or replacement.

GCRA Task Force: Scope of Work

The scope of the Gain-Change Readiness Assessment Task Force included the following tasks:

- To consolidate core business processes within concerned business areas.
- To identify the applications, functionalities and features of the (Upgrade option) that support the business processes.
- To identify the applications, functionalities and features of the (Replace option) that support the business processes.

- To identify cross-functional processes associated with both the (Upgrade option) and the (Replace option).
- To identify main issues, concerns and threats related to change resulting from selecting and adopting either option.
- To measure the anticipated business gain and level of readiness linked to the utilization of the functionalities of both the (Upgrade option) and (Replace option).
- To identify readiness gaps and readiness boosting measures and actions.

GCRA Task Force: Main Deliverables

- Definition of the scope of change associated with the transition and the impact of change on the business and end-users.
- Identification of major risks associated with the adoption of new applications and adopting new processes and practices.
- Identification of business gains associated with opportunities arising from the new applications and functionalities in resolving persisting problems, minimizing customization configurations, and introducing improvements.
- Development of a roadmap for the utilization of new applications, functionalities and features considering existing constraints (End-user acceptance, data availability and quality, resources, etc.).

GCRA Investigation Model: Terms and Principles

The investigation model adopted by the Task Force employed the following terms and principles:

- The term 'Usability,' to indicate the capability, potential, and preparedness of selected ERP module, application, functionality, or feature to be used in GTC.
- The term 'Usage,' to gauge the level of use (quantity) of a certain ERP modules, applications, functionalities, or features.
- The term 'Utilization,' to gauge the effective usage (quality) of selected ERP modules, applications, functionalities, or features.
- The term 'Opportunity,' to estimate the anticipated positive outcome, resulting from uncertainty-associated with change linked to either option (upgrade or replace). In a certain context, it corresponds to usability, business gain, and/or strategic value. For the purpose of Task Force, 'Opportunity' is correlated with business gain and strategic value and comparing the current 'Usability' with the anticipated boosting in usability of different functional-

ities and feature. The assessment used a 5-point scale that could be converted to %ages or to levels (Low, Medium, High).

- The term 'Risk Exposure,' to estimate the anticipated negative outcome resulting from uncertainty-associated with change linked to either option (upgrade or replace). Risk assessment of identified threats could be calculated using standard risk standards that combine the loss and probability to give a relative risk exposure level. For the purpose of the Task Force investigations, it was proposed to use business processes, data, and end-users as the contexts for risk identification and Risk Exposure levels are converted: Low, Medium, or High.

- The term 'Readiness,' to gauge the level of change readiness, or how ready is GTC to exploit anticipated opportunities and business gains, and mitigating risks that could hinder proper and effective use of new modules, applications, functionalities and features. For the purpose of Task Force investigation, and in order to measure level of readiness it was proposed to examine the status of items on a checklist list (management, end-users, resources, data, and business). The assessment could use a 5-point scale that could be converted to %ages or to levels (Low, Medium, High).

GCRA Investigation: Structured Approach

The approach that was adopted for executing activities of the Task Force towards achieving its key objectives is based on model that associates the uncertainty of change with opportunities and risks, and also with a conceptual insight to readiness, to check any hindering factors that can stand in the way of exploiting anticipated opportunities and mitigating identified risks.

The diagram in Figure 2 outlines the different activities and relationships that each Task Force stream would follow in assessing the impact of change in their respective areas. The main components of this approach and investigation framework comprised objective judgments by different members of Task Force streams, which in turn translate into a consistent rating.

GCRA Investigation: Execution Phase

Scope of Change

The definition of the scope of change by each stream (Finance, Human Resources, Procurement, and Technology) is a crucial for accurately examining the impact of change resulting from moving from the current version of ERP to either upgrading to a higher version of the same system (option 1) or Replace by new ERP. The

Figure 2. Investigation model: structured task force approach

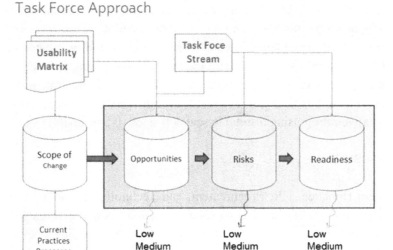

scope work is defined by revisiting the Usability Gains Matrix from the feasibility investigation (Part 1) to extract only the functionalities that are evidently of varying usability levels, ensuring that those which have the same usability levels are scoped out (excluded). Other functionalities that needed to be scoped-in were those which were being introduced in the new versions of the current system and had no equivalent in the current system version and which could be supported manually (this was evident in the (Procurement) area.

The scope of change for each stream was a subset of the Usability matrix listing the functionalities subject to change rolled up under different processes or functions. Stream leaders with members of their streams examined each of the functionalities for the extent of change and rated it using a suitable scale (% ages, 1-5 or LMH).

Change Impact

Derived from the Risk Management Utility Theory, the impact of change is associated with the opportunities and risks linked to the uncertainty surrounding the change. Therefore, each stream (Finance, HR, Procurement, and Technology) identified and assessed the opportunities and risks pertaining to each functionality item in the scope of change.

Opportunities

Each Stream (Finance, HR, Procurement, and Technology) scanned through all the items in the scope of change and reviewed the usability levels brought forward from the Gain-Usability Matrix in Part 1. The revised usability equated to the anticipated business gain associated with the opportunity arising from upgrading to either option 1 or option 2. Where appropriate a judgment of the strategic value was combined with the business gain to give an overall opportunity gain level to reach a representative rating using a suitable scale (% ages, 1-5 or LMH)

Risk Exposure

Each Stream (Finance, HR, Procurement, and Technology) scanned through all the items in the scope of change and examined each for potential threats that could jeopardize the effective usage and utilization of these functionalities. The risk assessment could use suitable contexts such as data, resources, or processes. The streams used a proposed risk matrix from Risk Management Australian Standards, which combines the consequence and probability of the threatening event as the basis to reach an overall judgment on the level of risk exposure using (LMH) rating scale.

Level of Readiness

Each Stream (Finance, HR, Procurement, and Technology) scanned through all the items in the scope of change and examined each for level of readiness to adopt and utilize these functionalities. As a measure of how ready is GTC to exploit anticipated opportunities and business gains and mitigating risks that could be hindering proper and effective use of new modules, applications, functionalities and features. To measure level of readiness a checklist of readiness-related factors (management, end-users, resources, data, and business) was used in conjunction with a suitable rating scale (% ages, 1-5 or LMH)

GCRA Investigation: Analysis Phase

The analysis included the processing of collected data in all work streams to reach meaningful conclusions associated with multiple perspectives of upgrade options, business disciplines, and way forward strategies. The categorization and prioritization of the collated functionalities in view of their business gain (opportunity) ratings and level of readiness was made possible by using a quadrant matrix approach (Figure 3).

Figure 3. Business gain-change readiness quadrants matrix

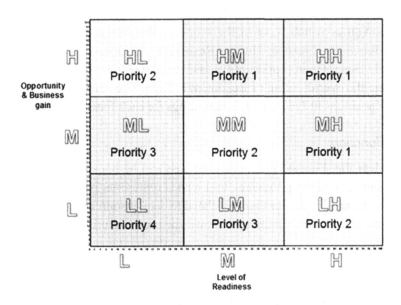

The combination of the level of business gain (Low, Medium, or High) combined with the level of Change readiness (Low, Medium, or High) were used to indicate which quadrant the examined functionality item would be fitted into. For instance High gain and High readiness equate to HH which corresponds to upper right quadrant of priority (1). A functionality items with medium gain and medium readiness corresponds to the MM middle quadrant, which is of priority 2 and so on.

The analysis was mainly concerned with:

- **Prioritization:** This is about combing the business gain ratings and change readiness ratings of each functionality and mapping them to the appropriate quadrant and priority (for instance High Gain and Medium Readiness to quadrant HM of priority [1]).
- **Way Forward Strategy:** This is about identifying the readiness gap and the means to boost readiness of each functionality items to take it to a higher readiness level (for instance from HM to HH).

GCRA Investigation: Findings

The main findings of the Task Force investigations were presented for both upgrade options (1) and option (2) as follows.

Option 01 (ERP Upgrade) Findings

The functionalities which were in the scope of this investigation belong to the following functions: Finance, Human Resources, Procurement and Technology. The overall business gain (opportunity) associated with the upgrade option to was Medium and the overall rating of Readiness is High. The gain/readiness combination of *MH* positions in *Priority 01*. The findings for each function were as follows.

Finance Functions

It is also clear that Finance functions readiness can be boosted from Medium to High resounding the strong message by Finance representatives in the Task Force that there was a need to address issues related to data, resources and end-user training to ensure that the new functionalities will be used and utilized as shown in the quadratic matrix.

Human Resources Functions

The business gain ratings of Human Resources functions are *Low* but the readiness is High putting in *Priority 02*. However, these functions are of strategic value as they will replace some of the current customizations and workarounds and also they are part of the overall integrated solution.

Procurement Functions

The business gain ratings of the Procurement functions do not exist as the upgrade option will not provide a suitable solution to replace the procurement application, which is currently interfaced with the ERP.

Technical and General Functions and Features

This stream includes three areas as part of its investigation:

- **General Features:** Low Gain / High Readiness → Priority 2.
- **Workflow features:** Medium Gain / High Readiness → Priority 1.
- **Technical Features:** Low Gain / High Readiness → Priority 2.
- **The Overall Ratings:** Medium Gain / High readiness → Priority 1.

The risk was estimated as low across all areas—the functionalities in this stream will be part of any upgrade options as they part of the overall solution.

The following are the technical issues that have been highlighted by Information Technology function as important to attend to as part of the upgrade:

- **Configuration:** An exact methodology is required for all processes during the Project cut over period and production environments are required in order to come up with an accurate configuration. However, considerable changes to the applications servers are required.
- **Workflow:** Current workflow processes are too huge such that they are not only tough to support and maintain, but also are causing extra burden on the application servers. It is highly recommended to undertake a modular approach while doing the new workflows for the new version of the system and maintain relevant documentations.
- **Interfaces:** Ensure that there is no disruption to all applications interfacing with the new version of the ERP.
- **Security:** ERP New version has added security for attached documents and the facility to encrypt sensitive data.

Option 1 (Upgrade): Overall Results

The overall Business gain / Change Readiness and Priorities associated with the option 1 (Upgrade) is shown in the Prioritization Matrix (Figure 4). Readiness needs to be boosted in relation to Finance functions and are Human Resources are included in the scope because of the high readiness, strategic value and their contribution to the integrated solution.

Option 2 (ERP Replace) Findings

The functionalities that were in the scope of this investigation belong to the following functions: Finance, Human Resources, Procurement, and Technology. The overall Business gain (opportunity) associated with the replace option to is *High* and the overall rating of Readiness is Medium. The gain/readiness combination of *HM* positions in *Priority 01*. The findings for each function are as follows.

Finance Functions

The business gain is *Medium* to *High* confirming the initial findings of part 1 feasibility. However, proper attention to data, resources, and end-users training is needed to improve the level of readiness to utilize the functionalities. It is also reassuring that the risk level is consistently Low.

Figure 4. Prioritization matrix

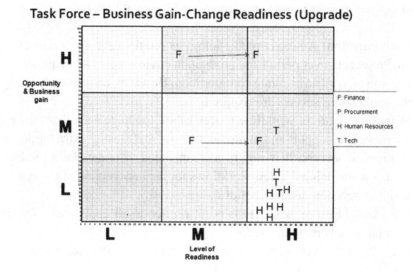

Human Resources

The anticipated business gain for different aspects of the Human Resources business in the new ERP is *Low*. However, the level readiness to implement and use the functionalities in the new system is High.

Procurement

The overall business gain ratings of the Procurement functions are High and readiness is Medium—putting in Priority 1. Therefore there is a need to boost readiness prior to the replace of the ERP through process definitions and data preparations.

Option 2 (Replace) Overall Results

The overall Business gain—Change Readiness and Priorities associated with the option 2 Replace is shown in the Prioritization Matrix (Figure 5). Readiness needs to be boosted in relation to Finance and Procurement functions. The Human Resources are included in the scope because of the high readiness, strategic value and their contribution to the integrated solution. The Technical and General stream functionalities, although low in gain but are included because of the High readiness and also because they are part of upgrade.

The status of option 2 as the preferred option is validated further by attending to the Business Processes, Data Preparations as they are critical activities to be taken into consideration:

Figure 5. Prioritization matrix

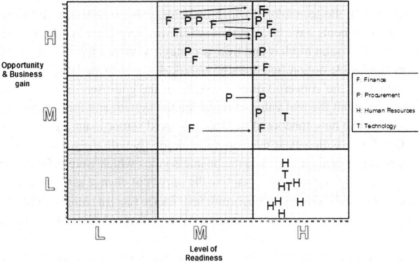

- **Business Processes, to be developed, reviewed, aligned as follows:**
  ○ Enhancement to the existing processes in accordance with new version.
  ○ Development of new processes for the new applications.
  ○ Creation of a Task Force to manage the above.
- **Data preparation as follows:**
  ○ Review the status of data and act accordingly with regards to new applications jointly with the vendor as part of the upgrade project (No resources available).
  ○ Review of existing data, cleansing, and enhancement (No resources available).

CONCLUSION AND RECOMMENDATIONS

The Task Force created for conducting Part 2 of the ERP investigation, *The Gain and Change-Readiness Assessment* (GCRA) was entrusted by senior management to carry out additional investigations building of the findings of Part 1 findings which were in favor of option 2 (Replace) justified by evidence of major business gains associated with this option, with the main beneficiaries being the Production functions Finance within as well as the introduction of some new applications that are currently supported by third party software and interfaced to the current ERP.

Although the option to replace the ERP was inevitable due to the anticipated improvements in the technology, which had changed over 5 years, and although general enhancements have been introduced, it was very clear that from usability and functionality point of view and from a strategic view the feasibility was favoring its most feasible option functionally, technically, and financially.

Nevertheless, the concern voiced by some of the end-users from the specific business area about the real value of replacing the system and their change readiness to utilize the new functionalities has prompted senior management to create a new Task Force with a clear mandate to work jointly with the stakeholders from relevant business areas (to validate the business gains which were indicated in the upgrade feasibility and to jointly examine the impact of change associated with the upgrade options considering the opportunities, risks to reach a realistic indication of the level of readiness by different business areas to undergo the transition associated with the upgrade or replacement of the current ERP.

A decision as important as this by senior management warranted the need for this additional Task Force to ensure the direct involvement of the stakeholders in assessing the technology solution, which will be serving GTC business function, processes, and employees in the coming years. This important aspect of the exercise has translated into a diversified team that represents all the stakeholders in the relevant business area including Finance, Human Resources, Production, and Technology.

The task force adopted a fast-track approach that has guided the efforts by members of the task force to reach the agreed goals and realize the objectives. It also provided an insight to the activities, tasks, issues, and challenges that were encountered and how they were managed. The task force report recommended to GM and senior management the most feasible option was option 2 to replace the current ERP supported by tangible evidence from the investigations that were carried out as part of the scope of the task force. The findings of the Task Force reflected the stakeholders' views, thoughts, and assessments of the impact of change associated with investigated options.

The outcome of the task force investigations strongly indicated that the replacement was the most feasible option due to the major anticipated business gains in Finance and Procurement in particular, the low risk exposure across all business functions and relatively high levels of readiness in most areas. Therefore, the Task Force members were unanimous in their recommendation to replace the current ERP by a selected new ERP.

KEY CHALLENGES

The onus is on the GTC ERP team and the stakeholders to take up the following key challenge to ensure success of the ERP replacement project by having:

- Enhanced Business Readiness (Business Process Alignment / Data).
- Comprehensive Scoping and Business Requirements Definition.
- Effective Project Planning.
- Effective Project Governance (Supportive Management / Sponsorship).
- Competent Project Team (Client's Subject Matter Experts [SMEs] and Vendor's Consultants).
- Effective Project Quality Control and Monitoring and Control.
- Appropriate Change Management.
- Role-Based Customized Training and Coaching.
- Post-Rollout Plan.
- Suitable Go-Live Strategy.

REFERENCES

Akkermans, H., Bogerd, B., Yucesan, E., & van Wassenhove, L. (2003). The impact of ERP on supply chain management: Exploratory findings from a European Delphi study. *European Journal of Operational Research, 146*(2), 284. doi:10.1016/S0377-2217(02)00550-7

Akkermans, H., & van Helden, K. (2002). Vicious and virtuous cycles in ERP implementation: A case study of interrelations between critical success factors. *European Journal of Information Systems, 11*(1), 35. doi:10.1057/palgrave/ejis/3000418

Al-Mashari, M., & Al-Mudimigh, A. (2003). ERP implementation: Lessons from a case study. *Information Technology & People, 16*(1), 21. doi:10.1108/09593840310463005

Ash, C., & Burn, J. (2003). A strategic framework for the management of ERP enabled e-business change. *European Journal of Operational Research, 146*(2), 374. doi:10.1016/S0377-2217(02)00556-8

Bernroider, E., & Koch, S. (2001). ERP selection process in midsized and large organizations. *Business Process Management Journal, 7*(3), 251. doi:10.1108/14637150110392746

Davenport, T. (1998). Putting the enterprise into the enterprise system. *Harvard Business Review, 76*(4), 121–131.

Gale, S. (2002). For ERP success, create a culture change. *Workforce, 81*(9), 88–92.

Hitt, L., Wu, D., & Zhou, X. (2002). Investment in enterprise resource planning: business impact and productivity measures. *Journal of Management Information Systems, 19*(1), 71.

Jacobs, F., & Bendoly, E. (2003). Enterprise resource planning: Developments and directions for operations management research. *European Journal of Operational Research, 146*(2), 233. doi:10.1016/S0377-2217(02)00546-5

Kumar, K., & Hillergersberg, J. (2000). ERP experiences and evolution. *Communications of the ACM, 43*(4), 23–26.

Lee, A. (2000). Researchable directions for ERP and other new information technologies. *Management Information Systems Quarterly, 24*(1), 3.

Mabert, V., Soni, A., & Venkataramanan, M. (2003). Enterprise resource planning: Managing the implementation process. *European Journal of Operational Research, 146*(2), 302. doi:10.1016/S0377-2217(02)00551-9

Parr, A., & Shanks, G. (2000). A model of ERP project implementation. *Journal of Information Technology, 15*(4), 289–304. doi:10.1080/02683960010009051

Sarkis, J., & Gunasekaran, A. (2003). Enterprise resource planning–Modelling and analysis. *European Journal of Operational Research, 146*(2), 229. doi:10.1016/S0377-2217(02)00545-3

Stewart, G., & Rosemann, M. (2001). Industry-oriented design of ERP related curriculum—An Australian initiative. *Business Process Management Journal, 7*(3), 234. doi:10.1108/14637150110392719

Stirna, J. (1999). Managing enterprise modeling tool acquisition process. In *Proceedings of the International Workshop on Enterprise Management Resource and Planning System*, (pp. 283-298). Venice, Italy: EMRPS.

KEY TERMS AND DEFINITIONS

ERP: Enterprise Resource Planning.
GCRA: Gain-Change Readiness Assessment.
GTC: Gulf Telecom Company.
ICT: Information and Communication Technology.

Opportunity: A measure of an anticipated positive outcome resulting from an uncertainty associated with change from the upgrade of current ERP version to higher version or Replace it by new ERP. In a certain context, it corresponds to usability, business gain, and/or strategic value.

Readiness: A measure of how ready is GTC to exploit anticipated opportunities and business gains and mitigating risks may be hindering proper and effective use of new modules, applications, functionalities, and features.

RFP: Request for Proposal.

Risk Exposure: A measure of an anticipated negative outcome resulting from an uncertainty associated with change from the upgrade of current ERP version to a higher version or replaces it by new ERP. Risk assessment of identified threats could be calculated using standard risk standards that combine the loss and probability to give a relative risk exposure level.

SOW: Scope of Work.

Usability: An indicator of the ability and preparedness of a certain ERP Modules, application, functionality, or feature to be used in GTC.

Usage: A measure of the level of use (quantity) of a certain ERP module, application, functionality, or feature.

Utilization: A measure of the effective usage (quality) of a certain ERP module, application, functionality, or feature.

Chapter 7
ERP Implementation:
A Project Manager's Tips for Success

Vladimir Kovacevic
Abu Dhabi Marine Operating Company, UAE

EXECUTIVE SUMMARY

Considering the high rate of failures in ERP implementation projects, there is an urgent need to identify the causes of such failures and the preventing actions associated with these causes. ERP practitioners and academics are unanimous that competencies and abilities of the ERP project manager have a direct impact on the project and its well-being. In fact, it is widely accepted that specific project manager's attributes such as oversight, leadership, communication, problem solving, and conflict-resolution are critical to the success of ERP projects. This case highlights some of the important issues and challenges that the author has encountered as a project manager of ERP system implementation in an Oil and Gas company in Kuwait. The focus of the case is on lessons learned and tips that can be handy and useful for people who may resume this important role in implementation projects.

ORGANIZATION BACKGROUND

The case is related to an Oil and Gas organization located in Kuwait, which will be referred to in this chapter as OGK. The activities of OGK include exploration, drilling, and production of oil and gas.

DOI: 10.4018/978-1-4666-2220-3.ch007

OGK manages the production and export of oil and gas from more than twelve developed oil fields in the state of Kuwait. The Company handles and maintains a comprehensive and fully integrated complex of production and export facilities that basically consist of: Oil Wellheads, Oil Flow-Lines, Gathering Centers, Gas Booster Stations, Pipeline Transit Systems, Water Treatment, and Injection Plants.

OGK is one on the leading world oil exporters.

SETTING THE STAGE

The case under examination is related to an OGK business-critical system implementation project that involved the replacement of the legacy systems previously used by the company with a fully integrated e-Business and Enterprise Asset Management System based on IBM Tivoli Maximo 7.1 software, a world leading Asset Management system.

The key project objective was to provide a total asset management initiative, geared towards moving the company from a fragmented situation, where numerous standalone systems were used in silos, to an integrated database solution. IBM Tivoli MAXIMO represents the center point of this configuration to integrate all facets of the business on a single unified platform and enabling effective Enterprise Asset Management, based on single version of asset data with its technical and financial history.

In addition to the basic software components, the scope of the project has also considered implementation of other software industry specific solution such as Transportation, Utility, Oil and Gas, MS Project and Primavera adapters and different mobile and asset specific solutions add-ons. In total, there were nineteen (19) different software components to be implemented.

The implementation project scope also included interfaces and integrations to fourteen (14) different business solutions as well as the design and development of eight (8) specific eBusiness solutions fully integrated with the core product.

The duration of the implementation project was originally planned for twenty four (24) months.

CASE DESCRIPTION

This project was considered one of the biggest (4,500+ users), and it was also regarded as one of the most complex implementation of IBM Tivoli MAXIMO EAM software ever, reflecting the requirements bundled in the scope of work. It was clear that projects of such magnitude required detailed and careful preparation by both vendor and client involving a comprehensive scope analysis, WBS development, the selection of a suitable implementation methodology, project organization set up, among other things. Unfortunately, many things did not start well from the beginning.

To start with, the vendor has failed to submit the vendors' resources histogram, project organization chart and personnel CV's to the client prior to the contract kick-off. Additionally, the client right to approve or reject the project team members combined with a very rigorous selection criteria specified, the project had to be started even though the project team had not been formed yet. Consultants were rejected one after another even though they had 3+ years of implementation experience working in complex projects. The harsh and unrealistic selection criteria, combined with the negative attitude of the client's project manager and the key stakeholders has delayed the resources mobilization and consequently start of initiation and planning phase.

Your client must be aware of the implementation methodology and standard you will apply much before project kicks off. On projects of this magnitude, the challenge will be to adjust it to accommodate client specific needs and you should do it along with the client during initiation and planning stage. However, this exercise must not transform into major changes to implementation methodology and documentation standards you use.

This has not only used up excessive time and efforts by the involved parties, but also had represented a potential risk for the delay of project deliverables.

The attitude of the client's project manager and many of the key stakeholders had a devastating impact on the project consistently, challenging consultants' competencies and knowledge while trying to hide their own weaknesses. This had a very adverse impact on the team moral and one by one would leave the project, leading to the resignation of four business lead consultants from the same work stream in less than 5 months, and during the one of the most important project phases, the Business Analysis and Solution Design phase. Surprisingly, nobody was much upset with this situation and even though this issue was escalated to the senior management, no action was taken as the issue seemed to be politically sensitive. So on one hand nothing was done to change the client's attitude and on the other hand, continuity of the key project resources was not secured.

An additional complexity was linked to the fact that the client did not have a fully dedicated project team and resources would be made available on "as and when required" basis provided that they did not have an important meeting. This has consequently made it difficult, ineffective, and inaccurate to obtain required input.

Since the project was already behind the planned schedule, the execution phase has started without having initiation and planning phase deliverables signed. This means there were no commitments from the client side. Later this even cascaded to commencing the development phase without having the 'To Be' business processes and functional specification documents signed off. For a lump-sum type of project this represented committing suicide and thus it was clear from the beginning that the project cannot be delivered successfully. And it was not.

PREPARATION PHASE

The preparation phase is very important in any implementation project as it defines clear project objectives and an efficient decision-making process. During this phase, a project charter is issued, an implementation strategy is outlined, and the project team and the work environment are established. Although it may sound, as a simple stage with no major issues, in a real life the time spent on proper project preparations is crucial as is the time to be spent on adequate project organization and roles set up. Unfortunately, there was a keen interest by some project parties to push for a speedy project kick-off and for a premature launch of the project activities without proper and adequate preparations. The risk of such an approach is very high, and it could lead to a high price to pay.

Project Organization Set-Up

Resource Selection

One of the key success factors for projects of this magnitude is to do proper resource selection. Before looking at his project resource pool and their viability, it is crucial that project manager has sufficient time to develop a full understanding of the project's scope in order to be able to identify the required resources' skills and competencies to ensure the successful delivery of the project. This time is needed and it is worth fighting for because it is the time for establishing a solid ground for the project, and its capabilities to cope with unplanned and unexpected events during the life-cycle of the project. It is of the utmost importance to convince senior management to provide adequate time to animalize the project requirements thoroughly. Once the required skills are identified and a draft of the project schedule is produced it is very important to define the number of all consultant profiles needed. There should be no hesitation by the project manager in presenting to senior management all the requirements in order to outsource activities/tasks for which there are no skilled personnel within the organization. Despite the huge pressure that would be applied to avoid this option, as it could impact gross margin, and despite the fact that top management might not look at that favorably as they did not plan for it, outsourcing in such cases is fully justified. Many would argue against the need for outsourcing using different rationale and irrationally contending that everything could be handled with internal resources. Many project managers would indeed hesitate to be involved in such a 'devious' act as they could be tagged as wimps.

Another important problem that would be expected, especially in projects that are executed abroad and which are of more than six months duration, is the availability of high profile consultants who would be normally reluctant to relocate unless tempted with incentives and financial rewards. What is different about running a project in a different country away from home compared to local projects is the difficulty to shuffle resources and move them from one project to another. It is common that vendor project managers tend to set high rates for high profile consultants and use them in other projects that run simultaneously.

This is the time for the project manager when steadfastness is required to defend and justify the need for project resource requirements of the right caliber and with the needed skills and competencies. There is no point of trying to be a hero at this stage, as not having a firm and clear stance on the resources issue could culminate in blame and possibly failure. The criticality of this issue to the success of the project qualifies it to be one of the important Critical Success Factors (CSFs) that can prevent a devastating impact on the project and on the morale of all resources from both vendor and client. In fact it would not count that attempts were made to address the resources issue since the kick off the project as what would be really considered is only the final outcome, which might have been impacted by any compromise on resources issue and the project manager would be certainly held accountable. The message here should be loud and clear that the project manager should fight for the required resources to successfully deliver the project.

Resource Qualifications vs. Client Requirements

It is normal before the resources selection process begins to check if there are any specific qualification requirements for the consultants who will work in the project in agreement between vendor and the client and such details must be included in the contract specification. This is another critical consideration not to overlook as it can put the project execution in serious jeopardy.

The project manager must refer to the contract specification and ensure that resources comply with the agreed consultants' profiles, although the client may insist on having a pool of high caliber consultants. Such requirements must be negotiated with the client, as they may be unrealistic and difficult to fulfill. If the requirements were viewed as unreasonable and were not considered essential to deliver the project successfully, the vendor's management support could be sought to define the best strategy to communicate that to the client. However, it is important to avoid making the mistake of ignoring the client's views, even if their requirement were unrealistic. The project manager's negotiation skills are crucial in such situations to convince the client to change position on the issue.

Secure Project Resources

Once a short list of suitable consultants to resource the team is finalized, it is highly recommended that the project manager make effort to understand their personality and capabilities. This can help the project manager to define a successful strategy to effectively utilize their skills as members of the project team. A proper strategy must be here and it is not appropriate to only inform the consultants of what they are assigned to do in the project. Improper handling of this issue could lead to costly consequences later when it may be impossible to solve that problem without affecting project milestones. Maintaining good relations with the project team members is another critical success factor. The project manager must find the best way to get their buy in. Experience indicates that forcing employee to accept project assignments always lead to devastating impacts on their moral and they would not produce even 60% of their capabilities and they would be the first to leave the project should things start going wrong.

In fact, on projects of this magnitude, what is needed is not 100% but 110% of project members' ability.

In order to have a better understanding of the project resources capabilities, strengths and weaknesses, the project manager might seek help from colleagues who have previously worked with these resources in other projects. The manager must know who is accompanying him in the voyage where turbulence is expected and one team spirit is critical to reach the shores of safety. This will allow the project manager to keep focus on the most critical resources.

Honesty is certainly an important attribute that should characterize the relationship between the project manager and the project team members as this will lead to mutual respect even in cases where there are disagreements, and even if they dislike anything about the project, place, client attitude, etc. Initially, project members should be introduced to the project scope, objectives, complexity, client culture, and obstacles in getting the project through. It is important not to conceal any facts that could negatively affect the convenience of member of the project because this could lead to a feeling of betrayal, which could later translate to project damage.

Resources discontinuity represents a risk with high potential impact on any project, and it is not possible to avoid this risk completely, thus a proper risk mitigation plan must be in place. Once the project team is finally set up, the emphasis should be shifted to the challenges of protecting the project, which can be primarily done by attaining the commitment of all resources to work as a team, and by ensuring common understanding among all team members of the project objectives, deliverables, and the methodologies and standards to leverage successful conclusion of the project.

Although it might not be a major issue for a project manager to replace a business consultant, a trainer, a report writer, or a technical consultant, a project resource pool would usually have enough consultants with the right skills to cover each others in case of disappearance of any of the resources or if the project manager opts to replace any one swiftly and effectively during the project lifetime. However, replacing a work stream lead consultant or senior consultant is not that simple, and it may have serious impact on the quality of the project deliverables, especially when there is not enough time for proper handover. Thus, the additional focus should be on securing their availability and continuity, by having them commit in writing that they will not attempt to leave the project at least until completion of "Initiation and Planning" and "Business Solution and Design" phases, as they are vital for project success. Failure to give effective measures to ensure their availability throughout the project can lead to delays and critical disturbance of the fluency and progression of the project in a way that is very hard to recover from. Unless key project team members' commitment is guaranteed, the moment they face first serious obstacle, they will leave the project manager with a nightmare scenarios. A smart project manager should not have on board people who are not ready to be loyal and dedicated to the project.

Resources Acceptance by Client prior to Kick-Off

It is appropriate that the project manager seeks the client's acceptance of the nominated project team members (resources). The vendor should submit consultants' CVs and professional profiles to the client with a request of the clients written approval before the project kicks off, allowing sufficient time for evaluating the candidates competencies and experience and making a judgment on the their suitability that will lead to their approval or rejection. In case of rejection of nominated resources by the client, a suitable replacement could take time, therefore it is not recommended that this task is deferred to the initiation and planning phase as it could become too late. Certainly, if this is not addressed it will be disruptive to the progress on other important tasks and activities when the project manager focus should be on proper planning and effective project execution.

INITIATION AND PLANNING PHASE

Implementation Methodology and Standards

A recipe for disaster in this phase could be associated with client's disagreement to the proposed project implementation methodology and the standards. A lengthy debate about the suitability of the methodology and standards can drag on with many challenges and counter challenges, and this could not only lead to delay but also to a negative team environment that can characterize the relationship between the vendor represented by the project manager and his resources and the client. Although there is no one solution for an awkward situation, delay can be avoided and damage minimized by the ability and wisdom of the project manager in conflict resolution, communication and leadership—this would certainly prevent the project be dragged into a twilight zone.

The project manager need to be firm and educative about the value of the proposed methodology and the standards, although they may at the same time decide wisely to give some grounds to the client by showing willingness to entertain client's ideas and thoughts without departing from the main theme.

It is a good practice to always educate the client of the value of what is being proposed and to have this little bit of space for minor adjustments that can satisfy the client or at least make him feel that he has an important role in this venture. This can also apply to document templates and other project plans and tools which could be expected to meet some of the client's specific requirements. The important tip here is that the project manager should get the approval of the client of what is believed to be right to the project, possibly with some compromise for the buy in, but certainly not ever accepting significant changes just to make it look like what was used in a previous system implementation at the client side.

Your client must introduced to your implementation methodologies and standards even during RFP stage proposing the methodology that will deliver project objectives set by the client.

Not standing firm on this issue can initiate a 'Master-Slave' relationship with a precedence that encourages the client to question and challenge everything in the project and would be very costly to the project on the long run. This can also lead to loosing the project manager's grip and control of the project and perhaps tarnishing the image of the project manager as a professional expert with credibility and integrity.

Usually, establishing 'One team working environment' with both (vendor and client) working together as partners is an important project critical success factor.

Involving Key Stakeholders

If an implementation project is successful many parties would jump to claim the credit, however if it fails, then only the project manager would be held accountable. That is just simply how it works in major projects. That is why identifying key stakeholders from the client side is very important.

During this phase of the implementation, it is critical that the project manager and his team does not work in isolation. It is of the utmost importance to have active participation of key management, knowledgeable users, and technical representatives from the areas of the business affected by the project's objectives, and right from the beginning. A smart project manager must be able to identify at early stage the 'Chief in Command' and to create channels of communication to get the direct input from him/her. He could be the client project manager, but then again it may be the person seating next to him/her. The project manager should be ready to answer questions about their source of the input and about its authenticity.

As a result, a lot of valuable time might get wasted on searching e-mails and trying to prove that the input for your documentation was really obtained from the nominated client personnel.

Managing Client Stakeholders

Managing Objectives

Sometimes, the client does not know exactly what they want and they expect the vendor to guide them. There is no problem with the project manager resuming such an advisory role if it is not excessive and if it is done with care to avoid ending-up with prototyping. The project manager must insist on having clear vision of what project will deliver. Otherwise, the project team will spend time developing a solution that does not necessarily meet the client's expectations and could be eventually enter an endless loop of client's rejections and vendors' modifications until the project is seriously behind the schedule. This could trigger frustration among all parties and may translate into finger-pointing and unhealthy blame project environment, which can have an overall negative impact on the project.

The best way to avoid such a situation is to stick to a clearly defined plan and to avoid wasting too much time on entertaining client's wishes on ad-hoc basis.

A formal signed-off initiation document spelling the approach and defining the relationship between the two parties can help both parties play their roles effectively in harmony and not lose focus on the important issues.

Common Conflicts and Resolutions

By resolving conflicts, the project manager moves the project along, and attempts not to make enemies at the same time, however regardless of the patience, leadership, and diplomacy he/she may demonstrate, there are no guarantees that all stakeholders will be always happy with decisions or even the project objectives. It is only normal that some will always be criticizing and blaming unless all their wish list of requirements are entertained and added to the scope of the project.

Conflicts may arise in many different forms but the most common for this case were:

Implementing Business Process vs. Business Process Re-Engineering

When implementing business system the project manager would be provided with the list of approved business processes/process flows. This would be followed by performing 'As Is' business analysis to identify all the GAPs between the business process and the system capabilities, and to decide on appropriate business solutions. There is no doubt that changes to business processes can potentially get the best out of the software being implemented, but care should be taken here to avoid falling into the trap of ending-up with process re-engineering unless it is unambiguously stipulated in the scope of work. Otherwise, the GAP analysis workshop would become a convenient forum for the process re-engineering and developing of new processes. These could consume a lot of time on the expense of other tasks pertaining to GAP analysis, as they require a lot of time to be aligned and agreed by the client. The time wasting becomes more critical in the case of inter-related and cross-functional processes. Adding to it very stubborn client and unclear scoping, the damage to the project could be huge and the project is hard to recover.

In projects of such magnitude, the project manager must not allow the client to use software implementation project for business process re-engineering or design of new business process if not included in the project scope.

The likelihood of having this kind of conflict is much higher in cases where additional industry specific software solutions are procured on top of the 'out-of-the box' product. In such cases, there is a need to make sure to plan for the time needed for design and implementation of new processes.

Resource

Even though the client is not eligible to decide what is an adequate number of resources needed for each phase, and when they should be mobilized, they will always try to interfere and put pressure to have bigger number of consultants mobilized than what was planned. Perhaps the client tends to feel more comfortable having an 'army' of consultants on site or possibly, because they know they are extending the scope and they are of opinion that there is a need for more manpower to address the scope creep.

'As Is' and 'To Be' Business Process Document

It is very important to ensure that the client accepts the format of the 'As Is' and the 'To Be' business process documents, whether using horizontal or vertical presentation layer and the level of details to present in the document. The risk here is that unless the client initially accepts the format, he/she may reject the format and may insist to redo the work using the preferred format, hence losing consultant's time that could be dedicated for other tasks.

Functional Design Document Content

The challenge here is linked to the level of technical details that the functional design document should contain. While the project manager interest is to have the document ready for the project developing team to work on, the client could insist on a document that is written in 'business language' describing in details each function. They would not be interested in how it is made to function that way. They would not feel comfortable signing a document that is flooded with technical details and which they do not understand. On the other hand, if the client refuses to endorse the functional design document this could lead to the huge risk of introducing the system prototyping instead configuring the system based on GAP analysis and functional specification document. In other words, there would be no commitment from the client side. The main risk is associated with spending months working hard to deliver very complex solutions that might not be accepted after all by the key stakeholders because it is judged as not what they expected and that it does not function on the way they wanted. This does not necessarily mean that consultants did not understand the requirements, but it is that once it comes to user acceptance testing they start realizing they could be held responsible for what will be delivered to the final "customer." To avoid such a nasty situation, a smart project manager would make sure that the functional design document describes functions in details rather than system configuration, enhancement and customization required to meet functional requirements.

Different skills that can be handy to resolve common conflicts include:

Resolve the Problem

Of course, the project manager will always try to resolve conflict with the client, but it requires both sides to work jointly to find a solution that is the best for the project and acceptable by both parties. It is ideal, win-to-win situation but in this case, it did not work.

Compromise

When the first option does not work, it is appropriate to consider a compromise by giving up on something that will not impact project deliverables significantly, although this could result in the need to put some more effort during execution phase. However, in the case where the client is not willing to give up on any of original requirements that resulted with the conflict, then the manager could try to

Minimize Conflict

This strategy could smooth out the conflict without offering a specific solution. Giving stakeholders the chance to talk 'loudly' enables them to minimize problems on their own. If this strategy does not work, the project manager last resort is to try Reinforcing Strategy. It is always better to resolve a problem or to compromise on a conflict, but in cases when this signaling a considerable change on the project scope then the manger must has a firm stance and force the client to accept that the reference is what was defined in the project scope of work. A good project manager knows his/her project team and the abilities of all its individuals, but if the resource demand spread the project team too thin, they would never be able to get their work done and their morale would crash down, leading to a situation that could put project's success in jeopardy.

Stopping the Project

Although not a fancy option, it is considered a very tough call for the project manager to suggest and for vendor management to support. Nevertheless, this card can be used conveniently when the client insist to exercise power unfairly. This could be thought of as a yield-lose scenario because one side of the argument yields to the other without anyone really considering what the best solution for the project may be.

Considering Resignation

If none of above resolution methods work and the project manager is not having the needed support from his management to put project on hold or stop it, and the project manager is convinced that the project will be in jeopardy due to unresolved conflicts, then it is the time when the resignation option could be used. This is not an easy option for the project manager because it is like quitting but it is justifiable in cases when the communication channel with the client ceases to work and no support is extended by the clients management. This could represent a 'shock' therapy that may help the senior management realize that there is something seriously wrong going on with the project warranting the need for action.

To conclude, the project manager must be equipped with adequate knowledge about conflict resolution, and then his/her experience will help to figure out which are the suitable and effective strategies, methods and techniques considering the situation on hand. An important factor however is to handle the situation calmly and confidently and be comfortable with in each situation.

Document Signing

The project manager should ensure that all planning phase documents, including document templates are approved and signed-off by the designated client representative. Failing to do that can be a potential recipe for more conflicts in the execution phase. It is very important that of the outcome of the business requirements analysis workshops is a stakeholder signed-off requirements document that identifies everything the project promises to create. Both the vendor and the client should sign-off on this document so that everyone involved agrees on their roles and expectations for the project deliverables. As a rule, the person who signs off on the project acceptance at the end of the project should also sign off on the project requirements.

The business requirements signing-off serve the following purposes:

- Identifies explicitly what the project manager and project team will create for the stakeholders.
- Identifies that the stakeholders are in agreement as to what the project requirements are for the project.
- Ensures that the project manager understands the software functionality the stakeholders are expecting as a result of your work.
- Allows the project manager and the stakeholders to fully share in the project buy-in by agreeing to the things that the project will create.
- Acts as a checklist to ensure that the delivered solution meets all agreed requirements.
- Serves in the future as historical information for other project managers in the vendor's organization.

Tough Decisions

What would a project manager do if his/her views are constantly ignored by the client, even though the project might be already in a serious trouble and any further delay could impact the project duration and quality? What if at the same time the client project team virtually exists only on the paper, as they are continually busy to genuinely and sufficiently engage in the project? What if the client manager is adamant that they do not need to be in the project on full-time basis and that they can be freed when and as needed? What if client resources designated to the project are left to go on leaves without any consideration to the impact of that on the project?

This is the time when the project manager should challenge the competency of the client project manager and escalate the issue the project sponsor and board as a major threat. The project manager must stand firm on this issue and lobby all parties to play an active role to correct the situation. If the project manager fails to convince the decision makers on the urgency of this matter and its threat to the success of the project, and if no genuine action is taken, then there are serious questions to answer?

Should the project be stopped? Or you put it on hold and pull the consultants out until the project issues are seriously attended by your client? Or continue at any cost because it is the biggest implementation ever, regardless of the fact that the 'S' curve does not suggest that. Big decisions have to be made before starting the execution phase, because otherwise all these persisting issues will cascade to much bigger and more complex issues that would be very hard to recover from and would almost certainly fail to finish within planned budget.

Early Setting of Stakeholders Expectations

One of the trickiest parts of the project manager's job is balancing stakeholder expectations. Everyone wants something and sees the project as opportunity for many things that are not part of project scope.

The bottom line is that all the inputs can be taken into consideration, but reality dictates that there are limitations hindering the delivery on all requirements, simply because it is not feasible to build super software that can all meet every user's most minute need. Attempting to build this do-all solution will certainly end up with a highly customized solution that does everything poorly.

It is important that the project manager and all the stakeholders must agree about the purpose of the project and then work backwards to their wish lists from there.

The goal of negotiation in project management is not to get the best deal for a particular party, rather it is to find the best solution for the project.

Through rounds of give and take, compromise, and negotiations, the project manager is bound to reach a consensus with the stakeholders on why the project is being executed and what the project will accomplish and through awareness to set the expectation realistically of the client about the life after the go-live.

It is very important early in the project life cycle, that stakeholders use the opportunity to define, own, and control the product scope to avoid later changes, that can adversely impact the project leading to project delay or budget over run.

Politics and Your Project

Internal politics within any organization can be a key factor in destroying any project. The favoring of unjustified system functionalities and features and against genuinely justified functionalities and features to serve self-interest or internal agendas is a major threat to the quality of the project deliverables and to the acceptance of the solutions by end-users.

The ability of the project manager to challenge and resist such politics-driven features and requirements depend on the party who is sponsoring and endorsing such a demand. Regardless if this demand is from senior management or even power centers within the organizations, the project manager has to do his utmost efforts to highlight the consequences and impact that it could lead to, especially in cases where there is evidence that time, cost or quality are impact. In such cases, the project manager must state clearly that impact and perhaps consider using a feasibility model or even create a solid risk assessment of the tradeoffs and present a valid argument.

Another approach is to prioritize a project's feasibility based on all of the objectives presented, by finding or creating the central goal of the project's deliverables and getting everyone to agree first on the primary goals of the project's deliverables and then treat every other requirement as additional.

If it is possible to treat any additional deliverables as items that either support or hinder the project goal, politics become more clear and easier to ward off. Therefore, the project manager should be wise and firm in neutralizing any politics that can affect the project.

Do Not Support Rumors

It is not uncommon that the client would try to conveniently use the project manager to side with him against other project team members or to endorse his views controversial issues and problems. The project manager should try to avoid any such informal and unhealthy dealing s as it unnecessarily creates enemies and may back fire in the future. A formal and professional approach by the project manager would gain everyone's respect and is in the best interest of the project.

Do Not Let Client Ruin Your Reputation and Credibility

Often the project manager is irritated by the challenges of some of client's stakeholders for no obvious valid reason, and which implies unfounded problems in the project schedule, planning, or methodologies. This kind of challenges could be driven by self-promoting and showing off in front of certain. As this can be damaging to the project manager credibility and image, he should smartly contain such challenges by addressing the issues with clear facts and enforcing the project manager's posture as the expert in his area. There might be nothing wrong with the project schedule, or implementation methodology, and the project schedule is detailed enough with a proper WBS, dependencies, resources and constraints defined, yet there would be someone out there willing to stand up and argue—for instance—that the critical path is not adequately visible because dependencies of the tasks are inaccurate. In essence, this is defaming the project manger as an incompetent, unknowledgeable despite the fact that he/she has successfully managed numerous complex projects before.

In such occasions, when diplomacy might not be the most suitable option, the project manager must take a very firm stance on the subject and do whatever needed to clear an ambiguities in the minds of the audience about the project status by presenting facts indicative of the well-being of the project and that everything is under control. For credibility and integrity, the project manager may also identify issues and problems, highlighting corrective actions and clear indication of how and when these issues will be resolved.

This approach is effective in reassuring the audience that the project is in safe hands, and it maintains the image and reputation of the project manager, which is critical to the project success. The project manager has to be perceived as a fair and experienced, knowledgeable professional, who is focused primarily on the projects objectives and deliverables and not be distracted by unfounded claims, gossips, or rumors.

Use Diplomacy

Often on large-scale projects such as this, the project manager would face situations when someone from the project team members or stakeholders who tend to be nuisance by propagating negative messages and creating disturbance. Although this category of people can be irritating, however the project manager must make sure that he /she treat everyone the same way when it comes to discipline, time off, and achievements. Perceiving the project manager as fair by the stakeholders can translate it into respect and trust, two tools that are very effective to counter negative politics especially if the project manager shows willingness to share constructive criticism openly, as he/she would certainly do by sharing compliments loudly and proudly.

Respect Client Key Stakeholders

The project manager should avoid getting involved in negative politics by focusing on the projects best interest as the highest priority and not to be dragged by stakeholders into issues that may be driven by other considerations. Negative politics can certainly obstruct project progress, therefore when dealt with correctly and ethically, politics may facilitate progress. Building positive, supportive working relationships with project stakeholders is an example of a positive aspect of politics.

Make Sure Your Business Partners Work for You

If the project is a sub-contracted, the project manager must pay special attention to the relations with the main contractor, and to understand the business partner's relations with the client. The project manager should know enough about the relationship between key stakeholders from both parties and be conversant with the project environment and the kind of people involved in the project. This understanding can be a useful input to manage working with the business partners and minimize friction and conflicts.

This is of a crucial importance when you run overseas project and your business partner and the client are from the same country. You must not underestimate the fact that they possible already have established good relation. So if something starts getting wrong do not be surprised if some of sensitive correspondence between you and your business partner ends up in the clients' inbox. At the end, if project fails it is you and your team who will go back home and they stay for the future business opportunities. They will still need each other.

REFERENCES

Aladwani, A. (2001). Change management strategies for successful ERP implementation. *Business Process Management, 7*(3), 266. doi:10.1108/14637150110392764

Cliffe, S. (1999). ERP implementation. *Harvard Business Review, 77*(1), 16.

Markus, M., Axline, S., Petrie, D., & Tanis, C. (2000). Learning from adopters' experiences with ERP: Problems encountered and success achieved. *Journal of Information Technology, 15*(4), 245–266. doi:10.1080/02683960010008944

Markus, M., Tanis, C., & Fenema, P. (2000). Multisite ERP implementations. *Communications of the ACM, 43*(4), 42–46. doi:10.1145/332051.332068

McAlary, S. (1999). Three pitfalls in ERP implementation. *Strategy and Leadership, 27*(6), 49.

Ribbers, P., & Schoo, K. (2002). Program management and complexity of ERP implementations. *Engineering Management Journal, 14*(2), 45.

KEY TERMS AND DEFINITIONS

BPR: Business Process Re-Engineering.
CFSs: Critical Success Factors.
ERP: Enterprise Resource Planning.
OGK: Oil and Gas Kuwait Company.
WBS: Work Breakdown Structure.

Chapter 8

The Selection and Deployment of System in Gulf Private School:
Issues, Challenges, and Lessons Learnt

Ahmad Fayez
Information Fort, UAE

EXECUTIVE SUMMARY

The high academic posture of Gulf Private School (GPS) and its outstanding students' performance in the gulf region is a translation of its vision to be the leading school in the region. Technology applications were always viewed by GPS as tools to leverage change and drive continuous improvement, and thus, the utilization of Information Technology applications was weaved into GPS strategy to maintain its high ranking among private schools in terms of the delivery of quality education and the provision of distinguished services to students and parents. This positive attitude to new technologies explains why GPS is always on the lookout for the latest advancements in educational technology aids and tools to support its functions and processes. This case reflects on the ups and downs associated with GPS decision to implement an ERP system with a promise for major business gains that can help GPS to reinstate its position in the leaders' quadrant.

DOI: 10.4018/978-1-4666-2220-3.ch008

ORGANIZATION BACKGROUND

Twenty years since the inauguration of its first branch in the region as a non-profit organization, GPS accomplishments were driven by its vision to be a regional leader in K12 education. In this limited time, GPS went through major expansion to cope with the multiplication of its students that was also paralleled by a substantial increase in the number and types of courses and the number of teachers and administration staff. GPS has also grown in popularity in the region as one of the important education institutes that provide both British and American system and curriculum.

The forward and positive approach by GPS board of directors towards continual improvement and opportunities has led to several wins to celebrate and has helped GPS position itself as a leader among other schools, evidently overtaking some of the prominent schools, which were historically pioneers in this small gulf country. However, the emergence of new technology and Internet applications and the introduction of new western learning models over the past years have meant tougher competition and has resulted in the decline in GPS ranking compared to other organizations who are more technologically oriented.

Today, GPS is credited by two international institutes for its American and British Curriculums-based programs in addition to K12 local program. It has 257—mainly expatriate—teaching and non-teaching staff and 2113 enrolled students.

SETTING THE STAGE

GPS administration had always had a positive attitude towards adoption of new technologies to support education and learning, and they have regularly budgeted for investment in both hardware and software to equip classes and facilities and to serve staff, teachers, and students. In fact, the school had always a specific interest to have technology rich classrooms with smart boards, personal computers, projectors, and educational aids. GPS also prides itself for being a pioneer among other private schools for creating a Local Area Network (LAN) connecting teachers and administration and using a standard operating system environment based on MS Windows and MS office applications. GPS has also had procured different standalone software for the accounting department, human resources department and the library.

Unfortunately, what could have been described as a lavish spending on technology did not include the connectivity of school with students and parents. In addition, GPS departments were not connected to each other and one simple report could take a very long time to produce because relevant information resides in different isolated software and databases. Furthermore, much of the hardware and software used in GPS were aging and in some case deemed obsolete or outdated compared to new

Internet technology applications and new computers with much faster processing, data storage, and reporting capabilities.

It was evident that although the basic infrastructure represented by the hardware and software were in place, the low level of utilization of suitable technology and the modest business gains were linked to a number of factors that are summarized as follows:

- Outdated technology.
- Lack of integration of the software applications.
- Lack of connectivity.
- Lack of analytical reporting tools.
- Lack of good quality data.

This resounds the findings of a task force that was delegated by the school board to investigate the current status and level of utilization of technology in GPS and to submit recommendation of corrective actions that could pave the way and provide the justification for investment in suitable information system and technology applications to support the school's drive to reinstate its role as a leader in the region.

Decision to Acquire a System

The school board was alarmed by the findings of the task force, in particular those related to the problems associated with the disparate nature of the existing software and the lack of connectivity between different stakeholders. The report also confirmed that the existing applications' inability to produce meaningful performance reports and indicators to support management decision making, budgeting and forward planning. It has also highlighted as critical the lengthy costly routine processes, the duplications of data and most importantly the security threats of unlawful access to information of sensitive or privacy nature.

The task force findings have prompted management to discuss and explore feasible solutions in consultation with GPS board of trustees. The need was identified and justified and unanimously agreed by members of the board to acquire and implement a new information system with the objective to link business support functions and primary education functions within GPS organization, and to connect all concerned parties including school administration and teaching staff with parents and students. The objective was linked with GPS mission to restore its leading ranking in the region.

The main features of the system to be acquired were extracted from the findings of the task force report and the directions of the board of trustees which indicated clearly the need for an integrated enterprise system that can support the primary functions of learning and education as well as the secondary enterprise functions such as human resources, finance, accounting, stores, and procurement. The sought enterprise solution should automate the processes, and can produce analytical reports and key performance indicators to support all stakeholders.

The functional integration and process automation in the new system seemed to provide the opportunity to optimize the enterprise and educational processes and improve planning and decision making which could in turn improve quality control, minimize cost, reduce time, improve customer (parents and students) services, and improve communication between school and the community of stakeholders.

The great majority of administration staff and teachers were excited about the prospect of having a new system that will connects all concerned parties, reduce process times, and that which is easy to use for searching and querying and producing analytical reports. However, there was another small but loud group of staff who were cynical and critical about this new venture, and have used every possible occasion to send negative messages and were outspoken about the risks of moving to a new system, highlighting failures of similar systems in other schools and doubting that there will substantial gains to the school.

CASE DESCRIPTION

The school principal has chosen the school celebrations of its 20th anniversary as an opportunity to announce a package of improvement measure that the school board has approved and that GPS was embarking on for the next phase. Standing in the school auditorium, in front of large group audience of dignitaries, parents, students and staff the principal announced that "the challenges for the future can be only met with the commitment to continual improvement and the utilization of new Information Systems and to Technology applications." He also highlighted that the vision of the school is "to be ranked number one in quality education in the country within 3-5 years." He highlighted that gains from technology can be realized only by knowing why we should use it and by knowing how to use it?

The Selection Phase

The announcement of the way forward by GPS principal was followed by the formation of a small selection team to be led by a team leader representing management and composed of a team of five persons representing management, finance, and Information Technology functions.

The selection team circular indicated that the main objective of the team is to understand the current situation and to identify all requirements that can be used as basis to investigate suitable integrated information systems to replace the existing software within HR, Finance, and Accounting departments, and which will integrate the core functions within the school two campuses and automate the business processes which will link all stakeholders as potential end-users.

Over a period of 2-3 months the selection team worked together to explore available systems in the market and those which are being used by other comparable schools. The team's aim was to select a suitable system that matches the school's requirements and has the features and functionalities highlighted by GPS management. The team did not follow a structured approach per-se, and members of the team did not have enough knowledge about schools information system or new educational technology applications, therefore they had to rely on the advice of friends, colleagues, or acquaintances for impressions and the different software applications and on information and technology trends.

The team was not well informed about the implementation methodologies; customization issues, end-users issues or hidden costs associated with the deployment of readily developed and packaged ERP applications such as Oracle, SAP and PeopleSoft. However, alarmed by reported ERP failures has prompted them to decided to exclude such systems and to look for a solution that can be tailored to GPS requirements—specifically equivalent features and functionalities to that provided by the existing standalone software used in finance and human resources.

The search process by the selection team was interrupted due to a direction by an influential member of the school board suggesting a specific software development vendor as a potential provider for the sought system. Accordingly, the selection team has met with XYZ, a local software development firm and after a number of presentations they reached they were reasonably satisfied that this company was capable of developing a system that can replicate the functionalities and features of GPS standalone software and integrate the relevant modules. They were mainly impressed with the flexibility to tailor the solution to match any requirements and also that the system would be creating the required connectivity and produce a variety of reports to serve teachers, administrators and the board members.

Although company XYZ was a small firm with limited resources (12 employees) and a modest profile (yearly turnover of $1.10) and had virtually no reference sites where such system was implemented, the selection team was comforted by the reassurances that the company was affiliated to a prominent International software development group and that they will benefit from their long experience in the area of ERP implementations.

The selection team has submitted the findings to the school board with a recommendation to award the project to Company XYZ, indicating the main features and functionalities that will be delivered part of the solution and provided indications of the project duration (18 months) and budget ($110,000).

The Acquisition Phase

The excitement about the anticipated gains from the recommended system has prompted management endorsement and the final approval of the schools board of trustees, who instructed the starting of the acquisition phase.

The same selection team was instructed to liaise with the procurement department to submit an official Request For Proposal (RFP) to company XYZ and to start at the same time working on consolidating the requirements by different departments. The board's approval of the selection team's recommendation has meant that no tendering was needed and that the selection of the vendor (company XYZ) as a single source was automatically approved. The rush to start seemed to correspond to pressures from the board on management and from management on the team, to the extent that the requirements that were being gathered to include in the scope of work were defined at high level only and many details were left to be negotiated with the vendor during the development. The same could be said about the analysis of the existing infrastructure and the profiling of the potential end-users of the system and what that means in terms of number of licenses to purchase.

The RFP provided a high level description of the sought functionalities and features associated with the main modules and applications that are expected to be bundled in the final delivered system, namely; Finance Accounting, Stores and Inventory, Payroll, Human Resources, Registration and Enrollment, Grading, Students Records, Email, and Communication.

The award of the project was completed in record time, and a small project team headed by the same management representative who led the selection team, has been created to work with the vendor in the development and implementation of the sought system. The acquisition phase was concluded with an agreement to deliver a working information system as per the specified features and functionalities for a total of 350 end-users (100 concurrent users) in duration of 18 months (3 phases) for an a lump sum of US$110,000 covering license fees, project management, Implementation consultancy, training, and first year maintenance.

The Initiation Phase

This phase is to ensure that the necessary preparations to kick-off the project are in place, including, project offices, infrastructure and logistics. In addition, during this phase the project organization, development methodology, project plans, and schedules were to be finalized.

- **Project Preparations:**
  This is about creating a suitable project work environment including:
  - Project team offices and facilities (meeting room, training rooms)
  - Development Infrastructure; servers, network, software
  - Personal computers, printers, scanner, photocopier, telephones, fax machine, network.
  - Logistics; stationary, filing, etc.
- **Project Organization:**
  Project organization describes the roles, responsibilities, and relationship of the project manager and resources. The project team was comprised of resources from both the client (GPS) and the vendor (XYZ). As illustrated in the diagram, the project manager (vendor) heads a project team that included a secretary, 2 lead consultants (vendor), 2 P/T business experts (client), 1 F/T IT officer (client) and a trainer (vendor) (see Figure 1).
- **Development Methodology:**
  Considering the shortage of resources and the inability of the client (GPS) to release enough numbers of employees to participate in the project on full-time basis, the vendor (XYZ) and the client (GPS) have agreed to adopt a phased-out approach projected on a standard development methodology based on a tailored Waterfall methodology with the development of the *enterprise functions* included in phase one and the development of the *educational functions* in phase two. The adopted project development methodology represented a road map for an iterative development process that included the following tasks: Define → Analyze → Design → Develop → Test → Train (see Figure 2).
  - **Define**: To collate and validate relevant functional requirements to the module/application under consideration.
  - **Analyze**: To investigate requirement using appropriate tools such as feasibility analysis tools that test the pros and cons of different solutions considering risks, impacts, cost, etc.
  - **Design**: To produce conceptual and functional design associated with the selected solution. To be signed-off by an authorized representative of the client.
  - **Develop**: To build an application in accordance with the functional design specifications using appropriate development and configuration tools or programming.
  - **Test**: To have the delivered application subjected to Unit testing and acceptance by client's authorized representative.
  - **Train**: To develop and deliver tailored role-based training to the intended end-users.

The Selection and Deployment of System in Gulf Private School

Figure 1. Project organization

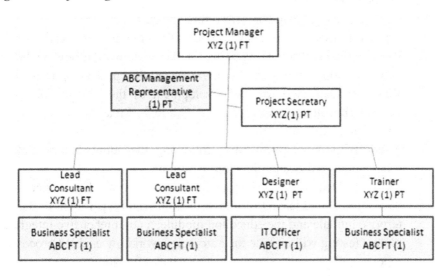

Figure 2. The iterative development process

Figure 3. Development roadmap

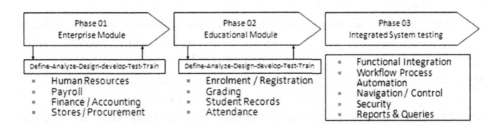

- **Development Roadmap:**

  The development road map comprised three phases:

  ○ **Phase 1:** Dedicated for the development of the enterprise applications (HR, Payroll, Finance Accounting, Stores, and Procurement) following the adopted development process (define-analyzed-design-develop-test-train).

  ○ **Phase 2:** Dedicated for the development of the educational applications (Enrollment, Registration, Grading, Students Records, and Attendance) following the adopted development process (define-analyzed-design-develop-test-train) following the adopted methodology (define-analyzed-design-develop-test-train).

  ○ **Phase 3:** Dedicated for Integrated System Testing. Upon successful development and testing of all applications (units) pertinent to the enterprise module and the education module, a comprehensive integrated system testing will include the automated workflow enabled processes, reports, and general system features such as navigation, control, searching, and querying. This will be followed by the 'Go-Live,' which will signal the start of the life of the system in GPS (see Figure 3).

- **Project Schedule:**

  Guided by the adopted methodology and roadmap, a project schedule was prepared by the project manager and endorsed by the client (GPS) with details up to the third level of the activities and tasks to be carried out by both the client and vendor personnel and the main deliverables at different project stages to achieve the project objectives. The schedule defines the stages, tasks, durations, dependencies, constraints, resources, and deliverables.

The Execution Phase: What Really Happened!

The project kick-off meeting was attended by the designated project manager and the project team members from both client and vendor. The project manager introduced the main objective and deliverables of the project and introduced the project team members and their roles. The team discussed the project schedule and other project related issues and agreed on progress reporting and frequency of meetings. The manager concluded with a message that "the success of the project is conditional to the dedication of all members of the project and to work as one team."

The first week of the project has witnessed issues related to the preparedness of the project's facilities and environments including personal computers, email, and Internet connections. In addition, there was no dedicated meeting room for the project team and the project had to compete with other school activities.

Despite these glitches, the team has resumed work by scheduling meetings with key 'functional' areas to collate requirements but this was hindered by the fact that everybody was very busy and people did not seem comfortable spending too much time in meetings discussing requirements. It was evident at this early stage that the Human Resources group was attempting to curtail the process of requirements definition by suggesting that a replication of the present HR software functionality would be adequate—with reluctance the consultants decided to go through the HR software functionality and use as a baseline for the development.

The consultants meetings with the HR personnel representatives were frequently interrupted due to other commitments and postponement of meetings and sessions were quite often. Additionally, there was an attempt to push a junior with limited knowledge of the organization processes and business to be involved in such meetings and act for the project member representing this business area.

Issues of this nature were raised in the weekly meetings to the project manager who reported to ABD management representatives generating a lot of unfulfilled promises.

The unavailability of a dedicated room to use for meetings has also contributed to delay in the finalizing of the feasibility and gap analysis sessions of the first enterprise application by nearly three weeks compared to the project schedule.

The late delivery of a development server and network problems in the project environment has meant that the consultants would often disappear to do work from vendor's office. This has encouraged members from the client to go back to their departments. It has become evident that that the project team was not behaving as a one team and that bits and pieces were done here and there. The meetings which were supposed to be held on weekly basis to report progress and to agree actions were less frequent and that any progress was not following the project schedule— rather an ad-hoc approach to attempt to address issues and to fix problems were prevailing. It was clear that any activities by the project team members were reactive and not following the schedule and frustration started to creep into all parties involved. The vendor was blaming the client for delays and lack of preparedness on all fronts and by not releasing personnel with the right qualities adequately to input to the project. On the other hand GPS was overloaded with other issues and was not seriously alarmed by the situation and was managing the conflict with promises and half-hearted solutions.

Four months after the project kick-off the project was in charade. The team was fragmented—neither the development or production servers were delivered and any activities have been shifted to the vendor's office. It was clear that the progress was very limited and that the project schedule was not being used any more—the relationship between the client and the vendor went into a phase distrust.

Busy with higher priority issues, the client has failed to be decisive on a situation, which was evidently deteriorating, when GPS management could have decided to take the concerns seriously and decide to take a corrective action, pressure the vendor to take a more practical approach or to dismiss the vendor's service all together.

This same situation has dragged on for a very long time with scattered work and minor progress on different modules based on replicating the existing software that serve different enterprise functions. During this period, members of the project steering committee, management, education, and support departments' staff had split on the subject with one group calling for the termination of the project and the other suggesting to take corrective actions.

This status quo was only interrupted by an initiative led by the Vice Principle to mandate an internal audit to investigate the status of the project and report the findings to the steering committee, reflecting on the real progress that has been accomplished and to put forward recommendations on how to put it back on track.

The findings of the internal audit were not to the liking of some of the stakeholders, prompting accusations and counter accusations between different groups, and eventually leading to ignore the report and not even consider the recommendations to dismiss the vendor and terminate the project—a certain group who were involved in the selection and initiation phase resisted this option as it amounted to accepting failure. Consequently and as a result of not taking a final and firm decision on the problem, the project was on hold for nearly two years.

Nearly two years down the track the GPS principal left the school with recommendation to the new principal to address and resolve the idle project. This has encouraged the new principal to create a new a senior level ERP Specialist post for technology oversight in the school with a specific prime responsibility to review the status and proceed with what is needed to resume work on the system, but giving priority to the supporting enterprise functions of Payroll and Accounting.

The new initiative to revive the project and to resume the development of the system was led by the ERP Specialist was backed up by the principal and the schools board.

The mission of the ERP Specialist has turned out to be a very strenuous and tedious process, including long meetings and discussions with stakeholders and with the vendor to assess the 'As-Is' and 'To-Be' statuses and explore effective strategies to revive the project and take the necessary measures to lead to success. The efforts included many presentations with reviews and revisions by representatives and end-users from all divisions and departments.

The new specialist has put his skills and experience behind the efforts to review the history of the project and to understand the root cause of the problems, and to come up with a strategy and a roadmap to move forward. Wisely, he recognized the importance of communication with stakeholders and end-users in all areas opportunity to understand their issues and pains and also to gain their confidence. This has culminated in an agreement to adopt a pilot approach to the development of the applications based on the initially proposed development process (define-analyze-design-develop-test-train) and also to phase out the development based on the business importance and agreed priorities.

It was agreed to include the development of the Accounting and Payroll applications in phase one, to be followed by other applications upon end-user testing and acceptance of the developed applications and their rollout.

Despite the initial success in creating the required momentum to revive the project through communication with the vendor and the stakeholders and despite his success to have an agreed strategy and roadmap, conflicts and disagreements came back to the surface as soon as end-users were given the chance to test and judge the suitability of the applications which were developed to replace their standalone legacy software. This has led to the resignation of the payroll section leader and the escalation of the issues to higher levels.

GPS had agreed with the vendor to have a fast track approach to complete the project and rollout the system. Although this has yielded a new system, it was not to the satisfaction of the end users. Today and after nearly two years since the project has started, the conflict persists with management attempts to impose the solution and end-users putting up a lot of resistance to have their legacy software replaced.

SITUATION ANALYSIS

Nobody questioned the wisdom of GPS board of trustees and management when they made the decision to acquire a new integrated enterprise system to leverage improvement and move back to the leaders' quadrant among other peer schools. Unfortunately, the high expectations from this system were not met, the anticipated gains were not realized and this has led to cynicism among stakeholders and resistance by end-users.

An appraisal of the current status of the system in GPS has clearly indicated that the majority of the developed applications and functions were not behaving as they should. It was also evident that there was a genuine problem with the integration between the different functions which seem to be virtually isolated from each other although in real life they were inter-related and cross impacting. The audit indicated also that non-standard and alien concepts were used to attempt to link the Human Resources function with other functions. The concepts adopted in the design seem to have overlooked important requirements such as labor regulations and standards, which were not clearly reflected in the solution.

Looking back at how the system development experience has evolved in GPS can provide an insight to the issues involved and indications of where and why things went wrong and what are the lessons learned from the experience. Follows is an overview of the main events and highlights of this journey:

- The decision was made by GPS board of trustees and top management to embark on an important track to reinstate GPS ranking as a leader in the region, by adopting state of the art technology and information system to support all functions and processes and serve a community of users including school administration, teachers, parents, and students.
- A selection team was delegated to select the most suitable system to match GPS requirements and has the potential to leverage the sought improvements and business gains. The selection was influenced by management interference.
- The RFP addressed requirements at high level due to management pressure to expedite the commercial process.
- The commercial process did not include any competitive tendering as management pushed for a single source acquisition.
- The project was kicked-off with a message from the project manager that only 'one team' spirit will ensure the success of the project.
- The project was adopted a suitable development methodology and a roadmap and schedule were prepared to guide the development.
- The project facilities, infrastructure and development servers were not ready for the team to resume work in accordance with agreed schedule—leading to consultants working from vendor's office.
- Although designated members of the project, GPS has failed to release them for the project and attempted in occasions to replace them with juniors with limited knowledge.
- Vendor consultants—although members of the project on Full time basis—assigned other tasks in other projects by the vendor and not available when needed.
- Initially assigned vendor consultants were replaced by inexperienced junior consultants.
- Consultants were pressured to replicate the functionalities of the existing software.
- The disagreements and distrust between the vendor and the client have led to lose project cohesiveness and teamwork, leading to inadequate testing of developed applications and improper training of end-users.
- A negative environment had impacted all parties and potential end-users who were not engaged or made aware of the issues allowing rumors and gossip to profile the scene. No change management efforts by the project team.

- During the project life, four GPS senior staff lost their jobs as a result of mishandling of the project.
- GPS principal attempted to gain the confidence of end-users to start using the system—efforts failed.
- New principal and assistant manager spent a lot of time and exerted huge effort to correct the situation by identifying the gaps and ensure that the system supports all areas.
- Management attempts to persuade end-users of the potential value of the system to the organization and employees at all levels—this was met with huge resistance by the end-users.
- Management tried a firm approach to impose the system and create a status quo whereby the system applications were rolled-out, informing departments that it is management expectation that any transactions should be done in the system rather than manually or using legacy software.
- The poor performance and the unreliability of the system, which was frequently failing has left even a worse impression on the end users—consequently the situation was in dire straits and management failed to move forward with the system.
- The internal auditor attempted to use the agreement terms and conditions as a leeway for appealing to the end-users to accept to use the system—failed.
- There were all kind of contractual issues and conflicts between the vendor and the client, leading to an exchange of emails with accusations and blaming—creating a further rift between the two parties and impacting the project team.
- The decision to recruit a new specialist with main mission to review the problems associated with the new system in the organization and to do whatever is need to properly deploy the system and utilize it for the benefit of the school.
- The new specialist, experienced, clever, determined, stubborn, and focused—reviewed the history of project and the developed components of the system in the school—pin-pointed where he thought the project was mishandled—drew a roadmap and a strategy to move forward towards proper development, implementation, and utilization of the system.
- The specialist attempted to reach out to users and creating new channels of communication with all areas—consulted with different sections about their perception and views of the system and noted the pains and issues.
- The specialist, in consultation with end-users agreed to start with the Accounting and Payroll department as a high priority, and to ensure that the system is reconfigured to match the requirements with special attention to the workflow automation of the processes and avoiding any major customizations.

- The specialist also agreed with end-users that the configuration of both Accounting and Payroll applications will be followed by end-users testing and adequate training and also to ensure that all concerned sections managers and key end-users are involved.
- It was agreed that the configured and tested applications will be run as a pilot for few weeks after training the end-users. The approval of the developed applications would be decided only after good level of stabilization and utilization are observed and end-users acceptance is evident.
- It was also agreed that the same pilot approach would be applied to the rest of the applications within the scope of the development project.
- Despite the initial cynical attitudes of the accounting participants at the beginning and the pressures on the end-users to accept the new application, the outcome of phase one was not positive as the Payroll section leader refused to sign-off acceptance of the application and he voiced concerns that the system was not working in accordance with the current practices and is not as easy to use as the existing payroll software. This has instigated a huge debate questioning the suitability and value of the new system and was concluded with a major clash between the specialist and the payroll section leader leading to the resignation of the latter.
- The resignation of the payroll section leader prompted more dissatisfaction and negative feelings among end-users and the debate and discussions started to have personal aspects.
- On the insistence of the management to use the new system in place of the legacy software, which was switched off, the Payroll staff were raged and had to use the new system unwillingly and ineffectively in addition to creating an uneasy environment.

LESSONS LEARNED

Although GPS made the right decision seeming to use technology to leverage improvement, the journey was bumpy and the outcome has not met the high expectations and the sought gains. Following are some of the lessons learnt from this experience and which can be useful to GPS and other schools who might embark on a similar track:

The most important lesson learnt is that senior management should play a supportive role throughout the life cycle of the system (selection – development – post rollout).

Related to the selection phase, an important lesson learnt is to ensure that the selected system and vendor are the most suitable based on agreed criteria that incorporate a clear definition and prioritization of the required functionalities and features and also considering the technology itself and the compatibility, resilience, scalability and security features of the selected system. The selection team has to be resourced by knowledgeable representatives from all core areas. In addition, it is an important lesson that the selection should be viewed as a professional exercise and no management influence should be disturbing or interrupting the approach or the output.

Related to the acquisition phase an important lesson learnt is to include a number of potentials to ensure competitive tendering which bases the award on technical and commercial evaluation to ensure that the award goes to the most suitable system functionally, technically and financially and that the vendor is a proven expert with references of similar projects.

Related to the Initiation phase, the lesson learnt is to ensure that the project is not pre-maturely kicked-off and that all preparations are done specifically those related to project offices and development environment. It is very important to ensure that the project is intact by having all members of the team work together and to have regular communication with all parties.

Related to execution, it is important that design solution should reflect accurately the requirements of the client and that adequate testing is done prior to training and rollout. The system integration is very important and representatives from all inter-related functions should be involved in the review and testing of the systems. It is very important to reach out to users by creating communication channels and awareness sessions to keep them up to date with the system development and share the anticipated gains from the system to the school and all parties involved.

KEY TERMS AND DEFINITIONS

CSF: Critical Success Factor.
ERP: Enterprise Resource Planning Systems.
GPS: Gulf Private School.
RFP: Request for Proposal.
Waterfall: Development Methodology.

Chapter 9
Managing Knowledge and Change in GCC Project:
ERP End-User's Perspective

Fayez Albadri
ADMA-OPCO, UAE

Salam Abdallah
Abu Dhabi University, UAE

EXECUTIVE SUMMARY

The "End-Users" factor is singled out as the one of the most important ERP Critical Success Factors (CSF). It is evident from reported ERP failure cases that commonly used approaches to ERP end-users' "training and competency building" are inadequate and ineffective. The case reports on an alternative structured approach that was developed and adopted in GCC Project. The new approach redefines the traditional role of "ERP Training" from isolated project activities that aim to introduce end-users to "how-to" use applications to an integral component of a comprehensive "knowledge and change management" strategy that advocates a holistic life-cycle approach to managing ERP. The proposed approach, which was successfully adopted in GCC ERP project, was built around "end-user characterization" as the main input into "competency building." It is also flexible enough to plug into standard ERP methodologies and could be projected throughout the ERP life cycle. The end-users characterization and Competency Building Approach (ECB) is expected to contribute to increased business gains and return on investment as a result of boosting levels of ERP usage and utilization.

DOI: 10.4018/978-1-4666-2220-3.ch009

BACKGROUND: MANAGING IT PROJECTS

Organizations of all sizes, profits, or nonprofits have adopted one form or another of Enterprise Resource Planning (ERP) applications. ERP systems are increasingly becoming a business enabler for organizations to remain successful and competitive in this turbulent and networked environment. ERP systems are enterprise applications affecting many aspects of the organization both internally and externally. Therefore, successful ERP adoption and its effective usage and utilisation are critical to the success of the organization's performance and survival. ERP implementation can be viewed as an organizational transformation endeavours, it imposes socio-technical transformation of the organization, and it involves a large number of stakeholders who may influence the success or failure of an ERP project. Boonstra (2006) in his study on the influence of stakeholder on ERP implementation argues that stakeholders have different interpretation of ERP systems and this may lead to differences about priorities and ways of implementations. Stakeholders are affected by the previous experience, interests, self-images, and prospects and views.

A typical ERP application may consist of 1,000 modules and 10,000 application program (Steven, 1997). The cost for deploying an ERP can range from 3 million to one billion dollar depending on the company's size, and the implementation may last up to 4 years (Chen, 2001; Weston, 2001). ERP projects can take years to implement and like other IT projects they are subject to budget over-runs, delayed deliveries and as a fatal consequence falling short of meeting expectations or abandoning the project altogether. Trunick (1999) states that only 40 percent of ERP implementations are effective and 20 percent have been abandoned. Numbers of other studies have argued that ERP failures have been reported more than 50 percent and 60 to 90 percent are not performing as expected (Scheer & Habermmann, 2000; Sarker & Lee, 2003; Escalle, et al., 1999; Trunick, 1999; Ptak & Shragenhe, 1999; Soh, et al., 2000). No one seems to be immune from an ERP project failure, Dell for example; after two years, they have abandoned their ERP project because of incompatibility with their business model. Others, like FoxMeyer, did not have the time to abandon their ERP project instead they filed for bankruptcy in 1996 (Davenport, 1998).

Interestingly, most often managers view ERP projects failures as technical while in fact at 50% of the failures are attributed to people related issues such as resistance to change, lack of appropriate training, awareness, and / or understanding the organization culture. The organization culture is probably the most difficult hurdle in the implementation of an ERP since it involves a complex marriage between people personal values, habits, skills and the business processes and how staffs are viewed. Ward et al. (2005) argues that organizational issues during enterprise applications implementations are more difficult to resolve than the technical ones.

ERP research continued to attract practitioners and academics interest to determine ways to engineer successful ERP implementations. Research into ERP at any given time of its life cycle is considered including, evaluation of software, effective user training or determining critical success factors.

For a compilation of critical success factors, see Sherry and Martin (2007) for 26 categories of CSF grouped by either strategic or tactical. The most reported CSF is top management commitment support (strategic), change management (strategic), BPR and software configuration (tactical), training and job design (tactical). An overstressed issue in the ERP implementation is to view ERP project as a business rather than technical solution. Reasons for failure have been attributed to poor planning, lack of user involvement and training, delays, over budgets and lack of skills (Summer, 2000; Umble & Umble, 2002; Wright & Wright, 2002). Resistance to change is also another main contributor to project failures; a study of 186 companies that implement enterprise system revealed that the second most important contributor to project overruns is resistance to change and it is the fourth factors that limit successful systems adoption (Cook, et al., 1998).

The size of the organization also matters; Sanna et al. (2007) argue that different sizes of organizations should not be treated as one homogeneous group when constraints of ERP systems adoption are investigated.

From the literature review and the authors' experiences, we found that change management and training are important critical success factors in an ERP project and should they be appropriately attended to, they can resolve important common problems faced by ERP project. Unfortunately, although some organizations recognise the importance of end users' training, often many companies treat it as a single step activity in the overall ERP implementation project. The subject of 'ERP training and evaluation' is evidently an under researched area although there is a greater need for such studies since managers are always on the lookout for new easy approach to evaluate their successes.

TRAINING AND EVALUATION

As highlighted earlier in this chapter, ERP training is one of the major determinants of successful ERP implementation. Everybody recognizes the importance of ERP training to the end-users, however, when it comes to budget, it is usually neglected or cut when projects are overrun. This imposes a challenge on the training to find innovative ways to be more effective and efficient. In addition, to the large amount of ERP investments in terms of human and financial efforts, executives require evaluation of the success of the implemented systems. Although training is generally related to users' ability to use the ERP applications, a more comprehensive view of the subject considers 'people' issues, which are evident throughout the life cycle of ERP including (pre-implementation, implementation, and post implementation). It is clear that people issues are widely recognized as important yet they are inadequately addressed and lower in the priority list of the decision makers.

Implementation methodologies of ERP systems usually incorporate training as one of their components, often designed on the basis of instructor-led classroom training and delivered towards the conclusion of the project. We contend this approach to training is inadequate because it does not address all the relevant issues and are not effective in preparing users to adopt and make effective use of the system. There is a clear need to consider an alternative holistic approach that is more result-driven, user-focused solution and to provide users with the competencies needed to drive value in the organization investment.

ERP TRAINING IN THE CONTEXT OF UAE

Three main ERP training approaches have been identified in a review of 22 ERP projects implemented in the United Arab Emirates (UAE), between 1998 and 2004. The review included major organization in the Oil and Gas, Utility, and Manufacturing industries. The review indicated that they have used one of three main approaches to address users' preparedness for using the ERP system, namely: 1) the traditional HRD approach, 2) the ERP methodology-prescribed approach, and 3) an integrated ERP end-user characterization-based competency-building approach.

Traditional HRD Approach

The traditional Human Resources Development (HRD) approach is a simple, subjective, non-robust, conservative, instructor-led class type where users' training requirements are superficially validated at job description level to reach gaps and to justify training expenditure. The approach is virtually consistently limited in effectiveness and suitability to ERP projects. The approach is generally vulnerable to influence by internal business politics, usually in favor of high-ranking employees (management) without a proper established need. The approach is mainly concerned with the delivery of specific knowledge points without much consideration to users' perceptions and attitudinal behavioural.

ERP Methodology-Training Approach

This approach corresponds to the sum of training activities included as component of ERP implementation methodologies that are primarily concerned with preparing end-users to use and utilize the ERP applications and tools. Almost all ERP implementation methodologies have a dedicated end-user training component which may vary in scope and details to include end users' awareness and change management. Methodologies such as SAP's ASAP, Deloitte and Touch's FastTrack, Oracle's AIM, and IBM's PRACTICOM also define user training as a main project deliverable. There is a strong evidence from most ERP projects that have applied such training style that this instructor-led class, vendor designed and delivered training tend to lack in business depth and relevance in both content and business, often ill-timed and quality compromised due to project time and cost constraints. In many cases, the gain from this training is marginal warranting the need in many cases to be followed by refresher-training, coaching and 1-1 mentoring in the post roll-out.

End-User Characterization-Based Competency-Building Approach

This approach refers to a more holistic and creative approach that is more comprehensive in addressing end-users competencies including knowledge, perceptions and attitudinal behaviour to ensure end-users' awareness of the business value of the system, understanding of their role as end-users, and perceiving the system usefulness at both organizational and individual levels. This is achieved through active involvement and partnering with end-users to play an active role throughout the life-cycle of the ERP project staring with ERP selection in the pre-implementation phase, going through implementation phase and most importantly during the post-implementation phase. The approach is user-focused, flexible, and diversified in terms of instructional design, role of users as a SMEs, and usage of different technologies for delivery.

TRAINING CYCLE AND EVALUATION METHODS

The Training Cycle

There are numerous versions of training / learning cycle definition in the literature, however a typical cycle would include as a minimum the following processes: 1) Identification of Training Need (ITN), 2) design of training solutions, 3) delivery of training, 4) applications of training, and 5) evaluation of training solution.

1. **Identification of training needs:** This is the process of identifying training needs and requirements and the target audience (end-users). As early as this

stage the impact success criteria could be decided upon. The main outputs of this stage are answers to why the training is needed, what is the expected outcome of the training and its impact (How to measure whether the training meets the identified need).

2. **Design of training solutions:** This process covers the planning, design and development of relevant training material. It is important in this stage to ensure that the training design solution approach is consistently adopted. The training solution design may include different delivery techniques including conventional class training, coaching, or e-learning.

3. **Delivery of training solutions:** This process of the training cycle is concerned with the effectiveness of the training delivery to ensure success of the learning process and knowledge transfer. This will involve the selection of most appropriate format and methods to meet training needs.

4. **Application of training:** This is concerned with applying learning outcomes and ensuring learning reinforcement through practice. This is specifically relevant to monitoring and reviewing the progress of individual learners.

5. **Evaluation of training solutions:** This deals with the collection, analysis and presentation of information to establish improvement in performance that results from this. The evaluation and assessment of the learning program is used to introduce improvements.

The Iceberg Competency

Competency can be defined as the technical capability which enables people to deliver superior performance in a given job, role, or situation. Competency can be acquired through talent, experience, or training, which are, which are important and needed because they represent the best way to understand, observe and predict people's performance. Competencies are only valid if they are visible, accessible and are linked to meaningful life outcomes describing how people should perform (Hay Group, 2003).

Different levels and types of competencies are formed through individual and organization's knowledge, skills and abilities and provide a framework for measuring performance. The "iceberg" Competency model (Figure 1), shows proposed levels of competency illustrating that while some elements above the surface (technical / hard competencies) are identifiable, measurable and known to others, others (behavioural attitudinal competencies) are usually unknown to others, more difficult to detect and measure, yet of significant value (De Wit & Meter, 2004).

Figure 1. Iceberg competency model

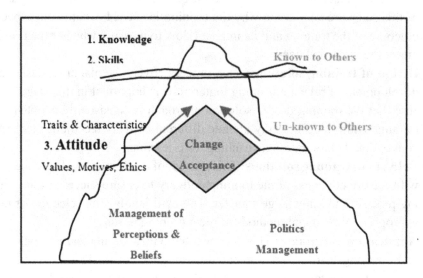

The competency iceberg model, at an individual level defines competency as a cluster of:

- **Knowledge:** Business processes, company policies.
- **Skills:** How to use system to make procure goods and services.
- **Attitude:** Behaviour, articulated perceptions (competitiveness, customer-focus).
- **Personal characteristics:** That influence job performance (carefulness, responsibility, ethics).

The Kirkpatrick Evaluation Model

Donald Kirkpatrick's Training Programs Evaluation Model is one of the most widely used and most popular models for the training evaluation. Although criticized, the four-level model is considered across training communities as an industry standard. The four levels of Kirkpatrick's evaluation model measure:

- Reaction of trainees (what they thought and felt about the training).
- Learning (The resulting increase in knowledge or capability).
- Behaviour (The extent of behaviour and capability improvement and implementation/application).
- Results (The effects on the business or environment resulting from the trainee's performance).

Table 1. Overview of Kirkpatrick's model

Level/ Evaluation type	Evaluation Description	Evaluation Tools and Methods	Relevance and Practicability
Level 1 Reaction	Gauges the trainees feelings about the training course and the learning experience	Feedback forms Verbal feedback post training surveys	Quick - Easy to obtain - Not expensive
Level 2 Learning	Measures the increase in the trainees knowledge	Assessments or tests before and after the training - interview or observation	Simple to set up; Easy for quantifiable skills - Less easy for complex learning
Level 3 Behaviour	Assesses the extent of applied learning on the job	Observation and Interview over time to; assess change, relevance of change, and sustainability of change	Measurement of changed behaviour Cooperation of line- managers
Level 4 Results	Estimate the impact on the business by the trainee	Measures are already in place via normal management systems and reporting - the challenge is to relate to the trainee	individually not difficult; unlike whole organisation Process must attribute clear accountabilities

These four levels should be applied comprehensively and together they should lead to meaningful learning evaluation within organization. Table 1 outlines the main characteristics of the four evaluation levels, provides examples of evaluation tools and comments on its relevance and practicability (Kirkpatrick, 1976).

The following section describes the case context and the components and features of the approach adopted by the Oil and Gas Company (GCC) to manage its ERP end-users characterization and competency building. The approach has its origins and theoretical underpinning in the relevant training cycle, competency model, and Kirkpatrick's Evaluation model all of which were defined and characterized in an earlier part of this chapter. The ERP End-User Characterization and Competency (ECB) approach was adopted by GCC as the vehicle to realize the sought business gains from the ERP system by systemically elevating end-users' knowledge, skills and attitudinal competencies leading to improved system acceptance and effective usage and utilization. In addition, in the following sections, we review the main components and features of the adopted approach (ECB) and review its results.

CASE STUDY: GCC COMPANY

The organization was a major oil producer and exporter company. Since its establishment, it had developed substantial business interests in all sectors of the Oil and Gas industries including exploration, production, and other products. The organization structure was composed of business and support services divisions. The business divisions were concerned with the areas of exploration, production, refining, and other services, whilst the support services divisions covered the areas of human resources, administration, finance, and management.

The organization embarked on a major project to replace its legacy system by state of the art integrated suite of ERP applications to support substantial part of the company's business function and processes. The selection of the system was reached after an extensive package evaluation carried out by a team of participants from different business areas.

The project's main goals included the establishment of a single centralized repository for assets, materials, and maintenance-related information and to utilize the best practice capabilities of the chosen system with minimum customization. The project duration was 12 months, with project procedures being derived from a standard ERP implementation methodology. The project major phases were analysis and requirements definition, design, development and implementation.

Alerted by reported ERP failures and recognizing the importance of the 'end-users' factor to the success of the ERP system in the company, senior management has approved the creation of a training advisory as part of ERP support team to specifically to manage end-users' issues throughout the life of the ERP system.

ECB Approach: Components and Features

The definition of the main components of the adopted model represent proven best practices and have their links as mentioned before to established theories and models pertinent to process change, learning and training evaluation. The ECB comprise the following components:

- Training and Change Management Strategy.
- **Training Cycle Processes:** Identification, Design, Delivery, Application, and Evaluation.
- **Training Programming:** Planning and Management.
- Training and Evaluation Tools and Methods.

The ECB approach was adopted to provide the mechanism and a guiding roadmap for planning and managing relevant programs to resolve ERP end-users' system acceptance, perception and knowledge issues in the post implementation phase which was anticipated to extend over 10-15 years. A summary of the main activities undertaken by the support team -guided by ECB is provided later on this section. The ECB approach had also adopted a number of quality attributes, namely, comprehensiveness, integration, continuity, diversification and reflective.

The attributes—described below—guided us also in designing the tools to deal with complex environment of ERP to ensure success in terms of system acceptance, usage, and utilization.

1. **Comprehensive (structured, modular and business aligned):** The ECB approach is not training methodology guiding the progress of training ERP end-users on how to use the new systems in isolation of the business strategic, tactical, and operational considerations. It is rather a comprehensive approach with components addressing important aspects pertaining to the 'human' component of ERP including end-users' perceptions, attitudes, knowledge gaps, and competencies, guided by a strategy with well defined objectives and goals, from different business perspectives; administrative, managerial and technical. It also sets clearly the roles and relationships between all involved parties.

2. **Integrated (integrates ERP planning, management, and control):** The ECB approach integrates training and competency building principles, concepts and practices tightly into the ERP planning and management. Standard training and competency building activities such as end-user characterization, training needs identification, content design, instructional design, instructional delivery and evaluation are woven into the planning, control, and management of ERP system.

3. **Continuous (applicable throughout the ERP Life-Cycle):** The ECB approach advocates continuity in managing end-user issues such as attitudes, perceptions, knowledge, and skills throughout the ERP life cycle, including: 1) ERP Pre-Implementation, 2) ERP Implementation Phase, and 3) ERP Post-Implementation Phase. Although the prime focus of the approach is mainly concerned with the ERP implementation phase but is also concerned with the links to the other two phases at both ends to ensure success is achieved. After all, the context of concern is to achieve the planned return on investment, which is outside the boundaries of the implementation phase.

4. **Diversified (adopts suitable methods, tools, and technologies):** The ECB approach is flexible in terms selecting methods, tools and technologies that are appropriate and fitting to the situation on hand considering: Target Audience, Business Culture, Organizations Specifics, ERP Environment, and the prevalent nature of the training subject. These include; instructor-led classroom training, online Web-based training, e-learning, computer based training, mentoring, coaching etc.

5. **Reflective (enter a learning cycle):** The ECB is systemic in approach where it attempts to learn from every action that has been taken in the process of the ERP implementation and attempt to learn and improve any future actions (Usually, conducted during formal and informal meetings).

The following describes the main ECB components, GCCs actions and the main results and deliverables.

ECB Component 1: Training and Change Management Strategy

GCCs Action: A strategy was formulated to address ERP end-user issues (in the post-implementation phase) at short, medium, and long term. The strategy highlighted the strategic nature of the ERP in the company and the criticality of the 'human' factor to the success of the ERP in the company and to the realization of business benefits and ROI. The strategy emphasized end-user characterization as the basis for competency building program. The strategy provided guidelines for the planning and management of training and change management programs. It has referred to the training development cycle, the evaluation methods and tools to implement and review the strategy and the associated programs. The strategy emphasized the alignment of the training strategy with the company's business goal. The strategy calls for the utilization of different types of training, coaching, mentoring, awareness and to utilize technology to achieve goals.

   Deliverables / Results: Strategy document was reviewed, updated, and approved by management.

ECB Component 2: Training Programming
– Planning and Management

GCCs Action: A training environment / facilities were created—a copy of the ERP production was setup to use for training purpose (without disrupting operations) in agreement with ITD to refresh on monthly basis. Special access accounts were arranged for use by trainees during the training and for post-training practice.

   A training coordinator assigned for administration of the training program and a representative from every business division to help in training analysis and in the nomination of trainees to different course. Training schedules were dispatched on monthly basis to divisions' representatives to nominate trainees for course. This network was also actively involved in site visits, divisional awareness sessions, and workshops. A training register was created, Different attendance, assessment forms, tests, questionnaires were prepared. Weekly and monthly reports formats were prepared.

   Deliverables / Results: Procedure, forms registers, schedules, programs, plans, reports, register, training ERP region

ECB Component 3.1: Training Cycle Processes – Identification, Design, Delivery, Application, and Evaluation

GCCs Action: The training cycle guided the end-user characterization and competency maps—and the identification of training needs through meetings and workshops involving management and ERP end-users. Subject Matter Experts from different business areas were designated to help in the content and instructional design (each course had a selling ERP awareness component, a business knowledge component and a step-by-step ERP application 'how-to' scenarios. Different training modules and courses were developed and copied on CDs rather than paper to give away. A number of competent resources from the support team were selected to use in a pool of trainees to deliver the training course. Quick Reference guides summarizing different training scenarios were deposited on the intranet and made accessible to all end-users—feedback assessment forms were used at the end of the training sessions to indicate trainees reaction and feeling about the course, the instructor, the material, and the training environment—pre-training and post-training test were also used to gauge level of knowledge. Regular evaluation and review of the training course content and duration were made on basis of trainees' feedback and reactions.

ECB Component 3.2: Change Management

GCCs Action: End-users attitudinal behaviour and perceptions related programs: awareness programs—site visits—newsletter—use different media for awareness—certification—rewards—motives—management support.

Deliverables / Results: Training material for different course—Web-accessible quick-reference—Guide—Assessment forms—Pre-training tests—Post-training tests—Evaluation forms—Reports.

ECB Component 4: Training and Evaluation Tools and Methods

GCCs Action: Instructor-led classes—Coaching, Mentoring, 1-1 management sessions, Train-the-Trainer, Computer Based Training, Recorded training macros, E-Learning, Web-based classes.

Deliverables / Results: Classes, training scenarios recorded macros—Web guides—Trainees feedback assessments—Questionnaires—Interviews—Online survey—Tests—Certifications Rewards—Motives.

Use of different evaluation methods and tools.

ECB-BASED TRAINING AND CHANGE
MANAGEMENT PROGRAMS AT GCC

Three years into the post-rollout stage of the ERP system in GCC, the support team has successfully contributed to improve end-users' attitudes, perception, and acceptance of the ERP applications leading to improved levels of system applications usage and utilization. Following is a summarized list of outcomes providing evidence of tangible positive resulting from the adopted approach. In addition, they may be viewed as performance indicators:

- **ECB Component 1:** Training and Change Management Strategy.
  - **Achievement:** The training and change management strategy (revised version 3) has successfully ensured the alignment of the programs to the business goals and has provided guidelines to the quality, standards and best practice processes used in the implementation of the training approach. Numerous quick reference guides are deposited on the Web and are accessible by end-users through the Web.
- **ECB Component 2:** Training Programming – Planning and Management.
  - **Achievement:** Skills were audited participants—End-users reactions and perceptions consolidated in a database and regularly analysed and acted upon.
- **ECB Component 3:** Training Cycle Processes.
  - **Achievement:** An elaborated end-user characterization is used as basis for the competency building programs.
- **ECB Component 4:** Training Evaluation Tools and Methods.
  - **Achievement:**
    - A foundation ERP training course and ten different specialized courses were designed, developed, delivered, and regularly modified based on end-users reactions and feedback (exclusively internal resources).
    - Several training scenarios were on recorded macros accessible to trainees.
    - Nearly 1400 trainees attended a total of 150 training sessions both on-site and off-site.
    - Nearly 30 'ERP Monitor' management reports and bulletins were issued with awareness messages, ERP knowledge tips, and ERP news reaching out to hundreds of end-users.
    - The trainees' feedback: 56% very good, 40% good, 4% average, 0% poor.

- Coaching and Train-the Trainer incorporated to complement formal classes.
- E-Learning feasibility study started and is planned for 2009.
- Pre-training and Post-training tests regularly used to evaluate the effectiveness of training.
- A major on-line survey of two parts: 1) to gauge end-users perceptions by answering 20 multiple questions, 2) to pinpoint knowledge weaknesses was implemented and results discussed with management and divisions.
- End-user audit including key users was conducted to observe the ability of trained users to transform their knowledge gain (by training) to action (use of the system application). This has helped us introducing more hands on practice additions to the training courses as well as 1-1 coaching.
- Survey results indicated increased end-user acceptance specifically among younger employees and those who attended training. Nearly 60% of participants are happy with the system, 15% unhappy, and 25% undecided. Suitable actions have been agreed for each of the groups.
- The knowledge tests provide clear evidence that those who attended training have higher results indicating the effectiveness of the training strategy and programs.
- The ERP support team has presented the survey findings to management who requested that the team launch a divisional awareness campaign to share the findings of the survey and agree jointly on suitable actions.
- Initial sessions of the awareness campaign (including four main divisions) indicate clear success in reaching out to users community, creating a positive environment of partnering and agreeing action for improvement including the introduction of management commitment for a rewarding program and certification.

CONCLUSION

It is clear that the adopted approach (ECB) through its structured, comprehensive, integrated approach has provided a useful integral framework for implementing a successful ERP end-users competency-building program with positive outcome. Considering the flexibility of the associated processes, the business relevance of the programs and the tangible gains accomplished through the exclusive use of internal company resources, it is suggested that such an approach can add real value to the outcome should it be adopted by organizations embarking on new ERP implementations.

Future research may offer the opportunity to have an elaborated investigation of the ECB approach to refine its components and features to validate its potential as a proven module that can be plugged onto standard ERP Implementation methodologies.

REFERENCES

Boonstra, A. (2006). Interpreting an ERP – Implementation project form a stakeholder perspective. *International Journal of Project Management, 24*, 38–52. doi:10.1016/j.ijproman.2005.06.003

Chen, L. J. (2001). Planning for ERP systems: Analysis and future trends. *Business Process Management Journal, 7*(5), 67–77. doi:10.1108/14637150110406768

Cook, Dudley, & Peterson. (1998). *SAP implementation: Strategy and results*. New York, NY: The Conference Board.

Davenport, T. H. (1998). Putting the enterprise into the enterprise systems. *Harvard Business Review, 76*(4), 121–131.

De Wit, B., & Meyer, R. (2004). *Strategy: Process, content and context*. New York, NY: Thomson Learning.

Escalle, C. X., Cotteleer, M. J., & Austin, R. D. (1999). *Enterprise resource planning (ERP). Technology Note*. Boston, MA: Harvard Business School Publishing.

Finney, S., & Corbett, M. (2007). ERP implementation: A complication and analysis of critical success factors. *Business Process Management Journal, 13*(3), 329–347. doi:10.1108/14637150710752272

Hay-Group. (2003). *High competencies to identify high performers: An overview of basics*. Working Paper. Retrieved Nov 2008 from http://www.haygroup.com/Downloads/uk/misc/Competencies_and_high_performance.pdf

Kirkpatrick, D. L. (1997). Evaluation of training. In Craig, R. L. (Ed.), *Training and Development Handbook: A Guide to Human Resource Development*. New York, NY: McGraw Hill.

Laukkanen, S., Sarpola, S., & Hallikainen, P. (2007). Enterprise size matters: Objectives and constraints of ERP adoption. *Journal of Enterprise Information Management, 20*(3), 319–334. doi:10.1108/17410390710740763

Ptak, C. A., & Schragenheim, E. (1999). *ERP: Tools technologies, and applications for integrating the supply chain.* Boca Raton, FL: CRC Press.

Sarker, S., & Lee, A. S. (2003). Using a case study to test the role of three key social enablers in ERP implementation. *Information & Management, 40,* 813–829. doi:10.1016/S0378-7206(02)00103-9

Scheer, A. W., & Habermann, F. (2000). Making ERP a success. *Communications of the ACM, 43*(4), 57–61. doi:10.1145/332051.332073

Soh, C., Kien, S. S., & Tay Yap, J. (2000). Culture fits and misfits: Is ERP a universal solution? *Communications of the ACM, 43*(4), 47–51. doi:10.1145/332051.332070

Stevens, T. (1997). Kodak focuses on ERP. *Industry Week, 246*(15), 130–133.

Summer, M. (2000). Risk factors in enterprise-wide/ERP projects. *Journal of Information Technology, 15*(4), 317–327. doi:10.1080/02683960010009079

Trunick, P. A. (1999). ERP: Promise or pipe dream? *Transportation & Distribution, 40*(1), 23–26.

Umble, E. J., & Umble, M. M. (2002). Avoiding (ERP) implementation failure. *Industrial Management (Des Plaines), 44*(1), 25–33.

War, J., Hemingway, C., & Daniel, E. (2005). A framework for addressing the organizational issues of enterprise systems implementation. *Strategic Information Systems, 14,* 97–119. doi:10.1016/j.jsis.2005.04.005

Weston, F. C. Jr. (2001). ERP implementation and project management. *Production and Inventory Management Journal, 43*(3), 75–80.

Wright, S., & Wight, A. M. (2000). Information systems assurance for enterprises resources planning systems: Implementation and unique risk consideration. *Journal of Information Systems, 16,* 99–113. doi:10.2308/jis.2002.16.s-1.99

KEY TERMS AND DEFINITIONS

AIM: ERP Implementation Methodology by Oracle Co.
ASAP: ERP Implementation Methodology by SAP Co.
BPR: Business Process Re-Engineering.
ECB: End Users Competency Building Model.
ERP: Enterprise Resource Planning.
FastTrack: Deloitte and Touch ERP Implementation Methodology.

GCC: Gulf Council Countries.
HRD: Human Resources Division.
ITD: Information Technology Division.
ITN: Identification of Training Need.
PRACTICOM: EIS Implementation Methodology by PSDI.
UAE: United Arab Emirates.

Chapter 10
Effective Implementation and Utilization of CMMS System:
Challenges and Solutions

Ali Sartawi
ZADCO, UAE

EXECUTIVE SUMMARY

Computerized Maintenance Management Systems (CMMS) are designed to manage asset maintenance in a professional manner, by means of integrating all related transactions (financial, material, purchasing) and maintenance activities (work requests, work orders) and converting them into high level information to drive users towards best practices and optimize cost and improve asset reliability. However, CMMS will only remain a tool with limited use unless proper attention is given to dynamic data feeding by end-users to build up a reliable asset maintenance history that can be used as a basis for managing assets over the life cycle. This investigation reflects on the challenges encountered in the cases of three UAE CMMS Projects, comparing the effectiveness and suitability of the dynamic data-feeding strategies and approaches adopted in the three cases and the level of business improvement through proper usage and utilization.

DOI: 10.4018/978-1-4666-2220-3.ch010

ORGANIZATION BACKGROUND

Abu Dhabi Water and Electricity Authority (ADWEA)

ADWEA is a government organization established in 1999 to implement the long term privatization program of the water and electricity sector on the basis of BOO "Build – Operate – Own" formula, designed according to the partnership agreement made between ADWEA and a number of international companies. ADWEA holds a 60% share of these, while 40% ownership is held by the foreign investor. In accordance with long-term arrangements IWPP's are committed to sell their production to ADWEC. Some of these international companies are:

- **Emirates CMS Power Company (ECPC):** The company operates a generation and desalination plant at the Al Taweelah site identified as "A2" of licensed capacities 710 MW electricity and 50 migd water.
- **Gulf Total Tractebel Power Company (GTTPC):** The company operates a generation and desalination plant at the Al Taweelah site identified as "A1" with licensed capacities 1350 MW electricity and 84 migd water. The 40% investors' ownership is shared equally between two international companies, Total Fina Elf and Tractebel.
- **Shuweihat CMS International Power Company (SCIPCO):** The company has been established to BOO a power generation and water desalination facility at Jebel Dhana, near Shuweihat, with licensed capacities of 1,500 MW and 100 migd. CMS owns 20% and International Power owns 20%.
- **Arabian Power Company (APCO):** APC, a private joint stock company, operates and maintains existing power generation and water desalination plants as well as BOO additional production capacity at Umm Al Nar. The licensed capacities are 2,200 MW and 160 MIGD, International Power owns 20%, Tokyo Electricity owns 14%, and Mitsui owns 6%.
- **Fujairah Asia Power Company (FAPCO)—F2:** FAPCO is the second company licensed to operate in Qadfaa at Fujairah with a capacity of 2000 MW of power and desalinates 100 MIGD of water in addition to 30 MIGD of potable water produced by reverse osmosis technology.
- **Shuweihat S2 Power Project:** ADWEA owned power plant, still under construction with anticipated production of 1600 MW of power and 100 MIGD of water. Expected completion on 2011/2012.
- **Emirates SembCorp Water and Power Company (ESWPC)—F1:** It is located at Qadfaa in Fujairah. The company produces 861MW of power and 100 MIGD of desalinated water. The majority of the water is being transferred to Abu Dhabi through a pipeline owned and operated by TRANSCO.

- **TAPCO-Taweelah Asia Power Company:** TAPCO became ADWEA's partner in 2005 owning 40% of the shares, the company operates and maintains existing plant (B and B-Ext). The Initial B Plant was commissioned between 1995 and 1997 with net power capacity of 619.9 MW and water capacity of 69.1 MIGD. An extension plant was constructed and completed by year 2001 with net power generation capacity of 308.3 MW and a net water production capacity of 22.5 MIGD, New B2 power plant has also been constructed under BOO license and commissioned in 2007 with net power capacity of 1000 MW and water production capacity of 60 MIGD.

Zakum Development Company (ZADCO)

In November 1977, Sheikh Zayed Bin Sultan Al Nahyan, promulgated Law No.9 for 1977 incorporating Zakum Development Company (ZADCO) to develop and operate the Upper Zakum fields.

The development of the Upper Zakum reservoir is considered as one of the major technical achievement in Abu Dhabi. As a result of ZADCO's continuous efforts exerted during the early years, the first shipment of Upper Zakum crude oil was exported on the tanker "Al-Ain" on 24th May 1983 marking a significant achievement in the company's progress. In April 1988, ADNOC decided to merge the operations of Umm Al Dalkh Development Company (UDECO), which was established in 1978, with ZADCO's operations in order to rationalize operations, avoid duplication of functions, and reduce cost. ZADCO Management has taken major steps in this respect, which resulted in the physical merger of the two companies. In May 2000, an Assets-Based-Organization structured was reformed which has in many areas changed the ways business has been run for more than two decades. Under the new organization, three Business Units were established, namely, Upper Zakum, Satah and Umm Al-Dalkh, and Zirku, in addition to two other Support Units, Technical and Operational Resources, and General Support Services that provide back-up to the three Business Units.

SETTING THE STAGE

Regional companies had been practicing businesses with brainstorming processes dominated by cultural thinking. In the last decay of the 20th century, some companies start to look for some management software as computers become within reach of individuals. The advantage of implementing management programs is to facilitate transparency, knowledge sharing, streamlining practices, and to retain skilled experiences within companies to be transferred from one generation to another. Moreover, management tools will enhance performance and optimize cost by maintaining bank data of high quality and implementing advance processes with transparency and control.

Management software developer have moved into the international market which later become a very tough competition between different providers due to growing demand and global inputs and investment in this type of technology.

Clients have also become more tempted to follow the technology advancement and to move forward towards best practice. It is now almost un-avoidable. There are many different management software applications for different business types, banking, accounting, stores, government departments, transportations, Oil and Gas producers, power (conventional and non-conventional) companies, etc.

Management systems are also considered to be a very powerful tool for security control and authority levels, as technology advances, Web-based management systems can be accessed from any spot on earth where Internet facility available.

Management systems have become strategic option for the majority of organizations to enhance their business performance. Upgrading existing versions to latest ones are also part of their strategies.

ADNOC (Abu Dhabi Oil Company) and its group companies in the oil and gas industry were the leaders in adopting management systems, this was initiated in the mid nineties, by 1999 ZADCO and other O&G companies have implemented their first management systems. MAXIMO, SAP, and PASPORT were the available systems in the market.

ZADCO had opted for MAXIMO (version 4.1.1). After few years, ZADCO decided to upgrade MAXIMO and had initiated a feasible study to evaluate the new versions and the added value. In February 2009, MAXIMO 6.2 (Oil and Gas Version) was launched. Further upgrades will be in due time and when decided by the company.

ADWEA was the next organization to invest in management system, they also opted for MAXIMO 4.1.1.

Project started in May 2000. Since ADWEA and its group companies had just been newly established, the project was centralized at ADWEA with link connections to its companies. First MAXIMO go-live was at ADWEA head quarters in July 2001, then Taweelah power company in Aug. 2001. By summer 2002 ADWEA group companies had MAXIMO up and running.

In 2005, MAXIMO 4.1.1 was upgraded to MAXIMO 5.2. Some of ADWEA companies were not part of the upgrade as they were already privatized and became independents like Umm Al Nar and Taweelah.

Five years later in 2010 another upgrade to Maximi7 was launched.

TAPCO had taken independent course since became private in May 2005. The company had inherited MAXIMO 4.1.1 from ADWEA but it had shown no willingness to follow ADWEA upgrade program.

TAPCO continued holding on MAXIMO 4.1.1 until MAXIMO 6 was released in 2006. The company had the upgrade to MAXIMO 6, which was launched in July 2006.

All above mentioned and other organizations can no longer avoid catching up with management systems developments and upgrades as it becomes a core element in any company's business management.

CASE DESCRIPTION

This part will be focusing on the projects and implantation cases of CMMS (Computerized Maintenance Management System). MAXIMO with its different versions and different clients was the main software implantation in which I have been deeply.

1. First project was in year 2000, for power and water sector, the project duration was 16 months. I was project team member in certain discipline (MAXIMO 4.1.1).
2. Second project was an upgrade to two higher versions (MAXIMO 6). The project duration was 4 months. I was deputy project manager.
3. Third project was also an upgrade, but for Oil and Gas organization. Project duration was 12 months. I was leading the maintenance team.

It is worth mentioning that field experience in maintenance and operation is quite vital in delivering successful project output. Other additional experiences will be an advantage.

Potential Challenges

Pre-Project Phase

When CMMS systems were first released, organization did not have clear vision of how much value such systems will add as a return for investments.

This led to the following challenges:

*   Weak scope of work.
*   Weak risk assessment.
*   Many concerns raised by both teams (Consultant and Client).

- Project duration was vulnerable to changes.
- Planned budget could not be accurate.
- Lack of reference examples.
- Setting up project team organization chart.

Project Phase

After project kickoff, some challenges could also be anticipated, including:

- Lack of awareness among the working team members of the main objectives of the project.
- Unclear road map of the project to the team members.
- Lack of CMMS concept.
- Lack of computer skills among some of the project team.
- Difficulties in allocating asset and plant technical information.
- Seeking support from site personnel to facilitate office document.

Implantation Phase

After go-live, more challenges were faced, including:

- The transformation to the new management tool.
- Users' resistance to change; most users by nature wish to stick to the way they are used to.
- Initial implementation functional malfunctions.
- Data integrity issues which had to be fixed after system go-line.
- Users and their access rights; some signature security profiles were to be reviewed.
- IT and networking issues: PCs configurations, connections.
- Change in culture and practices were the most lasting challenges the implementation and support teams are struggling with.

CURRENT CHALLENGES FACING THE ORGANIZATION

As mentioned previously, culture and the need for change in practice were the long-term challenge for the support team:

- Users are still keeping some vital data outside CMMS.
- Usage of the system is still at or even below acceptable level.

- Lack of awareness and the un-willingness to learn among some users.
- Poor concept understanding.
- Raising criticism and the tendency among some users to demote the system.
- Poor data (dynamic) quality due to feedback weakness by end user.
- Benefits and values of using the system are being felt and acknowledged by users.

Obstacles for Successful Utilization of CMMS

In the last upgrade to Maximo 6.2, our company top management had given strong construction to the project team to eliminate all customization, which was heavily applied in previous version. This scope has resulted in applying more configurations and change of practice, which was the most challenging task, many processes were reviewed by concerned teams, and alternative functionalities were presented, new approach for record creation and processing.

For commercial chain applications (purchasing and procurement), the company has applied many security controls on the application cycles which requires a lot of restrictions, validations and configurations by IT and the support team to be applied on the system, these requirements effected the system performance and its popularity among users.

In terms of users' feedback, users are still looking for shortcuts to close records with the mandatory information required, even though they can give more valuable input. This will have an impact on the data quality and KPIs (Key Performance Indicators) outputs.

IT, company IT department should have the proper hardware and networking infrastructure compatible with the CMMS software; moreover, IT should have the in-hose competency to manage and maintain the system reliability.

CMMS Best Practices Survey and Chronic Obstacles

Tour visits to sites' by users, mainly maintenance, were made to have face-to-face discussions and to highlight their concerns. The result of the discussions has clearly shown the following:

1. Lack of awareness in the MAXIMO features and very poor understanding in the application concepts. For example, users could not differentiate between different record's types and their relations. Work Order (WO) application is the main driver and the core of all maintenance activities, users could not differentiate between WO relationship types, understanding WO records relations

will definitely make maintenance users aware why and when they should create the right type of WO which will pour into better calculation of the reliability and availability of an asset. The relationship types are, Main WO, Child WO, Follow up WO, and Task WO.

2. Lack of awareness on the concept of an asset number and an asset location tag. This was a big confusion for them in tracking a particular asset.

3. Failure reporting was not very clear for the users; they totally undermined the importance of a proper selection and explanation of problem, cause, and remedy of experienced failures.

4. Lack of awareness on the procurement application sequence and their association with maintenance activities.

5. Lack of awareness on the concept of management systems CMMS in general. Users were treating MAXIMO as document processing platform where history data analysis was never utilized; only records' references were used.

6. Traditional communication means between users (all levels) is still dominating; it means that users were not using the CMMS—MAXIMO—as their main source of information and progress tracking. This has had a huge impact on the real time update of dynamic data and the quality of feedback, as users believe that none will need to see their input. In addition, this was and still is the most damaging attitude by users and must be changed. The change should be top-down driven with regular monitoring on data quality.

SOLUTIONS AND RECOMMENDATIONS

Based on the above findings, certain corrective measures are recommended as a solution to the chronic obstacles towards better utilization, best practice, and data quality enhancement.

Project Phase

*   Very professional team set up prior to implanting cmms to define a good scope.
*   Mature requirements and processes are to be in place as part of project implementation.
*   Deeper involvement of users' representatives (focal points) in the implementation.
*   Implantation team must lead the decision making while end-users" representatives would address their requirements and their practice needs.

- Minimize customization to near zero value, and move to standard features as this will help improving practice and hence business performance.
- Maximize training programs to cover as many users as you could.
- Management support to apply positive changes is vital.

Rollout Phase

- Proper effective campaign for CMMS MAXIMO go-live.
- Comprehensive roll-out plan with key support team members on call.

Post Go-Live Phase

- Dedicated support team member at each site for hand on support.
- Very professional business support team to utilize CMMS for best practice.
- Business team is to be accompanied with efficient technical members.
- IT support and prompt response to system issues is vital for buy in by users.
- Business practice enhancement and user role must be promoted.
- Continuous face-to-face contact with end users is quite essential.
- Educating users on how to improve performance and their input to enhance data quality.
- To continuously promote CMMS as the mean tool for driving the company business and for data enrichment to be a very fruitful source of information.
- Follow up and monitoring exercise to push utilization and data update is very much recommended.
- Define and develop business KPIs and benchmarking for continuous improvement and cost optimization.

CMMS Data Enhancement

Generally, all management systems are founded on two types of data, static and dynamic. The static data refers to all company assets information and details and defining the organization's policy and processes. The dynamic data is the data inserted, created, or entered in the system by end users as a result of their day to day activities.

For best implementation of the maintenance management systems, organizations must establish the following:

- **Maintenance Policy:** Which lays down the organization's guidelines, objectives, and compliance.

- **Maintenance Strategy:** Which defines the organization's maintenance philosophy.
- **Asset Hierarchy:** To be developed on parent child relation based on field process.
- **Asset Criticality:** To be defined on equipment /system level based their function.
- **Job Plan:** Which defines the procedure and tasks to be carried out on each asset.
- **Spares and Material:** All required spares and material must be cataloged and registered.

Maintenance Policy

The maintenance policy manual provides the principal guidelines for the management of maintenance activities for an organization. The document is a reference for the company's maintenance organisation, for use by the management and staff that forms the basis for determining the strategy and processes associated with implementing maintenance activities in a uniform and consistent manner. The maintenance policy manual also provides the organization, roles and responsibilities, and guidance necessary to ensure that all company facilities continue to function, as prescribed by their original design and for their planned life cycle. It also ensures that the maintenance activities carried out support the safe and efficient operation of the facilities.

Details are also provided for the individual and departmental responsibilities associated with the overall process of maintaining the systems, equipment, and procedures, which are essential parts of the maintenance management of the company facilities. The manual is considered as a living document, its issue and contents being controlled and updated as changes in safety, business or operational requirements dictate. The objective of maintenance policy is to maintain all company assets in a safe, effective and efficient manner while fully complying with organization's regulations and state legislation, without jeopardizing any asset technical integrity over its entire life cycle.

Maintenance Strategy

The maintenance strategy is the management method used in order to achieve the maintenance objectives. It is to define the principle and maintenance techniques to be applied on every asset based on its function and criticality within the process. The more critical the asset is, the more attention it is given. High critical assets must be well maintained to ensure their availability and reliability to safe guard the production line. Specific tasks with special tools and certified personnel may be required.

Asset Hierarchy

To define the methodology that shall be employed during the construction of the MAXIMO Location Hierarchy. This methodology must be employed when adding new locations to the database, to determine the parent of the new entry correctly and maintain the integrity of the location hierarchy.

The development of a structured equipment hierarchy, based on the ISO 14224 standard, is essential for the efficient operation of CMMS. The benefits of an effective hierarchy in CMMS can be summarized as follows:

- The locations table within the system provides the framework for many of the functions within the system. The structuring of the location records within the database in a logical manner is essential to the efficient and effective operation of various elements of the maintenance management system.
- The hierarchy enables both preventative and corrective maintenance activities to be scheduled (PM) and recorded (Work Order) at suitable levels in the hierarchy to assist in the execution, reporting monitoring and management of the maintenance activities.
- The hierarchal structure enables reports to be produced at various levels, i.e. installation, system, package, equipment unit, etc., to enable management to monitor performance and costs such as:
  - Unit Maintenance Cost.
  - Estimated versus Actual Costs.
  - Planned versus Corrective Maintenance.

When a location (tag) is entered into the MAXIMO database, it must be assigned to a parent to indicate its position within the hierarchal structure for the business unit and assets. As each location and its parent are entered into MAXIMO a structured hierarchy is created. For this reason, it is essential that the correct and consistent definition of the parent is employed when producing the hierarchy that meets the requirements of production, operations and maintenance (see Figure 1).

Asset Criticality

All assets/equipment are classified into a relevant maintenance and inspection criticality category, according to their primary function, with respect to company business, operational, safety, and environmental objectives. The equipment critical-

Figure 1. ISO 14224 hierarchy structure

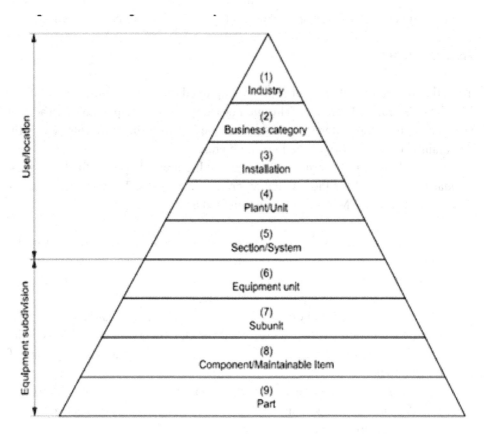

ity classification criteria must be applied and adhered to, as this will influence how the equipment would be maintained and will also determine the company's spares and inventory stocking policy for the equipment. The criticality classification for all equipment and systems shall be aligned with the company CRITICALITY MATRIX.

Four criticality categories, (defined below), shall be assigned to each specific piece of equipment in the system:

- **HSECES: (Highest criticality):** Catastrophic and Major
- **VITAL: (2nd highest criticality):** Big loss in business/production (value is defined by company)
- **ESSENTIAL: (Normal criticality):** Moderate and Minor to business
- **AUXILIARY: (Low criticality):** Insignificant

Figure 2. Criticality ranking procedure

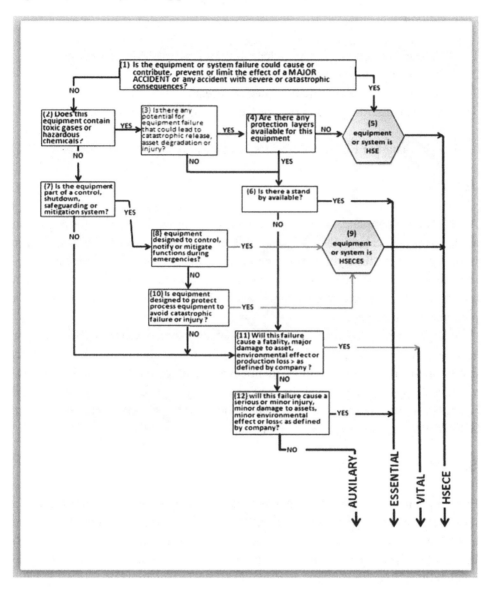

The criticality will be used to determine the equipment's maintenance strategy and accordingly its specific maintenance regime. Vital is prioritised over essential is prioritised over auxiliary. It will also determine the prioritization of work carried out on Facilities equipment and also the associated re-ordering and stock inventory policy for spare parts.

Criticality ranking will be reviewed and revised as necessary under the following conditions:

1. A change in Operating parameters and / or Potential Production rate.
2. Changes in environmental legislation.
3. Addition of new equipment or process stream.
4. Any increase /decrease in the consequence of failure (based on history).

The flow chart in Figure 2 describes the criticality ranking procedure.

Job Plan

A job plan is a template, with detailed description of work to be performed on an asset, item, or location. If you use job plans you do not have to enter the same information every time you want to carry out similar work. A job plan can be applied to an unlimited number of similar or recurrent work. When you use a job plan on a work order, its resource estimates and tasks are copied into a work plan as a procedure for the executer.

Job plans with predefined tasks and resources (labor, material, items, tools, or services) can be applied on all identical assets. Special attention or specific tasks can be applicable to some of those identical assets based on their function, the environment they operate in, and the time period they run are kept in service. When job plan template is used, changes and modifications can be made in the work order without affecting the original job plan template.

Spares and Material

Every organization performing maintenance and operation (O&M) must develop their own inventory to maintain certain level of stock material and spares to be available instantly when required as procurement and delivery may cause delay and hence affect the business revenue. Stocking material must be balanced to serve the availability of operating assets, overstocking is never recommended, as it will have negative financial impact on the organization.

Materials and Inventory Team will significantly contribute in minimizing inventory and reducing waste whilst ordering and carrying the correct materials for stock to maximize production efficient and service levels to all business units. The inventory team objectives are summarized as follows:

- To limit the range of stock items to the minimum necessary to ensure efficient operation of the business. In addition, to limit the value of stock items to the optimum for efficient business operations by striking a balance between carrying costs, order preparation cost and stock out costs. Ultimately, optimize the stock holding without jeopardizing the operations.
- To achieve a high degree of material consumer satisfaction in providing the stock materials and inventory—to the correct specification and quality and in time and thus achieving 99.5% service level.
- To contribute to the reducing in procurement cycle time in the total supply chain, by covering over 80% of stock purchases via Supply / Purchase Agreements.
- Enhance and develop CMMS functionality and reports so as to assist inventory team and the consumer in their business in so far as Materials and Inventory are concerned.
- Ensure that the newly purchased materials / equipment shall conform to the technical requirements of the Purchase Order specifications and good engineering practice so that customer demands are satisfied.
- Ensure to add value in every process related to the Materials and Inventory and proactively manage the Company Inventory.

All above mentioned enhancements of static data, in addition to predefined organization's processes and procedures are considered to be the core elements to implement Computerized Maintenance Management System (CMMS) in an efficient manner.

Work Management

CMMS is equipped with all necessary applications, facilities, and features to enable an organization to perform its maintenance activity in an optimized efficient method.

Most CMMS packages have some configuration or customization flexibilities to allow clients to comply with their cultural, country and regional rules and legislations.

All maintenance activities conducted in an organization shall be controlled and managed via an associated CMMS record (Work Order). Work Orders provide the means of identifying the work required, the resources required to complete that work and the equipment status required to enable the work to go ahead.

The Work Order is also the conduit to enable maintenance planning and scheduling activities as a suitably prepared Work Order contains details of all resources, spare parts, special tools, labor hours, and durations.

Effective Work Order management is therefore a cornerstone of successful maintenance management.

Figure 3. Maintenance overview

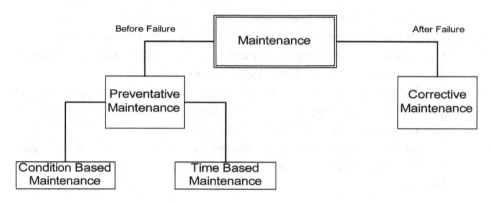

Work Orders mainly come under two types, Planned Maintenance (PM) and Corrective Maintenance (CM). Each type will follow different process. Maintenance overview is illustrated in Figure 3.

PM work orders have predefined tasks and resources with compliance window during which the work can be scheduled, they can still be rescheduled if the situation or process dictates. Whereas CM work orders may have to be scheduled as per their priorities.

The work priority is determined by the asset criticality and reason for work. To systemize the priority ranking, organization should develop its own priority matrix. Figure 4 is an example.

Corrective Maintenance refers to work where failure has already occurred, even CM is classified into different categories, some type failures which equipment can live with for sometimes (low priority) till work is planned, second types may force maintenance to act within short time, third type may require immediate response

Figure 4. Priority matrix

Work Priority Matrix									
PRIORITY CLASSES OF MAINTENANCE WORK									
CLASS									
Asset Criticality	Immediate Danger to life & Health	Environment Safety	Safety	Breakdown	Predictive & Preventive	Corrective & Nuisances	Process Improvement Minor Safety	Minor maintenance (Grees,Paint)	House Keeping (Cleaning)
	9	8	7	6	5	4	3	2	1
4	A	A	A	A	B	B	B	C	C
3	A	A	A	A	B	B	B	C	C
2	A	B	B	B	B	C	C	C	C
1	A	B	B	B	NA	C	C	C	C

Priority A	Priority B	Priority C
(7 Days)	(30 Days)	(60 Days)

176

by maintenance especially if it causes safety threats or jeopardize the production line or unbalance the process, this is called Break Down (BK) or it may be classified as Emergency (EM). In such cases, all preparation formalities are skipped until after the situation is restored.

Different types of work have different procedures and preparation steps. PM type comes as a result of forecast for all assets due for maintenance, some factors are reviewed before PM jobs are scheduled, availability of manpower, availability of materials, tools, and outsource services if required; if all resources are made available, one more factor must be considered by operation which is the possibility of releasing the equipment/system/plants (i.e. shut down and isolation). Process and production line have higher priority providing assets lives are not at risks. PM work order will be generated in the CMMS having all the steps/tasks to be carried out with all required resources predefined. Maintenance team will have to follow the instructions, process the work order record through status change to reflect the work condition in the field and to give their feed back where appropriate.

For CM work type, work priority (urgency) and the possible release of asset from the process to execute the work will dictate the work schedule. Work instructions in the form of tasks with duration should be developed by maintenance engineer/ supervisor to the best of their experience and anticipation of failure, crafts/labor should be assigned and estimated material required. This is done at the planning stage of the work, however, when work starts, some un foreseen requirements in the resources or new tasks may arise and that can be incorporated if possible; otherwise, the work has be re-scheduled or frozen until the remedy is fully matured.

All types of activities require approved Permit-To-Work (PTW) to be issued by the asset custodian (Operation) to the work executor (Maintenance team). Currently, our CMMS does not cater for it, it is being done outside the system on a hard format, it is believed that future versions—soon—will contain PTW application.

The PTW is very essential document between the two parties to comply under company safety rules and work conditions. The purpose of the PTW is to ensure the work will be carried out in a maximum secured and safe environment. Full safety assurances are all parties' objectives, but never 100% guaranteed.

There are different types of PTWs, which defines the condition under which the work is being carried out. The most common permits are 'Live and Normal (Cold).' Live means that the maintenance team can work on the equipment/system while it is in operation, of course, precautions and safety measures must be applied. Normal permits are normally issued to work on an isolated equipment/system with also precautions and safety measures in place based on risk assessments. Other PTW types can be applicable like "Hot, Excavation, Confined Space, Ionization, Diving." All permits must be CLOSED/CANCELLED upon normalization and clearance of work site, and equipment/system/plant is ready to be handed back to PTW issuer.

Work Order Completion

The supervisor shall ensure that the maintenance tasks are completed as defined within the Work Order.

The Maintenance Technician shall ensure that any unused materials or storeroom items are returned to the stores.

The Maintenance Technician shall enter all work history against the Work Order in CMMS. Work feedback shall be clear and unambiguous and shall contain sufficient details that a reader can fully appreciate the condition of the equipment before the work, the actual work conducted, conditions found during the work, issues relating to access, spares, etc., and the condition of the equipment after the work.

The Maintenance Technician shall accurately enter, in CMMS, all appropriate readings required, correct Failure Code information, actual hours expended on the maintenance task, actual materials used etc. If the work is being reported against multi disciplines Work Order (Mechanical, Electrical, Instrumentation, etc.), all Maintenance Technician shall ensure that the correct method of reporting against Parent, Child, and Task Work Orders is followed.

If the Maintenance Technician, through the course of executing the Work Order, has identified any change or improvement to the specified work instructions, e.g. changes to the work conducted, the materials supplied, the time estimated etc., he should detail the reasons for review in the Work Order history and escalate the requirement to the his Supervisor.

Incomplete Work

If for any reason completion of the activities detailed in any Work Order cannot be achieved, the Maintenance Technician, after ensuring the worksite is left in a safe condition, shall update the Work Order history within CMMS, recording all conditions and actions found to date, the condition the equipment has been left in, the actual hours and materials, etc., used to date and shall include in the Work Order Log the reason for incompletion and the details of the actions being taken, or required, to enable completion and shall change the Work Order status to HOLD or to the appropriate 'waiting' code, e.g. waiting for spares, that reflects the reason for incompletion.

The Discipline Supervisor shall consider the next required steps to facilitate the resources and work conditions to re-attend the job and complete the work.

When all Work Order history has been recorded, the Maintenance Technician shall change the Work Order status to 'Complete'

If repairs (Corrective Maintenance) or other follow-up activities are required, the Maintenance Technician shall create an appropriate follow-up Work Order within

CMMS ensuring that the details of any such follow-up Work Order accurately reflect the further work that is required and the resources, materials, time, and access, etc. that is required to conduct.

Finally, Computerized Maintenance Management Systems (CMMS) have become the spinal cord and business driven best practice, when utilized in a proper manner, maintenance performance boosts and optimize cost, which is the objective of any organization performing Operation and Maintenance.

REFERENCES

Everdingen, Y., Hillengersberg, J., & Waarts, E. (2000). ERP adoption by european midsize companies. *Communications of the ACM, 43*(4), 27–31. doi:10.1145/332051.332064

Huang, Z., & Palvia, P. (2001). ERP implementation issues in advanced and developing countries. *Business Process Management Journal, 7*(3), 276. doi:10.1108/14637150110392773

Koch, C., & Buhl, H. (2001). ERP-supported teamworking in Danish manufacturing? *New Technology, Work and Employment, 16*(3), 164. doi:10.1111/1468-005X.00086

Mirchandani, D., & Motwani, J. (2001). End-user perceptions of ERP systems: A case study of an international automotive supplier. *International Journal of Automotive Technology and Management, 1*(4), 416. doi:10.1504/IJATM.2001.000049

KEY TERMS AND DEFINITIONS

Asset (physical): A formally accountable item.

Availability: The ability to be in a state to perform as required, under given conditions, at a given instant or over a given time interval.

CBM: Condition Based Maintenance.

CMMS: Computerized Maintenance Management System.

Compliance Test: A test used to show whether or not a characteristic or a property of an item complies with the stated requirements.

Condition-Based Maintenance: Preventative maintenance which include a combination of condition monitoring and/or inspection and/or testing, analysis and then carry out active maintenance action.

Corrective Maintenance: Maintenance carried out after fault recognition and intended to put an item into a state in which it can perform a required function.

Criticality: The numerical index of the severity of a failure or a fault.

Disc: Discard Task.

Evid: Evident Failure.

Failure Analysis: A logical and systematic examination of item failure modes and causes before or after a failure to identify the consequences of failure as well as the probability of its occurrence.

Failure Mode: The manner in which the inability of an item to perform a required function occurs.

Failure: The termination of the ability of an item to perform a required function.

FF: Failure Finding.

FMEA: Failure Mode and Effect Analysis.

Inspection: The examination for conformity by measuring, observing, testing, or gauging the relevant characteristics of an item.

Item: Any part, component, device, subsystem, functional unit, equipment, or system that can be individually described and considered.

Maintenance Management: All activities of the management that determine the maintenance objectives, strategies, and responsibilities, and implementation of them by such means as planning, control, and the improvement of maintenance activities and economics.

Maintenance: The combination of all technical, administrative, and managerial action during the life cycle of an item intended to retain it in, or restore it to, a state in which it can perform the required function.

MMS: Maintenance Management System.

MSS: Maintenance Strategy Selection.

OC: On Condition.

OEM: Original Equipment Manufacturer.

Planned Preventative Maintenance: Maintenance carried out at predetermined intervals or according to prescribe criteria and intended to reduce the probability of failure or the degradation of the functioning of an item.

RCM: Reliability Centered Maintenance.

Reliability: The ability of an item to perform a required function under given conditions for a given time interval.

Rest: Restoration Task.

RTF: Run To Failure.

SIL: Safety Integrity Level.

Time-Based Maintenance: Maintenance carried out in accordance with an established time schedule or established number of units of use.

Chapter 11
E–Government and EIS Change Management and Critical Success Factors:
An Omani Success Story

Wafi Al-Karaghouli
Brunel University, UK

Ahmed Al Azri
Ministry of Higher Education, Oman

Zahran Al Salti
Sultan Qaboos University, Oman

EXECUTIVE SUMMARY

Transformational e-government projects and large-scale Enterprise Information System (EIS) implementation projects have one thing in common: they both over-run their time and budget due to unclear vision and unrealistic expectations. The aim of this chapter is to report on a success story of implementing e-government in the Higher Education Admission Centre (HEAC) that is beneficial in providing an insight to both categories of projects. The case is unlike many other case studies that look at project failures; it is concerned with exploring and discussing the key critical factors that facilitate the success of the projects of both categories (Brady & Maylor, 2010). The research is a qualitative approach, and the investigation uses a single case study, with data collected by means of semi-structured interviews

DOI: 10.4018/978-1-4666-2220-3.ch011

and organisational documents from the Ministry of Higher Education in Oman. The research findings suggest that there are three paradigms with a set of factors that impact the success of projects, namely organisational paradigm, technology paradigm, and end-user paradigm.

INTRODUCTION

This chapter discusses the effect of change and the use of e-government in the Omani Higher Education Admission Centre (HEAC), and through a large and complex transformational process. In addition, the chapter will look at the Critical Success Factors (CSFs) that can be effectively adopted to manage such change and transformation.

During the last 15 years, the public sector worldwide has embarked on a wide range of reforms and has witnessed a steady growth in the adoption of new ICT solutions and the number of Web-enabled Enterprise Information Systems and e-government transformational projects (Rinderle-Ma & Reichert, 2009; Pham & Teich, 2011). Public Sector Organisations (PSOs) are increasingly seeking new tools to improve their performance and to provide better services to their citizens (Quartel, et al., 2012). For example, Sharifi and Manian (2010) contended that many governments around the world are greatly supporting the electronic delivery of public services to the citizens and the enterprises, enabling them to make most of their transactions within the government via electronic channels, i.e. e-government. In its basic definition, e-government is "the use of Information and Communications Technology (ICTs), and particularly the Internet, as a tool to achieve better government" (OECD, 2003). Rose and Grant (2010) explained that more and more PSOs are implementing e-government initiatives in order to transform the way citizens and governments interact with each other. With e-government, PSOs have opportunities to do their jobs better, cheaper, and proved 24/7 hours access to citizens (Al-Fakhri, et al., 2008). Furthermore, citizens have the potential to interact electronically with government agencies anytime and anywhere (Terpsiadou & Economides, 2009). However, there are continuing cases of failure to realize expected benefits of such initiatives, resulting in significant losses (Ke & Wei, 2004; Heeks, 2004). According to Heeks (2004) who conducted studies on e-government projects in developing countries up to 35% of such projects have resulted in total failures, 50% have partially failed, and only 15% are considered successful. The picture is as gloomy considering the implementation of Enterprise Information Systems (EIS) and Enterprise Resource Planning (ERP) system with Standish group (2012) reporting up to 70% failures. Nevertheless, there are few EIS, ERP and e-government projects that have been deemed successful (Strang & Macy, 2001; Brady & Maylor, 2010;

Nour & Mouakket, 2011). It is worth mentioning that implementing change and transformation from a large and a complex physical government (brick-and-mortar) to e-government is not an easy task, and similarly a major ERP implementation across different government departments to support the enterprise functions and automate cross-functional processes could yield a major change to the processes and practices (Pham & Teich, 2011). The process of change (transformation) in both cases may include not only a new structure of Information Systems (IS) but changes in job tasks, management style, organisations, culture, etc.

Change is not a new challenge facing management. Heraclitus (540 – 475 BC) stated that, "There is nothing permanent except change" (cited in Bechtel & Squires, 2001, p. 249). Therefore, change is constantly happening and never stops. Niccolo Machiavelli in the 16th century noted that "There is nothing more difficult to take in hand, more perilous to conduct, or more uncertain in its success, than to take the lead in the introduction of a new order of things" (cited in Kotter & Schlesinger, 1979). Throughout the centuries, thinkers, researchers and philosophers were completely correct in holding that change, though omnipresent, uncertain, and indeed difficult, is nonetheless achievable.

SETTING THE SCENE: RESEARCH BACKGROUND

During recent years, there has been an upsurge of interest in ICT technology adoption including e-government transformation and change management. Change management is a complex issue facing both private and public sector organizations (Yeo, 2009; Shurst & Hodges, 2010; Jaros, 2010). Globalization and relentless development of technology have increased the rate of change, which has directly or indirectly affected human society (Oakland, 2007; Moran & Brightman, 2001). There is also a considerable body of literature providing studies of change and restructuring in organizations. Moreover, change management is a strategic action aimed at receiving the best outcomes from change (Balogun & Hailey, 2008; Holden, et al., 2008). Hence, managing change is a vital action at every level of an organization in order to maintain growth and survive. Over the past few years, there have been many attempts to implement change successfully in organizations, but many change programs and projects in organizations fail, including few e-governments. Some scholars, such as Michael Beer, have asserted that most organizational change efforts fail in their early stages (Beer, et al., 1990; Wateridge, 1998). More recently, Kotter, who has been observing the change process for more than 30 years, stated that "a few of these corporate change efforts have been very successful" (Kotter, 2006, p. 33). In addition, a full understanding of conditions and factors that contribute to failure and those which result in success is vital to lead change successfully in organizations and is the key to reducing the risk of failure in managing change (Zink, et al., 2008).

Many models and guidelines have been proposed, Dunphy (1996, p. 541) stated that, "there is no one all embracing, widely-accepted theory of organizational change and no agreed guidelines for actions by change agents." The reason behind this debate about universal applicability stems from the premise that "turbulent times demand different responses in varied circumstances" (Dunphy & Stace, 1993, p. 905). A similar conclusion was offered by Dawson (2003), who defines change as a transition to future circumstances where the context and time evolve and remain uncertain. Moreover, Todnem (2005) argues that there is a need for more empirical studies to be conducted in the area of change management in order to enrich the literature with empirical investigations. The rationale for that, from Todnem's perspective, relies on the reported high rate of failure, the great pace of change and finally the inconsistency between the existing approaches to change management.

From a contextual stance, this research is conducted in the public sector; compared with the private sector, the public sector has received little attention in the change management literature (Coram & Burnes, 2001). Rees and Althakhri (2008) argue that there is a lack of change management studies in the Arab region and in particular pertaining to ICT applications generally, and e-government in particular. Therefore, it is important to bridge such gaps by conducting empirical studies that can help in understanding the phenomena of change in non-western society where many cultural, societal, political, economical contexts are different from the western context. Moreover, the selection of the Higher Education Admission Centre (HEAC) as a case study stems from the dimension mentioned above. It is considered as a transition from paper-based services to digital-based methods, representing a case from public sector reforms and changes, and finally representing the Arab region. On the other hand, it is perceived as a successful implementation, which has been rewarded and recognized internationally. Consequently, identifying key success conditions and factors will develop our understanding of how successful change works and evolves.

This chapter addresses key studies in the change management literature in relation to e-government transformation of the HEAC. Moreover, through primary data collection, this research sets out to find out the answer by interviewing key informants in the HEAC in Oman. Finally, based on a review of the literature on CSFs and interviews with key informants in the HEAC, critical success factors have been proposed in implementing the change of e-government with a proposition to scale to include other large scale EIS/ERP implementations with far-reaching organisational and human impacts (Nour & Mouakket, 2011; Pham & Teich, 2011).

LITERATURE REVIEW: CHALLENGES OF ORGANISATIONAL CHANGE AND E-GOVERNMENT IMPLEMENTATION

The literature has presented several types of change. The two common types of organisational change are planned and emergent. According to Gomez-Mejia *et al.* (2005), planned change within an organization is normally prepared for in advance. One could argue that in light of the current economic mayhem, General Motors Plc (GM) and many others are indeed facing a mammoth task to plan and apply changes that are in response to the unprecedented event that the world is going through. Emergent change, by contrast, refers to change that happens rapidly and for which organizations are not prepared (Burnes, 2004; Linstead, et al., 2004).

It is always easier for leadership to cope with planned change than emergent change (Burnes, 2004). Thus, deliberate planned change can be seen in many forms and shapes. This may include change in people (culture), structure, and technology. A change in technological methodology is used in order to survive and prosper. Changes within the organizational structure can be interpreted as direct or indirect changes to the organization strategy (Daft & Marcic, 2007). However, the critical success factors in change lie with the needs and motivation of people—key executives—within the organization, as this determines the limits and constraints of what an organization can achieve (Porter, 1998; Hitt, et al., 2009). An illustration of such an Organisational change can be seen in Figure 1.

As for ICT and e-government initiative projects, many have been planned, developed and implemented worldwide, but relatively few projects have been investigated in the developing countries, such as Oman. The implementation of big and complex e-projects should cover the political and strategies that a government has already implemented and those that might be implanted in the future. Change

Figure 1. Type of planned organisational change (source: Hitt, et al., 2009)

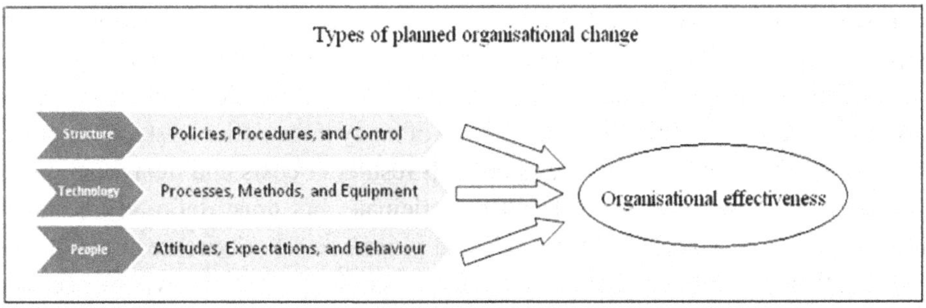

resistance is the outcome of inadequate awareness and lack of training across departments in using IT and coping with this e-change (Norris, 1999; Irani, et al., 2006; Ke & Wei, 2004).

LINKING THEORY TO PRACTICE: RESISTANCE TO CHANGE

Resistance to change is a phenomenon that has been extensively discussed in the change management literature. Resistance results from differences: whether ideas, plans, motives, or priorities (Bovey & Hede, 2001). Management should recognize and accept the fact that every change creates some resistance (Malhotra & Galletta, 2004). Therefore, change leaders need to integrate the differences in order to minimize potential resistance and be able to create adequate resolution.

There are two types of resistance, active and passive resistance. According to Lientz and Rea (2004), resistance is active when the resistors express their point of view openly and offer their reasons for disagreement. Passive resistors may actually express support for change, but when change is getting closer to being implemented, the resistance starts to emerge. Additionally, there is a third form of reaction to change, namely 'indifference.' Okafor (2007, p. 164) noted that indifference occurs when "an employee decides to sit on the fence." He or she neither gets involved nor opposes the change. However, he or she would not be bothered whether there is a change or not. People resist changes for many reasons. Aladwani (2001) presented two sources of resistance to innovations, namely perceived risk and habit. Perceived risk refers to one's perception of the risk associated with the decision to adopt the innovation. Thus, many employees resist changes and try to keep the current situation because they are anxious about how the change will affect their jobs. Habit, by contrast, refers to current practices that one is routinely doing. Employees become accustomed to performing a task in a certain manner and resent any effort by an outside influence asking them to experiment with other methods.

The adoption of new ICT solutions such as ERP systems and e-government represent a major challenge for many organizations. Many information system implementations fail due to non-acceptance by end-users (citizens) as they do not satisfy their needs (Al-Karaghouli, et al., 2005; Niu, et al., 2011; Pham & Teich, 2011). According to Joshi (2005), the failure of many information system initiatives can be directly traced to users' resistance. It results in costs and delays in implementation processes that are difficult to anticipate, but must definitely be taken into consideration. Craine (2007) stated that if users resist or become angry at new systems, then it is unlikely that even the best technology strategies will be successful. Furthermore, users tend to oppose some new information systems because they believe they are going to introduce new ways of doing their everyday routines. There

Figure 2. Methods for dealing with resistance to change

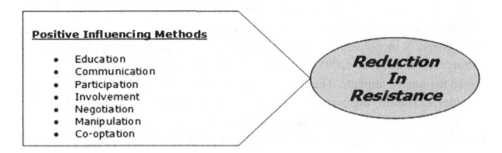

are some important strategies that should be considered when implementing a new change in order to minimize the risk of users' resistance (citizens). These include education, communication, participation, involvement, negotiation and manipulation (Kotter & Schlesinger, 1979). One could argue that co-optation is an empirical way to deal with resistance (see Figure 2).

REASONS AND CAUSES OF ICT PROJECT FAILURES

Putting change into effect is not easy, over 60 percent of changes are unsuccessful (Burnes, 2004; Oakland & Tanner, 2007; Song, 2009; Burnes & Jackson, 2011; Lofquist, 2011). This is partly due to general resistance to change (Washington & Hacker, 2005). But also due to the fact that much of planned change are based on a 'theory of change that is fundamentally flawed' (Beer, et al., 1990). Often, attempts to introduce change are based on the idea that attitude and behaviour patterns of individual employees need to be altered first of all so as to foster organisational change. It is more correct to say that individual behaviour depends on the positions and roles of people within the organisation. This concept can be used to make changes in behaviour more feasible through the insertion of employees into a new organisational context, which is not dealt with ahead of time, but takes place alongside the general organisational changes (Beer, et al., 1990).

Many reasons of change failures are linked to management (Beer & Nohria, 2000). Kotter (1996), in his book 'Leading Change,' examined why change attempts fail. He identified eight reasons for failure in implementing change, starting with lack of education about the validity of change, weakness in cooperation within the organization to lead efforts and to clarify the organisation's new direction, ambiguity of vision and poor communication channels. The other reasons are not having sufficient reasons to change, poor planning and aiming for short gains, hasty announcement of success, and indeed organization culture, which plays a key role in change failure.

Issues that ultimately result in failure have their roots in existing organisational culture and the struggle to break through it (Balogaun & Hailey, 2008). Burnes (1996) and Burnes and Jackson (2011) consider change failure as stemming from the manager's incompetence to consider or take into account the organisational culture. Jørgensen et al. (2008) stated that most failures in implementing change are linked to human elements. They also list seven factors: (1) modifying mindsets and attitudes, (2) modifying corporate culture, (3) undervaluing complexity, (4) lack of resources, (5) lack of commitment on the part of top management, (6) shortage of knowledge of the change process (known-how), and (7) lack of transparency due to missing or incorrect information. Consequently, it is to be stressed that social and human factors are significant factors that can influence the change process.

CRITICAL FACTORS FOR SUCCESSFUL CHANGE IMPLEMENTATIONS

There are several systemised models for the successful implementation of change that are based on CSFs that often propose step-by-step models (Lahti, 2005). In the six-step approach proposed by Beer *et al.* (1990), the first three steps are concerned with creating a shared understanding of vision for the proposed change. Firstly, a common appreciation of the problems involved must be identified, and the related change process must be developed to do so, while management must drum up the commitment to change. This should be followed by building up a shared vision of how to manage change successfully, thus promoting the new vision, along with the methodology to put it into effect and the coherence to enact it. The revitalisation should be institutionalised by means of formal policies, systems, and structures. The final step is to put into effect corrective actions after examining the results.

Kotter (1996), in his book 'Leading Change,' outlined eight critical factors for successful change, which are similar to Beer's (1990) step-by-step model. He proposes that it is necessary to establish the following: (1) bring about a sense of the importance of change, (2) set up a powerful partnership to lead the efforts and to clarify the company's new direction, (3) create a clear vision, (4) communicate this vision, (5) empower others to take action regarding the vision, (6) create obvious short-time wins, (7) establish the improvements, and (8) institutionalise the new initiative. In essence, Kotter suggests that a leader of an organisation should ascertain the process of implementing successful change. In doing so, the leader has to consider the eight steps as guide to coping with the proposed change. He also emphasises that the concept of leadership is different from management in that the former is to deal with change and the latter is to deal with complexity (Kotter, 1996).

Many CSFs have been identified by change management researchers, such as: continual ample communication, clear change message, belief of employees that the organisation can deal with change, clear vision of the benefits of the change, unequivocal support and commitment on the part of senior management, strong and competent leadership, staff participation and involvement, cooperation involving people from all levels of the organisation and staff motivation by means of empowerment and rewards (Salminen, 2000; Armenakis & Harris, 2002, 2009; Chrusciel & Field, 2005; Graetz, 2000; Graetz & Smith, 2010; McBain, 2006; Weber & Weber, 2001). Therefore, one could argue that there is no standard or a predetermined model that organisation must follow to implement a successful change. However, management should take into consideration the elements of the environment that play a major role within the organisation.

Kettunen (2007) argues that rather than following a sequential steps, which are normally a predetermined process, organisations should mould the steps needed to implement a successful change. In her work, which is based on the work by Burke *et al.* (1993), she proposes six dimensions for the successful implementation of change, each with its own critical factors. The six dimensions are: (1) response to change by individuals, (2) general nature of change, (3) planning change, (4) managing the human element of change, (5) managing the organisational side of change, and (6) evaluating change. Kettunen's proposal attempts to highlight the key factors that may lead organisations to implement a successful change from infancy—i.e. the preparation phase—to the maturity/evaluation phase. She also advocates the importance of individuals, management, and understanding of the environment. Accordingly, the assessment of the change is imperative not only to implement but also to learn. A summary of the key studies on CSFs on change management can be seen in Table 1.

Therefore, this section presents a list of CSFs, predominantly based on the literature review. A summary with explanation of these factors is illustrated in Table 2. In addition, it is worth noting that these listed factors will be combined and examined with the primary research findings at the end of this study and will be presented as a new list of proposed critical success factors list to give the final comprehensive list of CSFs in change management in general and in Oman in particular.

RESEARCH CONTEXT: THE SULTANATE OF OMAN

The Sultanate of Oman is situated on the southeast corner of the Arabian Peninsula. It has an area of 309,500 square km and covers a variety of topographic zones—mountain ranges, deserts, and fertile plains—as well as several small islands (MOI,

Table 1. Summary of key studies on CSFs literature in implementing organisational change

Authors	CSFs Description
Beer et al. (1990)	Commitment to change Develop a shared vision Foster consensus for vision Spread revitalization
Kotter (1996)	Sense of change Set up a powerful partnership Create a vision. Communicate & empowerment. Improvement & Institutionalize Create obvious short-time wins
Clarke and Garside (1997)	Commitment Social and culture issues Communication Tools and methodology Interactions
Salminen (2000)	Leadership & management support Need for change Participation Planning & goal setting Control & training Communication & motivation
Sirkin et al. (2006)	Duration Integrity Commitment Effort
Kettunen (2007)	Individual response General nature Planning Managing people Managing organization Evaluating

2005). It has borders with the Kingdom of Saudi Arabia, the Republic of Yemen, and the United Arab Emirates. Its coastline extends more than 3,165 kms from the Arabian Sea and the main entry to the Indian Ocean in the southwest to the Gulf of Oman and Musandam in the north (MONE, 2008). According to the preliminary population census of 2010, the Sultanate's population is 2,694,094m of whom 742,994 are expatriates (MONE, 2010).

The government's vision for the Omani economy, ''Oman 2020," is designed to shift the country to an advanced level by creating a digital society and e-government (MOD, 1995; MOE, 2008; MOHE, 2006; ITC, 2008). Therefore, in 1998, the Omani ministers' council made a decision to design a national information technology committee to develop the IT sector in the country which contributed to the e-government transformational projects.

Table 2. Description of factors of the conceptual framework

Factors	Descriptions	Authors
Need for change	The necessity of change.	Beer et al. (1990); Kotter (1996).
Vision	Clear vision is the bedrock for change.	Kotter (1996); Kettunen (2007).
Leadership	Strong leadership provides both security and transparency to employees.	Beer et al. (1990); Salminen (2000).
Commitment	Commitment and support from senior management are imperative in order to provide and allocate sufficient resources.	Sirkin et al. (2006); Clarke and Garside (1997).
Culture	Environment is a key in the process of change.	Clarke and Garside (1997); Robbins (2009).
Communication	A continuous stream of relevant and succinct information is one way to reduce resistance to change.	Kotter (1996); Salminen (2000); Al-Karagouli et al. (2005)
Involvement	Consultation, participation and voicing of the opinions of all members within the organisation.	Kettunen (2007); Salminen (2000).
Competence	The know-how.	Sirkin et al. (2006); Fortune and White (2006).
Motivation	The intrinsic needs and satisfaction.	Sirkin et al. (2006); Kenny (2003)

THE NEEDS OF HIGHER EDUCATION IN THE SULTANATE OF OMAN

Since 1970, the government has given high priority to developing an educated domestic work force (MOD, 1995). Prior to the foundation in 1986 of Oman's first public university Sultan Qaboos University (SQU) (SQU, 2011), the government sent students to universities in neighbouring Arab countries, UK, and USA (MOI, 2008). Currently, the Ministry of Higher Education operates two teachers' training colleges, five specialist colleges (MOHE, 2008) and the Ministry of Manpower operates seven technical colleges (MOMP, 2009). In addition, the Ministry of Health provides various training to nursing staff. The number of students who have completed their study in 1975 was 4,400, comparing to 41,812 in 2005 (MOI, 2005). Due to this big increase, public colleges could not cope with the demand and competition for places is still high. In the mid-1990s, more families have sent their children to study abroad. As a result, the government has encouraged the private sector to establish universities and colleges (MOHE, 2008).

Figure 3. The new HEAC system workflow

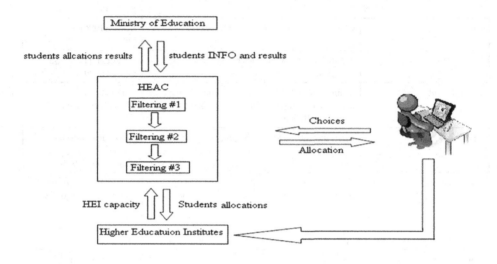

The Central Admission Workflow

In 2006/2007, the applications for higher education for both public and private universities were merged into one new and unified online system (HEAC). This was the birth of the e-government initiative in Oman's higher education. Prior to this, secondary schools students had to put up with the inconvenience of submitting in person their applications and supporting documents to the different institutes (HEAC, 2008). An illustration of the workflow of the new HEAC can be seen in Figure 3. Today, both Bachelors' and Masters' degrees in some subjects are offered by SQU and other private universities. From September 2008, SQU introduced PhD programs in some of its colleges, in Medicine, Engineering, Agriculture, Marine Sciences, and Natural Sciences (SQU, 2009). Normally only Omani students enrol in public university.

E-GOVERNMENT: HIGHER EDUCATION ADMISSIONS CENTRE (HEAC)

The Higher Education Admissions Centre (HEAC) was established by the Higher Education Council in November 2003 (MOI, 2004). Today, the HEAC is the largest centre in the Ministry of Higher Education (MOHE) in Oman. The MOHE has invested a lot of time, knowledge and resources into encouraging HEAC to switch from a manual to an electronic system (HEAC, 2008). The HEAC is responsible

Figure 4. Applications and acceptances for Omani students though the HEAC

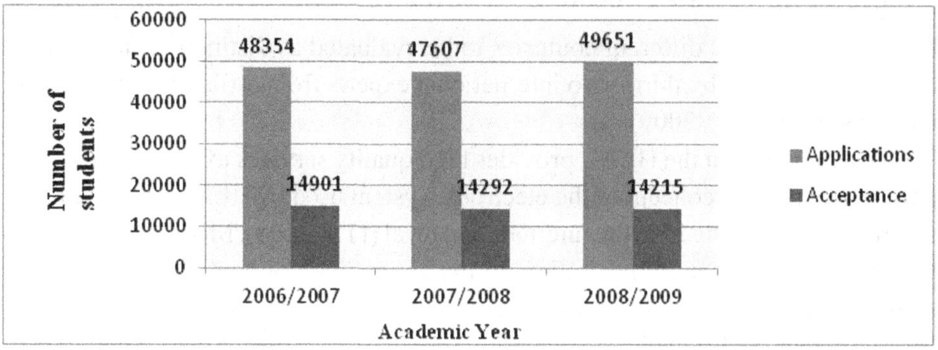

for processing applications from Omani students who have finished their General Certificate Examination (GCE) or its equivalent for admission to Higher Education Institutions (HEIs) and, as the Internet can be used for processing student's application, is the first e-service for students in the Omani public sector (ITA, 2008).

The goals of the Higher Education Admissions Centre are that students can effortlessly submit their applications to Omani Higher Education Institutions and to ensure that all students' applicants are treated fairly (MOHE, 2008). An electronic system allocates places to students in their preferred institutions and programs according to GCE exam results in an accurate, fair and transparent way, which has been managed by high skilled staff (HEAC, 2009).

The new HEAC system is designed to provide the student with his or her first choice as much as is possible, depending on his or her results in the General Certificate Exam, with students having to meet the minimum requirements in each chosen program (HEAC, 2008). The Admission Centre attempts to ensure that the student is treated fairly in the allocation process. Furthermore, students can apply to the Appeal Board if they feel their applications have not been processed justly and transparently. An illustration of applications and acceptances for Omani students though the electronic system of HEAC from 2006 to 2009 can be seen in Figure 4. In the academic year 2006/2007, the HEAC new system was implemented and has contributed to many advantages, including social, administrative, psychological, and economic.

RECOGNITION AND ACKNOWLEDGMENT

In November 2007, the Ministry of Higher Education received a World Summit Award recognising the Higher Education Admission Centre as one of the best five in the e-inclusion category (HEAC, 2009). The World Summit Award (WSA) is given once every two years and goes to the best electronic systems from around the world that benefit society (WSA, 2009). In 2007, WSA received 650 electronic products from more than 160 different countries to be evaluated as distinctive and creative electronic products by thirty-two international experts from different countries and background (HEAC, 2009).

It was agreed that the HEAC provides high quality services to students and their parents and that the concept of the electronic system used by HEAC added value to information committees on the international level (ITA, 2008). Moreover, receiving this award is evidence of the successful implementation of new electronic admission systems and the hard work done in successfully improving and upgrading the HEAC system. Additionally, the success of the HEAC is evidence that Omani society can competently implement any electronic systems and handle digital technology.

METHODOLOGY: CASE STUDY

This study concentrates on a specific context, i.e. the Higher Education Admissions Centre in the Sultanate of Oman, making the case study method most appropriate (Yin, 2009). This type of approach is closely linked with qualitative research, which also frequently uses Semi- structured interviews. This approach allows a broader assessment of a particular and real situation (Brewerton & Millward, 2001; Yin, 2004). The objective of this research is to develop theory rather than to make any generalisations and is focusing on HEAC, it is undoubtedly a single case study method (Bryman & Bell, 2011). It must be said that the work is exploratory in character and seeks a fresh perspective and understanding of a situation that has received little attention (Saunders, et al., 2009). The chance to study something that had not been widely investigated was also an added incentive. It is also important to highlight that the established similarities in patterns and causes of failure of transformational e-government projects and those of large-scale EIS projects justifies the initial assumption that the findings of this investigation would apply to the EIS and ERP implementations(Pham & Teich, 2011).

PRIMARY DATA COLLECTION: SEMI-STRUCTURE INTERVIEWS

In addition to obtaining secondary data from relevant databases that are available in Brunel University library. Today, there are many sources of primary data, e.g. questionnaires, interviews, and focus groups, are the most widely used primary data collection methods (Sekaran, 2003; Bryman & Bell, 2011). Therefore, primary research can be either quantitative or qualitative or both. This research adopted semi-structured interviews as the most suitable data collection methods for this type of research. Saunders et al. (2009, p. 245) described semi-structured interviews as "a discussion between two or more individuals in which a set of questions are posed." Therefore, to give the interviewee more flexibility and obtain greater insights, a list of possible questions is generally used by the interviewer as a guide. The contents of the interview can be adjusted according to which areas the interviewer deems significant and worthy of further investigation (Bryman & Bell, 2011). Semi-structured interviews were used for data collection in this research to provide insights into people's experiences and how they interpret them. Such insights are essential in answering the research question and emphasising critical success factors (Nour & Mouakket, 2011). This flexible approach allows a more detailed exploration of issues that the interview questions have exposed, resulting in further, often unexpected, insights, and information (Saunders, et al., 2009). The participants have been chosen for this study were key informants in the Ministry of Higher Education (MOHE). Moreover, they were directly involved in the change implementation project and therefore were able to provide adequate information about the implementation of change in the HEAC in Oman. The interview participants were chosen based on their capacity working within the Ministry of Higher Education in general and the HEAC in particular.

EMPIRICAL ANALYSIS AND INTERVIEW FINDINGS

After the interviews were conducted with the key informants and to ensure the richness of the data obtained, the transcripts were immediately available for analysis. As a result of the semi-structured nature of the interviews, it was crucial to highlight factors that were of interest and were relevant to the findings, which facilitated the ability to answer the research question. This method is called "inductive" and eliminates the need for hypotheses and deductive method analysis. To ensure and maintain the richness of the data obtained, tape recordings were made during the interviews, which were then available to be analysed at a later stage. Thereafter, great efforts were made by author in transcribing the data. The medium used was a tape recorder: the advantage of such a medium is that it ensures that accurate information is not lost or forgotten.

In this study, semi-structured interviews were conducted with four key informants from the HEAC in Oman. The duration of each interview was about 25 minutes and they were conducted in a friendly manner. The interview questions were designed to obtain answers to the research question and in-depth information. The interviewees were asked seven questions in order to answer the research question. The interviews were conducted in comfortable and quiet surroundings in order to ensure that participants paid full attention and to avoid any interruptions. The subsequent section will present the key findings from the interviews.

HEAC PROJECT PROFILE

Types of Change

Prior to addressing the research question, which set out "To identify the Critical Success Factors (CSFs) that ensue to the success of the implementation of change in HEAC," respondents were asked about the type of change that HEAC has made. All interviewees believe that Information Technology (IT) is a key factor in change in all manufacturing and services providers. To keep up with the rapid progress of IT, many organisations have allocated a substantive budget in order to provide very good services to the customers keep the public informed and raise confidence in the application of IT. Furthermore, the Omani leadership insists on implementing e-government projects in order to facilitate the usage of IT in day-to-day official government business. As one of the interviewees stated:

The introduction of IT systems to process students' applications in all higher education institutions in the Sultanate is the first step of many towards moving the country in the digital world. Using Web-based application through the Internet for processing students' applications is the first e-service for students in the Oman public sector (Interviewee 4).

Forces of Change

In today's competitive environment, the forces for change can be either external or internal or a mixture of both. Those forces differ from one organization to another. Naturally, customers' needs also differ and are diversified. According to one interviewee, the forces for change in HEAC were a mixture of both external and internal factors, as he clearly explained:

There are many forces: first the time span between secondary school results and HEIs registration is too short… Additionally, they have to follow a proceduralised timetable for applying …. Another example is that occasionally, students from the south & north of the country have to travel long distances accompanied by their parents to register in one of the HEIs, and you could see the cost element in such

Table 3. A summary of key drivers for change in HEAC

Internal Drivers	External Drivers
Improving the quality of service provided by MOHE. Continuous process improvement (time and cost) Operational performance Corresponded with MOHE objectives and innovation strategy.	Demand from government as a stakeholder. Students' (customers') requirement and satisfaction. Keep up with technology. Competition

endeavour.... There is a need for a system and manpower to accommodate the need of such increase. Therefore, there is a need for an e-system to lessen the admin work and reduce the travel time which by itself is an eco-friendly solution (Interviewee 1).

A summary of all forces mentioned by the interviewees can be shown in Table 3.

THE ROLE OF CHANGE AGENTS

To facilitate the implementation of change and increase the rate of success, change agents come into play. Today, various organisations pay more attention to those individuals who are able to facilitate the process of change and can improve the effectiveness of an organisation in a competitive market. According to the interviewed participants, change agents play a significant role, in that their skill and know-how lead to experience, which is the mother of wisdom. This view is echoed by one interviewee:

The role of a change agent is a core element in implementing a planned change: in HEAC, the concept of change was and is in motion. However, we wanted to expand our horizons and capitalise on an experienced change agent from outside the region, hence we have contracted the role of change agent to a skilled and experienced individual form Ireland (Interviewee 4).

BARRIERS AND CHALLENGES TO CHANGE

To increase the rate of success, the barriers to change must be identified, as this facilitates the process and reduces the challenges of resistance to change, as the latter is the main cause of change failure, a view that one of the interviewee stated:

In many organisations, members are reluctant to change and feel insecure and that causes them to challenge and resist any change. They are also concerned about issues of time, the decrease in interactions, there is a term in the UK—'file and rank'—that is insufficient communication between the layers of management (Interviewee 2).

In terms of challenges, one of the interviewees pointed out that the lack of education and communication, which both engender user awareness of the benefits of change, may backfire and act as a barrier to change. He clearly stated in his answer below that:

...users sometimes do not see the need and the benefits of change, and are therefore unwilling to move out of the comfort zone and accept change to keep up the progress in all its aspects (Interviewee 3).

Facing the challenges of resistance is central to the success of change, in that management should be aware of members of the organisation who would resist such policy—i.e. change—and one could argue that participation is the key. As one interviewee mentions:

Motivation, training, involvement, and communication: all these make an employee feel valued, which contributes to the eradication of resistance to change (Interviewee 3).

CRITICAL SUCCESS FACTORS (CSFS)

In the context of change, there have been many attempts to implement change successfully in organizations, but many change programs and e-government projects in organisations fail. In question (6), the interviewees were asked whether or not the change in the HEAC had been implemented successfully. All four interviewees agreed that the change had been a success, as evidenced by its receipt of an international award (see Figure 5). As one interviewee emphasised:

Of course we succeeded and receiving the World Summit Award (WSA) is evidence of our success ... (Interviewee 1).

All interviewees answered the previous question "yes" and one of the researchers asked for more details on the key factors that had led to the successful implementation of this change from their experience. The factors mentioned most frequently were:

Figure 5. Key factors that most frequently mentioned by interviewees

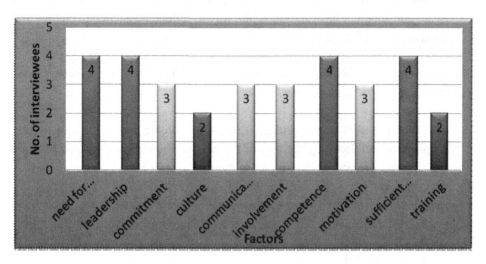

- **The need for change:** All of the interviewees asserted that having clear reasons for the need for change is the first step.

Communicating and explaining why change is vital from the beginning (Interviewee 2).

- **Leadership:** All interviewees believed that strong leadership can provide both security and transparency to employees.

Strong leadership is very important to ensure successful implementation of change. An effective leader can influence the organisation's employees (Interviewee 3).

- **Commitment:** Commitment and support from senior management are imperative in order to provide and allocate sufficient resources as well as discourage resistance. As one interviewee commented:

Top management commitment and support gives us motives to work hard and to create new ideas (Interviewee 4).

- **Culture:** A supportive culture is a key to facilitate the process of change, as one of the interviewees explained:

Organisation culture can facilitate the change process and help expedite the achievement of organization objectives (Interviewee 1).

- **Communication:** All interviewees consider that a continuous stream of relevant and succinct information is one way to reduce resistance to change and to save time and reduce costs.

Effective and direct communication can help to expedite the change as well as avoid resistance to change (Interviewee 1).

- **Involvement and participation:** Employee involvement is crucial to help employees feel that they are part of the change. In addition, participation by the right people will help to increase the rate of success.

Involving employees in the change process from the beginning of the change gives them a feeling of ownership and a sense that they are part of the change (Interviewee 4).

- **Competence:** All interviewees emphasise that competency (know-how) is the key factor:

Having competent employees who have good knowledge of the change process is vital... (Interviewee 3).

- **Motivation:** The intrinsic needs and satisfaction of employees must be addressed.

Without it, the wheel of change will be extremely slow and that is not cost effective (Interviewee 2).

- **Training:** Most of the interviewees considered that appropriate training plays a central role to expedite the pace of change. As one of the interviewees emphasised:

Appropriate training before the change is very important in order to have the necessary knowledge and capacity to cope with change (Interviewee 3).

- **Sufficient resources:** All interviewees agreed that the availability of resources is a key factor in implementing change successfully.

Successful implementation of change requires adequate resources in order to support the change process (Interviewee 4).

DISCUSSION

This section will include the discussion and analysis of the empirical findings of this study and will be supported with data from the literature review. Moreover, this part will include a discussion of the types of change, forces for change, the role of change agents, challenges faced in the implementation of change and CSFs that have led to successful change. After this discussion, a new list of critical success factors will be presented.

It is difficult to reach any definite conclusion based upon such a small number of interviewees from different backgrounds. Nevertheless, some comments can be made here as follows:

Planned change can be seen in many forms and shapes. This change may include change in one or more aspects of an organization's structure, technology, and people (culture). Changes in technology are frequently used these days in order to compete and prosper in the competitive market. The findings of the interviews show that the change that the HEAC has made was mainly in technology, which directly affects the organization structure and culture. Technological change is considered to be one of the key elements needed in order to gain and sustain competitive advantage. These findings are in line with those of Porter (1998), Robbins and Coulter (2009) and Lussier (2006), who have found that political and technological factors are the most influential drivers for change.

These forces can be either external or internal or a mixture of both. The findings of the interviews show that both external and internal forces have driven the HEAC's change. Technological force comes into play in implementing the e-government project and the speed of technology transfer. Further, socio-cultural forces are involved as population demographics increase, as well as in management forces for change. Thus, the forces for change in general were in accordance with the literature introduced in the change management field (Robbins, 2009; Hitt, et al., 2009; Johnson, et al., 2006).

Barriers faced by the HEAC during the implementation of change were not surprising because the change that the HEAC has made is directly linked with employees and users (citizens). All barriers and challenges that reported by all interviewees were similar to those stated in the change management and the IS literatures. Indeed, all challenges are in line with research findings published recently by Jorgensen et al. (2008), who found resistance to change, insufficient resources, lack of trust and lack of education to be the key challenges during the change implementation phase. However, none of the interviewees mentioned shortage of resources as an obstacle, contrary to the Jorgensen et al. (2008) findings. Perhaps this is because the MOHE allocated a massive budget in order to achieve their goal. Even the HEAC understands that users' awareness and trust is significant, but they do not give this issue enough attention: this might be because the HEAC planned to run many awareness programs at the end of the implementation stage. When asked, "where did the resistance come from?" the findings show that about 70% of resistance faced by the HEAC was from users (citizens) and less than 30% was from employees, including middle management. However, according to Craine (2007), users' beliefs and values are good indicators of what may cause their resistance to change, as well as helping to identify and evaluate the attitudes of users and influential groups. Therefore, change can be seen as a positive phenomenon.

Moreover, most of the interviewees mentioned that education, communication, participation and training were the methods they used most to cope with resistance. All of these methods are consistent with the research findings of Kotter and Schlesinger (1979), who advocate all of these methods to deal with resistance to change. Further, there are another methods not mentioned by the interviewees, such as negotiation, agreement, manipulation and co-optation.

Critical Success Factors CSFs

Change happens constantly and never ends: it is the nature of the life cycle. In term of increasing uses of technology, diversified products, and global competition, change comes into play in order to survive and prosper in a competitive market. Indeed, successful implementation of change is driven by many critical factors and focusing on these factors can lead to the successful implementation of change.

The discussion below presents the critical factors mentioned by interviewees that should be considered when implementing a new change in order to minimize the risk of users' and citizens' resistance and to contribute to success:

- **The need for change:** When implementing planned change, first of all leaders and managers require clear reasons for the need for the change. Ensuring the need for change was reported as a significant factor in ensuring full attention and priority from leadership. An interesting result was that all interviewees considered that having clear reasons for change would help to communicate and engage with organisational members. These finding is in accordance with the research findings of Kotter (1996) and Kettunen (2007), which indicate that having clear reasons for change makes it easier to convince leaders as well as organisation members. The commitment and support from top management that the HEAC received was presumably because of having clear and realistic reasons for the need to change.
- **Leadership:** Strong and active leadership is vital to implementing change successfully. Not surprisingly, all interviewees believed that strong and close leadership gives organisation members high motivation, commitment and

confidence during the implementation phase. This finding is in line with Salminen (2000), Sloan and Soosay (2005) and Kettunen (2007), who have emphasised the need for strong leaders and the role they play to motivate employees, bolster their confidence and allocate resources, all of which are regarded as critical success factors. Perhaps this type of leadership reduces the potential for resistance to change.

- **Communication:** Effective communication is essential to ensure that every member is kept informed and understands the meaning of the message. All interviewees believed that organisational communication and a continuous stream of relevant information is vital during the change process to achieve change successfully. Apparently, this is consistent with the change management literature, which emphasizes the need for communication during the change process (Kotter, 1996; Clarke & Garside, 1997; Salminen, 2000; Kettunen, 2007), which advocates for effective communication in order to control behaviour, motivate and encourage the emotional expression of employees' feelings. Perhaps the HEAC leadership understands that communication facilitates change and saves time in its implementation.

- **Culture:** The way of doing things is reflected in members' behaviour. An interesting result was that only half of the interviewees mentioned organisational culture as a critical success factor. This finding contradicts the literature as well as general views of change (Beer, et al., 1990; Clarke & Garside, 1997), which advocate that culture is a very supportive factor in implementing change successfully. Maybe some interviewees did not emphasise the importance of culture because they considered it as facilitative to change rather than being a crucial factor.

- **Commitment:** Top management support and commitment play a special role in change. One result that will not come as a surprise was that most of the interviewees considered that top management commitment was a critical factor. This view is supported by the literature (Beer, et al., 1990; Clark & Garside, 1997; Sirkin, et al., 2006): this might be because top management provided and allocated sufficient resources.

- **Involvement and participation:** Ensuring that employees feel part of the change and participation by the right people were reported as critical factors by most of the interviewees. This finding is in line with the research findings of Kettunen (2007), who found that involving employees from the beginning and participation by the right people is one method to avoid resistance and indeed to successfully implementing change.

- **Competent, suitable staff and motivation:** It was emphasised by all of interviewees that having people who know-how and retaining them as well as having suitable staff are significant in order to implement change successfully. In addition, the intrinsic needs and satisfaction of the employees are critical. This finding is in accordance with Salminen (2000), who advocates the role of competent personnel and motivation in success.

Proposed New CSFs

The interpretation of the interviews with key informants in the HEAC has led the researchers to identify additional factors that led the HEAC to successful change; these factors were not included in the conceptual framework. The additional factors are sufficient resources and appropriate training.

- **Sufficient resource:** According to the HEAC interviewees, the requirement of adequate resources when launching any change programme in organisations is imperative. Availability of resources during the change process is the engine of the process. Management should pay full attention in prioritising and planning for sufficient resources.
- **Appropriate training:** Most interviewees believed that appropriate training and hands-on practice before change is a critical element that needs to be incorporated into any change management strategy. It improves the skills and quality of employees: "new systems require new skills" (Pasmore, 1988, p. 135). Furthermore, it enhances employees' performance and creates a more productive atmosphere during the change process. Additionally, end user training is an effective tool to reduce resistance caused by embedded routines.

CONCLUSION

This chapter has presented a case of successful implementation of e-change in the e-government public sector within the Omani context. Despite the fact that many organisations have implemented change successfully, many change programs and projects in organizations fail. Therefore, the main purpose of this research was to identify the critical success factors that led the HEAC in the Sultanate of Oman to implement e-change successfully. In addition, a full understanding of these factors is imperative to lead change successfully in organizations. Secondary research was conducted to investigate the factors that lead organisations to have more success when implementing change and in particular e-government initiatives. The most prominent critical success factors supported by the empirical research are, ensuring the need for change, strong leadership, effective communication, supportive culture, top management support and commitment, involvement and participation of stakeholders, competent, suitable staff, and motivation.

The primary research, which was carried out in the form of semi-structured interviews, found that the majority of the interviewees emphasised all of the critical success factors that were identified in the secondary research. However, most of interviewees believed that sufficient resources and appropriate training are two additional critical factors that were not proposed in the conceptual framework. Although the findings of this study provide meaningful implications, but there was insufficient time to explore in detail all the aspects of the factors that may contribute to enabling Omani organizations to have more successes in managing e-change (e-government). Therefore, it seems worthwhile outlining some proposals for future research on this topic.

The authors are of the conviction that the same conclusions from the e-government case study can be extended to large-scale enterprise information system implementation in terms of the types of change, forces of change and the role of change agents, although a process of validation might applicable to consider the context and some of the differences between the two important and complex technology-based undertaking (Niu, et al., 2011). Finally, this study contributes to the area of e-change in EIS including e-government and could be generalised to other similar area in other gulf states.

FUTURE RESEARCH

This study is based on a qualitative method (semi-structured interviews) with key informants from the HEAC. The single case study presented has explained the change phenomenon at the HEAC in Oman. To get a clear picture of the change phenomenon in Oman, a wider research needs to be conducted. As with everything, evolution takes place on a day-to-day basis; therefore, the implementation of change especially in e-government projects where technology moves very fast should always be evaluated at the time and tuned to the need of the organisation. Moreover, a mixed-method approach using both qualitative and quantitative methods would provide a better insight into the phenomenon under investigation. On reflection on this study, quantitative approaches might provide an impact of certain issues that qualitative approach falls short in addressing. Additionally, despite the fact that some HEAC data is not yet published, the researchers have attempted, through their best efforts, to present up-to-date data. The sample in the interviews was small and limited only to current HEAC key informants, and interviews had to be conducted in a limited length of time.

It is also strongly recommended that the conclusions of this study can be used as an input to EIS / ERP cases for validation and refinement.

REFERENCES

Al-Fakhri, M., Cropf, R., Higgs, G., & Kelly, P. (2008). e-Government in Saudi Arabia: Between promise and reality. *International Journal of Electronic Government Research, 4*(2), 5–82. doi:10.4018/jegr.2008040105

Al-Karaghouli, W., AlShawi, S., & Fitzgerald, G. (2005). Promoting requirements identification quality: Enhancing the human interaction dimension. *Journal of Enterprise Information Management, 18*(2), 256–267. doi:10.1108/17410390510579945

Aladwani, A. (2001). Change management strategies for successful ERP implementation. *Business Process Management Journal, 7*(3), 266–275. doi:10.1108/14637150110392764

Armenakis, A., & Harris, S. (2002). Crafting a change message to create transformational readiness. *Journal of Organizational Change Management, 15*(2), 169–183. doi:10.1108/09534810210423080

Armenakis, A., & Harris, S. (2009). Reflections: Our journey in organizational change research and practice. *Journal of Change Management, 9*(2), 127–142. doi:10.1080/14697010902879079

AShurst, C., & Hodges, J. (2010). Exploring business transformation: The challenges of developing a benefits realization capability. *Journal of Change Management, 10*(2), 217–237. doi:10.1080/14697011003795685

Balogun, J., & Hailey, V. (2008). *Exploring strategic change* (3rd ed). London, UK: Harlow.

Bechtel, R., & Squires, J. (2001). Tools and techniques to facilitate change. *Industrial and Commercial Training, 33*(7), 249–254. doi:10.1108/EUM0000000006001

Beer, M., Eisenstat, R., & Spector, B. (1990). Why change programs don't produce change. *Harvard Business Review, 68*(6), 158–166.

Beer, M., & Nohria, N. (2000). Cracking the code of change. *Harvard Business Review, 78*(3), 131–142.

Bovey, H., & Hede, A. (2001). Resistance to organisational change: The role of the defence mechanism. *Journal of Managerial Psychology, 16*(7), 534–548. doi:10.1108/EUM0000000006166

Brady, T., & Maylor, H. (2010). The improvement paradox in project contexts: A clue to the way forward? *International Journal of Project Management, 28*, 787–795. doi:10.1016/j.ijproman.2010.08.001

Bryman, A., & Bell, E. (2011). *Business research methods* (3rd ed.). Oxford, UK: Oxford University Press.

Burke, W., Church, A., & Waclawski, J. (1993). What do OD practitioners know about managing change? *Leadership and Organization Development Journal, 14*(6), 3–11. doi:10.1108/01437739310047038

Burnes, B. (1996). No such thing as…. a "one best way" to manage organizational change. *Management Decision, 34*(10), 11–18. doi:10.1108/00251749610150649

Burnes, B. (2004). Emergent change and planned change – Competitors or allies? The case of XYZ construction. *International Journal of Operations & Production Management, 24*(9), 886–890. doi:10.1108/01443570410552108

Burnes, B., & Jackson, P. (2011). Success and failure in organizational change: An exploration of the role of values. *Journal of Change Management, 11*(2), 133–162. doi:10.1080/14697017.2010.524655

Chrusciel, D., & Field, D. (2005). Success factors in dealing with significant change in an organization. *Business Process Management Journal, 12*(4), 503–516. doi:10.1108/14637150610678096

Clarke, A., & Garside, J. (1997). The development of a best practice model for change management. *European Management Journal, 15*(5), 537–545. doi:10.1016/S0263-2373(97)00033-9

Coram, R., & Burnes, B. (2001). Managing organisational change in the public sector: Lessons from the privatisation of the property services agency. *International Journal of Public Sector Management, 14*(2), 94–110. doi:10.1108/09513550110387381

Craine, K. (2007). Managing the cycle of change. *Information Management Journal, 41*(5), 44–48.

Daft, R., & Marcic, D. (2007). *Management in the new workplace*. New York, NY: Thomson-South-Western.

Dawson, P. (2003). *Understanding organizational change: The contemporary experience of people at work*. London, UK: Sage Publications.

Dunphy, D. (1996). Organizational change in the corporate settings. *Human Relations, 49*(5), 541–552. doi:10.1177/001872679604900501

Dunphy, D., & Stace, D. (1993). The strategic management of strategic change. *Human Relations, 46*(8), 905–922. doi:10.1177/001872679304600801

Gomez-Mejia, L., Balkin, D., & Cardy, R. (2005). *Management: People, performance change* (2nd ed.). New York, NY: McGraw-Hill Companies, Inc.

Graetz, F. (2000). Strategic change leadership. *Management Decision, 38*(8), 550–564. doi:10.1108/00251740010378282

Graetz, F., & Smith, A. C. T. (2010). Managing organizational change: Philosophies of change approach. *Journal of Change Management, 10*(2), 135–154. doi:10.1080/14697011003795602

HEAC. (2008). *Website.* Retrieved from http://www.heac.gov.om/heac_en/index.asp

Heeks, R. (2004). *eGovernment as a carrier of context.* IGovernment Working Paper No.15. Manchester, UK: University of Manchester. Retrieved from http://www.heac.gov.om/heac_en/index.asp

Hitt, M., Black, S., & Porter, L. (2009). *Management* (2nd ed.). Upper Saddle River, NJ: Prentice Hall.

Hultman, K. (1995). Scaling the wall of resistance. *Training & Development, 49*(10), 15–18.

Irani, Z., Al-Sebie, M., & Elliman, T. (2006). *Transaction stage of e-government systems: Identification of its location and importance.* Paper presented at the Hawaii International Conference on System Sciences (HICSS-39). Hawaii, HI.

ITA. (2008). *Oman digital society report.* Retrieved from http://www.ita.gov.om

Jaros, S. (2010). Commitment to organizational change: A critical review. *Journal of Change Management, 10*(1), 79–108. doi:10.1080/14697010903549457

Johnson, G., Scholes, K., & Whittington, R. (2006). *Exploring corporate strategy: Text and cases* (7th ed.). Upper Saddle River, NJ: Prentice Hall.

Joshi, K. (2005). Understanding user resistance and acceptance during the implementation of an order management system: A case study using the equity implementation model. *Journal of Information Technology Case and Application Research, 7*(1), 6–20.

Ke, W., & Wei, K. (2004). Successful egovernment in Singapore: How did Singapore manage to get most of its public services deliverable online? *Communications of the ACM, 47*(6), 95–99. doi:10.1145/990680.990687

Kettunen, H. (2007). *Change management in implementation of strategic initiatives. Seminar in Business Strategy and International Business, TU-91.167.* Helsinki, Finland: Helsinki University of Technology.

Kotter, J. (1996). *Leading change*. Boston, MA: Harvard Business School Press.

Kotter, J. (2006). Leading change: Why transformation efforts fail. *Harvard Business Review.* Retrieved from http://cerc.stanford.edu/leading_change.PDF

Kotter, J., & Schlesinger, L. (1979). Choosing strategies for change. *Harvard Business Review, 57*(2), 106–114.

Lahti, C. (2005). *Change management in pay systems implementation: Case study from chemical industry companies on job evaluation and the evaluation of an employee's competence and performance based pay systems change processes.* Helsinki, Finland: Helsinki University of Technology.

Lientz, B., & Rea, K. (2004). *Breakthrough IT change management: How to get enduring change results*. Oxford, UK: Elsevier Butterworth Heinemann.

Linstead, S., Fulop, L., & Lilley, S. (2004). *Management and organization: A critical text*. New York, NY: Palgrave Macmillan.

Lofquist, E. A. (2011). Doomed to fail: A case study of change implementation collapse in the Norwegian civil aviation industry. *Journal of Change Management, 11*(2), 223–243. doi:10.1080/14697017.2010.527853

Malhotra, Y., & Galletta, D. (2004). Building systems that users want to use. *Communications of the ACM, 47*(12), 89–94. doi:10.1145/1035134.1035139

McBain, R. (2006). Why do change efforts so often fail? *Henley Management Update, 17*(3), 19–29.

Ministry of Information MOI. (2008). *Oman: 2008-9*. (266), Al-Nahda printing press, Muscat.

MOD. (1995). *Vision for Oman's economy: 2020*. Muscat, Oman: MOD.

MOE. (2008). *Education indicators: Academic year 2007/8*. Muscat, Oman: MOE.

MOHE. (2006). *Summary of the strategy for education in the Sultanate of Oman: 2006- 2020*. Muscat, Oman: MOHE.

MOI. (2005). *Oman: Years of progress and development*. Muscat, Oman: MOI.

MOMP. (2009). *Technical colleges in Oman*. Retrieved from http://www.manpower.gov.om/

MONE. (2008). *Statistical year book*. Muscat, Oman: MONE.

Moran, J., & Brightman, B. (2001). Leading organizational change. *Career Development International, 6*(2), 111–118. doi:10.1108/13620430110383438

Niu, N., Jin, M., & Cheng, J.-R. C. (2011). A case study of exploiting enterprise resource planning requirements. *Enterprise Information Systems, 5*(2), 183–206. doi:10.1080/17517575.2010.519052

Norris, D. F. (1999). Leading edge information technologies and their adoption: Lessons for US cities. In *Information Technology and Computer Applications in Public Management* (pp. 137–156). Hershey, PA: IGI Global.

Nour, M. A., & Mouakket, S. (2011). A classification framework of critical success factors for ERP systems implementation: A multi-stakeholder perspective. *International Journal of Enterprise Information Systems, 7*(4), 56–71. doi:10.4018/jeis.2011010104

Oakland, J., & Tanner, S. (2007). Successful change management. *Total Quality Management and Business Excellence, 18*(1), 1–19. doi:10.1080/14783360601042890

OECD. (2003). *OECD e-government studies: The e-government imperative.* London, UK: OECD Publishing.

Okafor, E. (2007). Globalization, changes and strategies for managing workers' resistance in work organization in Nigeria. *Journal of Human Ecology (Delhi, India), 22*(2), 159–169.

Pasmore, A. (1988). *Designing effective organisation. London, UK.* London: Taylor and Francis.

Pham, L., & Teich, J. E. (2011). A success model for enterprise resource planning adoption to improve financial performance in Vietnam's equitized state owned enterprises. *International Journal of Enterprise Information Systems, 7*(1), 41–55. doi:10.4018/jeis.2011010103

Porter, M. (1998). *Competitive strategy: Techniques for analysing industries and competitors.* New York, NY: The Free Press.

Quartel, D., Steen, M. W. A., & Lankhorst, M. M. (2012). Application and project portfolio valuation using enterprise architecture and business requirements modelling. *Enterprise Information Systems, 6*(2), 189–213. doi:10.1080/17517575.2011.625571

Rees, C., & Althakhri, R. (2008). Organizational change strategies in the Arab region: A review of critical factors. *Journal of Business Economics and Management, 9*(2), 123–133. doi:10.3846/1611-1699.2008.9.123-132

Rinderle-Ma, S., & Reichert, M. (2009). Comprehensive life cycle support for access rules in information systems: The CEOSIS project. *Enterprise Information Systems, 3*(3), 219–251. doi:10.1080/17517570903045609

Rose, W., & Grant, G. (2010). Critical issues pertaining to the planning and implementation of e-government initiatives. *Government Information Quarterly, 27*(1), 26–33. doi:10.1016/j.giq.2009.06.002

Salminen, A. (2000). *Implementing organizational and operational change – Critical success factors of change management. Industrial Management and Business Administration No. 7.* Helsinki, Finland: Helsinki University of Technology.

Saunders, M., Lewis, P., & Thornhill, A. (2009). *Research methods for business students* (5th ed.). Upper Saddle River, NJ: Prentice Hall.

Sekaran, U. (2003). *Research methods for business: A skill building approach* (4th ed.). New York, NY: John Wiley and Sons, Inc.

Sharifi, M., & Manian, A. (2010). The study of the success indicators for pre-implementation activities of Iran's e-government development projects. *Government Information Quarterly, 27*(1), 63–69. doi:10.1016/j.giq.2009.04.006

Sirkin, H., Keenan, P., & Jackson, A. (2006). The hard side of change management. *Harvard Business Review, 84*(3), 142–143. Retrieved from http://www.iconlogicgroup.com/pdf/HBR%20The%20Hard%20Side%20of%20Change%20Manag

Sloan, T., & Soonsay, C. (2005). Driving change: Innovate management in distribution centers. *Journal of Asia Entrepreneurship and Sustainability*, 1-21.

Song, X. (2009). Why do change management strategies fail? Illustrations with case studies. *Journal of Cambridge Studies, 4*(1), 6–15.

SQU. (2011). *Colleges*. Retrieved from http://www.squ.edu.om

Strang, D., & Macy, M. W. (2001). In search of excellence: Fads, success stories, and adaptive emulation. *American Journal of Sociology, 107*(1), 147–182. doi:10.1086/323039

Terpsiadou, M., & Economides, A. (2009). The use of information systems in the Greek public financial services: The case of TAXIS. *Government Information Quarterly, 26*(3), 468–476. doi:10.1016/j.giq.2009.02.004

Todnem, R. (2005). Organizational change management: A critical review. *Journal of Change Management, 5*(4), 369–380. doi:10.1080/14697010500359250

Washington, M., & Hacker, M. (2005). Why change fails: Knowledge counts. *Leadership and Organization Development Journal, 26*(5), 400–411. doi:10.1108/01437730510607880

Wateridge, J. (1998). How can IS/IT projects be measured for success? *International Journal of Project Management, 16*(1), 59–63. doi:10.1016/S0263-7863(97)00022-7

Weber, P., & Weber, J. (2001). Changes in employee perceptions during organizational change. *Leadership and Organization Development Journal, 22*(6), 291–300. doi:10.1108/01437730110403222

Yeo, R. K. (2009). Electronic government as a strategic intervention in organizational change processes. *Journal of Change Management, 9*(3), 271–304. doi:10.1080/14697010903125506

Yin, R. (2004). *The case study anthology*. Thousand Oaks, CA: Sage publications, Inc.

Yin, R. (2009). *Case study research: Design and methods* (4th ed.). Newbury, CA: Sage Publications.

Zink, K., Steimle, U., & Schroder, D. (2008). Comprehensive change management concepts: Development of a participatory approach. *Applied Ergonomics, 39*, 527–538. doi:10.1016/j.apergo.2008.02.015

ADDITIONAL READING

Al-Karaghouli, W., AlShawi, S., & Fitzgerald, G. (2003). A framework for managing knowledge in requirements identification: Bridging the knowledge gap between business and system developers. In *Knowledge and Business Process Management*. Hershey, PA: IGI Global.

Bocij, P., Chaffey, D., Greasley, A., & Hickie, S. (2003). *Business information systems* (2nd ed.). Edinburgh, UK: Pearson Education Limited.

Burke, R. (2003). *Project management planning and control techniques* (4th ed.). New York, NY: John Wiley.

Castka, P., Bamber, C. J., Sharp, J. M., & Belohoubek, P. (2001). Factors affecting successful implementation of high performance teams. *Team Performance Management: An International Journal, 7*(7/8), 123–134. doi:10.1108/13527590110411037

Cavell, S. (1999, February 16). Salespeople buck the system: Survey finds software failure fails to take account of culture. *Computing*.

Davies, C. T. (2002). The real success factors on projects. *International Journal of Project Management, 20*, 185–190. doi:10.1016/S0263-7863(01)00067-9

Gray, C., & Larson, E. W. (2008). *Project management* (3rd ed.). New York, NY: McGraw Hill.

Hanafizadeh, P., Gholami, R., Dadbin, S., & Standage, N. (2010). Paper. *International Journal of Enterprise Information Systems, 6*(2), 82–111. doi:10.4018/jeis.2010040105

Kuruppuarachchi, P. R., Mandal, P., & Smith, R. (2002). IT project implementation strategies for effective changes: A critical review. *Logistic Information Management, 15*(2), 126–137. doi:10.1108/09576050210414006

Lakshminarayanan, A. S. (2007, June 14). On IT project delivery: UK IT projects running late. *Computing*.

Lewis, W. E. (2000). *Software testing and continuous quality improvement*. London, UK: CRC Press. doi:10.1201/9781420048124

Macaulay, L. A. (1996). *Requirements engineering*. London, UK: Springer-Verlag. doi:10.1007/978-1-4471-1005-7

Marble, R. P. (2003). A system implementation study: Management commitment to project management. *Information & Management, 41*(1), 111–123. doi:10.1016/S0378-7206(03)00031-4

Sankar, C. S. (2010). Factors that improve ERP implementation strategies in an organization. *International Journal of Enterprise Information Systems, 6*(2), 15–34. doi:10.4018/jeis.2010040102

KEY TERMS AND DEFINITIONS

Change Management: Combinations of processes, techniques and tools to manage people, which can be applied to many business organisational change to improve the rate of success and Return On Investment (ROI). In addition, it could include Processes systems, organisation structure, job roles.

Critical Success Factors (CSF): A number of key factors that identified by executives to be critical to the success of the enterprise, usually key areas where successful performance will assure the success of the organisation to achieve its goals.

E-Government: Refers to the use of the Internet and related technology, including ICT to digitally enable government, other public sectors, citizen, and business to interact 24/7.

Enterprise Information Systems (EIS): Applications provide an information infrastructure for an enterprise, i.e. a well-defined set of services to its customers. These services are provided to customer as local or remote interfaces or both. An example of enterprise information systems includes enterprise resource planning systems.

Enterprise Resources Planning (ERP): A large, highly complex software that integrates many business functions, including database under one applications. In e-government, ERP is a system that handles the data infrastructure, e.g. a tailored system to fit a particular function, such as an automation system to hand its documents.

Oman: An Arab county in the Middle East, known as the Sultanate of Oman, which is situated on the southeast corner of the Arabian Peninsula Arabian Gulf region.

Project Success: Projects that finish on time and within budget to achieve the set business goals.

Transformation: A marked change, usually for the better, i.e. a process of change from one state or phase to another. In business, transformation could lead to transformational change of process, procedure or culture to another, and it is usually linked closely to business strategy readiness and vision.

Chapter 12

Implementation of Integrated Enterprise Asset Management Systems (IEAMS):
Key Challenges and Lessons Learned

Asim Hussain
KOC, Kuwait

EXECUTIVE SUMMARY

The chapter focuses on the challenges encountered and strategy used during Integrated Enterprise Asset Management (IEAMS) project from its inception to Go-Live. It has integrated all of the related processes from the project initiation to Asset Write-off (project initiation/ approval, asset creation/ operation/ maintenance/ write-offs, contract initiation/ execution/ payments) with the involvement of all concerned stakeholders.

IEAMS has replaced over 100 legacy, standalone, and custom applications with Maximo®. The consolidation of these applications and associated data represented a challenge in data integrity, cleansing, transformation, migration, and upload to Maximo® as a unified data repository.

DOI: 10.4018/978-1-4666-2220-3.ch012

A comprehensive training program was carried out before Go Live of the system to train all prospective users of the system. The extensive change management program included comprehensive campaigns, game shows to promote awareness about IEAMS in the company. A number of key personnel in their respective organizational units were designated as Change Agents to promote IEAMS and to ensure smooth transition upon Go Live.

ORGANIZATION BACKGROUND

It is a major oil and gas company having the responsibilities of exploration, drilling, and production of hydrocarbon resources. The company is also involved in the storage of crude oil and its delivery to tankers for export.

The company maintains a wide variety of asset types including:

- Sub Surface Facilities (Reservoirs, Wells).
- Surface Facilities (Gathering Centers/ Booster Stations, Water treatment, and Injection Plants).
- Export Facilities (Tank Farms, Export Terminals/ Marine Fleet) .
- Infrastructures (Pipe Lines/ Cables, Roads, Office Building, and Staff Accommodation).
- Workshops (Machining/ Fabrication/ Repairs).
- Transports (Heavy Equipment/ Light Vehicles).
- IT (Communication, Computers [Servers, Workstations], Accessories, and Software).
- Medical services for the staff.

All of these asset types and their distinct process for asset management have been covered within the scope of IEAMS project.

SYSTEM BACKGROUND

The company has always been at the forefront in using information technology for business process and productivity improvements. Prior to year 2000, separate applications were used for Supply Chain, Maintenance, Finance, and Human Resources.

A project to transform all of these applications and associated processes was initiated in late 1990s with the aim to implement the best of breed applications to meet growing business requirements and make use of the latest technologies available at that time. The project consisted of the following streams:

1. Maintenance and Inventory Management System (MIMS) had the objective of defining requirements for an integrated MIMS, reviewing the existing business processes and implementation of an application meeting the requirements with minimum changes in the business processes. A leading Asset Management application having best fit to the requirements was selected.

2. The Financial System was aimed at reviewing the existing business processes, selection, and implementation of an application meeting the requirements of General Ledger, Projects, Fixed Assets, and Accounts Payables. Oracle Financials was found to be the best fit for these requirements.

3. The Human Resource System was aimed at reviewing the existing business processes, selection, and implementation of an application meeting the requirements of Human Resources, Training, and Career Development. Oracle Human Resources was found to be the best fit for these requirements.

The implementation of these applications was a major change in the company culture in making use of online applications and associated processes. These applications were commissioned in early 2000, coinciding with Y2K changes.

Since its implementation, all of these applications have gone through a number of minor and major upgrades to make use of additional features and functions in order to meet growing business requirements.

With the increased usage of these applications the users became more experienced and conversant with the usage of computer application technology and process automation which led to the growing business requirements and the need to address these through configuration or customization to the applications.

The product support from MIMS vendor did not live up to the expectations of the company. The vendor was not able to develop local or regional support desk for the provision of timely functional and technical support of the application.

The company support staff was not able to address all of the user requirements due to lack of proper support from the vendor and since a number of the user requirements required customization to the application. Although, certain less complex customizations were carried out by company support staff, certain other customizations could not be implemented as the changes needed were to be carried out/ developed by the product vendor. It forced various users to develop their own standalone and disjointed applications.

The need to streamline processes and usage of e-Business within core business to become a more customer-focused organization was identified as one of the strategic objectives of the company. It required major transformation with regard to the tools and technologies being used for organizing the work. In order to achieve the objectives, the management decided to assess the possibility of replacing the existing MIMS application with more powerful Enterprise Asset Management software.

It led to a review on the utilization of MIMS software and associated vendor support services. The review resulted in recommendations to replace MIMS due to the following factors:

- A lower than average performance and inadequate support from application vendor thus hampering effective utilization of MIMS.
- Diminishing presence of application vendor in the region.
- The vendor product strategy and rigidity of the application to adapt to growing business needs.

INTRODUCTION

A task team was established to define the high-level requirement, evaluate, and recommend the most suitable product meeting these requirements to replace MIMS as per recommendations of the review carried out earlier.

The evaluation of various options was carried out through extensive market research and benchmarking with other Oil & Gas companies in the GCC to identify the business solution that provides the best fit to the business requirement of the company . It culminated in the selection of Maximo® as the software of the choice. The project was named "Integrated Enterprise Asset Management Systems" and known in the company by its acronym as IEAMS.

Upon commencement of the project, the Managing Director designated his Deputy Managing Director as the Project Sponsor, appointed a Project Manager, and established a Project Steering Committee and a Project Task Force. It demonstrated the top management's support for the project, which is vital for the projects of such magnitude and complexity.

The IEAMS project has brought a paradigm shift in terms of the work organization by moving from a Work Management to Enterprise Asset Management concept. It has integrated all of the related processes from project initiation to Asset Write-offs (project initiation/ approval, asset creation/ operation/ maintenance/ write-offs, contract initiation/ execution/ payments) with the involvement of all the related organizational units with the company.

The IEAMS project has resulted in the replacement of MIMS and more than 100 legacy and standalone applications by providing additional features, better built-in processes and workflows. The solution has been tailored to suit company business requirements so as to extract the benefits in the best possible way but without diluting the identity and significance of any of the current processes and functions.

The IEAMS is interfaced and integrated with other applications that are currently being used, such as Oracle Financial, Human Resources, Hospital System, Document Management System, Primavera, Work Permit system, and many more applications.

The eBusiness component of the project is currently being rolled out. It will provide suppliers / contractors (Business Partners) with Web-based online, secured, and round-the-clock access to the business opportunities offered by the company. It will leverage IEAMS infrastructure and underlying applications to advance, automate and streamline the current processes of purchasing and contracting by providing secure and fast communication channels between company and its Business Partners. It will also provide collaborative tools to Contracts and Purchasing professionals to conduct strategic activities (requirements definition, tendering, negotiation, award, and administration) of the procurement cycle, online with Business Partners.

INTEGRATED ENTERPRISE ASSET MANAGEMENT (IEAMS) PROJECT

The Integrated Enterprise Asset Management Systems project or IEAMS was launched after obtaining approvals from the senior management to replace MIMS with more powerful Enterprise Asset Management software covering full cycle of asset management. After a thorough selection process, Maximo® was selected as the product of choice and contract was awarded to a leading regional Maximo® implementation partner.

It was a major initiative taken by the company and in line with company strategy; initiative was also taken to implement eBusiness system as part of this project to enable electronic interaction with its business partners.

The implementation of IEAMS was to lead the company towards making use of the leading technologies in improving its business processes, employee productivity, reduced downtime and maintenance costs on field equipment and improved governance as one of the identified benefits.

The system was also expected to brings in a paradigm shift in the philosophy of work organization by moving towards Enterprise Asset Management concept from Work Management principles by integrating all of the related processes from project initiation to Asset Write-offs (Project initiation/ approval, Asset creation/ Operation/ Maintenance/ Write-offs, Warehouse operations and Supply Chain, Contract initiation/ Execution/ Payments) with the involvement of all the related stakeholders.

The IEAMS implementation also expected to result in the following benefits:

- Elimination of various legacy systems and standalone applications resulting in application consolidation and process standardization.

- Interfacing with other applications will result in seamless integration of the workflows.
- Business process automation in company departments where MIMS was not in use.
- Streamlining and alignment of operations through best practices and improved business processes.
- Reduced lead-time in provision of materials and services with increased efficiency.
- Faster decision making based on real time, timely and online information.

The senior management realized the importance of the project for company operations and provided sponsorship and support to the project at the highest level. The Managing Director of the company established IEAMS Steering Committee under the sponsorship of a his Deputy Managing Director to provide leadership and support for the implementation activities of IEAMS project across the company to ensure provision of the required resources from across the company for its successful implementation.

IEAMS: Project Organization

The IEAMS project teams and committees were established by Managing Director of the company. The project was sponsored by deputy Managing Director and supervised by Steering Committee consisting of key stakeholders from across the company and IEAMS project manager.

The project task force was headed by the project manager. The functional leads responsible for their specific functional areas were its members.

Each of the functional lead was also leading its own sub functional team responsible for the implementation within each of the specific application functionality.

The project organization structure is shown in Figure 1, which is followed by a brief description on the roles and responsibilities of various committees and teams.

Steering Committee

IEAMS Steering Committee was responsible for providing leadership and necessary support to the project team for the successful implementation by championing business process changes and ensuring required resource availability from across various organization units in the company.

Figure 1. IEAMS organization structure

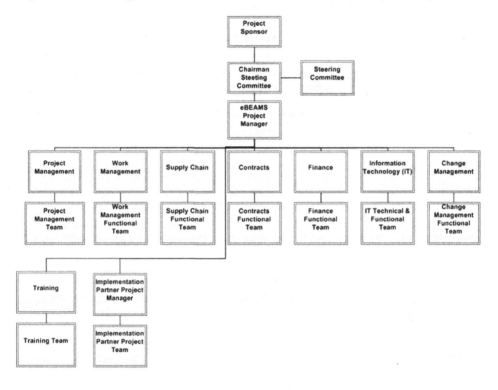

IEAMS Task Force (TF)

IEAMS task force was headed by IEAMS Project Manager reporting to Chairman IEAMS Steering Committee. The TF was responsible for the actual implementation of the project, establishment of various sub task forces, coordinating and directing various teams involved towards the achievement of the objectives, approval of the deliverables and addressing and resolving project and cross-functional issues.

Functional Teams (FT)

Each of the functional area (Work Management, Contracts, Supply Chain, Finance, and Information Technology) in the project was controlled by the respective functional team whose team leader was represented in the TF. They act as the bridge between the project teams and the respective end users. It was the responsibility of the respective functional teams to ensure that all the user requirements are addressed properly. The functional teams were also responsible to review and approve project deliverables for their respective functional areas.

Project Management Team

IEAMS Project Management team was responsible to coordinate IEAMS project activities with FTs and Contractor to achieve the successful implementation of project. It was also responsible to continuously monitor the progress of the project to ensure its compliance to the quality, standards, scope, cost, and time frame. It was also to act as single point of contact with the contractor, perform quality assurance for all project deliverables, identify, and mitigate risks.

Training Team

The training team was responsible to ensure that adequate end user training is provided to all company personnel those need to use the system just in time and prior to Go Live to ensure smooth switch over from MIMS. The training team was to coordinate with FTs and Contractor to finalize the training curriculum, prepare, and organize the training based on the outcome of training survey. The training team was to further coordinate with the user team to obtain enrollment, organize logistics for the training, and arrange for the training to be conducted.

Change Management Team

Change Management Team was entrusted to make the transition smooth by creating awareness and acceptability among end-users, reducing the level of resistance by addressing end-user concerns, ensuring adequate training, and communicating a 'positive image' of the change across the company. The Change Management Team was assisted by the Change Agents from users group to work towards the achievement of its goals.

The Change Agents were responsible to act IEAMS Champions within their respective organization units and promote knowledge and awareness by conducting information sessions and seminars within their working domain.

IEAMS: Project Scope and System Overview

The IEAMS project envisaged replacement of existing MIMS with Maximo® and many of the standalone applications developed independently by users to support their day-to-day operations.

The project scope includes configuration and tailoring of Maximo® to suit business requirements so to achieve the business benefits in the best possible way but without diluting the identity and significance of any of the current processes and functions.

The project scope included the following main functional areas:

Work Management: It includes complete life cycle management of assets from the project initiation to asset write-off including asset acquisition, maintenance and write-off processes.

Supply Chain: It includes all warehouse and supply chain management functions including procurement, replenishment of material, and management of stock levels.

Contracts: It includes complete Contracts Management Cycle from the initiation of a Contract Requisition from users to preparation of RFP, issuance of Tender Document, evaluation of bids, contract award, and contract administration.

Finance: It includes:

- Allocation and management of funds and budgets.
- Management of projects and asset capitalization upon project completion.
- Payment of invoices to contractors and suppliers.

eBusiness: It include provision of Web-based online secured round-the-clock access to the Business Partners (Contractors, Suppliers, Manufacturers) to access their Contractors/ Purchase Orders, invoices. The website is also available to prospective Business Partners to review the business opportunities offered by the company and submit their bids online through eBusiness.

IT Services Management (ITSM): it includes management of all IT assets including servers, workstations, communication equipment, software and Service Desk activities.

Integration with other applications: IEAMS is integrated with a number of other applications within the company to ensure timely, transparent and secure exchange of information between applications.

IEAMS PROJECT IMPLEMENTATION

After establishment of the project teams and award of contract, the project commenced with the work to be carried out in accordance with the project stages as shown below:

Stage 1: Initiation and Planning

The project initiation and planning activities were carried out during this stage that includes:

- Establishment of project management standards and preparation of the project implementation plan and all other related plan including communication plan, risk management plan, configuration plan, change management plan.
- Forming the strategies on training, testing, data migration, and conversion.
- Maximo® software installation.
- Infrastructure requirements study to assess the requirements for infrastructure components required to successfully host Maximo® application.
- Familiarization of Contractor Consultants with As-Is business processes.
- Existing application discovery.
- Maximo® training for project teams.

Stage 2: Analysis and Design

The main activity during this stage was the preparation of the To-Be processes, other activities include:

- To-Be Processes, business impact, and related process changes.
- Fit - Gap Analysis to identify changes required in Maximo®.
- Integration and Interfaces between Maximo® and other applications, study and functional specifications, and implementation plan.
- Data cleansing, conversion, and migration related tasks and preparation of data migration plan.
- Design of workflows.
- Preparation of training plan in accordance with the revised processes and training strategy.
- Preparation of testing plan in accordance with the testing strategy.
- Infrastructure and Security plan.

Stage 3: Configure and Build

Most of the work in this stage was technical in nature such as:

- Maximo® configuration including enhancements, customizations, workflow and interface development.
- Development and setup of data extraction, conversion, migration, and data load programs.

Stage 4: Testing and Training

During this stage, the data was migrated, actual testing of the application was carried out and users were trained on Maximo®.

- Data migration, conversion, and upload to Maximo®.
- Testing and verification of Maximo® including Unit, Integrated, User Acceptance, and performance testing.
- Go Live planning and Mock Cutovers.
- End user training

Stage 5: Cutover and Go-Live

During this stage, necessary environments were setup to ensure smooth system operations upon and after Go Live. The main activities during this stage were:

- Go Live assessment and Go-No-Go decision.
- Final Data Migration and upload to production.
- Go Live.

APPLICATION DISCOVERY

A number of standalone and disjointed applications were developed independently by the users to meet their day-to-day requirements. In order to address users requirements it was extremely important to ensure that all such applications are identified, studied, evaluated, documented with all of the required details and its dispositions strategy is formed that includes:

- The current and recommended status of the applications.
- Summary migration strategy for the application to be decommissioned.
- Identification of interfaces and integrations for the applications not to be decommissioned.

These following steps were taken for the achievement of these objectives:

- A survey for the identification of these applications was conducted across the Company. It resulted in discovery of more than 150 applications.
- Each of the identified application was analysed for further consideration for additional study and analysis. It resulted in identification of 120 applications.

- After obtaining additional details from concerned user groups on these applications, 81 applications were identified for detailed analysis and as candidate for replacement or integration/interface with Maximo®.

As-Is workshop sessions were then used to ensure the processes/process steps where a standalone application was being used to support day-to-day business were identified. Using the basic information gathered during these sessions, additional workshops were arranged to discuss details of these applications requiring additional input from users. It is to be noted that there was not enough information available for most of the identified application and clarification on the following was required:

- Why the standalone application was developed/ used and not MIMS?
- What is the functionality and the process behind each information tracked using the application?
- Who provides this information and at what stage?
- What is the usage of the information kept in the application?
- Are there any interface to other system(s), and if so how information is exchanged between them?
- Are there any security constraints?

Based on information gathered during the sessions following analysis was performed:

- Possibility to replace standalone application by Maximo® standard or new application and its potential benefits.
- Estimate configuration effort required to bring a standalone application into Maximo®.
- Estimate data conversion and customization efforts.
- Interface needs to other system(s) and effort required to develop them.

The application discovery provided valuable input and insight into the user requirements that led them to develop standalone applications. It also provided detailed information on various data sources for data migration to Maximo®.

IEAMS PROCESSES

During the Analysis and Design stage of the project (Stage 2) a number of workshops with functional teams were conducted to define the To-Be business processes.

The approach used in defining the To Be Business Process was to conduct the process workshops with the functional teams for corresponding functional areas and work streams. These workshops were intended to specify the standard business process using Maximo® for the related functional areas. These were based on the existing As-Is processes, current business practices, suggested best practices, current and future integrations with other systems, functionality and capabilities of Maximo®.

The outcome of theses workshops were documented and additional requirements identified during the workshops were analysed based on three major aspects

- Business Priority
- Complexity
- Business Benefits it may bring.

Table 1's key design principles were used during the To-Be process design.

The findings of the workshops, the analysis of the identified additional requirements and identified gaps with the functionality of Maximo® were then presented to the functional teams for their review and confirmation.

These workshops, their findings, and user confirmation formed the basis for the To-Be business processes for each of the functional area and work stream. The gaps identified during these workshops were documented for further analysis and resolution by configuration, enhancement, or customization to Maximo®.

IEAMS high-level processes are shown in Figure 2.

Table 1. Design principles

IEAMS Design Principle	Rationale
Re use existing knowledge and processes	• The functionality must be repeatable and deliver value to reduce risk and implementation costs • Leverage on the standard business process • Reduce cost • Reduce risk
Adopt a minimal customization approach	• Improve the management of change • Permit localization to suit specific needs • Reduce risk (performance and upgrade)
Adopt the best practices	• Adopt industry practices • Standardize practices

Figure 2. IEAMS high level processes

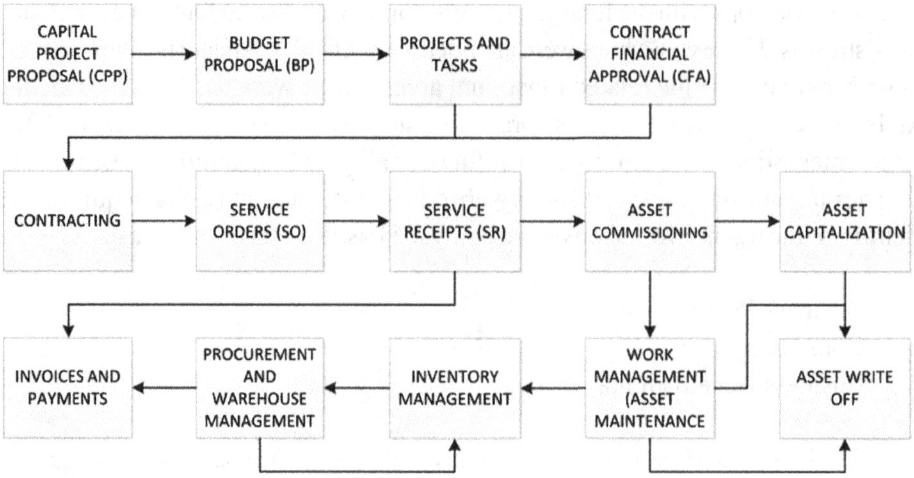

DATA MIGRATION/CONVERSION AND CLEANSING

Data is one of the most important assets of any organization. The company has been using various systems for the past many decades, these systems have produced a vast amount of data and information. The migration of the data from existing applications to the application being implemented is one of the most important tasks to be carried out in any application implementation project.

The objectives of the data extraction, cleansing, migration and conversion were to upload the new system with data that is accurate, cleansed, standardized, and required for business operations and to meet regulatory requirements. Any data that was not required for business operations and meeting regulatory requirements was to be archived and not to be uploaded to Maximo®.

The key tasks carried out during data migration are:

1. Data source identification: to identify various sources of data so as to carry out its amalgamation and standardization.
2. Data conversion and transformation: the data that needs to be converted to meet Maximo® application requirements and based on the To-Be business processes.
3. Manual data gathering: Identification of the data elements that are required by Maximo® and revised To-Be business processes but do not exist electronically in any of the existing applications of data sources.
4. Data Mapping: A mapping scheme to map each data element from various data sources into Maximo® data elements.

Data Migration Approach

The overview of the data migration approach is shown in the Figure 3.

All of the probable sources of data to be migrated to Maximo® were identified early in the project. The task of identifying the data sources began from Stage-1 with the application discovery. More than 80 applications were identified from which data needed to be migrated, amalgamated or interfaced to Maximo®.

After identification of the data sources, the analysis of data from each of these data sources was carried out. It resulted in the data sources and specifically data elements that need to be migrated to Maximo®.

The To-Be business processes resulted in identification of the requirements for data transformation with the new coding schemes to be used in Maximo®.

Data cleansing is extremely important during data migration to a new application. During day-to-day operations of the application, due importance is generally not given to the quality of data. The data quality suffers if proper validation controls are not applied through the application and standard business practices are not followed.

Over a period of time, huge amount of data was accumulated in the applications. The migration of each and every data element and record to the target system was not a preferred approach. Rather, the migration of historical data was based on the regulatory and reporting requirements.

After a detailed and in-depth analysis, a staging area was designed to be used to take input in a standard format from all of the identified data sources for any of the transaction and data element to be uploaded to Maximo®.

Figure 3. IEAMS data migration overview

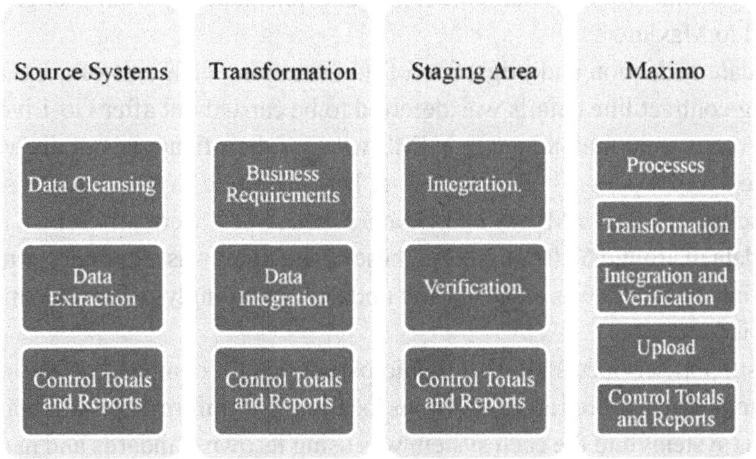

229

The mapping schemes from the source systems to the staging area and from staging are to Maximo® were developed. Subsequently, data extraction scripts to extract data from the source systems and data upload scripts to upload data from the Staging Area to Maximo® were developed. Consideration was given to the business and transformation rules defined in the To-Be business process documents.

The data verification reports, control totals and checksums were used at every stage to verify and confirm the accuracy of the migrated data.

The procedures were used and applied repeatedly to refine the data migration process until Cutover and Go Live.

Data Cleansing

A major task was undertaken to cleanse and standardize the data of 115,000 catalogue items out of a total of 200,000 items. A company specializing in such a task was engaged to carry out this task. It required manual verification of some of the items at the warehouse and then standardizing their specifications. The Catalogues items all of its associated data including Manufacturer/ Part number, Description, Commodity Codes etc. was cleansed and reformatted in accordance with Petroleum Industry Data Exchange (PIDX) standard templates conforming to United Nations Standard Products and Services Code® (UNSPSC®).

The migration of Contracts data was a challenging task. Minimum amount of information was kept in MIMS to allow for administration of contracts and payment of invoices. Other contractual details were either kept in paper files or various scattered data sources. The business processes designed in Maximo® require in-depth and detailed information regarding each contract.

The data was collected from multiple data sources, at times, these sources provided conflicting information. This information was manually verified. The remaining mandatory data elements were collected manually from user groups and migrated to Maximo®.

The data collection and migration of the remaining elements of contracts data including contract line details was deferred to be carried out after Go-Live.

The Assets were maintained in MIMS whereas their financial details were kept in Oracle Fixed Assets. There was no link between these two data sources and the coding schemes used in MIMS and Oracle Fixed Assets were different.

The data of around 67,000 assets in these two sources was mapped manually and the existing asset data was cleansed and updated accordingly before data migration was carried out.

The support services including municipal service for company offices and staff accommodation scattered around various location. This information was maintained in various systems and the each system was using its own standards and naming for various locations and buildings. A standard location hierarchy was created and data from various sources was mapped, converted, and migrated using the new hierarchy.

The various systems were used to maintain IT assets, associated user requests, and incidents. The data from these systems was also standardized, amalgamated from multiple sources, converted, and migrated using the standard location hierarchy prepared for company offices.

Data Migration: Cutovers

A number of data migration cutovers were planned during IEAMS project. The objective of these cutover was to identify issues related to data migration early in the process, address and resolve the issues. This process was repeated a three times before Go Live to ensure that all issues have been addressed and resolved.

The following is the list of activities carried out in each of the data migration cutover:

- Execute and review output of each of the migration and upload scripts.
- Review the quality of cleansed data.
- Refine extracted data based on the modified business rules and To-Be processes.
- Identify and resolve any exceptions.
- Review control total and checksums and resolve any differences.
- Execute reports in source and target systems to ensure the correctness of data, specially related to financial related information.

This process was repeated and three data migration cutovers were carried out:

- The first cutover took three months. Most of the issues related to the quality of data, extraction, and upload procedures were addressed and resolved.
- The second data migration cutover took two months to ensure all data is migrated successfully.
- The third data migration cutover took two weeks, which was a significant improvement and an indication that the processes and procedures being used for data migration are working properly.
- The final data migration cutover at the time of Go Live took three days. Thus minimising the system downtime required to switchover from the old MIMS to the new IEAMS—Maximo®.

TESTING AND VERIFICATION

The testing and verification is an integral part of any implementation project to ensure that the system is working in accordance with the expectations. The following approach was adopted and used for system testing and verification during IEAMS project.

- Each of the modified configuration item (screen, program unit, database item, etc.) modified was tested independently by persons responsible for making the changes.
- Unit Testing was carried out on an application/ module basis. It included testing each unit independently after completing its configuration. It ensures that all configurations have been applied, the module and related applications are operational and producing expected results.
- Integrated Testing was carried out by the project team and contractor resources jointly after completing the unit test. It included testing all modules, related interfaces, and integrations to ensure proper functioning of all modules, related processes, and workflows. It was carried out using the testing scenarios developed jointly during the project.
- User Acceptance Testing was carried out after completing the integrated testing. It included testing all modules, related interfaces, and integrations to ensure proper functioning of all modules, related processes, and workflows. It was to be carried out independently by the functional teams.
- Performance Testing was to ensure that the system is performing properly and to identify and address any issues related to infrastructure components including servers, databases, networks, and application environment configuration.

The integrated testing and user acceptance testing were the most important testing and verifications steps carried out during the project. It involved the use of cross-functional teams for Integrated Testing. Functional team members from all functional areas like Work Management, Supply Chain, Contracts, Finance, and IT were involved in the process.

Each team member was assigned specific responsibilities as part of the testing process. It was to capitalize on the core functional competencies of functional team members and to ensure cross-functional issues are dealt with immediately. They were assigned specific roles for testing the workflows and validations in the system.

The testing was carried out at a location that was specially configured to host integrated and user acceptance testing. Thus co-locating key functional users from all functional areas and carrying out testing in accordance with test scenarios and test cases until successful completion of the testing process to the satisfaction of key functional users.

TRAINING

The training strategy used during the project, as detailed below, was to ensure smooth rollout of the system to end users.

- All users should be trained on their system processes and operations prior to using the system in a live environment.
- All users should be trained as close as possible to the Go Live date to ensure utilization of application soon after completing the training.
- Training will be carried out on the configured system and following the typical processes and workflows that are used in specific job roles by the users.
- The End User Training will be led by trainer provided by the contractor and assisted by a super user.

The training team was responsible for organizing and scheduling the training courses, staff enrollment in the courses and training logistics.

The training curriculum was prepared by the contractor in consultation with the respective functional teams. A total of 35 distinct training courses were finalized. These were ranging for generic courses regarding Maximo® to specific and specialized training in functional areas.

A training survey was conducted to assess the expected number of trainees that are expected to attend these courses. As a result of the survey, a total number 542 sessions for the 35 courses were organized.

These sessions were held over a period of five months with two months before Go Live targeting heavy users of the application. This extensive training program was conducted in 16 different class rooms across the company. Six of these classrooms located in the field areas in close proximity to the work location of operations and maintenance staff. It helped the training team in organizing 16 parallel sessions during peak times of the training program. All efforts were made to organize the classes close to the workplace of the trainees.

The training program was a success and training team succeeded in organising training as close as possible to the Go Live date.

CHANGE MANAGEMENT

It was also recognized in IEAMS Project organization structure and Change Management Team was entrusted with providing a structured approach to transit from MIMS to IEAMS as the desired future state.

The Management of Change is the key to success of any project. Change Management Team was entrusted to make the transition smooth by creating awareness and acceptability among end-users, reducing the level of resistance by addressing end-user concerns, ensuring adequate training, and communicating a 'positive image' of change across the company. The Change Management Team was assisted by the nominated Change Agents from users group to work towards the achievement of its goals.

The Change Agents were responsible to act as IEAMS Champions within their respective organization units and promote knowledge and awareness by conducting information sessions and seminars within their working domain to ensure smooth transition from MIMS to IEAMS.

The Change Management team laid out their detailed strategy to spread awareness on IEAMS across the company. The first step in this regard was branding IEAMS. A logo was created with indicative yellow colors that could be easily recognized and attentive for all company staff. This logo was subsequently used throughout the project in all communications, presentations, newsletters, billboards, leaflets, screen saver, articles and publications. It was one of the key initiatives in driving awareness.

An IEAMS project site was created on company portal containing all IEAMS related material to help all stakeholders, end user, and company staff in obtaining any of the information from a single source.

The Change Agents were assigned to deliver messages by conducting presentations, workshops, seminars, and surveys within their areas of responsibility to keep the staff informed of the project progress and status on a continuous basis.

The change agents were briefed by selected functional leads during their monthly meetings on the progress in specific functional areas so as to convey the same message back to the end users.

The change agents were required to regularly update the team with their progress within their areas of responsibility. The change agents with high level of contribution were recognized throughout the project.

The company offices are scattered in a vast geographical area. In order to reach the maximum number of employees, outdoor advertising campaign was launched by the team. During these campaigns, company billboards were used to spread awareness for IEAMS and posters were supplied to various offices to be posted at key locations. Three such campaigns were held during the course of the project

In preparation of the Go Live of IEAMS project, efforts were made to create more interest amongst employees to enhance their knowledge and awareness regarding IEAMS. A roadshow was launched throughout the company in all directorates. It was based on game shows and inspired by a few well-known popular television game shows. The game show was entitled by the change management team as, "Who wants to be an IEAMER."

The material to be used during the competition was carefully prepared by the team members with assistance from the functional leads of respective functional teams. The preparation material was made available to the users through the competition website.

Key members of the functional teams, who were also members of the change management team, were selected to prepare a question bank to assess the awareness and knowledge level of the employees participating in the competition. A sufficient number of questions and answers for the competition were prepared by the sub team. All questions prepared by the sub team were based on the functionality of IEAMS, related company processes and the changes that being introduced and implemented.

The competition was divided into three rounds as:

- The Qualifying round, it was open to all employees of a specific directorate with top 10 employees from each of the directorate of the company for the Directorate round. It was based on online questions through website.
- The Directorate round was held for directorate of the company, the qualified employees from qualifying round participated in a competitive sessions in front of audience including senior management. Top three employees were awarded prizes and the winner qualified for the Corporate round.
- The Corporate round, Grand Finale
  - The winners of the Directorate round from participated in this round played in front of company senior management and invited guests.
  - The winner of this round was crowned as "IEAMER"
  - This round was scheduled to coincide with the Go Live of IEAMS project.

The Grand Finale was an extravaganza; all competitors were fully prepared with the knowledge of IEAMS. It also provided the audience an opportunity to gain knowledge on IEAMS. After a tough and entertaining competition, the winner was recognized by the Managing Director and the project sponsor.

The change management team was able to achieve a high level of awareness regarding IEAMS across the company through the innovative change management program.

CUTOVER AND GO LIVE

The cutover and Go Live of IEAMS project followed the user acceptance testing and a decision by the Steering Committee to Go Live.

A cutover and go live plan was prepared with clearly specifying the tasks and associated responsibilities. The plan was detailed enough to plan tasks and activities by the minute. It was to ensure that the objective of minimising the downtime is achieved.

An awareness campaign to the users was launched two weeks in advance to prepare them for Go Live. It included awareness messages, the tasks to be carried out during system unavailability and other related information.

Some of the key activities carried out during this period include:

- Production server configuration.
- Application environment setup and tuning.
- Database setup and tuning.
- Data migration, conversion, transformation, and verification.
- Application and workflow testing and verification.
- Final verification of processes with the migrated data.

A new internal IEAMS application portal was developed and launched with all relevant material for users to assist is utilization of IEAMS. In addition to the links to IEAMS – Maximo® application, the portal site included:

- IEAMS training manuals.
- To-Be business processes.
- Step by Step instructions to carry out key transactions using IEAMS.
- Quick reference guides.
- Frequently asked questions.

All stakeholders were kept well informed with the progress of the cutover. The manual procedures to be followed during the cutover period were also communicated to the users. The outgoing application—MIMS—was made unavailable on the well-advertised date and time.

The cutover tasks were carried out during four-day period including weekend. During this period, the project team members worked round the clock went smoothly and the system was launched as per the plan.

CONCLUSION AND LESSONS LEARNED

IEAMS project was of a complex nature with a huge scope of work covering varying types of assets, functionalities, and processes by a single software application product. The efforts exerted and the innovations carried out during IEAMS project were recognized and company was awarded the Maximo® Asset Management Maintenance Best Practice award.

The project achieved its objectives by automating the majority of identified processes related to Asset Lifecycle. A number of changes in the processes and business practices were introduced through IEAMS. With the Go Live of IEAMS, the adaptation of new processes and associated changes by the users started and with the passage of time, the utilization of IEAMS has gained momentum.

Innovative strategies were used during the project for change management to keep the stakeholder and end users well informed, be involved in upcoming changes to enable a smooth rollout of the system.

The following are some of the lessons learned and improvements that can be carried out in future similar projects:

- The project of such magnitude consists of a number of sub projects that need to be completed independently while keeping track of dependencies to achieve the main objective. A dedicated project management office will enable smooth handling and coordination between sub-projects.
- A small dedicated core project team consisting of key personnel will ensure key decisions are taken in timely manner.
- Co-locating the key project personnel will result in better coordination and faster resolution of project issues.
- Although an extensive change manage program was carried out during IEAMS project. More effective communication to ensure user ownership of the change is required.
- Despite training a large number of users, a number of end-user were not able to attend the training courses. The training program should include continued refresher courses. The refresher courses should be launched prior to Go Live to allow users to refresh their knowledge. This program should continue for some time (6 months to one year) after Go Live.
- Train the Trainer approach should be applied to such project by training key business users to conduct awareness and training sessions within their domains.
- A continued training program including Computer based training should also be made available.

- Support from the line management of the users is required to ensure attendance during the training.
- Develop cross: functional skills in project team resources. Functional users within the project team tend to concentrate on their specific functionalities and the bigger picture of the entire system remains unexplained.
- The project scope should be controlled in a better way by defining the scope in unambiguous manner. The ambiguities in the scope definition can be interpreted differently by different people.
- Business processes should be streamlined by making use of the best practices. There is a general tendency in such projects to adopt the individual business practices that lead to customizations to the application.
- The customizations to the application should be kept to the minimum and all efforts should be made to make the changes through configurations that can be ported to the new release by automated processes.
- Phased implementation of different asset clauses will help in the better management of process and project complexity and better utilization of resources.
- Go Live is the beginning of a journey and not end of the project. The post Go-Live support structure including establishment of support desk needs to be carried out much before the Go Live date to ensure smooth transition.

REFERENCES

Motwani, J., Mirchandani, D., Madan, M., & Gunasekaran, A. (2002). Successful implementation of ERP projects: Evidence from two case studies. *International Journal of Production Economics, 75*(1/2), 83. doi:10.1016/S0925-5273(01)00183-9

Olhager, J., & Selldin, E. (2003). Enterprise resource planning survey of Swedish manufacturing firms. *European Journal of Operational Research, 146*(2), 365. doi:10.1016/S0377-2217(02)00555-6

Robey, D., Ross, J., & Boudreau, M. (2002). Learning to implement enterprise systems: An exploratory study of the dialectics of change. *Journal of Management Information Systems, 19*(1), 17.

Sheu, C., Rebecca Yen, H., & Krumwiede, D. (2003). The effect of national differences on multinational ERP implementation: An exploratory study. *Total Quality Management and Business Excellence, 14*(6), 639.

Tatsiopoulos, I., Panayiotou, N., Kirytopoulos, K., & Tsitsiriggos, K. (2003). Risk management as a strategic issue for the implementation of ERP systems: A case study from the oil industry. *International Journal of Risk Assessment and Management, 4*(1), 20. doi:10.1504/IJRAM.2003.003434

Trimmer, K., Pumphrey, L., & Wiggins, C. (2002). ERP implementation in rural health care. *Journal of Management in Medicine, 16*(2/3), 113. doi:10.1108/02689230210434871

KEY TERMS AND DEFINITIONS

CM: Change Management.
FT: Functional Team.
HSE: Health, Safety, and Environment.
IEAMS: Integrated Enterprise Asset Management.
ITF: IEAMS Task Force.
ITSM: IT Services Management.
MIMS: Maintenance and Inventory Management System.
RFP: Request for Proposal.
SC: Supply Chain.
TF: Task Force.
WM: Work Management.

Chapter 13
ITIL Implementation in a Major Arabian Gulf Company:
Approach and Challenges

Mohamed Elhefnawi
UDEAL, UAE

EXECUTIVE SUMMARY

The experience of many organizations that have automated their business capabilities using enterprise information systems indicates that the realization of the sought business gains and promised returns on investment are conditional to having in place an effective strategy to support and maintain such systems technically and functionally during the post-implementation phase. It is argued that the proper implementation of Information Technology Infrastructure Library (ITIL) represents an ideal forum for providing effective support tools that include service/help desk and incident reporting functions for end-users to report problems and issues or request enhancements, change management and configuration management functions to manage and document changes to the applications and functionalities, as well as IT infrastructure inventory and tracking applications. ITIL framework is widely used as a best-practice framework for IT services management. It outlines a set of integrated processes and procedures that will structure and re-engineer IT services activities, shifting IT function to be enterprise-wide business-focused while making the best use of the deployed technology. The case described in this chapter reflects the approach adopted by the IT function of an Arabian Gulf Company (AGC) used for ITIL implementation, highlighting the main challenges that have been encountered in this project.

DOI: 10.4018/978-1-4666-2220-3.ch013

INTRODUCTION

ITIL is used as a framework of IT services best practices that define a set of integrated processes and procedures that will structure and re-engineer IT services activities. ITIL redefines the scope and role IT function from a limited discrete function to an enterprise-wide, business-focused function that links effective technology adoption to business strategy and vision.

The main benefits associated with ITIL solution include the following:

- Greater alignment of IT services, processes and goals with business requirements, expectations, and goals.
- Improvement of availability, reliability, and security of mission-critical IT services.
- Higher quality of IT services.
- Increased IT productivity.
- Permanently lowered Total Cost of IT Ownership (TCO) including services costs.
- Minimizing risk due to IT infrastructure changes.
- Provision of demonstrable IT performance indicators.

The case is concerned with the issues and challenges encountered by AGC as ITIL was being implemented and is concluded with lessons learned from this experience.

The implementation has followed a phased approach. The first phase established the core services support processes: Incident Management, Problem Management, Change Management, Configuration Management, and Release Management. The second phase had focused on the implementation of additional ITIL processes (Service Level Management, Financial Management, Capacity Management, Availability Management, and IT Service Continuity Management). A post-implementation review was conducted after two months from completing the two project phases to ensure stabilization of introduced ITIL activities prior to assessing improvements in the delivered IT services.

BACKGROUND

Business has become strongly dependent on IT solutions to enable it to deliver its products and services. In fact, IT has become pivotal for any Company to accomplish its business goals and objectives. ITD is continuously aiming to improve their services and streamline their operations through adopting international standards and best-practices. ITIL has emerged as the industry de-facto standard and best-

Figure 1. ITIL: aligning people, technology, and process for continuous improvement

practices for IT services management that is widely used nowadays. ITIL provides a comprehensive framework for IT services support and delivery processes that align people, technology and processes to achieve performance excellence and meet stakeholders' expectations as depicted in Figure 1.

ITIL has undergone various version upgrades. The first ITIL version was introduced in the 1980s. The second version was released in the late 1990s, with a strong emphasis on operational process maturity Current ITIL V3 focuses on the entire IT service life cycle, taking the ultimate consumer of the services—the business—into consideration. Thus, ITIL V3 paves the way for making IT a business partner by providing technology and components to support the business and enables ITD to shift its focus from producing IT capabilities to delivering business technology services and from the management of IT silos to holistic governance of IT services. The ITIL V3 life cycle phases are:

Service Strategy: This phase primarily focuses on the planning aspects of a service strategy and the inclusion of key organizations inside and outside IT to provide true service delivery. The key activities of the service strategy phase are:

- Defining the various customers that will consume IT services
- Understanding customers' expectations and needs
- Building a funding mechanism to support customer needs
- Determining methods for managing customer demand
- Developing an IT service portfolio

Service Design: The second phase has more structure and explains a step-by-step approach to designing services. This phase focuses on designing the services to support the strategy defined in the first phase as part of the planning cycle. Many of the puzzle pieces were already addressed by ITIL v2 with the exception of security management—an excellent addition. The key activities of the service design phase are:

• Developing an IT service catalog
• Building the service assets
• Creating processes to support the delivery of service

Service Transition: This phase is concerned with configuration, change, and release management. Change management focuses on how to assess and plan for changes. To effectively manage change, IT must know what configuration items exist, how they are related to each other, and what services are supported via these configuration items. The subject of configuration management has been extended to include service assets, or IT assets, which are also important for IT to be aware of. IT organizations have funded asset management processes and tools in the past with a strong financial focus. This new phase describes the need to manage configuration items as part of the change, release, and capacity management process. The subject of service validation, testing, and quality assurance is introduced along with knowledge management. The key activities of the service transition phase are:

• Providing the capability to smoothly move new IT services from design in to production
• Providing for the deployment of enhancements to existing IT services
• Managing the integrity of configurations

Service Operation: Like Service Transition, Service Operation focuses on the "Do" in the PDCA cycle. This phase focuses on the restoration of services and mostly incorporates all of the key pieces from the service support in ITIL v2. The key activities of the service operation phase are:

• Supporting the successful operations of services that are in production
• Leveraging incident management and problem management to improve the mean time to restore service and to reduce the reoccurrence of problems
• Managing the fulfillment of IT service requests
• Providing guidance on operating an effective and efficient service desk

Continual Service Improvement: The concept of continuous improvement is not new, although it generally receives more praise than action. This phase makes it clear that, for organizations to become more proactive, assessment must be a continual process, rather than one that only happens when a failure occurs. The key activities of continual service improvement phase are:

- Provide methods to iteratively improve the effectiveness and efficiency of services
- Structure the use of service measurement and service reporting processes
- Leverage advice on the definition of critical success factors, key performance indicators, and metrics

The five ITIL phases encompass 23 IT processes making it difficult to implement in one project. Therefore, ITD has decided to follow a phased approach for implementing ITIL in the Company. This approach resulted in manageable project activities and allowed us to gradually introduce the new concepts making it easier to adapt and follow by all the ITIL stakeholders.

CURRENT IT SERVICES MANAGEMENT STATUS

ITD was delivering a range of valuable services to the wider business community. However, this was based on relatively informal relationships between the Business and IT. There were definite operational risks from a process perspective where processes are not formally documented, processes were not integrated, or were executed on ad hoc basis. Particularly concerning were those processes where large amount of time, effort, and expenditures had been invested; but they were not currently delivering the full-expected benefits to the Company's business units.

ITD had taken some good tasks in deploying some activities of the Information Technology Infrastructure Library (ITIL) based best practices, without naming them as ITIL tasks. Recently, the Company had selected ITIL as its IT services management framework and decided to embark into ITIL implementation in 2009. This approach had capitalized on those existing ad hoc ITIL activities and aimed to achieve full ITIL implementation by end of this project.

The project team had examined and assessed all service support processes affecting the Company's IT services from two main perspectives: risk to reliable service support, and process maturity. The assessment had identified areas of potential improvement in both of these areas and these should be addressed to ensure ITD will

Figure 2. Graphical summary of the company's services support processes maturity

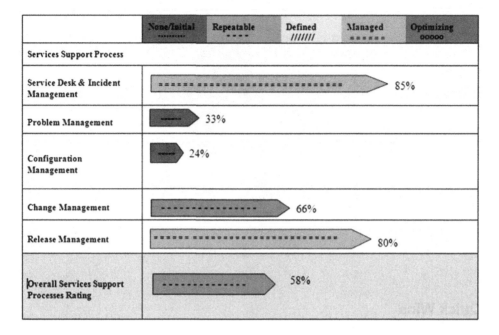

be able to reliably meet the future IT requirements of the business, especially given the planned growth of the business, and the subsequent pace of change required within the IT environment to support this growth.

Figure 2 shows that the Company has achieved an overall IT Service Management score of 58%, as an average of the maturity rating for each individual IT services support process. The average ITIL Capability Maturity Model (ITIL/CMM) based maturity rating is "Initial/Repeatable."

Figure 3 shows that the risk associated with reliable service support of two services support processes has been assessed as being High. This means that the Company had a relatively notable risk of missing their business objectives and service level commitments for IT activities depending on those high-risk processes.

It was recommended to give high priorities to improvements related to the high-risk processes in order to increase the effectiveness and efficiency of the overall IT service support processes. In addition, it was proposed that the improvements suggested within this report to be addressed in next project activities as per their business priorities.

Figure 3. Graphical summary of risks to reliable service delivery

Quick Wins

Standardize on the creation of Request for Change records for all changes to production services.

Currently software changes to the production environment are done through a paper Change Request Form. Other changes (networking, Hardware, etc.) are carried out through e-mails and are approved by the Section Heads/Team Leaders via email as well.

All Change requests should only be approved via the Change Management process and the deployed Change Management tool to be used to record and publish the planned change. This will be imperative when the Configuration Management Database is populated and deployed to ensure the content of the Configuration Management Data Base (CMDB) is accurate and up to date.

Recommendation

Develop 'Service' Focused Awareness within ITD

The current mindset within ITD is focusing primarily on the technology side of the IT services. While this has previously been a valid approach, the complexity of the current IT environment mandates that ITD should pay the highest attention to the availability of an IT service rather than the individual technical components that support the service.

It is important that individuals working with the technical support areas understand the impact of decisions they make and actions they complete on the business users. Effective methods of altering this view can include:

- IT staff experiencing life from a business user perspective (site visits, etc.).
- 2 level support staff experiencing the life of a Help Desk agent.
- ITD Department 'Open Days' to show the business users what happens within the ITD/CISD department.
- ITD Road show to emphasize the Service Provider's role of the Department.

Focused ITIL Process Resources

Proper implementation of ITIL processes mandates clear formal assignment of ITIL process roles. Non-fulfillment of this requirement will result in a lack of dedicated focus to the development, implementation, and enforcement of the defined ITIL processes.

It would be recommended that as a minimum the role of 'Service Management Champion' be created and assigned. This individual would be responsible for the review and enhancement of the existing processes, until they are at the level of maturity that they are considered the 'normal' operational method of the Company, when they can be handed over to another resource (IT process owner) for on-going activities, process maintenance, and enhancements. The intention is that the 'Service Management Champion' would then progress to defining and implementing additional ITIL processes.

The title of Service Enhancement Manager can be assigned to this role if required, with a long-term goal to transition the role from a focus on implementation of new processes, to overall control and integration of the different ITIL processes until a specific maturity level of addressed process is reached.

Ideally, all process owner roles should be defined and assigned in coordination of all concerned stakeholders. In light of the current structure within the Company, the Incident Manager role would be assigned to the Help Desk Section Leader. The Problem, Change, Configuration, and Release Managers roles would require further study of ITD activities and workloads for choosing the proper candidates for these roles.

Configuration Management: Data Population of the CMDB

There is an ad hoc Configuration Management process in existence within the Company, which does not currently provide much value due to the lack of stored content within the CMDB. To define the content required for the CMDB the following questions need to be answered for the environment:

- **Q1:** What information details of a Configuration Item (CI) should be captured and stored?
- **Q2:** How will the data be collected?
- **Q3:** How will the data be managed?
- **Q4:** How will the data be audited?

In very simplistic terms the answers could be:

- **A1:** What would (or should) be the lowest level of independent change in the environment? For hardware, this is generally relatively simple to define. Data center elements are limited in number and are critical to service delivery and as such can be recorded in some detail without generating too much data. Applications can be viewed differently, with application 'modules' defined. If a change is made to an element within the module, then the new module would be implemented and controlled via Change Management. The desktop environment depends on the level of Standardization within the Company. If there are a small number of 'standard' machines, then these can be recorded in some detail and repeated for each physical entity. If there are a number of different types of machines then the overhead of capture and subsequent management would be considerably higher.
- **A2:** Currently, the Company has BMC Remedy as the Configuration Management toolset, and Altiris as a software distribution product. Altiris has the ability to capture the inventory information of the IT environment and populate the CMDB.
- **A3:** The role of Configuration Manager has not been assigned to an individual. This role would be recommended to ensure that the appropriate focus on the day to day activities of Configuration Management is in place to manage all IT infrastructure data.
- **A4:** The appropriate exploitation of automated collection tools (Altiris as described above) will allow for a consistent audit process to be defined from an 'uncontrolled change' perspective. Physical audits would also be required to ensure the physical location of Configuration Items has not been altered.

Develop the Release Management Process

Develop the Release Management process Of the ITIL Service Support processes. The Company has not formally deployed Release Management process, although the majority of the reactive activities of this process are being covered in 'normal' activities.

The element of most risk is the Release Management process, and most particularly the control of the source software used in the production environment. Currently the development areas retain all of the software control, and each area uses different methods to achieve this control.

The ITIL Best Practice requires a formal, controlled, Definitive Software Library (DSL) where ALL software used in the live environment (O/S, utilities, in-house developed applications, packaged applications etc.) is stored, and access to this area is controlled. The goal of this approach is to ensure that all elements of the environment are available for recovery purposes, and testing of planned changes to the live environment is completed against a test bed representative of the production environment.

PROJECT APPROACH

The scope of work that was addressed of the project comprised the following tasks:

- Review of assessment of current IT services support environment including processes & tools.
- Design "To Be" IT services support processes using recommended software tool (s).
- Implementation of IT Services Processes.
- End-user Training.
- Project Closure.
- Post Implementation Assessment.

The selected implementation approach had taken into account the requirements of AGC to drive excellence in IT services. The approach aimed that the ITIL processes are developed with the involvement of the respective support teams to ensure that there was adequate consensus and ownership to make the project a success. Further, the approach also had a phase to collect feedback and improve on the requirements of the support team or management team as may be required.

The project was divided into the stages shown in Figure 4.

Figure 4. Project stages

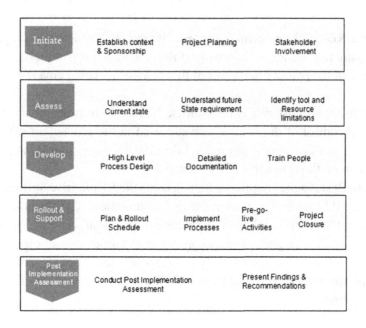

Initiation Phase

Establish Context and Sponsorship

- **Objectives:** To mobilize the project team and agree the objectives and approach.
- **Inputs:**
  - Invitation for discussion.
  - Expression of Interest.
  - Dates for meeting Project stakeholders.
- **Activities:**
  - Conduct Kick-off Meeting with key stakeholders to understand expectations and agree upon objectives of the engagement.
  - Set Context and Establish Sponsorship.
  - Develop and Agree upon Engagement Project Charter.
  - Perform Project Analysis.
- **Outputs:**
  - Letter of Engagement.
  - Engagement Project Charter.
  - Agreement on set of deliverables.

Project Planning

- **Objectives:** To agree on the list of activities, ownership, and timelines.
- **Inputs:**
  - List of deliverables.
  - Project Charter.
  - List of project team members.
- **Activities:**
  - Identify and categorize tasks.
  - Obtain AGC agreement on tasks.
  - Identify potential task owners.
  - Contact and communicate tasks and responsibilities to owners.
  - Agree on expected completion dates.
- **Outputs:**
  - List of activities.
  - Ownership assigned for activities.
  - Agreement on dates of deliverables.

Stakeholder Involvement

- **Objectives:** To ensure that there is a clear understanding of the objectives, roles, and responsibilities of AGC.
- **Inputs:** Project Objectives.
- **Activities:**
  - Agree on the roles and responsibilities of all stakeholders.
  - Agree on risk logging.
- **Outputs:**
  - Communication plan.
  - Roles and responsibilities matrix.
  - Risk log.

Assessment Phase

To Understand Current State of ITIL Processes at AGC

- **Objectives:** To understand current state of ITIL processes in AGC.
- **Inputs:** Existing Current State Assessment Report.
- **Activities:**
  - Study current state assessment report, in addition to process also assess current state of resources and tool.

- ◦ Review existing process documentation.
- ◦ Conduct further interviews to understand level of implementation.
- ◦ Identify / assign process owners.
- ◦ Use techniques like workshops, questionnaires, etc., as required.
- **Outputs:** Revised current state assessment report.

To Understand Future State Requirements and Identify Tool and Resource Limitations

- **Objectives:** To understand the Company expectations out of to-be processes.
- **Inputs:** Revised Current State Assessment Report.
- **Activities:**
  - ◦ Study current state assessment for gaps.
  - ◦ Conduct interviews with staff to understand to-be requirements.
  - ◦ Identify any limitations of the tool or existing resources in achieving to-be state.
- **Outputs:**
  - ◦ The Company considerations for to-be processes.
  - ◦ Resource and Tool Limitations.

Development Phase

High Level Process Design

- **Objectives:** To create high level process maps and confirm understanding.
- **Inputs:**
  - ◦ Current State Assessment
  - ◦ AGC inputs for to-be state.
- **Activities:**
  - ◦ Create High Level Process Maps.
  - ◦ Develop list of processes and corresponding procedures.
  - ◦ Conduct workshops/meetings to confirm process maps.
- **Outputs:** Confirmed High Level Process Maps and corresponding procedures.

Detailed Documentation

- **Objectives:** To detail the processes into process descriptions and procedures.
- **Inputs:** High level process maps.
- **Activities:**
  - ◦ Detailed Documentation of Process Description and Procedures.

- ○ Obtain agreement with process owners.
- **Outputs:** Finalized ITIL service management processes.

Train People

- **Objectives:** To detail the processes into process descriptions and procedures.
- **Inputs:** Revised ITIL service management processes.
- **Activities:**
  - ○ Identify participants.
  - ○ Create Training Material.
  - ○ Conduct process-wise sessions to process owners and IT end users.
- **Outputs:**
  - ○ ITIL Training material.
  - ○ Trained staff.

Rollout and Support Phase

Plan Rollout and Schedule and Implement Processes

- **Objectives:** Implement processes on the workflow tool and support AGC during trial period.
- **Inputs:** ITIL service management processes.
- **Activities:**
  - ○ Define schedule for implementation.
  - ○ Agree with stakeholders and communicate schedule.
  - ○ Configure tool and Implement processes on the tool.
  - ○ Monitor KPI's and produce process reports.
  - ○ Collect and record feedback from team for improvement actions.
  - ○ Modify configuration/workflow as required.
- **Outputs:**
  - ○ Implemented process on tool.
  - ○ Process Reports.
  - ○ Team Feedback on Tool Performance.

Pre-Go Live Activities

- **Objectives:** Conduct pre-go-live activities to ensure readiness of tool to go-live.
- **Inputs:** Successfully rolled out tool.

- **Activities:**
  - ◦ Obtain Project Sign Off.
  - ◦ Communicate Project Closure through Project Closure Meeting.
  - ◦ Document Project Closure Report—record final status, list of handover documentation, good practices, lessons learnt, and opportunities.
- **Outputs:**
  - ◦ Users trained on tool.
  - ◦ User Acceptance Report.

Project Closure

- **Objectives:** Obtain Project Sign Off and debrief team.
- **Inputs:** Workflow implemented on test environment.
- **Activities:**
  - ◦ Pre-go-live process training on tool and implemented workflows for tool users.
  - ◦ Conduct user acceptance testing to ensure readiness.
- **Outputs:**
  - ◦ Project sign off.
  - ◦ Project closure report.

Post Implementation Phase

Conduct Post Implementation Assessment and Recommendations

- **Objectives:** To obtain an understanding of process maturity after an identified implementation period and to identify improvement areas.
- **Inputs:** Successfully rolled out tool.
- **Activities:**
  - ◦ Conduct post implementation assessment for ITIL processes.
  - ◦ Identify gaps and improvement opportunities, develop recommendations.
  - ◦ Present findings and recommendations.
- **Outputs:** Post Implementation Assessment Report.

PROJECT CHALLENGES AND SOLUTIONS

Management and Organization

The adoption of ITIL in the Company was accompanied by a major ITD functional transformation. The purpose of this transformation was to design, develop, and implement a corporate-wide improvement plan for the Company and ITD that supports the Company's vision and strategy. The transformation project was primarily focused on the following key areas within ITD and their direct relation and impact on the core business:

1. IT Strategy.
2. Enterprise Architecture.
3. Data Management / Information Management.
4. IT Governance.
5. IT Standards.
6. Quality Assurance Strategy and Framework.
7. Information Security Management Framework.

The introduction of the new ITIL processes during such major transformation required careful attention when designing the ITIL processes, getting stakeholders endorsements and assigning the process roles to designated staff. ITD had decided to proceed with the ITIL initiative and deferred the allocation of the process roles after the formal announcement of the new ITD organizational structure. However, wide management consensus on key ITIL decisions were always sought to avoid any changes to the process activities following the completion of the functional transformation.

In addition, the project team conveyed the organizational requirements that were required to successfully implement ITIL based on the RACI matrices of the deployed the ITIL processes to the transformation project. As a consequence, the newly designed organization catered for the required ITIL processes roles. This resulted is a more effective rollout of the ITIL processes.

Interfacing ITIL with Other IT Management Framework

Companies adapt different frameworks to streamline its IT services. Adopting ITIL requires more than just five phases describing Service Management best practices. It is clear that ITIL is does not stand alone, and in fact, can only succeed when used with other best practices. The ITIL's Continuous Service Improvement Program

(CSIP) should be tied in with the Company's Business Process Management (BPM) Program and the Quality Management System (QMS).

The CSIP must tie back to key business drivers. Common business drivers include regulatory compliance with industry regulations like The Gramm-Leach-Bliley Act (GLBA), the Health Insurance Portability and Accountability Act (HIPAA), and others. All regulatory compliance business drivers require reporting and auditing. Common audit schemes include Statement on Auditing Standards (SAS) No. 70, is for Service Organizations, including IT service providers. Another popular audit is for compliance with the Sarbanes-Oxley Act of 2002. Auditing connects the business driver to the organization. The CSIP must steer IT toward systems and methods that support successful audits. For ITIL to succeed you must clearly identify business drivers, auditing required, and most importantly affected stakeholders organization. This is a proven method for obtaining senior management commitment.

QMS ITIL calls for a QMS as the "how to" to manage quality improvement and implementation. There are numerous QMS options including Deming, Six Sigma, LEAN, and others. ITIL provides the "what" to consider, the BPM provides the "where and when" and the QMS provides the "how to" for managing. The QMS provides step-by-step analysis and improvement. For ITIL to succeed you must choose and use a QMS consistently.

Discovering that the Biggest Obstacle is Culture Change

Repeatedly, successful ITIL implementers mention that their success came from their people. They attribute their success to not just the commitment of management, but also to the commitment of the line staff who perform ITIL duties day in and day out. Remember that ITIL is a process-based best practice, and as a process, it requires people do things in a certain manner. People often do things how they choose to do things, not how you tell them to do things. The ability to gain the active support, commitment, and enthusiasm of line staff workers is a key requirement.

People do not like change. IT staff work in what is arguably the most dynamic, fast-paced and rapidly changing of fields, and IT staff is some of the most resistant people when it comes to change. The only proven method to gain the commitment of staff required to change is involving line staff in the adoption process. You must lead by example; involving line staff in the entire process from the initial decision to implement, through process design and into process establishment. For ITIL to succeed you will need to use sound interpersonal management skills to involve and empower staff at all levels during the entire adoption process.

Remembering that ITIL are Processes

ITIL is a set of operational processes process, not a project. Any process, including ITIL, requires roles (owner, manager, implementer, auditor, etc.) responsibilities (outputs, conformance to requirements, etc.), authorities (ability to direct or perform activities, etc.) activities (actions required to meet responsibilities, etc.) and procedures (documentation of how to perform actions required, etc.)

For ITIL to succeed you must:

- Define roles and responsibilities clearly.
- Select and empower a process owner with cross-silo management scope.
- Select and empower a manager responsible for establishment, auditing and day-to-day operational oversight.
- Define process workflow responsibilities in enough detail for workers to follow.
- Implement process reporting and auditing in order to improve the efficiency, effectiveness, economy, and equity of the process continuously.

Key here is to establish a sound framework without going overboard. You must not spend too much time trying to create perfect workflow diagrams and all-encompassing procedures. For ITIL to succeed you must adopt elements of your existing workflow, process, and procedures while molding new behaviors into existing workers. Good enough is perfect.

Technology Concerns

Prior to the commence ITIL project, the Company had used packaged Help Desk software for about 5-6 years for managing IT incidents and user request. However, this was conducted without catering for the other ITIL related processes. A key constraint for the ITIL implementation project was to capitalize on existing software and to redesign the new ITSM framework using the same tool with the possibility of adding new service management modules from the same vendor. Fortunately, the selected Help Desk software was among the leader ITSM packages as rated by international market researchers. The project team has added two new modules to cater for the additionally introduced processes.

RECOMMENDATIONS

IT Service Management is a main segment of the operating model of IT divisions. Successful implementation of ITSM will improve both the internal efficiency and effectives of IT as well as end-use satisfactions. Here are some key points that were followed during the project implementation that facilitated accomplishing the project objectives:

- Executive Management emphasis and communications during meetings and presentations were important to draw all staff attention to the project during its implementation and roll-out phases. Senior IT managers had stressed how ITIL could help to improve performance by regularly promoting its benefits and positive results, and constantly linking these back to business goals and objectives.
- New job descriptions and Key Performance Indicators (KPIs) for IT employees were amended, formalized and communicated to reflect IT Service Management roles, responsibilities and accountabilities.
- These job descriptions and KPIs were considered during performance appraisals, compensation systems, and reward and recognition programs.
- ITIL process owners were be formally appointed and held accountable for specific outcomes and deliverables.
- New/updated measurements and Management reporting were be implemented to track and communicate required ITIL process goals and outputs.
- Recruitment and selection criteria for new IT employees and HR hiring practices have been changed to reflect the required levels of ITIL experience and knowledge, and IT service management attitudes.
- Cultural changes were being passed on to new employees. Orientation and training programs for new IT hires should include IT service management and ITIL education and awareness.
- Education and training are ongoing. As operational level IT staff is promoted to tactical and strategic management roles, education have gone beyond the ITIL IT Service Management Essentials course. Managers have participated in advanced certification: ITIL Service Manager, ITIL Practitioner Courses, and IT executive management education.

LESSONS LEARNED

The main lessons learned from the ITIL implementation project are summarized as follows:

- As ITIL is a process-based framework of best practices, its implementation should be tailored to the specific requirements of the implementer. Companies differ in their dynamics of organizational goals, priorities, leadership, maturity, etc. Thus, ITIL project management should counsel all ITIL stakeholders to commence a successful transition to the process-driven ITSM Lifecycle.

- A holistic view of the IT division operating or functional model will clarify the interfaces and relationship of the ITIL processes with other IT processes and will ensure smooth rollout and adherence of ITIL activities by all concerned parties.

- Changing the IT staff mindset and focus from being technology-oriented to service-oriented usually requires a company-wide extensive Change Management program. It is the responsibility of the project team to follow up the adherences of the IT staff and end-users to the newly introduced concepts and to tailor their change Management program accordingly to address any rollout shortcomings or pitfalls.

- ITIL is a transformation rather than an implementation project, i.e. the cultural change of the staff is the ultimate objective and the most important part. Therefore, do not get fixated on processes or, worse still, technology. Make sure the major target is on people-change else, failure or atrophy is the result.

- Some Companies choose to concentrate on a single ITIL process, such as incident management. However, ITIL processes are by nature inter-related and inter-dependent. Therefore, if you want to drive down the number of incidents, you need to quickly find the root-cause of persistent problems. To reduce the number of problems, you will need to consider change management. Organizations that get too far down the path with one process before considering related processes may spend significant time and money in constantly revisiting and refining the initial process as they implement others. Therefore, the best way to improve service is to simultaneously work on enhancing two or three process areas.

- Understand your position in the ITIL Process Maturity Model and set a goal to help you best support the business. Use the model to help plot a strategy for sequential improvement by investing in IT operations management tools, people and processes to achieve higher maturity levels.

- The main EIS post-implementation strategy requirements should be used as input to the ITIL project to reflect EIS specifics and to ensure that both are ITIL implementation and ERP configuration are aligned.

REFERENCES

Earl, M. (1994). Viewpoint: New and old business process redesign. *The Journal of Strategic Information Systems*, *3*(1), 5–22. doi:10.1016/0963-8687(94)90003-5

Kettinger, W., & Grover, V. (1995). Toward a theory of business process change management. *Journal of Management Information Systems*, *12*(1), 1–30.

Kotter, J. (1995). Leading change: Why transformation efforts fail. *Harvard Business Review*, *73*(2), 59–67.

Mintzberg, H., & Waters, J. (1985). Of strategies deliberate and emergent. *Strategic Management Journal*, *6*, 257–272. doi:10.1002/smj.4250060306

Schniederjans, M., & Kim, G. (2003). Implementing enterprise resource planning systems with total quality control and business process reengineering: Survey results. *International Journal of Operations & Production Management*, *23*(3/4), 418. doi:10.1108/01443570310467339

Sheng, Y., Pearson, J., & Crosby, L. (2003). Organizational culture and employees' computer self-efficacy: An emperical study. *Information Resources Management*, *16*(3), 42. doi:10.4018/irmj.2003070103

Voordijk, H., Van Leuven, A., & Laan, A. (2003). Enterprise resource planning in a large construction firm: Implementation analysis. *Construction Management and Economics*, *21*(5), 511. doi:10.1080/0144619032000072155

KEY TERMS AND DEFINITIONS

BPM: Business Process Management.
CMDB: Configuration Management Database.
CSIP: Continuous Service Improvement Program.
DSL: Definitive Software Library.
ERP: Enterprise Resource Planning.
ITIL: IT Infrastructure Library.
ITSM: IT Services Management.
QMS: Quality Management System.
TCO: Total Cost of Ownership.

Chapter 14
Managing the Replacement of Legacy HR System

Nabil Ghalib
Business International Group, UAE

EXECUTIVE SUMMARY

Application software projects have always been viewed as a massive challenge by companies, particularly when it comes to replacing legacy in-house developed systems with package solutions. Challenges start by the resentment to change typically demonstrated by a good percentage of the user community, followed by the many pitfalls encountered due to the changes that are included / excluded while the project progresses with user hesitance to accept the new system. The project had many challenges that are not typical of a properly managed one and to make matters worse, it had challenges that were related to poor priority settings that were attached to some non-professional aspects. Cultural issues came as a bonus in this project. The challenges and the counter measures taken to ensure the timely delivery of the project with minimum damage possible will be addressed as the chapter progresses, reflecting on how the objective shifted towards the end of its life to a win/win scenario.

DOI: 10.4018/978-1-4666-2220-3.ch014

CASE STUDY OBJECTIVES

The case at hand is an example of how a project could take a dangerous turn from what was agreed on. It also reflects on the results from additional detours that were made during its life cycle until sign off.

This case study highlights issues and challenges pertaining to the different phases of the "Project Life Cycle," with emphasis on the cultural constraints and challenges encountered during each phase. It aims at providing the audience with examples of how cultural and regional factors affected the Project and the overall impact it had on the project. It also addresses methods and practices used to counter measure the impact of factors that were seen as major threats to the Project success.

For organization, the case study is divided into the following (6) sections: 1) Setting the Stage, 2) Background of the Business Requirements, 3) The Project Structure, 4) System Implementation and Challenges, 5) Reflecting on the Project/ Achievements, and 6) Lessons Learnt.

SETTING THE STAGE

The Customer

A multi-site company with operational sites distributed over a wide geographical area. The company employed thousands of employees and contractors under different schemes such as direct hire, contractors, and personnel from shareholding companies. The list of shareholders included some highly reputed international oil and gas giants.

The company had an in-house developed legacy HR system that served its needs during the eighties and early nineties of the twentieth century.

The HR Division (the custodians of the new system) consisted of eight functional areas (Departments) that covered Recruitment, Personnel and Employee Relations, Job Evaluation, Career Development, Training, Payroll, Compensations, and Payroll Budgeting.

The Vendor (Main Contractor)

An IT company reputed as a leading professional services provider in the Middle East. It had a customer base of companies serving a myriad of industries such as Telecommunications, Banking, and Commerce. It represented a number of International IT companies in the Middle East.

The Product

The system was one of the leading HR systems used by a number of companies in Europe. It had functionality exceeding that required by the Customer but had one major challenge since it was a non-English-based system.

There were other challenges that related to the product structure, which imposed limitations on the flexibility needed to deliver customized functional requirements. There were additional complications due to the lack of qualified resources that knew the product and were capable of supporting it in the region.

The Product Owner (Sub Contractor)

A European company based in Pairs, with a huge customer base in Europe. This was their first implementation of the product in the Middle East using English as the system language.

The Project

The Project was a thirteen-month's project starting from September 1st 1997 with the scope of delivering a new customized HR system in English with one year warranty / support agreement starting from the day of commissioning the new system.

The project team consisted of resources from all stakeholders. The number and skill mix of resources varied at different intervals of the project (depending on the needed skills during the phase).

The work was executed in the Customer HQ on an environment that was specified in the contract with most of the technical support (hardware, network, database, client PCs, and PC tools) provided by the Customer on need basis at no extra cost.

BACKGROUND OF THE BUSINESS REQUIREMENT

The HR Division of the company required a system that would facilitate maximum process automation possible to serve its different Departments while maximizing data integration. The requirement was for an English based system that could support some Arabic fields required for local official authorities. The system had to be based on Client Server topology but was later shifted to Web enabled. A fully functional Employee Relations suite that handled functions and data pertaining to the Employee, the personal records and historical data related to his/her job progression in the company was the core of the requirement. A payroll suite of modules, which handled monthly salaries and maintained records of salaries paid to every employee with its allocation against different cost centers complemented the Employee Relations core.

The system also included satellites modules for employee training attended, career development / progression and annual budgeting per cost center, etc. The system had to meet the following criteria (as part of the agreed scope of work):

- User friendly.
- Easy to configure (label names on forms / screens).
- Easy to customize (change system functionality to meet business requirements).
- Easy to parameterize (particularly for what if analysis / scenarios).
- Easy to enhance (new functionality requiring functional and database change).
- Utilizes a specific environment (operating system and database brand).
- Allows for dynamic assignment of user profiles / privilege settings.
- Capable of delivering the performance criteria stated.
- Facilitates proper audit logs and security measures / features.

THE PROJECT STRUCTURE

The project had the following structure with a summary of its characteristics:

The HR Division team consisted of a Team Leader, a HR Coordinator and members from the different HR Departments (numbers varied according to the project phase). They were active in terms of delivering the requirements and discussing possible ways of implementation and attended all scheduled sessions; however, when it came to endorsing the "Requirement Specifications" document. The team demonstrated concern due to the history of delays in the project. There concern was genuine due to the delays encountered so far, but the hesitance they demonstrated was only adding to the overall delay. None of the team members wanted any of the delays encountered to reflect badly on their performance appraisals at the end of the year. They also were skeptical of the progress after all the delays and issues encountered. Most of the sign off documents were obtained after escalating the issue to HR management.

The Finance Division team consisted of representatives from the Payroll section and the Budgeting Section. Additional resources were required at different intervals to address issues related to decisions. The team had clear requirements that were presented neatly in quantitative and qualitative terms. Endorsements were obtained smoothly. The time for this team involvement was an advantage used positively. The plan had the involvement of this team scheduled about five months from the project start date. The team was not very concerned with a month or so of delays.

The Maintenance groups (consisting of many Divisions) nominated a resource who was expected to contribute by addressing labor details that were not maintained b the HR Division but related to other systems serving the area of site maintenance. These details were basic in nature and related to personal information of contracted resources, their cycle leaves, contract details such as start and end dates ... etc. The individual assigned to the task of scoping the requirements in both systems (HR and the Maintenance system) could not clearly identify the requirements. This added to the delays as will be seen later.

A fourth group of users was assigned the tasks of addressing requirements related to the official documentation requirements for expatriate employees and their dependents.

This group was clear about their requirements; however, the system lacked functionality in this area and attempts to include such functionality within the system were seen as suicidal in terms of efforts and cost. There were additional challenges in this area that were envisaged due the continuous change in local regulations since the system had to allow for maximum flexibility to accommodate such changes. A compromise was presented by the new Project Manager to facilitate the way forward.

The IT group consisted of staff assigned on full time and part time basis. Two members were assigned to the project from day one. One resource was assigned on need basis. Specialized technical resources were utilized on need basis particularly when challenges related to the Customer environment were encountered.

The Software Owner team (Sub Contractor) consisted initially of a full time Project Manager (referred to as the old Project Manager), one full time Consultant, and one full time Contractor who worked on behalf of the Software Owner. They all knew the product very well.

The Vendor (Main Contractor and Local Agent) team consisted initially of three full time developers who were not familiar with the system. They lacked experience in the HR business areas of and were not fully capable / privileged to handle customer relations.

SYSTEM IMPLEMENTATION AND CHALLENGES

This case will neither address the activities related to the awarding of the project nor the tasks that took place prior to the "Mobilization" of the resources.

Below is a summary of the project status when the new Project Manager (will be referred to as the new Project Manager) took over:

The original mutually agreed project plan (the one signed between the Vendor and the Customer) had all the phases properly defined, with milestones (deliverables) clearly defined per phase. Each phase had a clear set of tasks with proper start and finish dates and resource were assigned to the tasks with the time required by each resource per task were mostly realistic.

The project plan applied a waterfall approach of the System Development Life Cycle (SDLC). Requirements were supposed to be defined very early in the project during the "Analysis" phase. This would later be translated to a formal document referenced as "Functional Requirements" document. Although waterfall is not the best practiced project planning technique, there was a reason for placing the activities in the plan in a waterfall structure. It was purely to allow the initially assigned old Project Manager of this project to work on multiple projects at the same time. The plan would enable him to assign part of his time to other projects once the ball started rolling in a project. In simple words, the Software Owner aimed at minimizing the time allocated by the old Project Manager to each project so that he could manage a number of concurrent projects. This was primarily due to the limited availability of qualified "Business Analyst" resources in the region with skills covering the business and technical aspects of the product and of course, to optimize cost. Four months down the track with this approach applied, the project plan was completely out of track due to the improper handling of the project as the priorities assigned by the old Project Manager were influenced by "Fire Fighting" and his time management skills were defeated by the numerous challenges and issues encountered by the two projects he was managing. The status of this project was taking a sharp detour towards legal action, as the Customer could not see any progress.

The Customer gave the Vendor an ultimatum of one month to demonstrate a more serious attitude in managing this vital project.

The Vendor had to recruit a competent Project Manager on full time basis. Although product knowledge was essential, the priority was given to competence in Project Management under crisis when the candidates were interviewed. An added bonus was the good knowledge of HR business as well as the ability to handle extreme pressure.

With all the challenges laid in front of him and realizing that time was a factor that played against him; the newly assigned Project Manager (new Project Manager) had to apply a fresh approach to the project. The starting point was to obtain the Customer endorsement for major changes to the plan. These changes meant revamping the approach used. There were other challenges that could be envisaged by the new Project Manager in terms of the available resources, the loyalty factor by all concerned, as well as the personal attitude that could be seen from some members cultivated by the lack of direction seen so far.

Below is a summary of the challenges that were given the highest priority to address:

The first challenge was establishing an agreed roadmap for the project. The second was to demonstrate how seriously committed he was to deliver the project with the minimum losses. For this, he adopted a simple management philosophy known as "Management by Example."

Being on site very early in the morning of every working day, setting weekly goals, and converting them to daily assignments that were clearly conveyed to each member of the team were some of the simple techniques he used to ensure clarity of authority and objectives.

Ensuring that workloads were properly distributed amongst the team members taking into consideration that the work assigned was within the level of knowledge / skill each member had so far and presenting new challenges to each member so that new skills were acquired were two other examples of the tools used by the new Project Manager to demonstrate how determined he was to the success of the project delivery.

Having established grounds with the team representing the Vendor, work shifted to produce an acceptable roadmap for the way forward with the Customer representatives. This task was an extremely challenging task as the change was in every direction and it was vital that all concerned parties were supportive of what will be required to achieve success. Below is a summary of the agreed roadmap:

1. Revisit the number of resources required for the rest of the time available to establish the need for additional resources (based on the contract guidelines).
2. Compile and produce the "As Is Analysis" document to reflect a clear understanding of the current practices, systems, and data used.
3. Compile and produce a new "To Be Analysis" document to reflect the requirements from the new system.
4. Produce the final Gaps Analysis (Identifying the Gaps between what is required versus what is currently there) prioritized by Division / Department.
5. Produce the detailed "Requirements Specifications" by Division / Department including the "Interfaces" between Departments / Divisions. This will be referred to as the "Agreement" between the Vendor and the Customer for all deliverables from that point onwards.
6. Identify the "Acceptance Criteria" including test scenarios. This would be used as an appendix to the "Agreement" and would be the reference for how the deliverables will be tested for completeness, correctness, and accuracy. This was later used as part of the "Quality Plan" for Audit purposes.
7. Implement the agreed "Requirements Specifications." This was divided to three major disciplines:
    a. Enhancements, which included changes to the system such as database tables and forms.

      b.   Configuration tasks that affect the forms but do not require changes to the database tables or form definitions. Renaming filed names / labels was one example.

      c.   Interfacing tasks that handle relationships between different modules and / or functional areas.

8.   Administration tasks that relate to preparing test scenarios, documentation changes, and data requirements resulting from the changes to be implemented.

9.   Identify and agree the "Data Migration" requirements and plan.

10.   Update the plan to reflect all the above.

A brief discussion of the roadmap elements to clarify its purpose and how it was expected to serve the interest of all concerned is given beneath:

The Plan Update

This was seen as a waste of effort and time by some of the Customer resources who were of the opinions that the project is bound to fail (always referring to the history of the project).

The new Project Manager had to focus on preparing a plan that would handle the main concerns at hand. The first was to ensure no more slippage in deliverables, the second was to ensure recovering as much time as possible taking into consideration the many constraints / challenges he faced and will encounter in the future, while the third was to change the perception of all concerned, hence change the attitude towards the project.

Required Resources

The new Project Manager thoroughly revisited the contract terms and conditions to capitalize on the items that were open for interpretations in the areas of resource allocation. Using some of the gaps found, extensive efforts were exerted with all concerned parties to restructure the team with the aim of obtaining resources on need basis. Assigning needed resources on part time / casual basis proved very useful as will be seen later, but convincing the stakeholder of the "time gains" expected was not easy. By obtaining resources from the different stakeholders, the new Project Manager managed to establish a formula the will evenly distribute the cost of the additional resources on all parties concerned. The argument used was convincing to the Customer, the Vendor, and the Product Owner and that in turn meant that every stakeholder carried part of the resulting additional costs hence paused no additional cost on the project and all parties perceived this as a fair deal. The biggest achievement here was obtaining a highly skilled resource from the Product Owner from France to deliver training. This faced resistance by the product Owner initially, but the negotiation skills of the new Project Manager prevailed and the return on that investment he presented to the management Product Owner was very convincing.

As Is Analysis

The "As Is Analysis" was divided into multiple (parallel) tasks. Extensive hours were spent in discussions and orientation to explain the new approach. A by product was a unified template which was jointly designed and created by the team members. This template proved very useful when resources were assigned to complete this task. The project team was split between the different HR Departments to obtain the necessary details. Following the collection of details, a workshop was held over one week end (two days in a local hotel) to discuss the outcomes and agree on the format / structure to be used for the "As Is Analysis" document which would eventually be submitted to the Customer.

The project team was then split into (3) groups:

- The first group produced well structured simple and easy to use "As Is Analysis" document that was also easy to endorse (A Department per Chapter).
- The second group worked on preparing a "Presentation" that will explain and simplify the "As Is Analysis" document so that time given for reviewing and endorsing it would be focused and optimized.
- The third group filtered and categorized the list of issues that were obtained from the users so far so that they are addressed in the "To Be Analysis" phase.

The approach was exceptionally useful and considerable time was regained against the original project plan. Endorsements of the document were obtained in a timely manner and the issues for the next stage were well organized and under control.

To Be Analysis (Including Identifying Gaps)

The same approach was applied with one workday workshop held to establish the method of conducting the "To Be Analysis." It was noticed that involving the team (Vendor and Product Owner) in the decision-making process and project management was producing very positive results triggering competition between the team members to produce and apply better methods of executing tasks and delivering outcome.

A second weekend workshop was conducted and concluded successfully with the production of a well-structured simple and easy to use "To Be Analysis" document that was also easy to endorse (A Department per Chapter).

Requirement gathering sessions were held with different Departments. Details were filtered daily and ideas were shared and once again, the results were very positive.

It was agreed to divide the project team into two groups at this stage.

The first group attended extensive training on the software (a technical consultant form the Product Owner was assigned the task to train the Vendor team members) so that they can start using the development tools to configure and customize the software. This Product Owner resource was an outcome the new Project Manager renegotiating resources.

The second group was lead by the new Project Manager and the Customer resources assigned to the project (from HR and IT) with the aim of obtaining the endorsement of the "To Be Analysis" document and producing the "Gap Analysis" document.

Customer representatives (from HR and IT) were working jointly and knowledge was exchanged in the business area. This was essential for the IT staff assigned by the customer to support the package after the go live.

The project was now building momentum and it was viewed by all stakeholders as a source of pride since all members were participating in managing it. Lost time was regained, confidence was building up, and positive feelings started to replace the negative attitude that was hovering around earlier.

Requirements Specifications

Following the training, two weeks were spent in a workshop to review, filter, and prioritize the identified gaps. The outcome of this workshop included:

Designing a unified template used for the "Requirements Specifications" document.

The "Requirements Specifications" document was divided into chapters. Every chapter was assigned to a team member who was responsible for specifying the full requirements of one Department. In the mean time, the new Project Manager was producing the remaining components that would complement the document such as the "Executive Summary," the "Terms of Reference (TOR)" and the Appendices to reflect the agreed glossary used in the "Requirements Specifications." The task was completed in a relatively fast period of time and all chapters were ready within the set time period.

A couple of weeks were then spent with the different Department representatives to verify and conclude the chapters pertaining to their Departments. This approach was very useful once again, as it reduced the time needed for official endorsement of the "Requirements Specifications" document. The draft document was reviewed, edited to reflect a unified feel in terms of the language used (Business and Technical wise), and verified. The final document was compiled and was forwarded officially for endorsement.

The reviews and editing were very important for quality purposes and proved very useful when the project was later audited for ISO 9000 compliance.

The "Requirements Specifications" document was endorsed in time. By now, the overall delay of the project against the original plan was reduced from the inherited (5) months to (3) months, which meant a gain of (2) months.

Once again, the workshop approach was utilized to prepare for the coming tasks. This time, the team members were assigned to tasks related to the development and testing. At the end of the workshop and to ensure the adequacy of knowledge, a technical consultant was requested from the Product Owner for the first two weeks of the development stage so that he could assist the assigned development teams.

It was also time to request additional resources from the Customer. The Customer demonstrated his interest in familiarizing resources from his end so that they can later support the tool. One Customer resource was seconded to the project where he was assigned to the tasks of testing modules that were developed / enhanced and deemed ready for release to the live system. The main objective of their assignment was to pass comments on the quality of the product to the new Project Manager. The test scenarios were used to ensure that the set goals of correctness, completeness and accuracy were all adequately met.

Four major challenges were encountered during this phase.

The first related to the process flow and data sharing. Many functions were utilized by more than one Department with shared data. There were no clear boundaries for these shared processes and the shared data. "Resource Development" is one example, where its functionality is divided into two separate function areas. The first one addressed the development of experienced resources of the Customer staff members while the other addressed the development of graduates joining the company under the nationalization program.

The second example related to the details pertaining to an employee such as contact numbers and office details such as location and telephone extensions. This area required addressing with other divisions as the information existed in other systems but could not be accommodated in the HR system due to its nature (these details were populated in Microsoft Outlook).

It was clear that these shared functional and data areas were to be addressed outside the project to ensure no further delays. A new strategy was required for "Resource Development." The most appropriate suggestion was to maintain the development of experienced resources of the staff members of the Customer and create a new specialized module that handled the case for new graduates. This was discussed with the HR management and received appreciation.

In the later case (office and contact details), it was agreed that all "non HR details" were to be kept outside the system and it was the HR Division Management support that resulted in this decision being implemented.

The second major challenge related to the interfaces between the HR system and the financial system. The link to the financial system was straightforward since the users were very clear about the interface requirements. One-way communications was established, where information pertaining to payroll was passed to the financial system on regular basis.

Budgeting was developed as a standalone system that required very limited but specific interfacing with the HR and financial systems.

A one off annual data down load was designed to copy last year accumulated payroll amounts to the budgeting system, and that in turn was used with different "what if" scenarios to produce the appropriate next year Payroll Budgets.

The third major challenge was to address the interface with the Maintenance system. As was mentioned earlier, the engineer assigned from the Customer side to the task of identifying the data required for the interface between the HR system and the system used by the Maintenance groups failed to deliver the task. The Customer engineer did not demonstrate any interest hence no progress was made despite the many attempts to address this task. Informal concerns were raised with the Customer project sponsors but the failure to have any positive results lead to the removal of this task from the agreed scope of work. This is an area that relates to a cultural code used by many companies in the sector. When things do not work due to whatever reason, innovative methods are created to avoid conflicts. In this case, the resource management communicated their endorsement to changing the scope of work and the decision was made to drop the interface between the HR and the Maintenance systems.

The decision was mostly attributed to protectionism offered by certain influential individuals working for the Customer. In the case at hand, a compromise had to be reached to compensate the Customer with other features in return for dropping this requirement of interfacing with the Maintenance system.

The project team was not in agreement with this compromise; however, the change was inevitable and the compensation had to be negotiated with HR management.

Although the requirement was defined in the scope of work for the HR system, HR Division had very little to do with the case of contractors since the handling of all contracted resources was executed by the Contracts Department which is not part of the HR Departments.

An important issue noted here relates to the assignment of resources. It is important to ensure that the conditions pertaining to assigning resources to particular tasks (one off tasks in particular) should be scrutinized with extreme care since these tasks could prove fatal and cause massive risks including major project delays.

In this case, the HR Division Management was flexible enough to consider and apply a compromise. It is hard to predict what other measures could have been taken if the case was not handled wisely!

The fourth challenge was applying better practices with minimum impact on current policies.

Two examples are given here for demonstration purposes:

The company pays education allowance to all employees with children attending schools (number of children, age, and allowance amounts varied depending on many factors such as the Grade of the Employee, Employee Nationality, etc.).

The policy used was based on reimbursing the employee against receipts for payments made to the school up to the set limit.

Revisiting the policy lead to a major change where the company started paying the employees the full entitlement upfront in August of every year.

The second case related to the Annual Tickets allowance, and a similar approach was taken where all expatriate employees were paid the allowance at the beginning of every year (in January) while national employees were paid a relatively comparable amount under a different scheme.

Once all these issues were addressed and agreed, it was time for endorsing the "Requirements Specifications" document and moving forward. Endorsements were made within the set time and HR Division Management demonstrated great support and commitment hence paving the way for completing this task on time.

Development

Development started with classifying the tasks required to complete this phase. Tasks were classified as:

- **Configuration Tasks:** Changes to the look and feel of the application such as data field labels naming with no change to the database structure or the application functions.
- **Application Change Tasks:** Changes to the forms and / or system functions but not to the database structure.
- **Application and Database Change Tasks:** Changes to the database structure as well as the forms and / or system functions.

The tasks identified as "Application Configuration" were easy in nature and could have been executed by any team member, e.g. fields provided by the application were labeled and used to accommodate additional data requirements by the customer.

Changes to the forms, functions and/or to the database were referred to the new Project Manager and the consultant representing the Product Owner. These were properly logged as Changes under "Change Management."

Changes were reviewed on daily and weekly basis where priorities were assigned to each change depending on factors such as its usage, importance and its impact on other components of the system (a two dimensional matrix was used to establish priority). Each change was then assigned to a resource (starting with the easy ones for the Vendor resources). The actual development time was monitored and was improving on daily basis as the learning curve was taking an exponential upwards trend for all team members.

Changes that were identified as "Critical" in terms of their importance and priority were addressed with extreme care. These were further categorized to two groups, namely:

- Changes to the database structure and the application functionality but limited to one Departments / Division.
- Changes impacting many Departments / Divisions (interfacing functionality).

To ensure that the critical changes were properly tested, it was agreed by the team members that each critical change would undergo two stages of testing before it is released to the live environment. The first stage would be conducted by the developer and the consultant representing the Product Owner, while the second stage would be an attempt to make it fail (stress testing). The second stage of testing was conducted by the Customer staff members assigned to the project with help from HR staff.

To ensure that proper "stress" testing was conducted, nominal rewards were given for the team that scored most "system failures" on weekly basis. Nothing fancy, but a small gift and a bit of publicity amongst colleagues made HR staff eager to participate in this exercise. They viewed it as challenge to prove competence and skill.

This task of "stress testing" proved very useful in terms of reducing the time spent on training since most of the IT staff members were familiar with the system look and feel and were familiar with the functionality of the modules related to their daily tasks.

As things were looking brighter, a perceived major blow hit the project when the Private Contractor who knew the software well had to leave the project. Negotiations lead to an agreement where his services could be hired on need basis with a maximum of one month per quarter. Although this was not the best option at this point in time, the new Project Manager had to settle with this arrangement to minimize losses and potential further delays.

The departure of the Private Contractor seemed to have ignited a new kind of challenge amongst the remaining team members as if they were compensating for the loss of the resource on one hand and were trying to prove that they were up to the challenge they were facing and the commitments they were hired to meet. The process was gathering momentum as the team continued the development and testing of the changes. The resources assigned to the project were now taking the challenge to new heights and again the results were astonishing with a total reduction of the time lost in the project to almost two months (one-month gain).

During this stage of the project, the team was working on three parallel tasks and the challenge took a new dimension. Each team member was trying to ensure the robust delivery of the modules (sub-systems) assigned to him / her first.

The three parallel tasks were development and testing, parallel running with key users (stress testing) to obtain feedback and updating the documentation and online Help.

This required working extra hours but the team members took this as yet another challenge and this positive attitude enabled the team to capitalize on the achievements made every day.

Recognition and Gratitude

This positive attitude and the positive results seen lead the new Project Manager to think of a way to reward the team members (as an interim measure) particularly that all team members agreed to postpone their planned leaves until the project was over.

The new Project Manager approached the top management team of the Vendor who were in a different country via the Branch Manager. He requested a senior representative to visit the site with two objectives in mind for this visit:

1. The Customer was able to see positive results and some of the deliverables were labeled as "very good achievements" by the Customer Management so it was time for all concerned to meet in a positive atmosphere and get a better understanding of each other, hence open doors for future potentials.
2. The team efforts needed to be praised and appreciated and a senior member of the Vendor Management team would be the best person to deliver this.

A few days later and to everyone's surprise, the Managing Director of the Vendor arrived at the Customer site and the (3) days visit schedule included a business lunch with all team members of the project in the best sea food restaurant in town.

The visit schedule also included meetings with the Customer Management and some of the key users as well as a visit to new potential customers who were monitoring the project from a close distance and were advised of the achievements made by the project team. In principle, these customers wanted the same product applied since they had similar business requirements and identical processes.

The Managing Director of the Vendor invited all team members to a meeting in the Vendor's office to pass an official gratitude message and to discuss potential plans since he could see excellent potentials coming soon. The Branch Manager of the Vendor presented the team members with gifts at the end of the meeting. Although this gesture is not limited to this part of the word, it is seen in the Middle East as a huge honor when team members are rewarded with such a high recognition while still in the middle of the project.

Delivery

The hard work continued with the same enthusiasm and the team members were now enjoying the ride as they could see positive results, which made them feel like heroes in front of everybody else. They were racing against the clock to complete the project within the scheduled delivery time with an eye on higher position in the coming projects.

By the end of September 1998, all modules were either delivered or ready for delivery. In fact, some of the modules were delivered and accepted officially by the Customer representatives in August. User training and formal hand-over took place in October 1998, which meant that the total project delay was only ONE month.

The Go-Live Phase

On 1.11.1998, the new HR system was declared live and all functions were formally accepted with appropriate data migrated from the legacy system and all user online Help functions were active as well as an online version of a User Guide.

The only missing component was the paper based User and Technical Manuals which were delivered then in "French" and were delivered in "English" four weeks later.

System Support

Immediately after the commissioning of the system, the Product Owner representative had to leave for family commitments in France. This meant that post implementation system support (warranty) had to be carried out by the Vendor staff members.

By the time you are reading these lines, the system would have served the Customer HR Division for more than (14) years.

It was also acquired by five other companies in the region.

REFLECTING ON PROJECT/ACHIEVEMENTS

Many challenges were encountered that were mostly inherited and related to cultural aspects. Below is a summary of these challenges followed by a list of achievements:

Challenges

The structure of the project team was not clearly defined from the Customer end. The Customer Project Manager had no HR experience, limited IT knowledge and limited Project Management background and was assigned this task as an honorary reward for his long years of service in the company just before his retirement. The result of this appointment raised a challenge that was an on-going concern through the life cycle of the project. This challenge was resolved by passing the project plan to an engineer who had excellent planning skills but limited authority for change, which in turn restricted his project management skills. Issues and plan changes were discussed with the planning engineer who would escalate them to the Customer Project Manager for approvals. To ensure that the project plan was on track, weekly meetings were held with the Customer Project Manager and most of the time in this meeting was spent on repeating what was already agreed with the project engineer.

A second was the IT representative who was assigned by the Customer to handle IT requirements. His IT competencies were limited to the old environment but were not sufficient for the project in terms of technology changes. This added to the bureaucracy whenever a decision had to be taken at IT level. All IT related issues and requirements had to be escalated via him only to be repeated later with the IT member of staff who could address the issue.

The third and biggest challenge was to obtain user's confidence, since their experience was not positive for a fair percentage of the project time. Many users tried to avoid attending planned activities using excuses such as "the project will fail." Patience was the most important asset the project team needed then.

A continuous challenge was managing the debates between the different Department representatives, which took place in almost every meeting. Customer staff members would easily get into a highly tensed situation over issues that relate to business areas that had more than one interpretation. This was magnified even further when the issues were related to policy attributes that related to more than one Department. These debates are typical in the Middle East and are usually confused with personal emotions. It is mostly indicative of "who is in charge" or "who has the power."

The new Project Manager had to tackle this from two angles. The first angle was to isolate the issues that were not "Departmental" in nature hence issues were classified as "Intra" or "Inter" Departmental. The classification approach was discussed with the Customer HR Team leaders and with the Customer Project Manager and both parties supported the approach fully. The second was to limit the meetings (the weekly ones and the ones held on need basis) to ONE Department at a time. Each meeting was restricted in time and scope (agenda). At the end of every meeting, all attendees were requested to endorse the Minutes of Meeting prior to leaving the meeting arena. The new Project Manager took the responsibility of documenting all the minutes. Once all the items in the agenda were addressed and actions were agreed on, the closing of the meeting was narrating the Actions with emphasis on the expected outcome of every Action, the person who is accountable for its delivery/ completion and its deadline. Once all the items were narrated and agreed by the assignee, all attendees were requested to sign the Minutes of Meeting document.

The task of preparing and distributing the Minutes of Meeting them was given 24 hours to be completed. No changes were accepted after they were distributed. However, there were cases raised to modify some actions in the next meeting agenda.

This would typically be seen as an extra item of workload, but this approach proved extremely valuable in reducing conflicts, misunderstanding and personal issues.

Issues that were seen as potential for conflict were addressed in a different meeting that had clear options for the way forward. The Customer HR Team Leader and the permanent HR member did an excellent job to minimize conflicts by providing realistic options that were practical to implement; hence, they paved the way for moving forward at full speed.

The failure to meet the requirement to address the interface with the maintenance system was one issue that is worth revisiting. As was stated earlier, a compromise was made but reflecting back on the project, a red flag should have been raised, and the issue should have been escalated then as "lack of competence, not one of a compromise." Massive benefits were missed out due to the failure to create the interface.

On the contractual / formal side of the project, the "Contract" document should have included clauses that would allow for potential delays since there were too many parameters that were beyond the Vendor's control. Product Owner resources and Customer resources are just a few examples.

This is important from a cultural point of view, since personnel assigned to a project who encounter a new culture could have reservations / family challenges beyond their control and that could definitely cause delays. Relocating does not always work and family issues could have its shadows here.

Achievements

Below is a list of achievements:

1. A fully operational, ISO 9000 quality audited system was delivered (on time, within budget, and to the satisfaction of all concerned). This was a rare thing then.
2. A set of improvements were addressed and some of the most important ones were implemented with minor changes to the Customer policies.
3. Data that was important to the Customer was migrated smoothly, while data that had no impact on the system integrity and staff records was properly archived.
4. All Technology constraints were applied as per the customer environmental restrictions. The conformity was 100%.
5. The Vendor staff members were fully trained and by the end of the project, they were capable of supporting this project and contribute with higher responsibilities in other projects. The Customer staff members were fully capable of offering first line support including the production of new reports and business rule changes.
6. A structured approach was presented to the Customer HR Division. The approach was then adapted to better monitor and control the job progression of the national graduates. This approach was later translated to a fully computerized system that had a proper workflow.
7. A clear segregation of business functions (by Department) was further refined after the system was implemented. This reflected positively on the way specific functions were addressed and completed. An example was the splitting of the Employee Relations Job functions to a number of specific components including Job classification, Job Grade Range and Personal Grade that was linked to a Job Position.

ISO 9000 Audit

During the last few weeks of the project, an ISO 9000 audit took place on the Vendor Branch. Its scope covered the branch and the projects managed by the branch.

Hours were spent with the international Auditor with issues discussed at different levels and from different angles to validate the status of the project, its deliverables, and the quality of these deliverables. To the joy of all concerned in the project, the audit result was outstanding with "zero non-conformity." There were minor comments on the structure of the Quality Plan as it was mostly an extract of the milestones of the project plan.

This result added to the already established status and reputation of the project to make it the "Flag Ship" of the Vendor's projects in 1998 and 1999.

LESSONS LEARNED

The 7-S model is used to analyze the lessons learnt for this major project. This tool is typically used for analyzing organizations, but is used here to assist with the analysis of this case. It is normal to assume that using this tool here may be subject for debate, but it always a good challenge to find new ways of applying different tool and techniques!

Strategy

Taking the definition of strategy as the plan of action prepared by the organization to respond to the changes (the changes here include the demand for an automated solution to replace and enhance the continuity to deliver the Human Resources and Payroll service levels). This was handled fairly reasonably at all levels as it addressed the three basic questions:

1.   Where do we stand now?
2.   Where do we want to be?
3.   How to get there within the applicable constraints?

Initially, all concerned had a mutual agreement to one unified Strategy.

At the end of the project, the unified Strategy was translated to a working system.

The Customer failed to address a very critical strategy issue. The Project's scope of work did not include any clauses to ensure the compliance with the year 2000 (Y2K) issue although the project was executed at the right time for this. The same applied to the other ERP systems acquired by the Customer. This issue proved to be costly since this project and the other one in the ERP suite had to be revisited in 1999 to ensure compliance with the Y2K criteria.

Structure

Taking the definition as the structure as the hierarchy applied by the organization to respond to the changes (the changes here include the creation of a team to define, develop and implement a new automated solution to sustain and enhance the continuity to deliver the Human Resources and Payroll service levels). This was an on-going concern, as it had to respond to many changes during the life cycle of the project. The major concerns include but not limited to the following:

1. The structure of the inherited project.
2. What changes should be applied to improve the Structure?
3. Who are the main sponsors / players?
4. How to ensure changes are acceptable by all concerned?
5. When to escalate (if needed)?

Mutual agreements and the priceless HR Management support at the time facilitated the handling of other concerns and issues that were encountered as the project progressed. A properly defined structure and a supportive management team are two critical success factors for every project. In this case, both worked favorably.

Style / Culture

There were no major challenges in this area since the company has a clear and distinct style / culture.

However, cultural aspects related to individuals had to be handled with care as was stated in the case above.

Cultural aspects related to the country and region followed a clear code of conduct. The team members of the project had all this clarified in the company policy, which was easily accessible. Team members demonstrated full adherence and respect to the applicable cultural code and that was a very important success lesson.

Systems

HR Division had an automated system that was based on mainframes topology. It met the business requirements then but was definitely out of date and of limited value when it came to the new requirements dictated by the technology movement and business growth.

The system changes included enhancing the business processes to meet internationally accepted business practices. New technologies introduced (Client / Server) and the new equipment meant that networking and hardware systems had to be replaced. Finally, the requirements related to the continuous need for ad-hoc and management reporting was a side product of the change.

Business Process Re-Engineering (BPR) was applied in some cases. It was not easy to sell the idea of major changes to way HR staff worked, but eventually benefits outweighed resistance. The lesson here is to demonstrate the bright side of the change. Adopting new processes was confined to the core functions. This covered new functionality and was accepted with minimum resistance since the results were time and effort savings, which is very much in line with what every employee wants.

The prime improvement area was the capability to allow for future growth / expansion and change. These improvements were implemented as satellites to the system's core functionality. The Customer wish list was endless but the lesson here is simple, think of the process first, think of its practicality and its impact, then think of automating it.

Innovations were also used to simplify the way some processes were applied and some of these were translated to automated systems so that technology could be taken advantage of.

Staff

The staff issue was discussed extensively in the different sections above. The prime objective of the project was to deliver a quality and a robust system that replaced the legacy system used then. Staff discipline was the lesson to learn and if it was not for the dedication and sincere efforts exerted by each member, this project could have been a case for law students.

During the project life cycle, a daily morning coffee habit was established. Every member of the team had to tell the members something new. Nothing specific, but topics included new legislation issues that were published and could impact the project. Examples such as labor policy changes in the country, health and safety regulatory changes, issues pertaining to the technology and of course sports were amongst the many topics discussed over the 150 or so mornings during the project.

Allowing for a few minutes of "socializing" proved very effective in team building. It started as an idea that was not welcomed only to become a very important session that Customer staff members from different disciplines in close by offices attended. Team building could be costly, but in this case, it was achieved at a much optimized price.

Skills

Knowledge transfer was at the core of the skills aspect, and the project was used as a vehicle to deliver this. Product Owner staff members were to deliver this task at different times. This opportunity was presented to the Vendor and Customer staff members as a once in a lifetime chance (each member perceived the training as the vehicle he could use to achieve career progressions). Lessons learned here include three items:

New skills are important but knowing how to market them to each member of the audience requires investigating the ambitions of each member and being able to pass the right message that will make him / her eager to utilize the training to the maximum possible potential, hence use it as part of his / her continuous learning.

Apply every new skill immediately after it is learned. The learning curve will shoot sky high.

Pause new challenges (since one has the authority) so that the challenge is ignited amongst team members and always reward ALL. After all, they are a team that works to deliver the project you are responsible for and rewarding some while ignoring others is one of the worst practices in a project similar to the case here. The maximum possible efforts were obtained from all members of the team and the was really the secret of this project's success.

Shared Values

The prime values of the company were maintained with emphasis on integrity, and team work. All project objectives were met while the team members were all keen to participate and deliver to the best they could. Conflicts of interests were noticed early and were handled swiftly and decisively. The team was keen to make this project a success story to be used as a flagship.

The most important asset of this project was the team spirit. From a demoralized team that was haunted by the fear of failure to a team labeled as the "A" team meant much more that just success. Project management skills refer to teamwork as a critical success factor; however, the case at hand is a real example of how valuable this was.

Maintaining the image of the company was a prerequisite for this and other projects that were applied at the same time.

Finally, the 7-S model is a tool that was introduced for analyzing organizations, but as could be seen above, major projects such as the one at hand could be used as a case for applying it. Reflecting on the results may be subject for debate, but it always a good challenge to find new ways of applying new tool and techniques!

REFERENCES

Adler, P. (1990). Shared learning. *Management Science, 36*(8), 938–957. doi:10.1287/mnsc.36.8.938

Arrow, K. (1962). The implications of learning by doing. *The Review of Economic Studies, 29*, 166–170. doi:10.2307/2295952

Freeman, C., & Perez, C. (1988). Structural crisis of adjustment: Business cycles and investment behavior. In Dosi, G. (Eds.), *Technical Change and Economic Behavior*. London, UK: Pinter.

Guha, S., Grover, V., Kettinger, W., & Teng, J. (1997). Business process change and organizational performance: Exploring an antecedent model. *Journal of Management Information Systems*, *14*(1), 119–154.

Johnson, D., & Johnson, R. (1989). *Cooperation and competition: Theory and research*. Edina, MN: Interaction.

Keil, M., & Robey, D. (1999). Turning around troubled software projects: An exploratory study of the deescalation of commitment to failing courses of action. *Journal of Management Information Systems*, *15*(4), 63–87.

Kilman, R., Saxton, M., & Serpa, R. (1986). Issues in understanding and changing culture. *California Management Review*, *28*(2), 87–94.

Markus, M., & Keil, M. (1994). If we build it they will come: Designing information systems that users want to use. *Sloan Management Review*, *35*, 11–25.

KEY TERMS AND DEFINITIONS

As Is Analysis: This document depicted the status as is in terms of the current business processes, the rules / conditions per process, the data required as input and its out coming results. It also touched on how the process interfaced with other processes.

Gap Analysis: This document was the result f comparing the "As Is" against the "To Be" Analysis documents and contained a consolidated list of the differences "Gaps." The list had 7 sections addressing (business process, business rules, workflow conditions, input data required, output queries and reports, integration and interfacing with other processes / systems and exception conditions and methods of handling them.

International Organization for Standardization (ISO): An international body for setting standards in different disciplines of the world we live in including quality, ecology, safety, economy, efficiency, and effectiveness.

ISO 9000 – The Quality Assurance Certificate: This certification assists fulfilling customer quality requirements, ensuring the customer satisfaction of the deliverable while applying the relevant regulatory requirements. It also facilitates for continual improvements to meet best business practices.

Project Charter: The document that describes the project, its teams with the responsibilities assigned to each team member and agreed terms an conditions (including quality parameters).

SOW (Scope of Work): It is the document that specifies in sufficient details what the requirements are and that in turn is typically transformed into the more details "Requirements Specifications" document.

To Be Analysis: This document described the requirements in terms of the new business processes, the rules / conditions per process, the data required as input and its out coming results. It also touched on how the process interfaced with other processes.

Chapter 15
Automating Competency Development Program for Integrating Graduates in EDC Workforce:
Issues and Challenges

Moh'd Jarrar
Business International Group, UAE

EXECUTIVE SUMMARY

The project aimed at developing a system to manage the development of young university graduates and equip them with the experience and skills necessary for integrating them in the company workforce. The case study focuses on three sections. The first section addresses the development of the Proof Of Concept (POC) that aimed at creating a prototype that was then enhanced in terms of its functional capabilities and data management tasks to meet the set objectives. The second section addresses how the POC was transformed to a fully functional multi-user system that was later utilized by all the divisions within the company. The third section touches on how the experience obtained was later used to help in building a unified system for the oil and gas sector in the country. The case also discusses the challenges, measures, and counter measures taken to address them, and the lessons learned to ensure the project was delivered to stakeholders.

DOI: 10.4018/978-1-4666-2220-3.ch015

ORGANIZATION BACKGROUND

The company is multi-site Energy Distribution Company and will be referred to as (EDC) throughout this chapter. It belongs to a multi company group representing the Energy Sector in the country. The company has a policy to recruit young graduates and to prepare them to be integrated in the workforce, but the process was not formalized. In this case study, discussions will address how the process was perceived by different stakeholders in EDC, how it was analyzed then redesigned (many times) with numerous revisions until it became a mature, fully automated and easy to use system covering the process to meet and exceed the set objectives.

Initially, records of about (50) graduates from different disciplines of science and engineering were used in the POC. By the time the finished product was commissioned, data of over 200 graduates was populated.

SETTING THE STAGE

Initially and until 1998, the development of recruited graduates in EDC was a manual process, where a profile was created for every graduate to follow up on his / her progress. The technology utilized was based on Microsoft office tools, where the initial profile contained a list of development milestones that was superficial in nature most of the time. The development details were left for the individual divisions and the assignment of coaches and supervisors were not formal. The philosophy was simple and rotated around sending the graduates to as many courses as needed to assist them to execute the job each was assigned to do, then assign each graduate to tasks on weekly / monthly basis and follow up the progress he / she makes against these tasks. No formal assessments were carried out and there were no plans / benchmarks to refer to so that development schemes / patterns could be improved.

Issues and challenges encountered during the different phases of the "Project Life Cycle" are the core of this case study with emphasis on the cultural constraints and challenges encountered during each phase.

The case study aims at providing the audience with examples of how the cultural and regional factors affected the process of developing a formal system then automating it and the overall impact these constraints had on the project. In some sections, it touches on methods and techniques used to counter measure the impact of these challenges and factors, which were seen in some cases as major threats to the project success.

CURRENT CHALLENGES FACING THE ORGANIZATION

In brief, the challenges faced by EDC were mostly of control nature as the company was keen to manage the flux of young graduates on one hand and enable the HR division to administer the development plans of these graduates in a systematic and efficient way.

Eight challenges were identified at the beginning of the project and these were classified into two categories. The first category related to the administration of the process from the HR division point of view and that had the following challenges ranked in descending order according to their criticality to the business and their importance.

The first challenge was the lack of a methodical approach, where HR division heavily relied on processes applied by different divisions and that most of the time lacked critical details. In fact, the HR division was mostly facilitating training sessions while the divisions were dealing with graduates on case by case basis.

The second challenge was the difficulty of establishing a unified framework (including the identification of unified templates) for defining and classifying competencies, while the third challenges related to the complexity of defining the competencies at macro (EDC) and micro (divisional) levels.

The fourth challenge of this category was of course the need to establish a pan company standard for competencies that are common to all divisions including but not limited to the administration, formal communication, networking, and IT skills.

The remaining challenges were related to EDC management and were directly linked to the above challenges. They included the difficulty in obtaining feedback from stakeholders prior to having a systematic tool that enables the users to test the suggested solution. The second challenge was the problems expected due to the lack of clarity of the details, where what could work for some divisions may not necessarily be acceptable to the other ones and that of course would raise issues from management once the details are explored / addressed. The fourth challenge was the resistance expected from many users who could see this as a threat (in all divisions).

The challenges and problems identified above took some time to explore and although most of the issues were not related directly to technology, the IT team assigned to this project could envisage from the very first day that the success of this project would heavily rely on the design and development of a tool (system) that meets the characteristics of user friendliness (very easy to use by mostly novice users) while allowing maximum flexibility for change at any point in time (including design changes) and facilitating minimum data entry by users through maximizing the usage of data selection and look up data lists. The functional flow of the system must be smooth with minimum screens / tabs switching while allowing maximum ability to produce reports (including ad-hoc ones that are requested on need basis) and maximum potential for interfacing with other systems at input and output levels. This would allow for developing Application and Data Interfaces (API and DAPI).

The case study is divided into (8) sections with the aim of giving the readers the maximum benefit from the case in a structured method. These sections are:

- Background of the Project and its Stakeholders.
- Background of the Business Requirement.
- The "Proof of Concept" – POC stage.
- The Project Structure.
- System Implementation and Challenges.
- Project Achievements.
- Concerns and Risks Management.
- Lessons learned.

BACKGROUND OF THE PROJECT AND ITS STAKEHOLDERS

Recruiting, training, and integrating young graduates is one of the strategic objectives in the energy sector in the region. Policies to recruit young graduates with the aim of preparing them to become fully productive members of the workforce in the sector within a set period of time are continuously reviewed and enhanced to stream-line and sometimes expedite this process. EDC is no exception, where graduates applying for jobs in EDC are typically screened according to their skill levels in three areas, the English language, the education level and specialty and the number of years of experience (if applicable). A baseline competence assessment takes place as part of the recruitment process in EDC and the results are plugged into the applicant profile, which is used once the graduate is recruited to establish the career path in terms work discipline (job), the gaps in skills to be addressed hence closed.

The task of assessing graduates and assigning them to different jobs were carried out by the HR division as follows:

The graduate profile was checked against the relevant targeted jobs, where the competencies required for the targeted jobs were compared against the set of competencies acquired by the graduate and a gap list was created. Assigning the graduate to the job followed according to his / her academic specialty.

Once the recruited graduate was assigned to a job, he / she were assigned a supervisor, who would be responsible for preparing the graduate to become a productive member of staff within a set period of time.

Although the program was mostly based on time, many graduates were able to complete the set of development tasks in a shorter period than the time frame set. Integrating each graduate was subject to the supervisor's judgment of how ready he / she were.

There were two stakeholders in the project. The first stakeholder was the HR division and the second was the IT staff members.

Initially, there were four entities directly related to the project:

- The graduate, since the development plans focused on developing the graduates.
- The supervisor / coach, as he / she was the responsible entity for the development of the graduate.
- The development program, which was the vehicle to achieve the set goals.
- The assessor who was the entity to make the decisions hence facilitates the realization of the set objectives.

Because the development programs lacked the formal status at the company level, and due to their divisional nature where each program was prepared, administered, and managed by the division that created it, the relationship between the supervisor / coach and the graduate could not be benchmarked and that of course lead to conflicts and issues at different levels.

In some cases, graduates were placing strong claims that they were not receiving the right level of support / attention. Other claims included lack of supervisor assistance and purposely causing delays.

These claims were not easy to prove / deny hence HR division had to make many decisions that were based on minimizing damage rather than trying to investigate and establish root cause per claim. No professional solution could have been applied and that was a major challenge for all concerned.

Furthermore, and due to the manual nature of the process and its related data, it was not easy to obtain reports. The reports that were produced were mostly manual and they were soon out of date and viewed as useless and stakeholders could not make informed decisions based on the information presented.

BACKGROUND OF THE BUSINESS REQUIREMENT

This area was managed in two steps. The first was to develop the requirements by prototyping. The main reason for this was basically to utilize a tool that would facilitate maximum user flexibility (the HR division objectives were clear, but there were no clear standards yet and the exercise involved a long learning process to reach an adequate solution that would serve the purpose for all concerned.

Prototyping was later referred to as the POC stage which had five initial objectives, namely creating a unified structure for grouping and classifying the competencies, then establishing an acceptable competencies classification scheme followed by formalizing an acceptable benchmark for the competence level required per job and creating an acceptable mechanism for evaluating the competence levels set and comparing the competence levels achieved by the graduate against the required level and finally establishing a pan company structured process for assessments and approvals.

The outcome of that stage was a framework, which was to be used to create working templates for different graduates. The records of 50 graduates from different business areas / disciplines were used to ensure that a generic system could be developed to serves all gradates records.

Many new ideas were explored during the POC stage with the aim of enhancing the process and establishing a Quality Assurance mechanism for continuous process improvement.

The second step was to further enhance the framework by the users and IT, then design and develop an automated system that serves all concerned. During the stage of enhancing the framework, the ideas focused mostly on the creation of a methodical way so that the properties and details of the framework would be utilized by all. This meant that the framework had to be designed in a way that allowed for common competencies to be defined once but utilized by all, similarly, skills that were commonly used by many jobs / divisions had to be handled with care to ensure proper reusability.

The objective of the final product was put as: Producing a time based development plan per Job, which covers the competencies and the level of skill required per competency for this job, use the developed plan to assign the right graduate to the proper development plan (as per the job he is recruited for) then modify the development plan to meet the actual graduate development requirements as stated / required by the division and assign staff members to manage the graduate development / progress in supervision and coaching capacities as well as enabling the assessment process to achieve the set tasks, hence produce reports that would enable the HR division to manage the process more effectively.

PROOF OF CONCEPT (POC) STAGE

This section covers the POC in some details.

As stated earlier, the POC stage had five objectives:

1. Create a unified structure for grouping and classifying the competencies.
2. Create an acceptable competencies classification scheme.
3. Create an acceptable benchmark for the level of competence required.
4. Create an acceptable mechanism for evaluating the competence levels set and comparing the competence levels achieved against them.
5. Create a structured process for assessment and approvals.

The outcome of that stage was a framework, which was to be used to create working templates for different graduates.

From IT point of view, there were three aspects that were considered key success factors in the POC. These were identified as Organizational Concerns, which related mostly to meeting the requirement of the different divisions and at the same time respond to the Management Concerns of having a system that would answer all the queries raised. The third was the Technology Factors and that came in two flavors. The first related to the challenges expected while working on the Pilot (POC) development, while the second was the ability to design and implement a robust solution that would eventually meet all the functions defined during the POC.

Following the successful replacement of the legacy HR system in EDC in 1998, the HR division started looking for a solution that would complement the newly implemented HR system with a system that could assist the HR division in managing the intake of young graduates and follow up on their progress.

Searching for a tool that could meet the HR division requirements was not successful and since it was an issue the HR division wanted to address as soon as possible; the decision was made to approach the IT division with the aim of exploring different scenarios including the development of a tailor made system.

A team was formed from the two divisions and the objectives were presented in broad sense. There were no clear boundaries since the idea was not clear and the HR staff assigned members to the task were looking for a solution that could do everything!

The first cut roadmap was agreed. The next step was to manage the flux of issues, details, and changes to be included and to achieve the best results, the team agreed to follow a simple approach, which is summarized below.

Every member would state his view of the requirements to be included in the pilot.

Weekly, two meetings were held with the objective of discussing the different inputs (requirements) and then agreeing on the items and details to be included in the POC.

During the meetings, there were three major Organizational concerns raised. The first related to the mechanism to be used for identifying the detailed competencies required per job, the second was the way to identify the timeframe for covering specific competencies (start and finish time) and the third was how to establish a benchmark for evaluation?

Two Management concerns were presented:

1. Competencies may vary for similar jobs (jobs carrying the same name) depending on factors related to work location, division, etc.
2. How to ensure that the competencies and skill levels required were dynamic enough to allow for handling exceptions?

There was one technology factor, which related to data capturing and populating the POC database. It was clear that the data had to be reviewed, structured, and then filtered, which was a big manual task then.

One cultural issue was encountered during this stage, which was related to the data acquisition. Most required data resided in paper files, while some were maintained on MS-Word documents.

Lack of enthusiasm was a big challenge since this system was seen as a job security threat by many. The new classification of the competency had to take the following format:

"Verb followed by description of the task to be done," e.g. "Define input validation Process."

In fact, one of the cultural challenges during this task related to the skill level in English language while the other was the ability to build a meaningful competency. The resulting framework was later defined as a (4) levels structure, consisting of:

*   Unit
*   Sub Unit
*   Element
*   Competency (Sub Element)

The structure had the following relationships:

*   A Unit may contain one or more Sub Unit(s)
*   A Sub Unit may contain one or more Element(s)
*   An Element may contain one or more Competency

The next task was defining the skill levels, where three levels were defined. The first level was labeled as "Awareness," while the second level was labeled "Knowledge" and the third level was "Skill." The levels aimed at reflecting the skill level required to be achieved at that point in time in the development plan.

Figure 1. The competencies structure

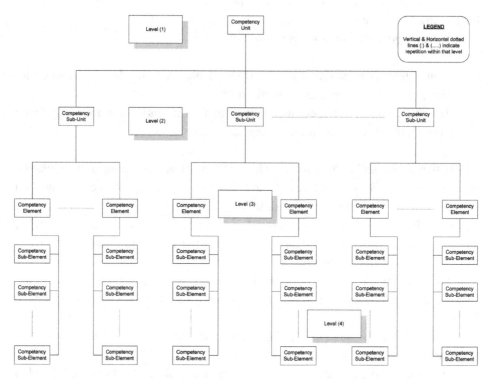

Competencies that were identified as "Skill" were then evaluated from a critical-ity viewpoint. Some of the "Skill" competencies were viewed as "Critical" to the job hence they were labeled as "Critical." This label meant that the graduate was very well prepared to execute this competency independent of others. To simplify, the structure below depicts the classifications and the levels attached to them (and see Figure 1):

Unit 1:

- Sub Unit 1.1
  - Element 1.1.1
    - Competency 1.1.1.1: Awareness
    - Competency 1.1.1.2: Knowledge
    - Competency 1.1.1.3: Skill
    - Competency 1.1.1.4: Skill--------Critical
- Sub Unit 1.2
  - Element 1.2.1
    - Competency 1.2.1.5: Skill--------Critical
    - Competency 1.2.1.6: Skill--------Critical

Unit 2:

- Sub Unit 2.1
  - ○ Element 2.1.1
    - ▪ Competency 2.1.1.1: Awareness
    - ▪ Competency 2.1.1.2: Knowledge
- Sub Unit 2.2
  - ○ Element 2.2.1
    - ▪ Competency 2.2.1.1: Knowledge
    - ▪ Competency 2.2.1.2: Skill
    - ▪ Competency 2.2.1.3: Skill--------Critical

The next step was to create the assessments and approvals process and its supporting structure. This had three components. The first one was establishing a method to identify and define the different roles required in the process. The second was defining a mechanism to link these roles so that each role acts in it is intended order. The third was to assign each role to the tasks attached to it in the workflow.

The examples below explain this part of the POC stage.

Some roles were related to supervising and mentoring the graduate during his / her development program, while there were roles that focused more on the assessment of the graduate after each stage of the development program. A third set of roles related to the overall verification of the process as a whole where the verifier's role varied from ensuring that the process was followed properly to verifying that a fair assessment was conducted.

From IT view point, it was not easy to establish a full automated system that was capable of delivering the this part of the system, but eventually all concerned parties agreed on formalizing the process as below:

During the preparation of the incumbent graduate development program, the division will nominate senior members of staff to act as the supervisor, the coach, the assessor, and the mentor for this graduate. The coach is the entity accountable for the success of the developer, while the mentor is the support entity that the graduate and the coach could refer to for issues and concerns. The assessor's role was defined to test and ensure that the graduate is ready and has fully acquired the required level of skills for that time period. The supervisor (usually the most senior member in the group) would conduct regular interviews with the concerned parties to ensure all is well and act on issues / concerns so that the road is paved for the integration of the graduate within the division. The verifiers were typically members of the HR division and they would attend as and when they choose or upon being invited by the supervisor. They also could have one on one or group sessions with the graduate, the assessor and the mentors to discuss the development of graduates (if needed).

Going back to the concerns raised by the IT team, it was agreed that the system would allow semi-automated functions to cover the workflow requirement. The designed function operated as follow.

The graduate would trigger a request in the system, which would include a list of the "Sub Elements" to be covered (using a tick against them). The request will include a suggested date and time. Such requests would typically be endorsed by the coach.

The assessor receives an e-mail notification of the request requesting the details to be explored. An accepted request by the assessor triggers e-mails to the coach, the HR pool of verifiers and the supervisor. It is important to note that the pool pf verifiers consist of many members of HR division staff.

One HR staff member would take ownership of the request and could attend the session (depending on the need, the history of the graduate and any comments that may demand the verifier attendance).

The assessment session could take as long as necessary to satisfy the objective it was defined for, and the graduate is informed of the result (skill level met / not met and the way forward).

The session is concluded by the signature of all attendees and the results are manually fed to the system by the assessor. To avoid conflicts, the system was designed to allow for a review by the supervisor prior to committing the assessment results. The assessor utilized this function to trigger an e-mail to the supervisor and the supervisor would in turn either endorse the results or conducts a review session with all concerned to decide on the next action with the assessment results. This function proved extremely useful in eliminating conflicts.

The next part of the building blocks was to allow for the flexibility of shifting competencies to a future date, which was a typical solution to avoid the use of "not met" for competencies that were assessed but the graduate could not demonstrate the skill level required.

A manual trial of the POC was conducted after the building blocks were in place and that went well. The next step was conducting a Quality Assurance exercise to review the classification the competencies, which was carried out in parallel with the development of the POC using PC tools and records of few graduates and few members of staff in the HR division to play the different workflow roles.

THE PROJECT STRUCTURE

Once the POC was successfully tested, the team was restructured as follows:

1. A team was assigned to collect and classify the competencies needed for every job in EDC. This team had to conduct lengthy workshops to thoroughly explain the requirements to EDC divisions and to work on some examples to clarify the requirements and to demonstrate how to create competencies according to the defined structure.
2. A second team was assigned to identify staff members in the different divisions in EDC to play the roles required for the assessment and approvals processes (Coach, Supervisor, Assessor, and Mentor). This team had to define the skills needed per role then check with the different divisions for potential candidates that could meet the necessary skills for every role. The progress flow process which was drafted during the POC stage was revisited to ensure its compliance with all the requirements it was designed for including the pre-requisite to enable the graduates to complete competencies ahead of schedule and move competencies to future dates and the ability to reflect such changes on the overall progress of each graduate.
3. A third team was assigned to verify and consolidate the information obtained from tasks (1) and (2) above.
4. The IT team was assigned to design and build the full application and the database for EDC.

There were a number of cultural issues encountered during this stage. Below are three examples.

Softening the Development Program

Due to conflicting opinions regarding the development program between HR and other divisions particularly when it came to the number of competencies, the skill level required per competency and the criticality to be assigned to the competency, cultural issue related to the two different views of the development plan arose, where the HR team wanted to ensure a systematic unified methodology was in place while operational divisions wanted a more dynamic approach that capitalizes on the opportunities arising from daily work conditions. The operational approach meant that the plan was a non-binding theoretical tool. There was no clear cut and solutions had to be devised to allow for flexibility hence avoid delays that could have taken place due to personal and / or work related conflicts.

Flexibility to Allow Switching the Development Program of a Graduate

This flexibility was requested by many divisions to allow graduates to move to better prospects while still under development. This is typical in companies like EDC where graduates could move to jobs that have better career potential in terms of job progression and that could mean switching the whole career of the graduate, switching the division or both. A big challenge here was the way to measure what was achieved in the current development plan against what is required in the new plan!

Verifying Acquired Skills

A third example was the absence of a standard mechanism to verify the skill level required. This was clear when the assessors list was prepared as it was clear that some assessors had the tendency to be softer in the assessment approach than others. It was also noted that graduates could see this as a gap in the system and would strive to arrange with the assessors that had this softer approach.

Furthermore, the team could see that graduates would arrange to cover a wide range of competencies based on theory or based on answers they could obtain from other colleagues with the aim of completing their development as fast as possible, which ignited yet another conflict between the different divisions. This issue was particularly interesting and usually led to heated debate between the HR division and some divisions when some graduates managed to capitalize on this gap and the assessors did not take the necessary measures during the assessments to ensure that the skill level was acquired. The issue was explored when the graduate could not demonstrate the required skill level when assigned to tasks that required him / her to work independently.

Two management concerns were raised during this stage. The first related to identifying graduates at both ends of the spectrum, namely; fast track and slow track ones. This requirement added to the complications already encountered in the assessment and verification processes.

The second was to review the assignments made by the different division for the different roles required from division staff to manage the development program of the graduates, particularly that staff members assigned were not always available.

Initially, there were many points of view regarding the roles, the responsibilities and the workflow, but once the system analysis started, ideas became clearer and a formalized process started to shape up to meet the management keenness to have a pool of skilled staff members who could act in multi capacities so that the process is always on track and does not get affected by individuals being present / absent.

SYSTEM IMPLEMENTATION AND CHALLENGES

Having the first cut release of the system ready and using the data collected so far, HR division decided to commission the system on September 1st 1998, with two objectives:

- To meet Key Performance Indicator of being the first company in the country to have an automated system for developing graduates. HR wanted to use the system to manage the intake group of graduates expected to join by the fourth quarter of 1998.
- To facilitate the use of decision support tools that would give EDC an advantage in recruiting graduates and integrating them at a rate faster than other companies in the group, hence position them as the flagship in that race, particularly for national graduates.

The plan was to implement the full system according to the following schedule:

1. Compile the development programs for graduates joining "back office" areas such as HR, Finance and IT divisions. The target date for populating the data and producing the first cut reports was the end of September 1998.
2. Produce the first assessment for the graduates defined in the system early in the fourth quarter of 1998. This was given a duration of (5) weeks.
3. Review the process fully during the fourth quarter of 1998 to identify gaps, enhancements and changes then implement as much as possible with minimum impact on the system / users.
4. Design and develop the workflow required for the system, which is to be ready by the end of 1999.
5. The remaining "Operational" divisions were to complete the data collection process and be ready for populating it by the end of 1998.
6. January 1st 1999 was set as the target date for all EDC divisions to use the system with a properly defined workflow.

To achieve this ambitious task, HR assigned some of the finest staff members to take responsibility of the system. They were trained to administer the system and were equipped with the necessary skills to train and supervise others company wide as well as manage the user expectations for future phases. However, two challenges were encountered during this stage:

- Many graduates were assigned to offshore / remote work locations and it was not easy to get their supervisors to attend planned training sessions, so a number of "one on one" sessions had to be arranged for all staff members who were unable to attend due to operational / logistical reasons.

- Competency definitions and skill levels continued to vary for offshore development programs although the jobs were the same (e.g. Mechanical Engineer on site "A" had a different set of critical skills to that used for a Mechanical Engineer on site "B"). The same applied to competencies and skill levels.

On the project management side, the project teams were getting closer than ever to having a unified vision of where they wanted this project to anchor.

An excellent "Change Management" methodology was applied which basically captured all requirements and changes was used for scheduling and implementing them smoothly and swiftly.

During the first six months of going live with the system, there were (5) major challenges encountered:

1. There were competencies that required the graduate to attend courses such as English Language, but it was clear that such competencies could not have been fully acquired hence could not be properly assessed after a course. Time was needed for most graduates to establish the language skills needed for the job and the graduate future career.

2. Graduates who decided to switch jobs were facing challenges in establishing a baseline for the new "Graduate Development Plan." It was never easy to compare the two sets of skills leave alone the issue of resolving the differences in the competencies required. This of course was even worse when graduates switched divisions / work locations.

3. Competencies that had to be completed as attachments to divisions other than the division the graduate worked for were encountering all kind of challenges. Divisions preferred attachments to be in groups / batches as this enabled the division to minimize the time they had to assign resources to assist the graduates but that approach was not practical since the development plans of individuals were not synchronized for divisional attachments. This resulted in time spent on organizing the graduates to attend a group attachment, which was a lengthy and time-consuming task. A cultural issue was noticed as some graduates capitalized on their relationships with key staff members to ensure meeting their planned attachment requirements without having to wait for group attachments. This was not easy to control system wise.

4. Initially, every graduate had a specific set of senior staff members assigned to his / her development plan, which proved to be impractical since the assigned members of staff were not always there during the time for supervision / assessments / verifications, etc.

5. Some assessors were allowing excessive shifting of competencies to future quarters with the aim of avoiding the use of the "Not Met" rating for planned competencies that the graduate did not actually meet. This meant that the development would take more than (2) years and that was an issue the system could not verify. To avoid such excessive usage, it was suggested that division management should emphasize the HR assessment guidelines by restricting any shifting of competencies to future quarters to the approval of the division managers.

On 1.1.1999, the system was commissioned with a well-formalized process. The bandwagon effect took place as divisions gradually started using the system to manage the development plans of their graduates.

During the first week of 1999, the project team was dismantled and staff members assigned to the project went back to their normal duties, but as with the case of most newly introduced system, HR Division started receiving new suggestions on regular basis for improvements and enhancements.

HR Division could see benefits from improvements suggested / requested by the users and it was not long before a small project team was established to manage the enhancements / changes with the aim of taking the system to a new dimension as a "Decision Support System—DSS." This new team established yet another "Change Management" process that revisited all the changes suggested / requested then a thorough analysis was made to evaluate and prioritize them, then they were scheduled as follows:

1. Business based (functional) enhancements were given highest priority.
2. Enhancements to techniques applied such as simplifying the system usage and facilitating more user flexibility were assigned second highest priority.
3. Application look and feel configurations were given third priority.
4. Issues that related to data attribute changes (data field properties and characteristics) were given second lowest priority (as long as they did not impact the system functionality). A typical example was allowing indexing on certain fields to allow faster search.
5. Lowest priority was given to labeling and renaming of attributes and fields names on the user entry forms / screens.
6. Suggestions related to grouping "Competencies" within "Elements" were included in the Change Management logs but were referred back to the concerned divisions for discussion and agreement since different divisions had different opinions (Mechanical Engineer is a job that is used by about half a dozen divisions) and the grouping suggested by one division does necessarily match what the other divisions wanted.

By the end of June 1999, the system was fully functional with the following tasks fully automated:

1. A full set of "Job Master Plan" were created in the system for every job.
2. The "Job Master Plan" was used to create a "Graduates Development Plan" for the first graduate recruited for that particular job.
3. "Graduate Development Plans" for the following graduates were either copied from the 'Job Master Plan" or were clowned from a previous "Graduate Development Plan," and that was later modified to reflect the job specific requirements.
4. Quarterly assessment dates were defined (according to the graduate recruitment date).
5. The assessments were conducted on-line with results automatically reflecting overall progress.
6. Changes deemed necessary to the "Graduate development Plan" were reviewed by the division management to ensure integrity of the process and fairness to all concerned.

Changes requested were particularly interesting as the learning curve went upwards exponentially, and it was noticed that many of the mature ideas came from divisions that had many graduates. Some positive ones came from supervisors who were responsible for the development of more than one graduate.

Some of the particularly interesting examples related to maintaining and meeting competencies that were of cultural and legislative nature. Examples included the stringent rules applied by EDC for Health and Safety, which are considered core competencies particularly for working offshore.

The Health and Safety competencies were continuously enhanced to meet best practices and Environment Protection regulations and that was a massive challenge. EDC holds international certification in Health, Safety and Environment protection, as well as Quality Assurance and that imposes stringent controls at the enterprise level in all these disciplines.

The second area of continuous change related to adopting and applying changes in EDC policies due to changes in the local regulations. This was particularly interesting as the country was moving very fast in adopting and implementing e-business and e-government culture and practices.

The final area of challenges related to the implementation came from internal factors that related to the continuous change and growth. As EDC grew bigger, new projects were introduced and these in turn brought along new practices / methods, new tools and new standards and that also meant more divisions and new jobs, etc.

The challenges here related to coping between the introduction of new jobs and defining the competencies required using the current framework (from similar or close enough jobs).

PROJECT ACHIEVEMENTS

This section highlights the achievements mad at the project level, which are grouped under three main headers, namely (IT, HR, and EDC).

IT Achievements:

1. The system design allowed a dynamic design that would allow for "n" levels. Only 4 levels were used in EDC but the flexibility offered allowed a tree structure that had no limits on the number of levels.
2. The semi dynamic workflow design allowed for a group of individuals to be defined in a pool and they could be used for the next task using different capacities. This structure had a default setting per graduate, but the pool of experts allowed the current member of staff to assign the next in route when the need aroused.
3. The data cloning procedure proved to be an efficient method of minimizing the time taken by the users to define competencies for both jobs and graduates.

HR Division Achievements:

1. The system allowed the HR division to have a formal development framework that had clear boundaries. The intake plans for graduates were clearer.
2. The Job related competencies were defined in a structured method and that in turn allowed HR division to manage all the competencies in a consistent method using a unified procedure.
3. The data cloning capabilities allowed the users great efficiencies in minimizing the time taken to define competencies for all graduates once the template was created. It was even faster to clone the graduate plan.

EDC Achievements:

1. Meeting EDC Key Performance Indicator of being the first company in the group to have an automated system for developing graduates.
2. The system was used as a decision support tool which gave EDC an advantage in recruiting graduates and integrating them at a rate faster than other companies in the group; hence, position them as the flagship in that race.

3.   The structured Job related competencies allowed HR division to produce proper progress, divisional, and management reports.
4.   Graduates could check on-line their progress against their development plans and that offered transparency that was not familiar to the relationship between the graduate and HR division.
5.   The produced "Dashboards" and "Charts" enabled EDC management to have "status at a glance" view of the progress of graduates and that in turn proved very useful for all concerned, particularly when it came to rewarding the fast lane graduates.

CONCERNS AND RISKS MANAGEMENT

Basically, there were many concerns and risks that were encountered during the project life cycle. The method used to address these issues was based on two factors. The first was to identify, classify, and properly record the concern / risk then attach the relevant details pertaining to it. The details included assigning a probability attribute (Low / Medium / High) and a severity parameter (Low / Medium / High) on a matrix to categorize the risk, hence act on the appropriate mitigation scheme.

A common folder was created with a spreadsheet that allowed the team members to log concerns and risks as and when encountered (see Figure 2).

Change management was applied to ensure that all the risks / concerns were addressed and resolved, as the project was getting closer to completion.

Some examples of the risks encountered and the actions taken to address and neutralize each risk are given below:

1.   Lack of clarity (objective were not clearly set) at the beginning of the project. This was the biggest risk and was addressed in a gradual manner, where the team applied a top down approach. Major objectives were designed and then these were broken down into more manageable components.

Figure 2. The structure of the spreadsheet

Severity

		Low	Medium	High
Probability	Low			
	Medium			
	High			

2. Lack of experience in such schemes. Visits were made to most of the group members of companies EDC belonged to seeking to learn from the experience and knowledge of others, but it was clear that there was no structured framework was available and each sister company had its own approach to address its needs.

3. Availability of resources in EDC. When management decided to formulate the team, it was very difficult to find the right mix of skills (technical and informal academics). Staff members did not want to be responsible for developing a program that was viewed by many as "yet another two years of study"! This perception was so strong that many members of staff could hide their relief when the apology reason they used was accepted and they were excused from participating.

4. The continuous change everywhere. The number of changes occupied a huge amount of space in the change logs as it was acceptable for the project to change. The concept of the POC was purposely executed on paper prior to developing a single line of code to ensure that a process was in place and it was possible to collect the data required.

5. During the POC stage, it was noticed that the PC tool was not offering the flexibility needed. PC tools are always restricting in nature and the IT team had to exert massive efforts to provide convincing solution / arguments that the final system will deliver the agreed requirement.

6. Other known risks such as personal conflicts, culture related risks (addressed earlier) and health and safety risks. The pattern applied for managing and eliminating risks was the same as the team always broke each reported risk into a number of manageable (smaller) ones. Decision trees were used to assess further the success and failure potentials of suggested solutions while "brainstorming sessions" were the carriage used to manage the exercise.

LESSONS LEARNED

There were many valuable lessons that were captured from this experience. These lessons varied from issues and challenges encountered to improper sponsorship to challenges and risks related to the approach used down to the risks related to incorrect interpretations of how a pilot could be transformed to a full system.

The first lesson was the lack of proper sponsorship: As was stated in the case, the objective was to meet top management directives to have a fully automated system for managing the development of graduates pan company; however, sponsorship was taken by the HR division, which meant that there were many constraints and restrictions encountered due to the lack of power on the HR division part. This was very clear when different divisions were requested to nominate representatives at different points in the project life cycle.

Lesson: Whenever the project crosses the divisional boundaries, sponsorship should immediately be taken over by top management who should nominate a top management representative (sponsor).

The second lesson was the lack of clarity of the scope of work: Initially, the scope of work was to manage the pilot (POC). This scope was changed immediately after the success of the POC. This switch dictated many changes including the creation of a project team that was efficient and effective, however, the team was taken away from other assignments, and that could have caused delays and interruptions to other projects / assignments.

Lesson: The clarity of the scope of work is a must for all projects. It is the management responsibility to ensure that a project has a clear scope prior to giving it the go-ahead signal.

The third lesson was the impact of the team structure: The team was formed from some full time and many part time members. The part time members belonged to many divisions and getting input from all concerned was not easy within the required time, particularly when members were either assigned to other important projects or were on duty / leave.

Lesson: The idea of having critical decisions depending on part time members of projects is a high risk that has to be addressed with project management for every project of a similar nature.

The fourth lesson related to the transformation from POC to a full system: This lesson relates to the methods used to address the transformation. The POC was very limited in nature and scope. Its success was a very commendable achievement, but the methods dictated by management to produce the full-fledged system from POCs do not always work. This is particularly dangerous when it is mixed with enterprise objectives and lack of authority.

Lesson: With projects that are developed using prototyping, the team involved in the process should be equipped with the right tools, resources, and power.

The fifth lesson: Although the project was critical from management point of view, uncertainty and lack of clear long-term strategy forced many qualified resources to avoid participating, as they feared job loss. Many issues that were encountered and took time to resolve (business and IT) could have been avoided if some of the skilled resources were included or represented in the team.

Lesson: Knowledge sharing is critical for such projects to reduce delays and risks due to the lack of clarity in the scope of work.

The outcome of the experiences was a mix of positive and negative lessons, but when linked to the events in the experience and the surrounding environment, resources, decisions and actions, one could say that it was a rich one with many lessons learned by all concerned. Recommendations for success with similar projects are simply placed as having the right level of sponsorship, negotiating a clear scope of work, recruiting the right skilled resources, and ensuring the buy in at the enterprise level.

The system utilization generated a number of business related improvements at EDC and its sister companies in the group. Some of these improvements were measurable while others were qualitative in nature. A summary of these changes follows:

As the job competencies were formally identified, and since jobs with similar nature were linked in job families, it was possible to define and refine the relationships between competencies, jobs and job families and that in turn allowed the HR division to produce some generic frameworks of competencies that are common amongst jobs within the job family. This simplified the process of creating development plans for newly recruited graduates.

The changes to the development plans of newly recruited graduates also became easier and mostly systematic as HR and the division that the graduate worked for had sufficient details to refer to for the required change.

On the level of formalizing the processes, the system had a clear roadmap for all concerned that takes the user in a step-by-step approach to complete the required tasks in a smooth way.

The assessment process had a clear path and staff members who were expected to conduct assessment sessions were trained to ensure that the process is adhered to and the likelihood of being subjective was eliminated to a large extent.

One more improvement crawled in slowly but surely, and that was related to the time factor involved in the development plan, where many graduates were keen to complete the assignments they were given in the quickest time possible hence close competencies of higher skill levels at an earlier date than that scheduled. This dictated a new factor in the process as it became more acceptable and adoptable and it was becoming clearer to all concerned that this was creating a win-win scenario for the graduate and the company particularly in the disciplines that knowledge and experience transfers needed to be completed as soon as practicable.

The final advantage came from sharing the experience itself with the sister companied to develop a generic system that served all the companies in the group. Staff members from IT assisted others in many other disciplines to comprehend the process and later develop a unified system that served the group.

REFERENCES

Amin, N., Hinton, M., Hall, P., Newton, M., & Kayae, R. (1999). A study of strategic and decision-making issues in adoption of ERP systems resulting from a merger in the financial services sector. In *Proceedings of the 18 International Workshop on Enterprise Management Resource and Planning Systems EMRPS*, (pp. 173-181). Venice, Italy: EMRPS.

Bingi, P., Sharma, M., & Godla, J. (1999). Critical issues affecting an ERP implementation. *Information Systems Management, 16*(3), 7–8. doi:10.1201/1078/431 97.16.3.19990601/31310.2

Brehm, L., Heinzl, A., & Markus, M. L. (2001). Tailoring ERP systems: A spectrum of choices and their implications. In *Proceedings of the 34th Annual Hawaii International Conference on Systems Sciences*. Hawaii, HI: IEEE.

Brown, J. S., & Duguid, P. (1991). Organizational learning and communities-of-practice: Toward a unified view of working, learning, and innovation. *Organization Science, 2*(1), 102–111. doi:10.1287/orsc.2.1.40

Cohen, W. M., & Levinthal, D. A. (1990). Absorptive capacity: A new perspective on learning and innovation. *Administrative Science Quarterly, 35*, 128–152. doi:10.2307/2393553

Cohen, W. M., Nelson, R. R., & Walsh, J. (2000). *Protecting their intellectual assets: Appropriability conditions and why U.S. manufacturing firms patent (or not)*. Working paper No. 7552. Washington, DC: National Bureau of Economic Research.

Conner, K. R., & Prahalad, C. K. (1996). A resource-based theory of the firm: Knowledge versus opportunism. *Organization Science, 7*(5), 477–501. doi:10.1287/orsc.7.5.477

Crosby, P. (1994). *Completeness: Quality for the 21st century*. New York, NY: Plume Books.

Damanpour, F. (1996). Organizational complexity and innovation: Developing and testing multiple contingency models. *Management Science, 42*(5), 693–716. doi:10.1287/mnsc.42.5.693

Davenport, T. H. (2000). *Mission critical: Realizing the promise of enterprise systems*. Boston, MA: Harvard Business School Press.

Holland, C., & Light, B. (1997). Critical success factors model for ERP implementation. *IEEE Software*. Retrieved from http://www.imamu.edu.sa/Scientific_selections/abstracts/Documents/A%20Critical%20Success%20Factors%20Model%20For%20ERP%20Implementation.pdf

KEY TERMS AND DEFINITIONS

Assessor: A senior Subject Matter Expert (SME) who is responsible for assessing graduates in one or more disciplines and provide the Supervisor with a clear picture of the status.

Coach: A senior member of staff who is assigned the responsibility of preparing the graduate to meet his / her development program.

Graduate: A new member of staff recruited upon graduation from an academic institute with a bachelor's degree. He / She is assigned to a target job and is expected to meet the development program competencies within the set time frame to take over that job.

Mentor: A senior member of staff who is assists the graduate with technical and / or personal issues.

Supervisor: A senior member of staff who is responsible for ensuring that the Graduate and Coach work closely to achieve the integration of the graduate in the fastest time possible.

Verifier: A HR member of staff who assists (when needed) to ensure the fairness of the process. The terms used in the four levels used in the competency structure had the following meanings:

Unit: Means the highest level which related to disciplines directly related to the business divisions. Examples included Administration, Engineering, IT, Finance, Projects, Communications, etc.

Sub-Unit: Means the level directly below the Unit. Examples included Analysis, Design, Development, Testing, Implementation, Support, and Maintenance, which were all Sub-Units of the Unit IT.

Elements: The next level of classification and using the IT example, the following Elements are siblings of the Design Unit—these are Logical Design, Data Model, Process Model, and Function Hierarchy.

Competency: The lowest level of the skill and is defined as a sentence that begins with a verb. The following are examples of the Competencies defined under the Data Model Unit: (1)Identify all data attributes required.(2) Apply First, Second and Third Normal Form. (3) Define / Name all Entities resulting. (4) Define all Relations between the Entities identified above. (5) Identify Validation Rules for each data attribute. (6) Identify the necessary sizing details such as initial data size, expected annual data growth, expected system life, etc.

Chapter 16
Business Intelligence Enterprise Solution at Abu Dhabi Finance:
Issues and Challenges

Salam Abdallah
Abu Dhabi University, UAE

EXECUTIVE SUMMARY

The challenge of transforming data and information in enterprise information systems into knowledge that can be rolled up and presented to management as key performance indicators is business-critical. The implementation of a business intelligence layer on top of the transaction processing systems and management information systems is viewed as an opportunity to move up a level to promote knowledge-based decision-making and strategic planning. This chapter attempts to examine the issues and challenges associated with the initiative by Abu Dhabi Finance to implement business intelligence solutions that extract information from the enterprise information systems, present them as KPIs for senior management, and produce knowledge that can be used to support decision-making and strategic planning.

ORGANIZATION HISTORY AND BACKGROUND

Abu-Dhabi Finance Trust (AFT) is Semi-government Company opened its doors in November 2008 with the goal to be the leading source of mortgages in UAE and then expand its services throughout the MENA province. It was built by four leading organizations in UAE.

DOI: 10.4018/978-1-4666-2220-3.ch016

AFT main strategy is to make clients expect more, as they are willing to dedicate their efforts to maintain a high quality standards and customer satisfaction.

The vision of Abu Dhabi Finance is stated as: "Our inspiration is to be the leading real estate mortgage company in the UAE and over time in the MENA region."

The mission of Abu Dhabi Finance is indicated as the purpose:

- To become a leading innovator in mortgage solutions and services with a specific focus on delivering superior client service.
- To enable real estate investment through offering financial solutions to individuals in pursuit of home ownership and wealth creation.
- To become an employer of choice, attracting and developing top talent.
- To promote and support the formation of the real estate sector in Abu Dhabi.
- To create value for our stakeholders.

The values of Abu Dhabi Finance include the following:

- Each of our clients is one of a kind.
- More than a supplier, we are a companion.
- The Abu Dhabi Finance experience is always memorable.
- We create value equally to our clients, our stakeholders, and our employees.
- We make a difference in our community.

The above vision, mission, and values configure that AFT devotes their services with high quality, as they care about their stakeholders and most of all their clients. They believe that organization success comes by dedicating strong rooted standards with superior customer satisfaction; as they are the drive towards achieving their goal to be the leading mortgage company and to sustain and grow more in the market.

SETTING THE STAGE / CASE DESCRIPTION

Business Perspective

AFT is a mortgage financer; therefore, they need to adopt software that will deliver effectiveness to their business activities. As they are financing their business activities lies between calculating the down payment, the interest rate as it varies between 5.75 and 8.5 depending on the market, method of repayment either a interest only mortgage loans, a part from the repayment and part of the interest, or a interest roll-up loans, and developing financial reports. Therefore, the required software must perform these calculations and every client data must have a separate report that presents their due payments, method of payment, requested product. The requested software must alert the mortgage advisor if any due payment were not placed and when is the next payment will be needed upon the client plan of repayment process.

Technology Perspective

By the above description of the company activities and work processes here comes the description of processes and systems they use to maintain the superior customer satisfaction and internal integrated company. Abu-Dhabi Finance Trust uses the SLAs; Sales Level Agreements software which is an Oracle Business Intelligence Enterprise Edition (OBIEE) that is primarily a business intelligence tool to report key performance indicators information and other relevant departmental and management reports. AFT chose this software as they need to have each client account information separately formatted in reports, as it has to do with finance; payments should be well organised and the interest rates adjusted to the amount remaining. Also, they chose this software as it integrates all company departments together and enable them to share documents and reports along together, to make sure that everything is moving on the right loop.

In addition to the above, it also allows the users to create and share ad-hoc reports to use them without requiring any technical assistance. The ad-hoc reports is a visualization approach it allows users to interact with the system easily and efficiently, as the reports goals is to seek out the answers to different questions and adjust the resources available according to current business requirements. The ad-hoc reports are easy to navigate and search through them, they are built easily through self-service; it demonstrates how each department in the company is functioning and what their activity level of business is. The ad-hoc reports as mentioned above are all about visualization as "a picture is worth a thousand words" it organizes the information in a clear concise form, it allows the users to view the required information in a powerful yet managed environment, the uniqueness of the ad-hoc reports is that you can filter out the data to the exact required field to measure and compare easily. In addition, it allows the users to build out hypothesis from what if scenario functions to visualize and analyse how changes will bring on growth and development to the organization. The ad-hoc reporting is a win-win process as it is a self-service both users and IT department are benefiting from it; it offers a strong robust enterprise to assemble all the present and future challenges and requirements.

Moreover, the dashboards in OBIEE are the overview of the information and pages; it is an interface that allows several reports to be viewed at the same time. The dashboards are like the warehouse, it is a container for reports that allows them to be interactive and retrieval; also, it can view data and reports in a summarized way and in graphical method if applicable.

The SLAs helped in managing the organization and the tasks required as the software allows the company to increase efficiency and accuracy by automating daily ad-hoc reports which provides effective communication tool and it also saves a lot of time and effort as they do not have to create those reports manually. In addition, it helped in getting the required information instantly by assessing the user definable fields. The hypothesis option id the SLAs helped the organization by improving their budgets and time spent on projects. The tools that are built within the system for financial plans helped a lot in managing the future plan for consumer's repayment process efficiently, as mistakes were minimized and ensure that everything is being handled accurately.

Issues and Problems before Implementation

The company had more than 30 legacy systems running at the same time on different databases including, Oracle, MS Access and SQL Server and were also running on different platforms. These legacy systems were used by nearly 2000 employees from different business areas, such as; Maintenance, Inspection, Inventory, Purchasing, Contracts, Finance, Human Resources, and Payroll.

New technology implementation and installation is compatibly easy as there is expert people who can implement it, but when it comes to staff and workers issues and problems starts to emerge. Changing people means and techniques in conducting work and behavior is the most challenging part. The human element is the essential to activate and work out the effectiveness of the new software, but it can lead to high costs with less productivity, hence leading to more mistakes, inefficiency, and longer time to implement the software. As the system was relatively new to the IT resources in Abu-Dhabi Finance, therefore there was a very steep learning curve involved, along with some teething problems during the initial setup. Workers at the initial stage lack the required and proper skills to adopt with the software. If the workers fail to communicate effectively with the new software, then this whole project and implementation process will be jeopardized. So, AFT realized those problems from the beginning and started to devote their efforts to ensure that each member attitude must be influenced to accept the new software; as well as, adapting the new necessary skills to guarantee a successful implementation. They started by conducting a systematic diagnostic approach, as they analyzed the areas of inadequate performance, then overcoming issues that emerged by the implementation the system. They had a prior training session to reduce errors and facilitate the process of adapting to the new software skills; however, prior training is not enough; they used the e-learning sessions for post implementation; the e-learning sessions and modules costs less and requires less effort from the IT resources, as this technique will be self service learning and engaging with the system. This type is better as its available always at any time with unlimited number of access, so each member can keep on learning and practicing by looking into the online sessions and modules until they become mastery in it.

ERP PROCESSES

Software Selection Process

AFT chose the SLAs after a Proof of Concept process (POC), which they first build the expectations by inviting various business intelligence software vendors to conduct on site workshops, the purpose of the invitation was is to determine if the software scope meets with the organizational goal and mission. After building the expectations, they started to filter out and weigh the presented software to locate the best suited one, this process was held by controlling the expectations; here comes the cancellation and incorporation of the presented software's. The proof of concept process will minimize the ambiguity of the software requirements and provide an understanding of the new software resources, potentials, and limitations. Also, it's a tool that helps in defining the design decisions at an early stage in the process, and it reduce the possibility of project failure as it minimize the uncertainty of adapting new software. However, the proof of concept does not provide the final deliverable as it only view and demonstrate the methods and functionality of the software, but not the requirements of the implementation process as it require specialised resources. AFT faced some issues that are mainly related to overlapping or missing features in the various options provided and considered.

Software Implementation Process

Abu-Dhabi Finance Trust went through four different phases to implement the SLAs software, the implementation phases were built to provide a faultless transformation; from a paper-based procedure to an electronic procedure, that ensure all the client information and operation has been inserted into the system; to supply and deliver superior high level of performance, support, and managing relations. The four phases are discussed below (also see Figure 1):

1. **Detecting the Software:** This phase is done after the proof-of concept process; that determines the organization needs and match to the right software. At this phase, a demonstration has been done to ensure that the SLAs applications and services are assessing in delivering the organization goals. It defines the software structure and explores the policy of operating the software, it also

Figure 1. Four implementation phases

provides more clear understanding about the software weaknesses and strengths, and it helps in collaborating the conversion process and software configuration.

2. **Training:** At this phase, a training session is done for the staff in form of a demonstration or by doing the daily activities, to learn how to enter data and interpret it. The training session is done before the Go-live phase to make sure that the staffs has been trained to optimize the system and get the best out of it, and ensure that they are being able to perform their tasks and activities effectively. AFT has used a tailored training session, which has been developed to deliver the requirements of the organization and the tasks that should be performed by their staff. After finishing the training, they made sure that each member of the organization has been trained properly to Go-live and use it with the clients, this way they will minimize faults and ambiguity while using the new software.

3. **Go-Live and Testing:** After performing the training session and system configuration and analysis for readiness, that gave the organization the green light to Go-live and initiate and the system. Here the system has been initiated and used actively by the staff, and then comes the testing phase to detect if the system has delivered the requested goals or not. Testing is very important to

make sure that the company has invested their money in a worthy valuable project, rather than keeping moving on it and at last turns to be a catastrophe.

4. **Feedback and Evaluation:** Following the testing a feedback and evaluating must be performed to demonstrate the effectiveness of the software on the organization and how it made the organization deliverables be performed in a better effective way. SLAs have taken the organization into a journey of continuous improvements and leveraging the organization into a new enhanced edge. The SLAs is not just software, it is a business strategy that has been adopted after an advanced planning and research, to promote effectiveness and efficiency through better integration channels and effective report development process.

Report Development Process

Figure 2 illustrates the summarization of report development process and how it moves through the organization to start the production phase. It views how the client information and operations are being inserted into the SLAs software and how it runs through several levels to be operated and optimized to reach high productivity level, and provide high level of performance in a manageable and convenient process.

The Cycle shows how the report being transferred in the management level and start producing, developing reports is which requires several phases in which some

Figure 2. Development process

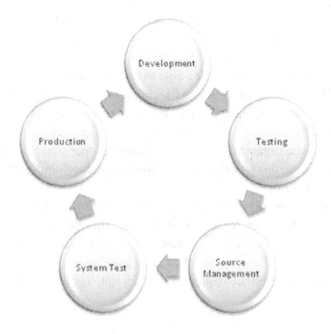

reports needs to be passed through departments to be build. Then reports must enter into a testing phase to make sure that data that have been entered are correct and reduce errors and redundancy. The third phase is to manage the resources that have been reported and interpret them to test them if they work with both client and business requirements, and then start the production phase.

BENEFITS AND CONCERNS

Software Benefits

Abu-Dhabi Finance Trust reveals the benefits that they have attained from the software. The software provided a full automation of the business critical; Key Performance Indicators (KPIs), by allowing the management to view how each department is growing and performing, as it automated the process of seeing how the organization is performing toward the goals and strategic objective, it also helped in making decisions in quicker time with less effort as there is an available accurate measures that can be looked into at anytime.

In addition to the above, it didn't automated the KPIs only but also the MI (Management Information) reports, by using the business information to build a measurement plans and forecasts. Also, it had a significant reduction on man-hours spent on developing manual reports, as the SLAs is all about having a formalized reports that can be also be changed easily into graphs if applicable. The SLAs has a connectivity with Smartphone's, so the time of sharing reports has minimized through auto notifications and auto alerts features that the SLAs send to the Smart-phone once the reports has been sent and the user can check it directly, this feature helped in having a fast rich interaction process. Moreover, the SLAs is the single source of truth for all data reported in the organization.

The software has changed the process of customer care, as there is enhanced auditing and monitoring by understanding how the users interact with the software and provide the feedback for the customers. The SLAs software is built on a uni-fied infrastructure, so it has reduced costs and improved productivity by having a system that delivers several services. Users' knowledge and expertise has increased; it is a task-oriented software and encourage users on self-learning by engaging themselves and interacting actively with the system features, reports, and innova-tive rich graphics. The SLAs software that provides a well integration between all organization departments and minimizes redundancy, also it avails a measurement and feasibility to reach organization goals; it is a reliable system that provides scal-ability and optimizes performance.

Technology Concerns

Abu-Dhabi Finance Trust had one technology concern; it was around running the software on a Microsoft Windows Server Platform, since the product is more stable on Linux Platform, they implement it on Microsoft windows Server due to the lack of the in-house expertise in Linux Administration, they have decided to deploy the software on a Windows Server. This is a challenging step to take as it may cause lots of problems and failures due to the failure to the system to function properly on the Windows Server, as it designed to be on a Linux Platform. The Platform is the framework for operating any system; it supports and limits its functionality. This may lead to having a poor investment, if the platform turns to be a failure; however, Abu-Dhabi finance have studied the challenges that can be raised by implementing the system, and till now no major problems has accord.

Management and Organization Concerns

The management was concerned about the steep learning curve involved, especially for the non-technical users, as they require lots of training and auditing process. They were aware if the no proper training is available, it will cause the system to fail, and the new investment will just collapse at once. In addition, they were concerned about the accuracy and data presented in the system database; even they have studied their choice precisely the concern was still there until they started to use it and optimize it.

TECHNOLOGY COMPONENTS

The SLAs implementation process required five different technology components to implement and initiate it.

1. **Microsoft Windows Server 2003:**
    Windows Server 2003 is a reliable and flexible server for the SLAs software, its features, visualization tools, resources, and management tools integrates with the SLAs to accelerate and enhance its functionality. The server saves time as its efficient and dynamic, and it delivers high quality features, valuable functions, and a powerful operating system. It provides with a solid infrastructure for the SLAs software system, it enables the system to operate on highly dependable, consistent, and scalable platform. Windows server has provided the organization with better solutions, as management concerns in

deploying a platform that is compatible with both management goals and the changing environment is solved.

In addition, the server has benefited the organization by reducing power consumption, as it is one server the initiates and supports organization computers. As well as, reducing power consumption it has improved management tasks as well, by enhancing command-line tasks and improving remote management by having better visualization and graphical integration process. Windows server has the ability to extend features and utility by integrating it with other software. In short, windows server 2003 increases productivity, efficiency, and provides rich experiences for users and management.

2. **Oracle Business Intelligence Enterprise Edition Answers:**
    As the business environment is always changing, an OBIEE Answers is a solution for all the operational and business intelligence tactics it has been developed by Siebel but provided as a part of OBIEE. This application allows users to find answers and build their own customized queries and reports without having any IT technical assistance. It is also the tool that business developers use it to build the reports and dashboards; it is a warehouse of retrieving information that answers business questions.

3. **Business Intelligence Publisher:**
    This is formerly called XML Publisher; it provides a powerful design and building structure for delivering information securely and in the correct format. Business Intelligence Publisher has new features that works perfectly with the SLAs software to leverage dashboards, data, calculations, and allows requesting for business intelligent services.

    In addition, it allows collecting data from multiple records and reports to display it in one single document, and it allows having fast communication and performing business tasks quicker by connecting to smart phones. It helps having a faster report interaction; it highly optimizes reports with using less memory space as it uses a compatible version of reports. So, BI Publisher results in better integration process and allows its reports to be designed in Microsoft word; as well as, Adobe Acrobat, this means it is easy, efficient, and most of all an intelligent technology component.

4. **Oracle Database 10g:**
    Oracle Database is a relational database that it's main goal to calculate resources and present the relation between them, its system architecture for the SLAs software. Oracle Database Features:
    a. Creating tables and views, to display sequences and consistent data modeling.
    b. Specifies attributes, relationships, and entities.
    c. Building Web-based applications.

    d.   Flashback features, to undo the mistakes that users perform.

    e.   Creates database backups to prevent massive failures.

    f.   Information management and managing its lifecycle.

    g.   Managing the unstructured data and it acts as a warehouse for reports and databases.

It enables to bring a change into the organization environment with a very low risk, as it has many features that benefit the organization in having great performance scalability, secured and centralized communication, and it helps to move from single to clustered open communications.

5.   **MS SQL Server 2005:**

SQL server developer is exclusively supported with graphical tool developing databases; it has many features that enhance business activities.

    a.   **Data Mining:** This is an option in the SQL server, it helps users to extract their required data, describe, save, and share it. In addition, it provide data in visualize and transforming data to graphics. It automates knowledge by allowing users to build and discover information and databases (Anonymous, 2011).

    b.   **Data Modeler:** SQL server allows users to design and build data models; it provides instructions for designing and building data models.

    c.   **DBMS Scheduler:** This feature provides the users to form a schedules, chains, jobs allocation, jobs authenticated, and databases targeted.

    d.   **DBA Functionality:** It enables users to review database arrangement and construction, and edit it to initialize their activity. It mange resource plans and prioritize them, and it identifies inspection settings and maintains users roles and profiles secured.

    e.   **Exporting and Importing Data:** It acts as an interface to have a dynamic secured data exchange.

    f.   **Menus:** It allows recompiling plans by connections, and generating API tables; which are tables builds based on user ID, it helps in having a dynamic and easy configuration process.

    g.   **Migrations:** All migrated tasks are managed by the project navigator; it delivers the tasks to right persons in the company as the users profiles are being captured, so it redistribute and migrate tasks by targeting the appropriate person for the task.

    h.   **PDF:** It generates PDF documents for the databases, to have a faster sharing process and maintain secured documents transfer as it is authorized to have different levels of document encryptions and a password-PDF document.

    i.   **Query Builder:** SQL worksheet is tightly integrated with the query builder; it allows automatic determination of connected and joint data, helps in grouping and sorting procedures of databases.

    j.   **Schema Browser:** This feature allows having easier navigation process between databases and objects, and it supports a filtering and narrowing information to display the précised requested information.

    k.   **Times Ten:** It supports the memory storage of the databases; it compresses databases to avail more storing space.

Therefore, the SQL Server helps in having accelerated database development, faster communication and productivity, and easier database designing process.

MAIN CHALLENGES

Current Challenges

Abu-Dhabi Finance Trust faced some problems regarding the SLAs software; the software is a combination of XML Publisher by Oracle Corporation and Seibel Analytics, it's marketed by Oracle as a single product; however, there are some integration and user management issues due to the coupling of these two corporations.

Future Challenges

Managing the various backend database connections, and report repository is becoming a bit tedious as the number of reports and the available data gradually increase. Therefore, upgrading to the newer version is a future concern, since it will involve a minor learning curve for the new features and system changes.

RECOMMENDATIONS

The software should be deployed and installed only after a thorough analysis of business requirement and after consulting the deployment guides provided in order to avoid issues arising post deployment. Also, finding the right software for the organization guarantee a successful investment, as it will help in achieving organizational goals.

REFERENCES

Adam, F., & O'Doherty, P. (2003). ERP projects: Good or bad for SMEs? In Shanks, G., Seddon, P. B., & Willcocks, L. P. (Eds.), *Second-Wave Enterprise Resource Planning Systems: Implementing for Effectiveness* (pp. 275–298). Cambridge, UK: Cambridge University Press. doi:10.1017/CBO9780511815072.012

Adler, P. S., & Kwon, S.-W. (2002). Social capital: Prospects for a new concept. *Academy of Management Review, 27*(1), 17–40.

Ahituv, N., Neumann, S., & Zviran, M. (2002). A system development methodology for ERP systems. *Journal of Computer Information Systems, 42*(3), 56–67.

Ahuja, G., & Lampert, C. M. (2001). Entrepreneurship in the large corporation: A longitudinal study of how entrepreneurial firms create breakthrough inventions. *Strategic Management Journal, 22*(6-7), 521–543. doi:10.1002/smj.176

Bancroft, N., Seip, H., & Sprengel, A. (1998). *Implementing SAP R/3* (2nd ed.). New York, NY: Manning Publications.

Barki, H., & Pinsonneault, A. (2005). A model of organizational integration, implementation effort, and performance. *Organization Science, 16*(2), 165–179. doi:10.1287/orsc.1050.0118

Baskerville, R., Pawlowski, S., & McLean, E. (2000). Enterprise resource planning and organizational knowledge: Patterns of convergence and divergence. In *Proceedings of the 21st International Conference on Information Systems*, (pp. 396-406). Brisbane, Australia: IEEE.

Boudreau, M.-C., & Robey, D. (2005). Enacting integrated information technology: A human agency perspective. *Organization Science, 16*(1), 3–18. doi:10.1287/orsc.1040.0103

Braa, K., & Rolland, K. H. (2000). Horizontal information systems: Emergent trends and perspectives. In Baskerville, R., Stage, J., & DeGross, J. I. (Eds.), *Organizational and Social Perspectives on Information Technology* (pp. 83–101). Boston, MA: Kluwer Academic Publishers.

Brown, C., & Vessey, I. (1999). ERP implementation approaches: Toward a contingency framework. In *Proceedings of the International Conference on Information Systems*, (pp. 411–416). IEEE.

Davenport, T. (2000). *Realizing the promise of enterprise systems*. Boston, MA: Harvard Business School Press.

Ross, J. (1999). Dow cornings corporation: Business processes and information technology. *Journal of Information Technology*, *14*(3), 253–266. doi:10.1080/026839699344557

Stebel, P. (1992). *Breakpoints: How managers exploit radical change*. Boston, MA: Harvard Business School Press.

Stoddard, D., & Jarvenpaa, S. (1995). Businesss process reengineering: Tactics for managing radical change. *Journal of Management Information Systems*, *12*(1), 81–108.

KEY TERMS AND DEFINITIONS

Ad-Hoc Reporting: Tools to allow end users to easily build their own reports and modify existing ones with little technical skills.

Business Intelligence (BI): A set of applications and technologies for gathering, storing, analyzing data to make better business decisions.

CRM: Customer Relationship Management.

Dashboards: A set of tools to allow business users to define, monitor and analyze business performance via Key Performance Indicators (KPIs).

DBA: Database Administrator.

ERP: Enterprise Resource Planning.

Key Performance Indicators (KPI): Quantifiable measurements to help an organization define and measure progress toward organizational goals.

MENA: Middle East and North Africa.

MI: Management Information.

OBIEE: Business Intelligence Enterprise Edition.

Proof of Concept (POC): The demonstration that a product is technically and financially viable.

SLA: Service Level Agreement.

SQL: Structure Query Language.

324

Compilation of References

Abdinnour-Helm, S., Lengnick-Hall, M., & Lengnick-Hall, C. (2003). Pre-implementation attitudes and organizational readiness for implementing an enterprise resource planning system. *European Journal of Operational Research*, *146*(2), 258. doi:10.1016/S0377-2217(02)00548-9

Abugabah, A., & Sanzogni, L. (2010). Enterprise resource planning (ERP) system in higher education: A literature review and implications. *International Journal of Human and Social Sciences*, *5*(6), 49–53.

Adam, F., & O'Doherty, P. (2003). ERP projects: Good or bad for SMEs? In Shanks, G., Seddon, P. B., & Willcocks, L. P. (Eds.), *Second-Wave Enterprise Resource Planning Systems: Implementing for Effectiveness* (pp. 275–298). Cambridge, UK: Cambridge University Press. doi:10.1017/CBO9780511815072.012

ADEC. (2010). *Enterprise student information system (eSIS) systems documents*. Retrieved from http://www.adec.ac.ae/English/Pages/NewsDisplay.aspx

ADEC. (2010). *Completes the ERP system in a record time*. Retrieved February 10, 2012 from http://www.ameinfo.com/222431.html

ADEC. (2010). *Implements enterprise resource management in Abu Dhabi institutions*. Retrieved February 11, 2012 from http://www.ameinfo.com/224841.html

Adler, P. (1990). Shared learning. *Management Science*, *36*(8), 938–957. doi:10.1287/mnsc.36.8.938

Adler, P. S., & Kwon, S.-W. (2002). Social capital: Prospects for a new concept. *Academy of Management Review*, *27*(1), 17–40.

Ahituv, N., Neumann, S., & Zviran, M. (2002). A system development methodology for ERP systems. *Journal of Computer Information Systems*, *42*(3), 56–67.

Ahuja, G., & Lampert, C. M. (2001). Entrepreneurship in the large corporation: A longitudinal study of how entrepreneurial firms create breakthrough inventions. *Strategic Management Journal*, *22*(6-7), 521–543. doi:10.1002/smj.176

Akkermans, H., Bogerd, B., Yucesan, E., & van Wassenhove, L. (2003). The impact of ERP on supply chain management: Exploratory findings from a European Delphi study. *European Journal of Operational Research*, *146*(2), 284. doi:10.1016/S0377-2217(02)00550-7

Compilation of References

Akkermans, H., & van Helden, K. (2002). Vicious and virtuous cycles in ERP implementation: A case study of interrelations between critical success factors. *European Journal of Information Systems*, *11*(1), 35. doi:10.1057/palgrave/ejis/3000418

Al Meshari, M. (2003). *Enterprise resource planning (ERP) systems:* A research agenda. *Emerald Industrial Management & Data Systems*, *103*(1), 22–27. doi:10.1108/02635570310456869

Aladwani, A. (2001). Change management strategies for successful ERP implementation. *Business Process Management Journal*, *7*(3), 266–275. doi:10.1108/14637150110392764

Al-Fakhri, M., Cropf, R., Higgs, G., & Kelly, P. (2008). e-Government in Saudi Arabia: Between promise and reality. *International Journal of Electronic Government Research*, *4*(2), 5–82. doi:10.4018/jegr.2008040105

Al-Karaghouli, W., AlShawi, S., & Fitzgerald, G. (2005). Promoting requirements identification quality: Enhancing the human interaction dimension. *Journal of Enterprise Information Management*, *18*(2), 256–267. doi:10.1108/17410390510579945

Allen, D., & Kern, T. (2001). Enterprise resource planning implementation: Stories of power, politics, and resistance. In *Proceedings of the IFIP TC8/WG8.2 Working Conference on Realigning Research and Practice in Information Systems Development: The Social and Organizational Perspective*. Boise, ID: IFIP.

Al-Mashari, M. (2003). Enterprise resource planning (ERP) systems: A research agenda. *Industrial Management & Data Systems*, *103*(1/2), 22. doi:10.1108/02635570310456869

Al-Mashari, M., & Al-Mudimigh, A. (2003). ERP implementation: Lessons from a case study. *Information Technology & People*, *16*(1), 21. doi:10.1108/09593840310463005

Al-Mashari, M., Al-Mudimigh, A., & Zairi, M. (2003). Enterprise resource planning: A taxonomy of critical factors. *European Journal of Operational Research*, *146*(2), 352. doi:10.1016/S0377-2217(02)00554-4

Al-Mudimigh, A., Zairi, M., & Al-Mashari, M. (2001). ERP software implementation: An integrative framework. *European Journal of Information Systems*, *10*(4), 216. doi:10.1057/palgrave.ejis.3000406

Amin, N., Hinton, M., Hall, P., Newton, M., & Kayae, R. (1999). A study of strategic and decision-making issues in adoption of ERP systems resulting from a merger in the financial services sector. In *Proceedings of the 18 International Workshop on Enterprise Management Resource and Planning Systems EMRPS*, (pp. 173-181). Venice, Italy: EMRPS.

Armenakis, A., & Harris, S. (2002). Crafting a change message to create transformational readiness. *Journal of Organizational Change Management*, *15*(2), 169–183. doi:10.1108/09534810210423080

Armenakis, A., & Harris, S. (2009). Reflections: Our journey in organizational change research and practice. *Journal of Change Management*, *9*(2), 127–142. doi:10.1080/14697010902879079

Arrow, K. (1962). The implications of learning by doing. *The Review of Economic Studies*, *29*, 166–170. doi:10.2307/2295952

Arunthari, S. (2005). *Information technology adoption by companies in Thailand: A study of enterprise resources planning system usage*. (PhD Thesis). University of Wollongong. Wollongong, Australia.

Ashbaugh, S., & Rowen, M. (2002). Technology for human resources management: Seven questions and answers. *Public Personnel Management, 31*, 7–20.

Ash, C., & Burn, J. (2003). A strategic framework for the management of ERP enabled e-business change. *European Journal of Operational Research, 146*(2), 374. doi:10.1016/S0377-2217(02)00556-8

AShurst, C., & Hodges, J. (2010). Exploring business transformation: The challenges of developing a benefits realization capability. *Journal of Change Management, 10*(2), 217–237. doi:10.1080/14697011003795685

Balogun, J., & Hailey, V. (2008). *Exploring strategic change* (3rd ed). London, UK: Harlow.

Bancroft, N., Seip, H., & Sprengel, A. (1998). *Implementing SAP R/3* (2nd ed.). New York, NY: Manning Publications.

Barki, H., & Pinsonneault, A. (2005). A model of organizational integration, implementation effort, and performance. *Organization Science, 16*(2), 165–179. doi:10.1287/orsc.1050.0118

Baskerville, R., Pawlowski, S., & McLean, E. (2000). Enterprise resource planning and organizational knowledge: Patterns of convergence and divergence. In *Proceedings of the 21st International Conference on Information Systems*, (pp. 396-406). Brisbane, Australia: IEEE.

Beal, B. (2003, October 15). *The priority that persists*. Retrieved February 14, 2012, from http://searchcio.techtarget.com/originalContent/0,289142,sid19_gci932246,00.html

Bechtel, R., & Squires, J. (2001). Tools and techniques to facilitate change. *Industrial and Commercial Training, 33*(7), 249–254. doi:10.1108/EUM0000000006001

Beer, M., Eisenstat, R., & Spector, B. (1990). Why change programs don't produce change. *Harvard Business Review, 68*(6), 158–166.

Beer, M., & Nohria, N. (2000). Cracking the code of change. *Harvard Business Review, 78*(3), 131–142.

Ben Zion, T. M., & Yaffa, G. (1995). Information technology in educational management: Maximizing the potential of information technology for management. In C. L. Fulmer (Ed.), *Strategies for Interfacing the Technical Core of Education*. London, UK: Chapman & Hall

Beretta, S. (2002). Unleashing the integration potential of ERP systems. *Business Process Management Journal, 8*(3), 254. doi:10.1108/14637150210428961

Bernroider, E., & Koch, S. (2001). ERP selection process in midsized and large organizations. *Business Process Management Journal, 7*(3), 251. doi:10.1108/14637150110392746

Bingi, P., Sharma, M., & Godla, J. (1999). Critical issues affecting an ERP implementation. *Information Systems Management, 16*(3), 7–8. doi:10.1201/1078/43197.16.3.19990601/31310.2

Boonstra, A. (2006). Interpreting an ERP – Implementation project form a stakeholder perspective. *International Journal of Project Management, 24*, 38–52. doi:10.1016/j.ijproman.2005.06.003

Compilation of References

Boudreau, M.-C., & Robey, D. (2005). Enacting integrated information technology: A human agency perspective. *Organization Science*, *16*(1), 3–18. doi:10.1287/orsc.1040.0103

Bovey, H., & Hede, A. (2001). Resistance to organisational change: The role of the defence mechanism. *Journal of Managerial Psychology*, *16*(7), 534–548. doi:10.1108/EUM0000000006166

Braa, K., & Rolland, K. H. (2000). Horizontal information systems: Emergent trends and perspectives. In Baskerville, R., Stage, J., & DeGross, J. I. (Eds.), *Organizational and Social Perspectives on Information Technology* (pp. 83–101). Boston, MA: Kluwer Academic Publishers.

Bradford, M., & Florin, J. (2003). Examining the role of innovation diffusion factors on the implementation success of enterprise resource planning systems. *International Journal of Accounting Information Systems*, *4*(3), 205–225. doi:10.1016/S1467-0895(03)00026-5

Brady, T., & Maylor, H. (2010). The improvement paradox in project contexts: A clue to the way forward? *International Journal of Project Management*, *28*, 787–795. doi:10.1016/j.ijproman.2010.08.001

Brehm, L., Heinzl, A., & Markus, M. L. (2001). Tailoring ERP systems: A spectrum of choices and their implications. In *Proceedings of the 34th Annual Hawaii International Conference on Systems Sciences*. Hawaii, HI: IEEE.

Brown, C., & Vessey, I. (1999). ERP implementation approaches: Toward a contingency framework. In *Proceedings of the International Conference on Information Systems*, (pp. 411–416). IEEE.

Brown, J. S., & Duguid, P. (1991). Organizational learning and communities-of-practice: Toward a unified view of working, learning, and innovation. *Organization Science*, *2*(1), 102–111. doi:10.1287/orsc.2.1.40

Bryman, A., & Bell, E. (2011). *Business research methods* (3rd ed.). Oxford, UK: Oxford University Press.

Burke, W., Church, A., & Waclawski, J. (1993). What do OD practitioners know about managing change? *Leadership and Organization Development Journal*, *14*(6), 3–11. doi:10.1108/01437739310047038

Burnes, B. (1996). No such thing as…. a "one best way" to manage organizational change. *Management Decision*, *34*(10), 11–18. doi:10.1108/00251749610150649

Burnes, B. (2004). Emergent change and planned change – Competitors or allies? The case of XYZ construction. *International Journal of Operations & Production Management*, *24*(9), 886–890. doi:10.1108/01443570410552108

Burnes, B., & Jackson, P. (2011). Success and failure in organizational change: An exploration of the role of values. *Journal of Change Management*, *11*(2), 133–162. doi:10.1080/14697017.2010.524655

Calisir, F. (2004). The relation of interface usability characteristics, perceived usefulness and perceived ease of use to end -user satisfaction with enterprise resource planning systems. *Computers in Human Behavior*, *20*, 505–515. doi:10.1016/j.chb.2003.10.004

Chen, I. (2001). Planning for ERP systems: Analysis and future trend. *Business Process Management Journal*, *7*(5), 374. doi:10.1108/14637150110406768

Chen, L. J. (2001). Planning for ERP systems: Analysis and future trends. *Business Process Management Journal, 7*(5), 67–77. doi:10.1108/14637150110406768

Chrusciel, D., & Field, D. (2005). Success factors in dealing with significant change in an organization. *Business Process Management Journal, 12*(4), 503–516. doi:10.1108/14637150610678096

Chung, S., & Snyder, C. (2000). ERP adoption: A technological evolution approach. *International Journal of Agile Management Systems, 2*(1). doi:10.1108/14654650010312570

Clarke, A., & Garside, J. (1997). The development of a best practice model for change management. *European Management Journal, 15*(5), 537–545. doi:10.1016/S0263-2373(97)00033-9

Clemmons, S., & Simon, S. (2001). Control and coordination in global ERP configuration. *Business Process Management Journal, 7*(3), 205. doi:10.1108/14637150110392665

Cliffe, S. (1999). ERP implementation. *Harvard Business Review, 77*(1), 16.

Cohen, W. M., Nelson, R. R., & Walsh, J. (2000). *Protecting their intellectual assets: Appropriability conditions and why U.S. manufacturing firms patent (or not)*. Working paper No. 7552. Washington, DC: National Bureau of Economic Research.

Cohen, W. M., & Levinthal, D. A. (1990). Absorptive capacity: A new perspective on learning and innovation. *Administrative Science Quarterly, 35*, 128–152. doi:10.2307/2393553

Conner, K. R., & Prahalad, C. K. (1996). A resource-based theory of the firm: Knowledge versus opportunism. *Organization Science, 7*(5), 477–501. doi:10.1287/orsc.7.5.477

Cook, Dudley, & Peterson. (1998). *SAP implementation: Strategy and results*. New York, NY: The Conference Board.

Coram, R., & Burnes, B. (2001). Managing organisational change in the public sector: Lessons from the privatisation of the property services agency. *International Journal of Public Sector Management, 14*(2), 94–110. doi:10.1108/09513550110387381

Craine, K. (2007). Managing the cycle of change. *Information Management Journal, 41*(5), 44–48.

Crosby, P. (1994). *Completeness: Quality for the 21st century*. New York, NY: Plume Books.

Daft, R., & Marcic, D. (2007). *Management in the new workplace*. New York, NY: Thomson-South-Western.

Damanpour, F. (1996). Organizational complexity and innovation: Developing and testing multiple contingency models. *Management Science, 42*(5), 693–716. doi:10.1287/mnsc.42.5.693

Davenport, T. (1998). Putting the enterprise into the enterprise system. *Harvard Business Review, 76*(4), 121–131.

Davenport, T. (2000). *Realizing the promise of enterprise systems*. Boston, MA: Harvard Business School Press.

Davenport, T. H. (1998). Putting the enterprise into the enterprise systems. *Harvard Business Review, 76*(4), 121–131.

Davenport, T. H. (2000). *Mission critical: Realizing the promise of enterprise systems*. Boston, MA: Harvard Business School Press.

Davison, R. (2002). Cultural complications of ERP. *Communications of the ACM, 45*(7), 109. doi:10.1145/514236.514267

Compilation of References

Dawson, P. (2003). *Understanding organizational change: The contemporary experience of people at work*. London, UK: Sage Publications.

De Wit, B., & Meyer, R. (2004). *Strategy: Process, content and context*. New York, NY: Thomson Learning.

Dunphy, D. (1996). Organizational change in the corporate settings. *Human Relations, 49*(5), 541–552. doi:10.1177/001872679604900501

Dunphy, D., & Stace, D. (1993). The strategic management of strategic change. *Human Relations, 46*(8), 905–922. doi:10.1177/001872679304600801

Earl, M. (1994). Viewpoint: New and old business process redesign. *The Journal of Strategic Information Systems, 3*(1), 5–22. doi:10.1016/0963-8687(94)90003-5

Escalle, C. X., Cotteleer, M. J., & Austin, R. D. (1999). *Enterprise resource planning (ERP). Technology Note*. Boston, MA: Harvard Business School Publishing.

Esteves, J., & Pastor, J. (2003). Enterprise resource planning systems research: An annotated bibliography. *Communications of the Association for Information Systems*. Retrieved from http://profesores.ie.edu/jmesteves/cais2001.pdf

Everdingen, Y., Hillengersberg, J., & Waarts, E. (2000). ERP adoption by european midsize companies. *Communications of the ACM, 43*(4), 27–31. doi:10.1145/332051.332064

Finney, S., & Corbett, M. (2007). ERP implementation: A complication and analysis of critical success factors. *Business Process Management Journal, 13*(3), 329–347. doi:10.1108/14637150710752272

Freeman, C., & Perez, C. (1988). Structural crisis of adjustment: Business cycles and investment behavior. In Dosi, G. (Eds.), *Technical Change and Economic Behavior*. London, UK: Pinter.

Gale, S. (2002). For ERP success, create a culture change. *Workforce, 81*(9), 88–92.

Gomez-Mejia, L., Balkin, D., & Cardy, R. (2005). *Management: People, performance change* (2nd ed.). New York, NY: McGraw-Hill Companies, Inc.

Grabski, S. V., & Leech, S. A. (2002). Complementary controls and ERP implementation success. *Information & Management, 40*(1), 25–40.

Graetz, F. (2000). Strategic change leadership. *Management Decision, 38*(8), 550–564. doi:10.1108/00251740010378282

Graetz, F., & Smith, A. C. T. (2010). Managing organizational change: Philosophies of change approach. *Journal of Change Management, 10*(2), 135–154. doi:10.1080/14697011003795602

Gray, C. F., & Larson, E. W. (2008). *Project management: The managerial process* (4th ed.). Burr Ridge, IL: Irwin/McGraw-Hill.

Guha, S., Grover, V., Kettinger, W., & Teng, J. (1997). Business process change and organizational performance: Exploring an antecedent model. *Journal of Management Information Systems, 14*(1), 119–154.

Gupta, A. (2000). Enterprise resource planning: The emerging organizational value systems. *Industrial Management & Data Systems, 100*(3), 114. doi:10.1108/02635570010286131

Hay-Group. (2003). *High competencies to identify high performers: An overview of basics*. Working Paper. Retrieved Nov 2008 from http://www.haygroup.com/Downloads/uk/misc/Competencies_and_high_performance.pdf

HEAC. (2008). *Website*. Retrieved from http://www.heac.gov.om/heac_en/index.asp

Heeks, R. (2004). *eGovernment as a carrier of context*. IGovernment Working Paper No.15. Manchester, UK: University of Manchester. Retrieved from http://www.heac.gov.om/heac_en/index.asp

Hitt, L., Wu, D., & Zhou, X. (2002). Investment in enterprise resource planning: business impact and productivity measures. *Journal of Management Information Systems, 19*(1), 71.

Hitt, M., Black, S., & Porter, L. (2009). *Management* (2nd ed.). Upper Saddle River, NJ: Prentice Hall.

Holland, C., & Light, B. (1997). Critical success factors model for ERP implementation. *IEEE Software*. Retrieved from http://www.imamu.edu.sa/Scientific_selections/abstracts/Documents/A%20Critical%20Success%20Factors%20Model%20For%20ERP%20Implementation.pdf

Hong, K., & Kim, Y. (2002). The critical success factors for ERP implementation: An organizational fit perspective. *Information & Management, 40*(1), 25. doi:10.1016/S0378-7206(01)00134-3

Huang, Z., & Palvia, P. (2001). ERP implementation issues in advanced and developing countries. *Business Process Management Journal, 7*(3), 276. doi:10.1108/14637150110392773

Hultman, K. (1995). Scaling the wall of resistance. *Training & Development, 49*(10), 15–18.

IBM. (2012). *Wikipedia*. Retrieved from http://en.wikipedia.org/wiki/Ibm

Ip, W., & Chau, K., & Chan. (2002). Implementing ERP through continuous improvement. *International Journal of Manufacturing, 4*(6), 465.

Irani, Z., Al-Sebie, M., & Elliman, T. (2006). *Transaction stage of e-government systems: Identification of its location and importance*. Paper presented at the Hawaii International Conference on System Sciences (HICSS-39). Hawaii, HI.

ITA. (2008). *Oman digital society report*. Retrieved from http://www.ita.gov.om

Jacobs, F., & Bendoly, E. (2003). Enterprise resource planning: Developments and directions for operations management research. *European Journal of Operational Research, 146*(2), 233. doi:10.1016/S0377-2217(02)00546-5

Jaros, S. (2010). Commitment to organizational change: A critical review. *Journal of Change Management, 10*(1), 79–108. doi:10.1080/14697010903549457

Jing, R., & Qui, X. (2007). A study on critical success factors in ERP systems implementation. In *Proceedings of the IEEE International Conference on Service Systems and Service Management*. IEEE Press.

Johnson, D., & Johnson, R. (1989). *Cooperation and competition: Theory and research*. Edina, MN: Interaction.

Compilation of References

Johnson, G., Scholes, K., & Whittington, R. (2006). *Exploring corporate strategy: Text and cases* (7th ed.). Upper Saddle River, NJ: Prentice Hall.

Joshi, K. (2005). Understanding user resistance and acceptance during the implementation of an order management system: A case study using the equity implementation model. *Journal of Information Technology Case and Application Research, 7*(1), 6–20.

Keil, M., & Robey, D. (1999). Turning around troubled software projects: An exploratory study of the deescalation of commitment to failing courses of action. *Journal of Management Information Systems, 15*(4), 63–87.

Kerbache, L. (2002). Enterprise resource planning (ERP): The dynamics of operations management. *Interfaces, 32*(1), 104.

Kettinger, W., & Grover, V. (1995). Toward a theory of business process change management. *Journal of Management Information Systems, 12*(1), 1–30.

Kettinger, W., Guha, H., & Teng, J. (1995). The process engineering lifecycle methodology: A case study. In Grover, V., & Kettinger, W. (Eds.), *Business Process Change: Reengineering Concepts, Methods and Technologies*. Hershey, PA: Idea Publishing.

Kettunen, H. (2007). *Change management in implementation of strategic initiatives. Seminar in Business Strategy and International Business, TU-91.167*. Helsinki, Finland: Helsinki University of Technology.

Ke, W., & Wei, K. (2004). Successful egovernment in Singapore: How did Singapore manage to get most of its public services deliverable online? *Communications of the ACM, 47*(6), 95–99. doi:10.1145/990680.990687

Kilman, R., Saxton, M., & Serpa, R. (1986). Issues in understanding and changing culture. *California Management Review, 28*(2), 87–94.

King, P., Kvavik, R. B., & Voloudakis, J. (2002). *Enterprise resource planning systems in higher education (ERB0222)*. Boulder, CO: EDUCAUSE Center for Applied Research (ECAR).

Kirkpatrick, D. L. (1997). Evaluation of training. In Craig, R. L. (Ed.), *Training and Development Handbook: A Guide to Human Resource Development*. New York, NY: McGraw Hill.

Koch, C., & Buhl, H. (2001). ERP-supported teamworking in Danish manufacturing? *New Technology, Work and Employment, 16*(3), 164. doi:10.1111/1468-005X.00086

Kotter, J. (2006). Leading change: Why transformation efforts fail. *Harvard Business Review*. Retrieved from http://cerc.stanford.edu/leading_change.PDF

Kotter, J. (1995). Leading change: Why transformation efforts fail. *Harvard Business Review, 73*(2), 59–67.

Kotter, J. (1996). *Leading change*. Boston, MA: Harvard Business School Press.

Kotter, J., & Schlesinger, L. (1979). Choosing strategies for change. *Harvard Business Review, 57*(2), 106–114.

Kremers, M., & van Dissel, H. (2000). ERP system migrations. *Communications of the ACM, 43*(4), 52–56. doi:10.1145/332051.332072

Kumar, K., & Hillergersberg, J. (2000). ERP experiences and evolution. *Communications of the ACM, 43*(4), 23–26.

Kvavik, R. B., Katz, R. N., Beecher, K., Caruso, J., King, P., Voludakis, J., & Williams, L. A. (2002). *The promise and performance of enterprise systems for higher education (ERS0204)*. Boulder, CO: EDUCAUSE Center for Applied Research (ECAR).

Kvavik, R., Katz, R., Beecher, K., Caruso, J., & King, P. (2002). The promise and performance of enterprise systems for higher education. *EDUCAUSE*, *4*, 5–123.

Lahti, C. (2005). *Change management in pay systems implementation: Case study from chemical industry companies on job evaluation and the evaluation of an employee's competence and performance based pay systems change processes*. Helsinki, Finland: Helsinki University of Technology.

Lauden, K., & Lauden, J. P. (2009). *Management information systems: Managing the digital firm* (11th ed.). Upper Saddle River, NJ: Prentice Hall.

Laukkanen, S., Sarpola, S., & Hallikainen, P. (2007). Enterprise size matters: Objectives and constraints of ERP adoption. *Journal of Enterprise Information Management*, *20*(3), 319–334. doi:10.1108/17410390710740763

Lee, A. (2000). Researchable directions for ERP and other new information technologies. *Management Information Systems Quarterly*, *24*(1), 3.

Lientz, B., & Rea, K. (2004). *Breakthrough IT change management: How to get enduring change results*. Oxford, UK: Elsevier Butterworth Heinemann.

Linstead, S., Fulop, L., & Lilley, S. (2004). *Management and organization: A critical text*. New York, NY: Palgrave Macmillan.

Lloyd, S. (2010). *Why use school information software: Keys to making sense of K-12 software*. Victoria, Canada: Trafford.

Lofquist, E. A. (2011). Doomed to fail: A case study of change implementation collapse in the Norwegian civil aviation industry. *Journal of Change Management*, *11*(2), 223–243. doi:10.1080/14697017.2010.527853

Mabert, V., Soni, A., & Venkataramanan, M. (2003). Enterprise resource planning: Managing the implementation process. *European Journal of Operational Research*, *146*(2), 302. doi:10.1016/S0377-2217(02)00551-9

Malhotra, Y., & Galletta, D. (2004). Building systems that users want to use. *Communications of the ACM*, *47*(12), 89–94. doi:10.1145/1035134.1035139

Mandal, P., & Gunasekaran, A. (2003). Issues in implementing ERP: A case study. *European Journal of Operational Research*, *146*(2), 274. doi:10.1016/S0377-2217(02)00549-0

Markus, M., Axline, S., Petrie, D., & Tanis, C. (2000). Learning from adopters' experiences with ERP: Problems encountered and success achieved. *Journal of Information Technology*, *15*(4), 245–266. doi:10.1080/02683960010008944

Markus, M., & Keil, M. (1994). If we build it they will come: Designing information systems that users want to use. *Sloan Management Review*, *35*, 11–25.

Markus, M., Tanis, C., & Fenema, P. (2000). Multisite ERP implementations. *Communications of the ACM*, *43*(4), 42–46. doi:10.1145/332051.332068

McAlary, S. (1999). Three pitfalls in ERP implementation. *Strategy and Leadership*, *27*(6), 49.

McBain, R. (2006). Why do change efforts so often fail? *Henley Management Update*, *17*(3), 19–29.

Mehlinger, L. (2006). *Indicators of successful enterprise technology implementations in higher education business*. (PhD Thesis). Morgan State University. Baltimore, MD.

Ministry of Information MOI. (2008). *Oman: 2008-9*. (266), Al-Nahda printing press, Muscat.

Mintzberg, H., & Waters, J. (1985). Of strategies deliberate and emergent. *Strategic Management Journal*, *6*, 257–272. doi:10.1002/smj.4250060306

Mirchandani, D., & Motwani, J. (2001). End-user perceptions of ERP systems: A case study of an international automotive supplier. *International Journal of Automotive Technology and Management*, *1*(4), 416. doi:10.1504/IJATM.2001.000049

MOD. (1995). *Vision for Oman's economy: 2020*. Muscat, Oman: MOD.

MOE. (2008). *Education indicators: Academic year 2007/8*. Muscat, Oman: MOE.

MOHE. (2006). *Summary of the strategy for education in the Sultanate of Oman: 2006-2020*. Muscat, Oman: MOHE.

MOI. (2005). *Oman: Years of progress and development*. Muscat, Oman: MOI.

MOMP. (2009). *Technical colleges in Oman*. Retrieved from http://www.manpower.gov.om/

MONE. (2008). *Statistical year book*. Muscat, Oman: MONE.

Moran, J., & Brightman, B. (2001). Leading organizational change. *Career Development International*, *6*(2), 111–118. doi:10.1108/13620430110383438

Motwani, J., Mirchandani, D., Madan, M., & Gunasekaran, A. (2002). Successful implementation of ERP projects: Evidence from two case studies. *International Journal of Production Economics*, *75*(1/2), 83. doi:10.1016/S0925-5273(01)00183-9

Nah, F., Lau, L.-S., & Kuang, J. (2001). Critical factors for successful implementation of enterprise systems. *Business Process Management Journal*, *7*(3), 285. doi:10.1108/14637150110392782

Nah, F., Lee-Shang Lau, J., & Kuang, J. (2001). Critical factors for successful implementation of enterprise systems. *Business Process Management Journal*, *7*(3), 285. doi:10.1108/14637150110392782

Niu, N., Jin, M., & Cheng, J.-R. C. (2011). A case study of exploiting enterprise resource planning requirements. *Enterprise Information Systems*, *5*(2), 183–206. doi:10.1080/17517575.2010.519052

Norris, D. F. (1999). Leading edge information technologies and their adoption: Lessons for US cities. In *Information Technology and Computer Applications in Public Management* (pp. 137–156). Hershey, PA: IGI Global.

Noudoostbeni, A., Yasin, N. M., & Jenatabadi, H. S. (2009). To investigate the success and failure factors of ERP implementation within Malaysian small and medium enterprises. In *Proceedings of the Information Management and Engineering*, (pp. 157-160). IEEE Press.

Nour, M. A., & Mouakket, S. (2011). A classification framework of critical success factors for ERP systems implementation: A multi-stakeholder perspective. *International Journal of Enterprise Information Systems*, *7*(4), 56–71. doi:10.4018/jeis.2011010104

O'Brien, J. (1999). Management information systems. In *Managing Information Technology: The Internet Worked Enterprises*. Boston, MA: McGraw Hill.

Oakland, J., & Tanner, S. (2007). Successful change management. *Total Quality Management and Business Excellence*, *18*(1), 1–19. doi:10.1080/14783360601042890

OECD. (2003). *OECD e-government studies: The e-government imperative*. London, UK: OECD Publishing.

Okafor, E. (2007). Globalization, changes and strategies for managing workers' resistance in work organization in Nigeria. *Journal of Human Ecology (Delhi, India)*, *22*(2), 159–169.

Olhager, J., & Selldin, E. (2003). Enterprise resource planning survey of Swedish manufacturing firms. *European Journal of Operational Research*, *146*(2), 365. doi:10.1016/S0377-2217(02)00555-6

Olson, D. L. (2004). *Managerial issues of enterprise resource planning systems*. Boston, MA: McGraw Hill.

Oracle Corporation. (2012). *Wikipedia.* Retrieved from http://en.wikipedia.org/wiki/Oracle_Corporation

Parr, A., & Shanks, G. (2000). A model of ERP project implementation. *Journal of Information Technology*, *15*(4), 289–304. doi:10.1080/02683960010009051

Pasaoglu, D. (2011). Analysis of ERP usage with technology acceptance model. *Global Business and Management Research*, *3*(2), 157–181.

Pasmore, A. (1988). *Designing effective organisation. London, UK*. London: Taylor and Francis.

Payne, W. (2002). The time for ERP? *Work (Reading, Mass.)*, *51*(2/3), 91.

Pham, L., & Teich, J. E. (2011). A success model for enterprise resource planning adoption to improve financial performance in Vietnam's equitized state owned enterprises. *International Journal of Enterprise Information Systems*, *7*(1), 41–55. doi:10.4018/jeis.2011010103

Porter, M. (1998). *Competitive strategy: Techniques for analysing industries and competitors*. New York, NY: The Free Press.

Ptak, C. A., & Schragenheim, E. (1999). *ERP: Tools technologies, and applications for integrating the supply chain*. Boca Raton, FL: CRC Press.

Quartel, D., Steen, M. W. A., & Lankhorst, M. M. (2012). Application and project portfolio valuation using enterprise architecture and business requirements modelling. *Enterprise Information Systems*, *6*(2), 189–213. doi:10.1080/17517575.2011.625571

Ragowsky, A., & Romm Livermore, C. T. (2002). ERP system selection and implementation: A cross cultural approach. In *Proceedings of the Eighth American Conference on Information Systems*, (pp. 1333-1339). Retrieved from http://www.davidfrico.com/rico04f.pdf

Compilation of References

Rao, S. (2000). Enterprise resource planning: Business needs and technologies. *Industrial Management & Data Systems*, *100*(2), 81. doi:10.1108/02635570010286078

Rees, C., & Althakhri, R. (2008). Organizational change strategies in the Arab region: A review of critical factors. *Journal of Business Economics and Management*, *9*(2), 123–133. doi:10.3846/1611-1699.2008.9.123-132

Ribbers, P., & Schoo, K. (2002). Program management and complexity of ERP implementations. *Engineering Management Journal*, *14*(2), 45.

Rinderle-Ma, S., & Reichert, M. (2009). Comprehensive life cycle support for access rules in information systems: The CEOSIS project. *Enterprise Information Systems*, *3*(3), 219–251. doi:10.1080/17517570903045609

Robey, D., Ross, J., & Boudreau, M. (2002). Learning to implement enterprise systems: An exploratory study of the dialectics of change. *Journal of Management Information Systems*, *19*(1), 17.

Rose, W., & Grant, G. (2010). Critical issues pertaining to the planning and implementation of e-government initiatives. *Government Information Quarterly*, *27*(1), 26–33. doi:10.1016/j.giq.2009.06.002

Ross, J. (1999). Dow cornings corporation: Business processes and information technology. *Journal of Information Technology*, *14*(3), 253–266. doi:10.1080/026839699344557

Salminen, A. (2000). *Implementing organizational and operational change – Critical success factors of change management. Industrial Management and Business Administration No. 7*. Helsinki, Finland: Helsinki University of Technology.

Sarker, S., & Lee, A. S. (2003). Using a case study to test the role of three key social enablers in ERP implementation. *Information & Management*, *40*, 813–829. doi:10.1016/S0378-7206(02)00103-9

Sarkis, J., & Gunasekaran, A. (2003). Enterprise resource planning–Modelling and analysis. *European Journal of Operational Research*, *146*(2), 229. doi:10.1016/S0377-2217(02)00545-3

Saunders, M., Lewis, P., & Thornhill, A. (2009). *Research methods for business students* (5th ed.). Upper Saddle River, NJ: Prentice Hall.

Scheer, A. W., & Habermann, F. (2000). Making ERP a success. *Communications of the ACM*, *43*(4), 57–61. doi:10.1145/332051.332073

Schniederjans, M., & Kim, G. (2003). Implementing enterprise resource planning systems with total quality control and business process reengineering: Survey results. *International Journal of Operations & Production Management*, *23*(3/4), 418. doi:10.1108/01443570310467339

Sekaran, U. (2003). *Research methods for business: A skill building approach* (4th ed.). New York, NY: John Wiley and Sons, Inc.

Sharifi, M., & Manian, A. (2010). The study of the success indicators for pre-implementation activities of Iran's e-government development projects. *Government Information Quarterly*, *27*(1), 63–69. doi:10.1016/j.giq.2009.04.006

Sheng, Y., Pearson, J., & Crosby, L. (2003). Organizational culture and employees' computer self-efficacy: An emperical study. *Information Resources Management*, *16*(3), 42. doi:10.4018/irmj.2003070103

Sheu, C., Rebecca Yen, H., & Krumwiede, D. (2003). The effect of national differences on multinational ERP implementation: An exploratory study. *Total Quality Management and Business Excellence*, *14*(6), 639.

Sirkin, H., Keenan, P., & Jackson, A. (2006). The hard side of change management. *Harvard Business Review*, *84*(3), 142–143. Retrieved from http://www.iconlogicgroup.com/pdf/HBR%20The%20Hard%20Side%20of%20Change%20Manag

Sloan, T., & Soonsay, C. (2005). Driving change: Innovate management in distribution centers. *Journal of Asia Entrepreneurship and Sustainability*, 1-21.

Sobotta, T., Sobotta, N., & Gotze. (2010, May 31). *Greening IT*. Retrieved February 14, 2012 from http://greening.it/wp-content/uploads/downloads/2010/06/greening-it_isbn-9788791936029.pdf

Soh, C., Kien, S. S., & Tay Yap, J. (2000). Culture fits and misfits: Is ERP a universal solution? *Communications of the ACM*, *43*(4), 47–51. doi:10.1145/332051.332070

Soliman, F., & Youssef, M. (1998). The role of SAP software in business process reengineering. *International Journal of Operations & Production Management*, *18*(9/10), 886–895. doi:10.1108/01443579810225504

Somers, T., & Nelson, K. (2003). The impact of strategy and integration mechanism on enterprise system value: Empirical evidence from manufacturing firms. *European Journal of Operational Research*, *146*, 315–338. doi:10.1016/S0377-2217(02)00552-0

Song, X. (2009). Why do change management strategies fail? Illustrations with case studies. *Journal of Cambridge Studies*, *4*(1), 6–15.

SQU. (2011). *Colleges*. Retrieved from http://www.squ.edu.om

Standish Group. (1995). *Website*. Retrieved February 14, 2012, from http://www.projectsmart.co.uk/docs/chaos-report.pdf

Stebel, P. (1992). *Breakpoints: How managers exploit radical change*. Boston, MA: Harvard Business School Press.

Stevens, T. (1997). Kodak focuses on ERP. *Industry Week*, *246*(15), 130–133.

Stewart, G., & Rosemann, M. (2001). Industry-oriented design of ERP related curriculum—An Australian initiative. *Business Process Management Journal*, *7*(3), 234. doi:10.1108/14637150110392719

Stirna, J. (1999). Managing enterprise modeling tool acquisition process. In *Proceedings of the International Workshop on Enterprise Management Resource and Planning System*, (pp. 283-298). Venice, Italy: EMRPS.

Stoddard, D., & Jarvenpaa, S. (1995). Businesss process reengineering: Tactics for managing radical change. *Journal of Management Information Systems*, *12*(1), 81–108.

Strang, D., & Macy, M. W. (2001). In search of excellence: Fads, success stories, and adaptive emulation. *American Journal of Sociology*, *107*(1), 147–182. doi:10.1086/323039

Stratman, J., & Roth, A. (2002). Enterprise resource planning (ERP) competence constructs: Two-stage multi-item scale development and validation. *Decision Sciences*, *33*(4), 601. doi:10.1111/j.1540-5915.2002.tb01658.x

Summer, M. (2000). Risk factors in enterprise-wide/ERP projects. *Journal of Information Technology*, *15*(4), 317–327. doi:10.1080/02683960010009079

Compilation of References

Swartz, D., & Orgill, K. (2001). *ERP project: Learned using this framework for ERP could save your university millions of dollars.* Retrieved from http://net.educause.edu/ir/library/pdf/eqm0121.pdf

Tarafdar, M., & Roy, R. (2003). Analyzing the adoption of enterprise resource planning systems in Indian organizations: a process framework. *Journal of Global Information Technology Management, 6*(1), 31.

Tatsiopoulos, I., Panayiotou, N., Kirytopoulos, K., & Tsitsiriggos, K. (2003). Risk management as a strategic issue for the implementation of ERP systems: A case study from the oil industry. *International Journal of Risk Assessment and Management, 4*(1), 20. doi:10.1504/IJRAM.2003.003434

Terpsiadou, M., & Economides, A. (2009). The use of information systems in the Greek public financial services: The case of TAXIS. *Government Information Quarterly, 26*(3), 468–476. doi:10.1016/j.giq.2009.02.004

Todnem, R. (2005). Organizational change management: A critical review. *Journal of Change Management, 5*(4), 369–380. doi:10.1080/14697010500359250

Trimmer, K., Pumphrey, L., & Wiggins, C. (2002). ERP implementation in rural healthcare. *Journal of Management in Medicine, 16*(2/3), 113. doi:10.1108/02689230210434871

Trunick, P. A. (1999). ERP: Promise or pipe dream? *Transportation & Distribution, 40*(1), 23–26.

Umble, E. J., Haft, R., & Umble, M. (2003). Enterprise resource planning: Implementation procedures and critical success factors. *European Journal of Operational Research, 146*(2), 241–257. doi:10.1016/S0377-2217(02)00547-7

Umble, E. J., & Umble, M. M. (2002). Avoiding (ERP) implementation failure. *Industrial Management (Des Plaines), 44*(1), 25–33.

Umble, E., Haft, R., & Umble, M. (2003). Enterprise resource planning: Implementation procedures and critical success factors. *European Journal of Operational Research, 146*(2), 241. doi:10.1016/S0377-2217(02)00547-7

Upadhyay, P., & Dan, P. (2008). An explorative study to identify the critical success factors for ERP implementation in Indian small and medium scale enterprises. In *Proceedings of the IEEE International Conference on Information Technology.* IEEE Press.

Voordijk, H., Van Leuven, A., & Laan, A. (2003). Enterprise resource planning in a large construction firm: Implementation analysis. *Construction Management and Economics, 21*(5), 511. doi:10.1080/0144619032000072155

War, J., Hemingway, C., & Daniel, E. (2005). A framework for addressing the organizational issues of enterprise systems implementation. *Strategic Information Systems, 14*, 97–119. doi:10.1016/j.jsis.2005.04.005

Washington, M., & Hacker, M. (2005). Why change fails: Knowledge counts. *Leadership and Organization Development Journal, 26*(5), 400–411. doi:10.1108/01437730510607880

Wateridge, J. (1998). How can IS/IT projects be measured for success? *International Journal of Project Management, 16*(1), 59–63. doi:10.1016/S0263-7863(97)00022-7

Watson, E., & Schneider, H. (1999). Using ERP in education. *Communications of the Association for Information Systems, 1*(9), 12–24.

Weber, P., & Weber, J. (2001). Changes in employee perceptions during organizational change. *Leadership and Organization Development Journal, 22*(6), 291–300. doi:10.1108/01437730110403222

Weston, F. C. Jr. (2001). ERP implementation and project management. *Production and Inventory Management Journal, 43*(3), 75–80.

Wikipedia. (2011). *Education in Saudi Arabia*. Retrieved 6 April, 2011, from http://en.wikipedia.org/wiki/Education_in_Saudi_Arabia

Wong, B., & Tein, D. (2004). *Critical success factors for ERP projects*. Retrieved from cms.3rdgen.info/3rdgen_sites/107/resource/ORWongandTein.pdf

Wright, S., & Wight, A. M. (2000). Information systems assurance for enterprises resources planning systems: Implementation and unique risk consideration. *Journal of Information Systems, 16*, 99–113. doi:10.2308/jis.2002.16.s-1.99

Wu, J.-H., & Wang, Y.-M. (2006). Measuring ERP success: The ultimate users' view. *Journal of Operations & Production Management, 26*(8), 882–903. doi:10.1108/01443570610678657

Xia, L., Yu, W., Lim, R., & Hock, L. (2010). A methodology for successful implementation of ERP in smaller companies. In *Proceedings of the Service Operations and Logistics and Informatics (SOLI)*, (pp. 380 – 385). SOLI.

Yeo, R. K. (2009). Electronic government as a strategic intervention in organizational change processes. *Journal of Change Management, 9*(3), 271–304. doi:10.1080/14697010903125506

Yin, R. (2004). *The case study anthology*. Thousand Oaks, CA: Sage publications, Inc.

Yin, R. (2009). *Case study research: Design and methods* (4th ed.). Newbury, CA: Sage Publications.

Zink, K., Steimle, U., & Schroder, D. (2008). Comprehensive change management concepts: Development of a participatory approach. *Applied Ergonomics, 39*, 527–538. doi:10.1016/j.apergo.2008.02.015

About the Contributors

Fayez Albadri is a well-established academic, educator, consultant, and manager for over two decades. He holds a Doctorate in Management from MGSM Macquarie University in Sydney Australia, Masters in Intelligent Information Processing Systems from University of Western Australia in Perth, Graduate Certificate in Computer Instructional Design from Edith Cowan University in Perth, and Bachelor degree in Engineering from University of Westminster in London, UK. He is recognized as IS&T Specialist and Management Expert for his record in managing IT projects, implementing ERP systems and e-business solutions. Dr. Albadri is a pioneer researcher and academic with important contributions in the areas of educational technology and instructional design, entrepreneurship and e-business, IT strategic planning, project management, and risk management. He is renowned for his development of (IPRM) the Integrated Project-Risk Model and the introduction of (IELCM) the Integrated ERP Life-Cycle Management approach. He has also delivered numerous seminars and training workshops to hundreds of academics and professionals in Australia and the Middle East.

* * *

Salam Abdallah is an IS&T academic and practitioner. Dr. Abdallah has a PhD in Information Systems from Australia and a MSc degree from the United Kingdom. He has over 15 years of experience working as an IT consultant before joining United Nations Relief and Works Agency for Palestine refugees overseeing ICT facilities and curriculum development at schools and vocational training centers in UNRWA's entire field of operations. He is a founding member of Special Interest Group of the Association of Information Systems: ICT and Global Development. Dr. Abdallah is also an active researcher in the field of Information Systems and has published articles in local and international conferences and journals. Currently, he is an Associate Professor of Management Information Systems at Abu Dhabi University, UAE.

Nooruddin Ahmed has nearly twenty years of experience in the information systems industry with stints in major companies like Tata Consultancy Services and DSQ Software in India, CITIBANK NA – Singapore, HAPAG LLOYD – Asia – Singapore, SEER Technologies, USA. He is currently working as the Head of the Information Systems Department in Abu Dhabi National Oil Company (ADNOC). Nooruddin has been instrumental in introducing the concept of green/sustainable information technology to key stakeholders with a focus on supporting ERP systems, software development, and data/database administration and management. Mr. Ahmed has a Masters Degree of Science in Strategic Business IT from the University of Portsmouth, UK, certified as a Software Manager (CSM) from SIIA, USA, and Member of the Greenhouse Gas Management Institute.

Ahmed Al-Azri has BSc Education (Nizwa) and has recently completed a Master of Science (MSc.) in Management at Brunel Business School, Brunel University, UK. Mr. Al-Azri is currently the Director of External Scholarships at the Ministry of Higher Education, Oman, and his main interest is in the areas of change managements and information systems.

Zahran Al-Salti has BSc Computer Science, MSc Business Information Technology Systems (Strathclyde), and PhD Information Systems (Brunel). Zahran is an Assistant Professor at the Department of Information Systems at Sultan Qaboos University (SQU), Oman. He has more than 11 years of academic and industry experience. Prior to joining SQU in 2004, Zahran spent five years with the Ministry of Higher Education, Oman, in different technical and managerial positions. He served as a Director of Postgraduate Studies at the Directorate General of Scholarships. His current research interests include Information Systems (IS) outsourcing / offshoring, knowledge management, and e-government issues. Dr. Al-Salti has published several papers in international journals and conference proceedings.

Amer Dabbagh was born in Amman, Jordan, where he received his elementary and secondary education in government schools. For his university education, he went to Ankara, Turkey, supported by the JFK scholarship. In five years, he had a Civil Engineering degree in his bag. He worked in Gulf Oil and Gas Company for over 25 years in various capacities. He worked in the IT division as a System Analyst and progressed to the position of Team Leader, responsible for a team of around ten members responsible for the maintenance of a number of commercial applications. Later, he moved to the Commercial Division and was responsible for the ERP system in use at the time. In this capacity of Senior Business Analyst, he represented the Commercial Division in the EIS Implementation project. Mr. Dabbagh played a key role in the preparation of the user requirements, in the formulation of the Commercial Business Processes, preparation of the user acceptance scenarios, data migration, and user training. His contribution in the book reflects his experience in the implementation project.

Ahmad Fayez was born in Amman, Jordan. He started his schooling in Western Australia and continued in UAE. He studied both his Bachelor's degree in Internet Sciences and Masters degree in Information Technology Management at Wollongong University, based in Sydney, Australia. He has worked as an IT instructor and analyst, and he is currently working as an Account Manager at Information Fort in Physical Record Management and Document Management.

Mohamed Elhefnawi worked as Lecturer and Assistant Professor in the Military Technical College, Cairo, Egypt, from 1969 to 1983. He joined ISC Department of Qatar Petroleum (formerly QGPC) in 1984 until 1996, where he worked in the information systems development area. From 1996 to 2012, he had several engagements with Qatargas, ADNOC, ADWEA, GASCO, and ADCO in the IT planning, ITIL Implementation, IT standards, Enterprise Architecture, and IT Strategy areas. Dr. Mohamed Elhefnawi has earned MSc and PhD degrees in Electrical and Electronic Engineering from VAAZ Academy, Brno, the Czech Republic, in 1975 and 1977, respectively. He also has a BSc degree in Electrical and Electronic Engineering with first degree honor from Military Technical College, in 1969. He is a Senior Member of IEEE, since 1986.

Nabil Ghalib's experience as an IT Specialist for over 32 years included the management of tens of projects in five continents and many countries since 1980. He has worked for some international companies in a myriad of industries, including manufacturing, telecommunications, banking, and investment, as well as the oil and gas industry. His accomplishments include many in-house developments in the areas of facilities management and medical services.

Asim Hussain is ERP Project Implementation Specialist and Project Manager with a diverse and in-depth 29 year experience in all phases of ERP project and application life-cycle from its inception to retirement on medium to large scale systems. He uses his techno-functional skills for the implementation and subsequent support of business solutions. He has carried out implementation of a number of ERP and EAM project. He has conducted presentations in a number of conferences and seminars. He is currently working with Kuwait Oil Company as TPL Senior Specialist. He holds Master's degree in Computer Sciences. He is also PMI certified Project Manager holding PMP certification.

Moh'd Jarrar's experience as a project manager, an enterprise architect for upgrading IT infrastructure and data centers, as well as the academic curriculum in one of the leading universities in the Gulf region accompanied with more than twenty five years of international experience of work with many of the IT giants enabled him to bring many projects home with achievements beyond the wildest expectations of the stakeholders.

Wafi Al-Karaghouli's academic qualifications include, BA Statistics, MPhil Statistics and Operations Research (London), PhD IS Failures (Brunel), MBCS, MElite. Wafi gained extensive experience with multinational companies. 12 years industrial experience including a Blue-Chip and 22 years in Higher Education. A qualified practitioner in TQM and Project Management Methodology PRINCE2. His interest and research revolve around IT systems failures, knowledge management, and civil aviation. Wafi has published extensively on the subject of IS failure. He contributed to the development of a Knowledge Management System at Merrill Lynch HSBC, BAA's fast-track check-in desks, and the Iris Recognition Immigration System (iris) at Heathrow Airport.

Eissa Khoori was born in Abu Dhabi, the cosmopolitan capital the United Arab Emirates. Upon the completion of his secondary schooling in Abu Dhabi, he pursued his university study and graduated from Al Hosn University with a Bachelor's degree in Industrial Engineering. He has been working as ERP Maintenance Specialist at ADMA-OPCO since his graduation in 2009. He also has taken a number ERP-related assignments including the replacement of HR legacy system with ERP HR module and a number of ERP task forces, business process re-engineering, and ERP post-implementation management of change.

Vladimir Kovacevic is a well-established management consultant with extensive experience in the business and IT industries. He holds a Master Degree in Chemical Engineering from University of Belgrade. For over 17 years he has covered operations engineering, operations management, number of feasibility studies, business process design/re-engineering, and business process optimization. He has successfully managed a number of complex asset management systems implementations and ERP project management. Vladimir has designed many proven business/e-business solutions for a variety of clients in Oil and Gas, Utilities and Fertilizer industries. In addition to his roles as a management consultant, he has held positions of principal business consultant, professional services manager, and deputy GM of an internationally recognized IT solution company. Vladimir is well-recognized expert in ERP strategy and implementation. He currently works as ERP Advisor at Abu Dhabi Marine Operating Company.

Firas Albataineh holds a BSc (hons) in Computer Studies and a Masters degree in Computing and Information Systems, both from the UK. He has 13 years of experience in enterprise systems and systems implementations across the gulf region and across different industries covering utilities, facilities, oil and gas, transportation, airports, airlines, and military. He was involved in tens of projects and gained the knowledge, experience, and the skills to deliver IT projects on time, within budget, and according to specifications. Firas had implemented systems from IBM, Oracle, and SAP, and was involved in many different implementation phases, where he played different roles relating to the implementation of ERP systems from one vendor or best of breed systems from different vendors.

Ali Sartawi is a Graduate Engineer in Electronics Engineering. He started his career in early 1985 with a European company in the field of electro-mechanical construction. He was mainly engaged in instrumentation and loop test as well as system and equipment commissioning. The project was an oil platform sponsored by an oil company in Abu Dhabi. Two years later, he joined the power sector in a power and desalination plant in Abu Dhabi and served in the operation department for 10 years, as control room operator, operation supervisor, and shift charge engineer. His assignment as maintenance instrumentation engineer in power plant (1996-2000) has given him the opportunity to represent his company in ADWEA CMMS implementation project in year 2000. In 2005, he was seconded to an AGPS (Asia Gulf Power Services) who took the plant ownership as part of ADWEA privatization scheme. The company approved an upgrade project for CMMS in which he was appointed as deputy manager and head of planning, providing business and technical support to all types of company users. After becoming an expert in asset management implementation systems, he joined oil company in January 2008 as Work and Asset Specialist, where he led the maintenance group in the upgrade team project of the CMMS. Ali's present role, since the completion of the CMMS upgrade, is to enhance maintenance performance using asset management system as the main tool. He also provides support and consultation for best implementation of CMMS facilities on commercial processes.

Rima Shishakly has PhD in Management Information Systems from University of Manchester, UK, and MBA, Belgium. Currently, she is an Assistant Professor in Ajman University of Science and Technology, UAE. Her studies focus on the role of Information Technology (IT) in organization change and innovation as well as implementation and development of Information System (IS) in different organizations. A current specific area of interest is information technology in educational management. She has published in different international journals and conference proceedings, and also gives professional training.

Index